W9-ADG-341

MARTIN R. DELANY

The Beginnings of Black Nationalism

MARTIN R. DELANY

The Beginnings of Black Nationalism

by Victor Ullman

Beacon Press Boston

Library of Congress catalog card number: 73–141877
International Standard Book Number: 0–8070–5440–2
Beacon Press books are published under the auspices
of the Unitarian Universalist Association
Published simultaneously in Canada by Saunders of Toronto, Ltd.

Printed in the United States of America

To Louise,
My wife, who shared the thousands of miles of travel, the thousands of documents examined, and did all of the typing.

Contents

Preface

I care but little what white men think of what I say, write or do; my sole desire is to so benefit the colored people; this being done, I am satisfied—the opinion of every white person in the country or the world, to the contrary notwithstanding.

—Letter from Martin R. Delany to
Frederick Douglass, July 10, 1852

In order to "tell it like it was" about Martin Robison Delany, certain sacrifices must be made.

For one thing, it is impossible to deal with Delany and satisfy, at the same time, the insatiable American appetite for hypocrisy. He simply cannot be classified with either the "good guys" or the "bad guys," which may be the reason historians and educators have neglected his part in American history. In telling of him, unpalatable truths must also be told.

Delany was America's first "Black Nationalist." In his day, he was a novelty, for countless times he told the whites to get out of his kinky hair or else deal with him as an equal. In the context of a Negro in the American 19th century, this was a revolutionary, an anarchist, a nihilist, a communist—familiar terms today—talking.

Those are the titles we award to thousands of black militants who repeat the words and attitudes expressed by Delany over some fifty years of the last century. Like that pioneer black nationalist, too, these young men and women were not born that way. White society molded them. In the words of the old song, we made them what they are today, and we're not satisfied.

Many were the titles earned and given to Delany during his lifetime. He was major-doctor-author-editor-orator-explorer-ethnologist, but the title he demanded and honored most was simply—*Man.*

But in his day, as today, no "nigger" was a man. He was either property or a nuisance, either profitable labor or a scorned dependent. Delany invited destruction every time he spoke or wrote, for, like his descendants of today, he jabbed the American conscience by his pretense of being every bit as able as any white man. Moreover, when he also demanded ". . . one nation, indivisible, with liberty and justice for all," he was going too far. He was being naive, believing the 4th of July speeches he heard and delivered himself.

And so Delany was destroyed, and the memory of him, too. His death certificate lists the cause of death as "lung trouble," but Delany—the *Man*—had been destroyed long before January 24, 1885, when his body was pronounced dead. The *Xenia* (Ohio) *Gazette* carried an item in its local news two weeks before:

Major Martin R. Delaney (*sic*) a quite noted colored gentleman, is at his home at Wilberforce, O. and in a rather pitiable condition—being, considerable of the time, in a very feeble condition of mind. The gentleman is now an old man and in his prime was a very brilliant one. Many think him to have exceeded Frederick Douglass in intellect in his palmiest days. He has been the guest of rulers and potentates of high degree, has taken a leading part in politics and is the author of several valuable books. . . . His old friends at Wilberforce are pained at his present condition, which may almost be denominated as a mental and physical wreck.

One fact is clear. There will always be Martin Delanys among our black people. We manufacture them daily, and they repeat, in new lingo and more defiantly, the first Delany who told his people in the *North Star* in 1849:

Be thou like the first apostle—
  Be thou like heroic Paul;
If a free thought seek expression,
  Speak it boldly—speak it all!
Face thine enemies—accusers—
  Scorn the prison, rack or rod;
And if thou hast truth to utter,
  Speak and leave the rest to God.

CHAPTER ONE

"Born Free"

Martin Robison Delany was "born free" in old Virginia on May 6, 1812.

The condition of his birth signified that he was but one step above the most degraded position of any human being in the world—that of slave.

The date of his birth was significant, too. Eight days later the United States annexed West Florida from the Spanish to create the black belt of Alabama and Mississippi and thereby establish the future kingdom of cotton. Six weeks later war was declared on Great Britain and the War of 1812 was launched, not just to protect American seamen, but to invade Canada with the purpose of annexation.

The language of American history politely defines both the condition and the events. Martin Delany was born free because no white man owned his body. The War of 1812 was "expansionist" not imperialist, because to the south, the Spanish were obstructing the expansion of American agriculture; to the north, in Canada, the Indians, who had traded fifty million acres of land for whisky, were sheltered and had something more. As Henry Clay said: "Is it nothing to acquire the entire fur trade connected with that country?"

The two events, Delany's birth and the War of 1812, are related. This first flexing of America's muscles and greed was to set the conditions of Martin Delany's boyhood, manhood, and old age. He was almost eight years old when the Missouri Compromise of 1820 established the ground rules for the Civil War, and he was within a month of age 65 in 1877 when the Confederate States finally won that war. The intervening years slowly raised Martin Delany and all other Negroes from abject despair to a brief burst of near-glory in freedom, and then catapulted them back into the kind of black despair only blacks can describe.

Martin Delany grew up in this sonorous, well-phrased era of broken promises to the theory of American democracy.

Throughout his lifetime Delany annoyed white audiences and readers with reference to the words of our Founding Fathers in demanding freedom first and citizenship second for the American Negro. Somehow, this was unfair, for how could any good American dispute the definitions of liberty spelled out by the Irreproachables? Delany knew the disadvantage in which he placed his white audiences, and he delighted in it.

Martin Robison Delany was born free in the ever-present shadow of George Washington, about twelve years after Washington's death. There were Revolutionary War veterans and countless friends of Washington among the old-timers in Charles Town in old Virginia, where Delany was born.

That hilly corner of what is now the West Virginia panhandle was once "Washington country," a feudal empire created out of government land bounties. The town itself was named for George Washington's youngest brother Charles, whose palatial plantation, Happy Retreat, crowned the hill dominating the tiny settlement. To the southwest, on Bullskin Run, were the plantations of two grandnephews; and still more Washingtons—another grandnephew and a grandniece—adjoined them. In fact, there are more Washingtons buried in the cemetery of the Zion Episcopal Church at Charles Town than anywhere else in the country.

When Martin was born there were fewer than 1,000 whites, slaves, and free Negroes living in Charles Town. In one way or another all were economically dependent on the Washingtons. When Martin's mother delivered her seamstress or laundry work "downtown" she had only a few streets to cross. She turned into Washington Street, crossed Lawrence (brother) Street, then Charles (brother) Street. She reached the courthouse at George Street and sometimes continued north across Samuel (brother) Street to arrive at Mildred (sister) Street.

Martin Delany's first ten years were spent in the midst of the Washington hierarchy. It is small wonder then, when grown, he would face the mayor of Allegheny and tell him: "Honorable Mayor, whatever ideas of liberty I may have, have been received from reading the lives of your revolutionary fathers."

There was no ghetto in Charles Town in 1812, possibly because there were only eleven free Negro households in the whole village. They lived scattered among the whites, and the children played together—while young.

Martin played with the children of Samuel Offut, the white baker, and with the Avis boys, sons of the cooper, William Avis. One of them, John, was later John Brown's kindly jailer in Charles Town.

When the neighborhood children grew old enough for school, there began the separation of blacks and whites which was to endure for life. In all the so-called Free States, as well as in old Virginia, while black and white children were too young to understand their parents, their relationships were natural and uncomplicated. But that fateful day when their white companions got all dressed up for school left the black children with their first bitter lesson. They had no schools to go to. They were black.

Martin's mother Pati was a tigress with five cubs, who was known around Charles Town as an uppity Negress who did not appreciate the tolerance of the whites in allowing her to live "free." According to a law passed in 1806, a Negro could either be sent to slavery, if he committed a crime, or exiled from the state, for committing a small crime. Pati committed a major crime—surreptitiously she taught her children to read and write. From an enterprising Yankee peddler she bought a copy of the *New York Primer and Spelling Book* which was a basic "bootlegging" item among blacks all through the South.

The crime of educating Negroes—slave or free—was comparatively new legislation in the Slave States at that time. In 1818 the cotton gin was only 25 years old and the broad reaches of West Florida were just being settled to form the black belt. If cotton was not yet king it was at least crown prince in the economy, and it was to change the United States from those first plans for a democracy into principalities known as states.

When Pati taught her children to read and write it was with the sternest warnings of secrecy. She was committing a crime that endangered the entire family. But she did not reckon on one development—that children will "play school." According to Delany's account, they were so eager to learn that soon even the youngest was able to read and spell, and the oldest, Samuel, was already forging passes for slaves in the area. They aped their former white companions, and in the garden established their own school while Pati was away. Except for the Webbs, also free Negroes, their neighbors were white.

One afternoon a white man known to them questioned them and wrote down their boastful answers. In a few days Pati was summoned to court and charged with the crime of teaching her children to read and write. The evidence was unquestionable and it was only due to the unexplained intercession of the village banker, a man named Randall Brown, that Pati escaped punishment by fleeing to Chambersburg, Pennsylvania, a Free State.

Delany's pride in self and race was never negative, never anything but a dynamic force in all of his relationships. It was assertive and sometimes arrogant, yet more positive than the turbulent reactions of most black militants today, though the pride is the same. Delany had the aplomb and hauteur of the royalty of his day. He was convinced and later proved to his own satisfaction that he was descended, on both sides, from African royalty.

In manhood Delany emulated the white society of his day by his manner and casual acceptance of the roles of leadership, for was he not of royal blood? On his mother's side the case seems clear, for Pati Delany would not have been a "free" woman in Virginia if her mother, Graci Peace, and her father, known only as Shango, had not satisfied the whites as to their royal lineage. On his father's side, too, Delany claimed high rank. Samuel Delany and his brother were born slaves, the sons of a Golah chieftain who was captured with his family in an African war. Delany's paternal grandfather was never reconciled to slavery, and once escaped to Little York, Canada, as Toronto was then named, with his wife and two sons. Delany claims that the family was returned to Virginia slavery "by some fiction of law, international policy, old musty treaty, cozenly understood." This would place the escape and return before 1793 when Canada, a royal possession, set an example for the new democracy in the South, by abolishing slavery in the colony. Since that date, Canada has returned no fugitive slaves to the United States by legal process, despite over sixty years of clamor and protest from Washington.

Delany's grandfather, the story continues, was killed by a

slaveholder when he resisted punishment. This is in keeping with the remarkable tale of Delany's father, Samuel. In 1822 he, too, refused punishment from an overseer named Violet, on a plantation near Martinsburg (now West Virginia), fifteen miles from Charles Town. Samuel, reported to be of enormous strength, must have been an unusual slave. He did not mangle or harm Violet in any way. He merely tore off his clothing. Nine times he stripped Violet without harming anything but his modesty, and that gentleman had the choice of shooting him or refraining from punishing him. A strong slave being too valuable to shoot, Violet called the sheriff. Samuel then armed himself with a wagon's "swingle-tree," defying the attacking whites. A stone knocked him out and Samuel bore its scar, a reminder to Martin through the rest of his father's life. Samuel was lodged in the Charles Town jail and certainly was marked for death but Violet's cupidity was too great to destroy such a valuable piece of property. Later, Samuel was allowed, with Pati's aid, to buy his freedom in 1823.

There was no doubt in Delany's mind that "Princes shall come out of Egypt; Ethiopia shall haste to stretch out her hands unto God" once more. He was one of the princes of legitimate descent.

Pati carefully planned the family's escape. She saw to it that all the white neighbors in Charles Town knew that the Delany family was moving, and their move was considered entirely natural. They were going to Martinsburg so that Pati could be closer to her fractious slave husband and possibly keep him out of trouble. Therefore, there was no hindrance from the authorities when Pati and her brood set out on the Martinsburg road in a rented wagon, and none knew they continued northward beyond that Virginia town and some sixteen miles beyond the Pennsylvania border. Had the authorities known that Chambersburg was their destination, the entire family could have been arrested as fugitives from Virginia justice before they crossed the state line.

There was another reason for Pati's planning. Samuel was determined either to be free or die. If he succeeded in achieving freedom from slavery, Virginia law required his departure from the state within twelve months, or else he could be subject to re-enslavement for any infraction at all, including the all-embracing vagrancy law of that day, being "unable to show visible means of support."

Samuel joined his family in Chambersburg in 1823, when Martin was eleven years old. The boy now had a complete family, and it was due to Pati's careful planning.

In spite of all the restrictions of being a free Negro in a so-called Free State, Martin Delany's horizons widened. He had his family, and he lived in a black "ghetto" of Chambersburg named Kerrstown, where 35 to 40 Negro families had grouped, at first in self-protection, for Franklin County (as well as all of the south Pennsylvania counties) were happy hunting grounds for slave stealers. In 1812 the colored people of Kerrstown bought an old log Catholic church and moved it, setting up their own Methodist Episcopal congregation; a Sabbath school followed naturally, and then a school for the colored children only.

None of this could have happened in Virginia. Martin could never have gone openly to school nor even carried books on the streets. Nor would he have been able to avoid working at the age of eleven in Virginia. He was able to go to school because his father worked at the old Holywell Paper Mill and proudly paid an annual Occupation tax of twenty-five cents to the Borough of Chambersburg. His older brother Samuel also worked and, by 1830, was married and in his own home.

Unfortunately, we do not know who or what influence launched Delany's youthful and expanding mind into the study of the economic, political, and social history of his race and of all known civilizations. The seed was sown in Chambersburg for, by the time he was 24, Delany had already mapped out his own plan for a Black Israel. By then he had a grasp of Latin and possibly Greek as well.

The pedagogical influence may have been Dr. Andrew M. McDowell who was in Chambersburg until 1826 when he moved to Pittsburgh. Years later in Pittsburgh he was to initiate Delany's long course of study toward the practice of medicine. But this is conjecture. We only know that books were made available to the boy, and that may have been sufficient, for he proved to be a self-starting student.

These nine years in Chambersburg were important to Delany. By 1830 he was committed to his people and had only to learn the method by which he would serve them.

One method was a practical education. Kerrstown was the natural goal of fugitive slaves following the North Star. Traffic across the Virginia line increased during Delany's residence in Chambersburg—and so did the proficiency of the Underground Railroad. It was there that Delany learned both the laws and the furtive skills so necessary in Pittsburgh later.

Pennsylvania had the distinction of being the first of the states to abolish slavery. In 1780 during the Revolutionary fervor the state recognized the contradiction of a Declaration of Independence from bondage to Britain while holding a whole people in bondage.

The Pennsylvania law was one of gradual abolition, and by the time of the 1820 census, there were only 211 slaves left in the state, and they were elderly.

Delany lived and learned among a homogeneous group of Negroes forming a tight-knit community, who venerated not only their God but an institution so long denied them—the family. From that dual worship came the remarkable dedication to the education of their children which was almost universal among American Negroes of the time, whether free or slave. Martin continued school until he was 15 when he was forced to go to work because Samuel, Jr., married and the family had lost one source of income. For four years Delany worked around Chambersburg and in nearby Cumberland County at various unskilled jobs, meanwhile reading.

On July 29, 1831, at the age of nineteen, Delany set out along the Western Turnpike on foot. His goal was more schooling in Pittsburgh, then wherever duty to his people called him.

By then Delany had achieved full growth. He was of medium height, with his father's broad shoulders and his mother's inexhaustible vitality. Later descriptions of him suggest perpetual motion in all directions. And while those motions held the eye, a deep, resonant voice easily caught the mind. When motion and sound halted, there was Delany's blackness—a vivid ebony that flashed back the planes of light, and when his hair receded early to leave the shining black dome, his prominent nose and mobile thick lips worked with stark black eyes to complete a commanding presence.

Whites, in describing Delany, declared him a black Caligula, but to his own people he personified their lost image of Ham, the black son of God. If his skin had been white, he would have personified the patented American image of the purposeful young man who went west—along the Western Turnpike, over three ridges of the Alleghenies—in search of his fortune. But he carried no musket to shoot his food. Instead, he stopped in Bedford for a month to earn enough money to carry him on to Pittsburgh.

CHAPTER TWO

The American Abolition Myth

The year 1831 was a time of ferment, political upheaval, and economic challenge to the status quo in young America.

The common people demanded change through the built-in means provided by the new Constitution. The bold experiment of democracy had become ossified through disuse of the principle, Progress through Change. In the forty years since adoption of the Bill of Rights in 1791 there had been only two amendments to the Constitution, the eleventh, defining the powers of the Federal Judiciary, and the twelfth, establishing the Electoral College. Both were designed to serve the burgeoning theory of States Rights and meant little to the common people. They wanted a piece of the action—land. To quiet them, in 1830 a frightened Congress handed out the first crumb of land tenure for those who had squatted on government land by 1829. They could buy up to 160 acres at $1.25 an acre, if they had cultivated the land by then.

Andy Jackson, by 1831, was in the final throes of his struggle with Nicholas Biddle, president of the Bank of the United States, which had controlled and stultified the national economy for a generation. Biddle was non-partisan in politics and bought and sold Congressmen of all parties. He once said: "As to mere power, I have for years been in the daily exercise of more personal authority than any President."

These events were white men's concerns, however. The events that lifted Negro hearts into faint hope of freedom had begun in 1830. *The free Negroes of America had, for the first time, found their organized voice and used it.* A handful from seven states had gathered in Philadelphia to unite in demanding a hearing from white America.

A course was set in April 1830, and Martin Delany followed

it for the rest of his life. The initiative came from a young black man, Hezekiah Grice, who lived in Baltimore, Md. He too had been "born free" and had been indentured to a Virginia farmer who punished him as though he were a slave. When the farmer's wife also whipped him, Grice ran away.

In Baltimore, Grice wrote a letter to prominent Negroes in New York and Philadelphia suggesting that they get together to discuss their common problems. His thought was that they should advise black people on the wisdom of two courses, (1) emigrate to Canada, (2) stay in the United States and fight.

Grice did not receive a reply for four months and then his hopes rocketed. An answer came from the founder and first Bishop of the African Methodist Episcopal Church in Philadelphia, the Bethel Mother Church. Bishop Richard Allen asked Grice to come to Philadelphia immediately.

While Grice had given up hope, in New York three prominent Negroes who had received his letter had printed a circular endorsing the idea of a convention of colored men.

The group convened in Philadelphia on September 30, 1830, and consisted of 38 delegates and honorary delegates from Pennsylvania, New York, Connecticut, Rhode Island, Maryland, Delaware, and Virginia. Their first conclusion was "that our forlorn and deplorable situation earnestly and loudly demands of us to devise and pursue all legal means for the speedy elevation of ourselves and our brethren to the scale and standing of men."

The convention discussed the advantages of migration to Canada where 1,100 fugitives from Cincinnati had been welcomed. But perhaps the greatest contribution made by this first group voice of free Negroes was to establish a permanent organization.

The same group met again in June 1831 and it was the inspiration for the birth of the white anti-slavery movement in the United States. Whites had been invited to participate and among those attending were Benjamin Lundy, a pioneer abolitionist; and the wealthy New York merchant, Arthur Tappan and his brother Lewis, who were to become a rare combination in any crusade, moral, as well as financial, mainstays of abolitionism. Also at this early convention was America's first hero of democracy, William Lloyd Garrison, who had begun publication of *The Liberator* six months before.

The year 1831 was remarkable. Courageous whites had

spoken up before *for* the Negro, slave and "free." But never before had white and black hands clasped in agreement to seek the same objective. Never before had whites spoken up in agreement *with* Negro voices.

Southern state legislatures recognized this combination as a far greater menace to slavery than a revolt like Nat Turner's. David Walker's *Appeal* and William Lloyd Garrison's *Liberator* were not only barred from the states but also from the Federal mails. Their recipients were hounded from their towns and "book-burnings" took place. The slave codes were tightened and free Negroes fled the South.

In the North the Free States tightened their Black Codes and raided abolition meetings. Yankee skippers and Yankee merchants easily convinced their legislatures that what was good for King Cotton was good for the country.

Pittsburgh, too, shared in the Negro awakening to an advanced degree. Young Delany just missed the first meeting of the Colored Citizens of Pittsburgh, held in the Wylie Street African Methodist Episcopal Church on September 1, 1831. But he did not miss the results of that meeting, for almost immediately he met John B. Vashon who had been its chairman. Young Delany was thrilled by both. In the accounts of the meeting, Delany found his head lifted higher and his eyes opened wider to the plots and plans against his race. Vashon's meeting concerned itself with the growing activity among whites in behalf of the American Colonization Society. Five years before, a group of white churchmen in Pittsburgh had organized a branch of the Society and collected funds with which to send Negroes to Liberia. The Pennsylvania General Assembly had endorsed the objectives of the Society and memorialized the state's Congressional delegation to vote in favor of all Liberian aid from the Federal Government.

Against this tide, the colored men of Pittsburgh who welcomed Delany to their ranks spoke up in no uncertain terms:

> *Resolved*, That "we hold these truths to be self-evident: that all men are created equal, and endowed by their Creator with certain inalienable rights; that among these are life, liberty, and the pursuit of happiness"—*Liberty and Equality now. Liberty and Equality Forever!*

That was the sacred citation and the goal set for young Delany.

> *Resolved,* That we, the colored people of Pittsburgh and citizens of these United States, view the country in which we live as our only true and proper home. We are just as much natives here as the members of the Colonization Society. Here we were born—here bred—here are our earliest and most pleasant associations—here is all that binds man to earth and makes life valuable. And we do consider every colored man who allows himself to be colonized in Africa, or elsewhere, a traitor to our cause.

A right was stated here as well as a bold condemnation of all who fled the scene of battle. But why the forthright assertions in these and the other resolutions? One of them defined it.

> *Resolved,* That we are freemen, that we are brethren, that we are countrymen and fellow-citizens, and as fully entitled to the free exercise of the elective franchise as any men who breath; and that we demand an equal share of protection from our federal government with any class of citizens in the community. We now inform the Colonization Society that should our reason forsake us, then we may desire to remove. We will apprise them of this change in due season.

This was almost an impolite rejection. It was a statement of the right of self-determination, and more, an assertion of a *right* to equality. Then there was a pledge:

> *Resolved,* That we, as citizens of these United States, and for the support of these resolutions, with a firm reliance on the protection of divine Providence, do mutually pledge to each other our lives, our fortunes, and our sacred honor, not to support a colony in Africa nor in Upper Canada, nor yet emigrate to Hayti. Here we were born—here we will live by the help of the Almighty—and here we will die, and let our bones lie with our fathers.

This militant expression far outstripped the negativity of the

Philadelphia convention held just two months before. That body's delegates deplored the situation of the Negro in the United States, rather than denouncing it. They reported on and encouraged a refuge in Upper Canada instead of rejecting it. As for colonization in Liberia, compare the Pittsburgh statements with that adopted in Philadelphia:

> The Convention has not been unmindful of the operations of the American Colonization Society, and it would respectfully suggest to that august body of learning, talent and worth, that, in our humble opinion, strengthened too, by the opinions of eminent men in this country, as well as in Europe, that they are pursuing the direct road to perpetuate slavery, with all its unchristian-like concommitants, in this boasted land of freedom; and, as citizens and men whose best blood is sapped to gain popularity for that Institution, we would, in the most feeling manner, beg of them to desist; or, if we must be sacrificed to their philanthropy, we would rather die at home. Many of our fathers, and some of us, have fought and bled for the liberty, independence, and peace which you now enjoy and, surely, it would be ungenerous and unfeeling in you to deny us a humble and quiet grave in that country which gave us birth!

There was a reason for the difference between the almost simultaneous statements and plans of the two groups. In Philadelphia, they begged. In Pittsburgh, Vashon, natural leader of the free Negroes of Pittsburgh, demanded. Those were his sentiments, his attitudes, and his determination, although he himself was not sufficiently educated to have written those balanced sentences. He was a successful barber, and one of the many Negroes who "fought and bled" in the War of 1812 and was captured by the British early in the war. In a general prisoner exchange two years later, he was returned for a white British soldier, an act of equality he appreciated throughout his life. John B. Vashon was an indomitable force among the Negroes of Pittsburgh for nearly forty years. For young Martin Delany he was a mentor who not only aided but shaped him.

It is not surprising that 1831 saw such a divergent approach among the first articulate Negro groups. The fundamental question in relation to both the colonization scheme and refuge in Canada had yet to be answered, or even faced. In 1831, as today, the question was: Should Negroes stay in the United States and fight for a share of the democracy, or should they seek a haven beyond its borders? In 1831, as today, there is division among the Negroes as to the answer. In 1831, as today, there is wish expression among the whites combined with pious double-talk—whites wish the question would go away.

In 1816, when the American Colonization Society was founded, its organizers may have been sincere in believing that two million slaves could someday be returned to Africa and that any slaveholder would surrender his property and labor supply. As the years passed and the Society founded Liberia, its adherents in the North became largely church-oriented. Perhaps white congregations actually were convinced that their annual dues of one dollar constituted a tithe to the eventual end of slavery. At least, it had to be an act of grace to make possible a voluntary return of Negroes to the land of their forefathers. Besides, in the northern congregations the speedy departure of the Negroes would remove a nagging matter of conscience concerning equality of worship. The theologians were beginning to disagree and churches were to split over the problem; thus, if black faces disappeared from the segregated galleries, the white congregations could worship more comfortably.

The enthusiasm of the slaveholding South for the colonization scheme provided the chief source of revenue for the American Colonization Society and revealed still another motivation. Manumission of their slaves, wisely chosen, was a humane act. If slaves were forced to go to Africa, and that was the condition of freedom, the malcontents among them—the aged and infirm, the inept and lazy, in other words, unprofitable labor—could be shipped off. More important, the monstrous situation of free Negroes in the southern towns and cities could be corrected by making their lives so miserable that they would welcome escape to Africa.

The white colonization movement had an active life of about 45 years, and the sum total of its achievement before it expired of its own futility was to export to Liberia approximately fifteen thousand out of the four million Negroes in the United States in 1860. This was but a minute fraction of the number of slaves imported into the South through the illegal slave trade.

Both so-called free Negroes and white abolitionists rejected colonization as a scheme to get rid of the unwanted blacks and thus render slavery more secure. William Lloyd Garrison spoke up on the question just before Delany reached Pittsburgh.

> Now, to these promulgators of unrighteousness, I fearlessly give battle. . . . The Colonization Society . . . , instead of being a philanthropic and religious institution is anti-republican and anti-christian in its tendency.

However, there was a useful political purpose in the colonization movement and the Society—perhaps its only purpose. It provided both North and South with a sanctimonious meeting ground and therefore received approval of all Congresses and Presidents from James Monroe through and including Abraham Lincoln. Getting rid of the free Negroes would leave the inarticulate mass of black slaves more secure and more profitable both North and South. That was the fact and the "charity"—the rationalization—of the colonization scheme.

One of the first of many lessons learned by Delany in Pittsburgh was that, no matter what the moral compulsion, whites do not stir in regard to Negroes until the Negroes themselves stir them.

He was deeply moved by the Negro awakening and depressed by the lack of collaborative response among the whites. Until 1833, three years after the first meeting of the free Negroes in Philadelphia, there was no organized anti-slavery movement among whites. There were individuals, of course, whose voices came out of the white wilderness, like William Lloyd Garrison, who wrote on July 4, 1831:

> It is not probable that I shall be able to satisfy the great body of the people of my own color, otherwise than by entirely abandoning the cause of emancipation. Those who do not hesitate to call me a madman, a fanatic, a disturber of the peace, a promoter of rebellion—among other charitable epithets,—for vindicating the rights of slaves, will natu-

> rally be offended if I presume to stand up in behalf of the free people of color, or to address them on a subject pertaining to their welfare.

But it took two more years for white abolitionists either to eat their pious words or follow the example set by the free blacks and, finally, organize the American Anti-Slavery Society. But by 1840 their organized abolitionist activity had split irreparably into two major groups and, finally, many other splinters. They divided on the inevitable how? of achieving emancipation.

It is questionable whether white abolitionists might have had any hearing at all without a newspaper like *The Liberator* and an editor like William Lloyd Garrison who had no obligation to the status quo. The first subscriber to *The Liberator* was a Negro, and the paper survived only as a result of free Negro support, not white. Garrison's many expressions of gratitude to his Negro friends are on record. James Forten, the wealthy sailmaker of Philadelphia, helped pay the first printing bill with $54 for 27 subscriptions. Within a single year (December 1832 to November 1853) Delany's mentor, John B. Vashon of Pittsburgh, sent Garrison $110 which the editor acknowledged as a loan. He and Vashon were fast friends. When Garrison was saved from the Boston mob by being jailed in 1835, he was brought comfort and a new hat by Vashon. From the first issue of *The Liberator* until Vashon's death in 1854, he was the Pittsburgh agent for subscriptions to the vital newspaper.

This isolated example of Negro support could be multiplied many times over. During the first few years of its publication, white subscribers to *The Liberator* never exceeded 25 percent. The historical belief that *The Liberator* was the voice of the mass of Americans who clamored to do right by the blacks is entirely false. Negroes—and Negroes alone—made this dominant anti-slavery organ possible and assured its survival. Not until Garrison set the example was there to be an abolitionist press. In this aspect, too, it was the Negro awakening that filled the vacuum.

As a result, in the 1830s Negroes could look nowhere for popular support in the cause of abolition and citizenship but to themselves. And so there appeared a group of untutored free Negroes whose valiant struggle has been blotted out by the fiction of the American anti-slavery and emancipation movement.

It was this fraternity of black men that Martin Delany joined in Pittsburgh. These were men who "had it made" in spite of a hostile white society. They existed singly or in groups throughout the Free States. The story of John Boyer Vashon of Pittsburgh differs only in business activities from those of James Forten of Philadelphia, Dr. James McCune Smith of New York, John Malvin of Cleveland, John Jones of Chicago, and Hosea Easton of Boston.

These men, and many others, became comparatively rich and could afford not only luxury for their families but also the purchase of white protection. Yet they were not satisfied. They wanted more for their children and for their race. They gave their money, risked their lives and their businesses, and made themselves the target of white attack—all for their race. Their unwillingness to accept anything less than citizenship sparked the Negro awakening which, in turn, set a feeble fire under the white abolitionists.

Vashon had had the best possible education for his position as a black man, an education for survival. By 1837 there were 37 Negro barbers in Pittsburgh. This menial profession was in those years exclusively Negro because it was considered socially unfit for whites. (Today a Negro cannot join the Master Barbers' Union.) In 1834 Vashon announced the opening of public baths on Third Street, between Market and Ferry streets, "for the use of all who may be disposed to enjoy the luxury of bathing."

The City Baths became a business and political club for whites who made up the leadership of the city, and Vashon assumed the position of middleman between the Negro population and the city's men of influence. He became invaluable in any crisis, such as white riots, in protecting his people. But he went further.

From the first Negro convention in 1830 until his death in 1854, Vashon was in the forefront of every effort of self-help sponsored by black men in Pittsburgh or nationally. There was scarcely a meeting or a declaration from black people without his chairmanship or signature. At night, when his white patrons were not bathing, fugitive slaves reaching Pittsburgh utilized the elegant quarters for food, rest, and the most opulent baths in their lives. When there was money to be raised to buy a family back from the slave catchers, Vashon's name was first on the list.

Vashon and "Daddy Ben" Richards between them made it possible to establish the first colored school in the cellar of the Bethel African Methodist Episcopal Church in 1831. "Daddy Ben" was another early settler in Pittsburgh. A butcher, by 1810 he was accumulating wealth as a reliable supplier of meats to the Army and to the city's first provision markets. This made him hated by white competition who preferred to cut corners on delivery of fresh meats. However, the purchasers dealt with "Daddy Ben" because his word and his meats were good. He too invested early in real estate and became wealthy. The story is told that after fugitive slaves had their luxurious baths in Vashon's emporium they boarded one of "Daddy Ben's" wagons or keel boats for the journey northward to safety, with the strictest orders not to wave to the slave catchers as they went by!

John C. Peck was another of the Pittsburgh free Negroes who "had it made." In his old clothing store on Market Street, he began selling ice cream in the summers when business was slack. This became so successful that Peck announced in the *Pittsburgh Gazette* that he "has concluded to open a House during the winter season for Oysters, where parties of ladies and gentlemen will be served with oysters in the various modes at short notice." Here, too, fugitive slaves dined.

Rev. Lewis Woodson was not a success as a barber in his early years because he had an avocation of preaching and teaching. As an itinerant preacher, Rev. Woodson was among the leaders of the national organization of the African Methodist Episcopal Church and was secretary of the first annual conference of that church west of the Alleghenies in 1831. He eventually owned five barber shops, all operated by his sons and sons-in-law, and finally could afford to devote himself to the AME Church. He was the first teacher for an entire generation of Negro youth, including Martin Delany.

These men and others in Pittsburgh were not an exception among free Negroes. The Negro awakening found them in all cities and even in hamlets.

The Vashons of the country were the leaders of their race. In Pittsburgh in 1830 the Negro community was a highly responsible group. The census of that year shows that there were 435 "Free" Negroes and eight slaves in the city. They were too few to be classed as "nuisances" by the whites, because they were not yet competing for available jobs. Nor had Pittsburgh yet become overtly pro-slavery. That was to come with its development into one huge blast furnace, dependent upon the southern markets down the Ohio and Mississippi rivers. Not until 1834 were the anti-Negro riots organized and the pro-slavery forces mustered, as they were all over the North, as a coalition of economic powers and new white immigrants. Pro-slavery and anti-slavery whites were too busy with each other to bother with the Negroes. It was a time of comparative peace between the races and an ideal incubation period for Martin Delany.

The Negro population of Allegheny County was to leap forward in the next seven years as a result of its established black community. These black men, women, and children were not dependents. The earliest tax information available—for the year 1837—contains a report from the Overseer of the Poor that exactly three Negro families had been given aid during the year. In the same period, Negro taxpayers in Pittsburgh alone had paid $422 in property and poll taxes and $400 in water taxes. In a concentration of 71 Negro families, on the fringes of the city, 36 owned their own homes which were appraised for tax purposes at approximately $36,000. This was true too in Allegheny Town, across the river, where Negro property owners paid taxes ranging from $3.40 to $10.40. In that year, too, over one hundred black men paid poll taxes of $1.25 each. And heading all tax lists were John B. Vashon and Charles Richards, son of "Daddy Ben."

Martin Delany was welcomed into Pittsburgh by black men of pioneer courage. He settled in a community more self-sufficient and independent than that of the other minority groups, such as the Slavs and Irish, who also poured into the already smoky city.

CHAPTER THREE

Beginnings in Pittsburgh

Within two months of his arrival in Pittsburgh, Delany was among the first students assembled by Rev. Woodson in the cellar of the Bethel African Methodist Episcopal Church on Wylie Street, the founding of the first Negro-sponsored school for their own children. Within one year Delany was studying the classics, as well as Latin and Greek, and sharing living quarters and books, and taking courses with young Molliston M. Clark, a black student at nearby Jefferson College.

Within two years, Delany had chosen the area in which he wished to specialize, the study of medicine, which would serve both as a livelihood and a means of helping his people who had no Negro doctors. He began his apprenticeship in the office of Dr. Andrew N. McDowell.

Three years after his arrival in Pittsburgh, Delany was both a founder and an officer in several organizations of young Negro men and women, all formed for the self-improvement of his race. A year later he accompanied Rev. Woodson as a delegate from Pittsburgh to a national convention of colored men. Thereafter, Delany was launched in the turbulent, heartbreaking national scene of the Negro awakening.

Like all other young free Negroes, Delany for years groped for an answer to a question still pertinent today. If there is no opportunity to utilize it, why bother with an education? Was he aping the whites? Is knowledge a weapon against any enemy whose methods are the simple exertion of force? What philosopher ever created the ideal society they all discussed? Was the slaveholder right in his protestations as to the blissful ignorance of his slaves? Would it be wiser for a black man to live out his span in acceptance of his position on the lowest rung of the human ladder?

In his later writings, Delany confesses to moments of discouragement but adds hastily that they were only moments, caused by the endless individual debates with Molliston Clark, his young black friend. Emigrate? Or stay in the United States and fight?

If the answer was to emigrate, then where on this benighted globe, except to Africa? Canada would do as a temporary refuge, but the only real safety and opportunity lay among other black men. This answer would do for him, Delany knew, because he was preparing himself to lead his people. But what of those black men and women who had been debased to animal ignorance by the institution of slavery? There would be little point in establishing them among other blacks if they were incapable of self-government. Besides, why go to Africa merely to set up a refuge? The only motivation should be to form "a more perfect union" for the blacks, a society that achieved the ideal democracy professed but not practiced in America.

Stay and fight? Delany knew that he could do that too, if there was the faintest hope that slavery could be ended and black men could achieve equal citizenship. Sometimes, there was that hope, and with it the haunting doubt that it might represent mere wish expression, a self-delusion. That mercurial vacillation between hope and despair for the United States has been a familiar torture to black men both before and after Martin Delany.

For instance, by 1833 white citizens of Connecticut, by group action in New Haven and in Canterbury, prevented the establishment of a manual skills college for Negroes and a boarding school for Negro girls. In Boston the New England Anti-Slavery Society was having trouble finding a meeting place and, in addition, holding a meeting that would not be broken up by white mobs. Free Negroes were fleeing the Slave States as a result of new legislation after the Nat Turner uprising. In Washington, due to Henry Clay, South Carolina was being kept in the Union *on its own terms.* In New York, Irish fugitives from the potato famines were beginning to displace blacks in menial and unskilled work. The only promise of hope, the new voice of the free Negroes, was still too feeble to be a source of encouragement.

On the other hand, in September 1833 news of a miracle swept through the Pittsburgh Negro community. Eight hundred thousand slaves had been set free! The British Parliament had finally emancipated West Indian slaves. True, the emancipation would not be effective until 1840, and the British people paid heavily (£20 million) to the West Indies planters. But it was a fact. Approximately half as many black slaves as were held in the United States would be set free. The British had kept their word ever since 1808 when they abolished the slave trade from Africa, although the United States had never honored the agreement signed then. Perhaps there was hope of emancipation in a democracy like the United States, if it could be accomplished by a monarchy. Should the blacks spurn emigration and stay and fight?

There was only one conclusion possible for Delany from the endless individual and group debates that occupied free Negroes in the 1830s. Whether to emigrate or to stay and fight was a decision for the future because both courses demanded, as fundamental to their success, a single course of action.

Delany called it "self-elevation" of the black Americans. But he meant more than education of his people. His concept was the creation of a distinct minority group, so changing itself as to become a pattern for the majority society around it. It was the idealistic concept of a living culture he found among the philosophers he was reading, and he was young enough to disregard the destructive influences of property, politics, and prejudice upon ideals. His black people could *lead*, not merely equal, the whites. This required a course of action and a way of life that was a clear departure from the patterns imposed on the blacks, free or slave. It required more than mere education: living habits which were purer than Caesar's wife's and an individual and collective commitment to strive for all that white America preached and failed to achieve.

First and foremost, however, was education, and Delany was almost immediately drawn into that organized effort. Once more John B. Vashon and Rev. Lewis Woodson set about the solution of a Negro community problem. They had founded a school in the AME Church cellar which was inadequate at once. Merely the news that a school had been established was enough to bring Negro families into Pittsburgh. But there was not sufficient money in the Negro community to provide an adequate school; and their children were barred from white schools. Most whites in Pittsburgh and throughout the country, had forgotten the accepted motivation of the Revolutionary War, no taxation without representation.

On January 16, 1832, in the AME Church, the Negro community met to discuss the education of their children. Vashon was chairman and Woodson was secretary. Martin Delany was in the audience.

Once more Vashon's thinking and Woodson's power of expression produced a constitution for a permanent organization. Its preamble read:

> Whereas, ignorance in all ages had been found to debase the human mind, and to subject its votaries to the lowest vices, and most abject depravity; and it must be admitted, that ignorance is the sole cause of the present degradation and bondage of the people of color in these United States; that the intellectual capacity of the black man is equal to that of the white, and that he is equally susceptible of improvement, all ancient history makes manifest, and even modern examples put beyond a single doubt.
>
> We, therefore, the people of colour, of the city and vicinity of Pittsburg (*sic*), and state of Pennsylvania, for the purpose of dispersing the moral gloom, that has long hung around us; have, under Almighty God, associated ourselves together, which association shall be known by the name of the Pittsburg African Education Society.

Annual dues to the organization were $2. A five-man Board of Managers was elected and authorized to purchase books, supplies, and if financially possible, to pursue plans for a schoolhouse. Vashon was elected president, and Rev. Woodson, secretary. It was not until 1849 that Pittsburgh whites finally were shamed into sharing some of the Negro tax money for black schools, but in the intervening years, the African Education Society was a communal effort to educate their children, sometimes makeshift and sometimes highly successful.

The quality of education offered the black children cannot be evaluated beyond the patent fact that it was better than none at all. Martin Delany soon outstripped Rev. Woodson's classes and went on to independent study. However, one conclusion is possible. Rev. Woodson and his successor John Templeton must have been inspiring teachers, for leadership in the Negro community and also in the national Negro awakening came from their classes.

It is satisfying to know that the efforts of two of the men most responsible for the founding of the first school were rewarded in their children, both "graduates" of that AME Church cellar. George Boyer Vashon, son of John, was to go on to Oberlin College from which he graduated in 1844, one of the first Negro graduates from that institution. He continued in the study of law, writing poetry, teaching in New York State and in Pittsburgh, and leading his race in many respects. The first Negro to run for public office in New York, he was the Liberty party candidate for State Attorney General in 1855.

Dr. David J. Peck, son of John C., was the first Negro in the country's history to be awarded, in 1847, a medical degree recognized in every state and abroad. He graduated from Rush Medical College in Chicago.

These young men, Peck and Vashon, were not only their parents' pride and joy, they were Martin Delany's too. They were the next generation who would provide a continuity of leadership among their people, and this they demonstrated to him at an early age.

While Delany was busily organizing among his own age group and adults, Peck and Vashon went ahead on their own. On July 7, 1838, they organized their own age group into the first Juvenile Anti-Slavery Society in the country. Peck was elected president and Vashon was secretary. This group set the precedent for the national movement among youngsters to contribute the "cent a week" dues for anti-slavery causes.

In later years Delany was to work with both of them, as adult equals in many efforts for their people. They are only the outstanding examples of the generations of children to receive their first lessons in the little Wylie Street church, founded, sponsored, and continued for some eighteen years by the Negro community of Pittsburgh.

There were other community activities, and in them Martin Delany became the leader of the city's black youth, recognized as such by both blacks and whites. For him they were exciting years. He was discovering himself as well as being discovered. He found that he could capture an audience, that he could write his most abstruse thoughts in the typically florid manner of the day, and that he was capable of influencing even adults. In other words, Delany learned that he could communicate with his fellow man.

The order in which he entered the many community activities is not certain but Delany's initiative is definite. An example was the outgrowth of his studies with Molliston Clark, with whom he lived while attending the AME Church school. Clark was to rise high in the AME Church and at one time was the editor of its official newspaper still published today, the *Christian Recorder.*

While the two were students in Pittsburgh, almost inevitably they encountered the bread and salt of the classical education of their time, the Greek and Roman philosophers. Delany read avidly and was both surprised and delighted to learn that the Greeks and Romans, exciting as they might be, were merely annotating an earlier culture, an earlier set of philosophical concepts.

The city of Thebes in Upper Egypt had had a golden age many centuries before Pericles and Athens, he learned. The great Rameses II brought the city to its greatest splendor as a capital, a fountainhead of a new culture—*made by and for the black man.* The wonders of Thebes, the wisdom of its people, and the fact that it was an *African* civilization had the young enthusiast agog. To him Thebes was a three-mile-square Acropolis, inhabited only by poets, philosophers, musicians, and men of science whose expression became the intellectual heartbeat of all Africa and on whose words of wisdom the white barbarians to the north founded their own cultures.

That discovery was the cause of one of Delany's many activities. He and Clark founded the Theban Literary Society, a pretentious group of young black men whose offices had Greek appellations and whose meetings were occupied with reading and criticism of each other's literary efforts and intellectual wanderings. No doubt the rarefied atmosphere of the Society was quite divorced from the immediate problems of the day, but in 1832 it was a miraculous accomplishment to draw together these youths who were fumbling for mental armor against a predictable and difficult manhood. This was the first demonstration of Delany's leadership, and the members of the Theban Literary Society were to provide the nucleus for other efforts. By 1837, when the organization had adopted a new name, the

Young Men's Literary and Moral Reform Society of Pittsburgh, their sights were expanded. They declared as their objectives "the literary, moral and intellectual improvement of the young and rising generation, the establishment of a library, the promotion of education and morality and instruction in the mechanical arts, so far as in our power lies." In that year, Delany was elected librarian.

The members of this group had also joined Delany in 1834 when he founded the Young Men's Moral Reform Society of Pittsburgh. This "uplift" organization was an outgrowth of the third convention of free Negroes held in Philadelphia that year. It marked the beginning of diverging thought among the participants as to actually programming the national Negro awakening, between those who wished first to build a moral arsenal to persuade the American people and those who wished an aggressive assertion of demands. Delany agreed with all of its constitutional tenets, such as the creation of manual labor schools, establishment of a Negro press, a study of Africa so as to "endeavor to establish in our people a correct knowledge of their own immortal worth," and even to their stand on integration as opposed to emigration. Delany had not yet suffered his first disillusionment.

The Moral Reform Society in Pittsburgh was another useful forum for the young people but accomplished little beyond that. Perhaps its greatest accomplishment was the successful conclusion of a somewhat juvenile competition in 1839. Delany apparently was not sufficiently proud of it to report it but the organ of the American Reform Society, the *National Reformer*, did:

> ACTION! ACTION!
>
> The Young Men's M.R. Society of Pittsburg (*sic*) appear to be *practically* carrying out their principles, for while fools are running foot races, they are running with their pens. There were several competitors for a prize medal, to be given to the one what could write the Lord's Prayer in the smallest space. The prize was awarded M. R. Delany. A sample of the same has been sent us: it is about the size of a sixpence.

In still another activity Martin Delany was eminently successful. He himself never had to swear off the use of tobacco or liquor since he never used either. However, there was a tendency among black people to copy the white example throughout the country and the temperance movement found fallow ground among them. In Pittsburgh, drinking was as much of an institution as anywhere in the country and the newspapers of the 1830s recorded all the Negro drunks picked up by the night watch, particularly in the taverns along the wharves. This did not signify that whites did not drink, only that either they were not arrested or not reported in the newspapers. Usually, Negro arrests were made only when Negro drunks fought with white drunks.

The demon rum aroused Delany almost as much as his pride of ancestry. His speeches for total abstinence were as impassioned as his speeches for African elevation. The Temperance Society of the People of Color of the City of Pittsburgh was the first temperance organization among Negroes in the country. By its third year, in 1837, there were 170 members, and the annual report was written by Martin Delany, the recording secretary. It states that 500 copies of the constitution and by-laws had been printed and distributed; eighty copies of the monthly *Pennsylvania Temperance Recorder* had been circulated in the Negro community; and 333 *Temperance Almanacs* and $7 worth of temperance tracts had been given out. The funds, amounting to $30 in these expenditures had been raised through voluntary contributions in the city.

Delany was an officer in the above organizations at one time or another, but throughout his life in Pittsburgh there was one activity which gave him great personal satisfaction. Its title was misleading—the Philanthropic Society. For many years Delany was to be the secretary of its executive board, and, as a result, was recognized by the whites as the Negro representative in aid to the poor. He was named to the city's charity committee.

But the Philanthropic Society was not founded for philanthropy in the familiar sense, for there were four community mutual aid groups taking care that black families did not become public charges. The Philanthropic Society was a highly efficient fugitive slave organization that made Pittsburgh almost as safe a haven as the ultimate Canadian destination. Once the escaping slave had reached the city and made his contact, the numerous slave catchers were easily baffled. There were few captures in the city itself, yet in one year, Delany reports, the Society had sent 269 fugitives to the North Star. Their operations expanded to rescues, to organizing the re-purchase of captives and intervention in the courts to force return of kidnaped free Negroes.

His work for the Philanthropic Society led Delany into the position of heir-apparent to John B. Vashon's relationship with the city's white leaders. It was in those early years that he succeeded in establishing a most unusual status with whites, one that was to survive his death. No matter how often he aroused opposition, disagreement, dislike, and positive hatred in the whites by his arrogance in the spoken and written word, Delany never lost their respect of his demand that they deal with him as an equal, not an inferior supplicant.

He spoke his mind, sometimes totally without tact. The whites soon learned that he would not stoop to lie or dissemble and, of course, would never beg. As a result, while they respected his mind, they admired his pride. This was particularly true among the members of the medical profession in and around Pittsburgh.

Perhaps men of Hippocrates were different in those early years before the American Medical Association became a trade union barring Negro membership and holding "life or death" power over national health legislation through its lobby. The physicians of new America did not claim absolution from social responsibility because of their profession. In fact, one of the heroes of American medicine, Dr. Benjamin Rush of Philadelphia, not only signed the Declaration of Independence but was one of the first white abolitionists in the new country.

This was also true of Dr. F. Julius LeMoyne of Washington County, Pa., bordering on Allegheny County. In 1833 Dr. LeMoyne founded the Anti-Slavery Society of Washington County and was its chairman; and in February 1837 he helped to found and was elected the first president of the Pennsylvania Anti-Slavery Society established in Philadelphia. Among the first officers elected were Dr. Joseph P. Gazzam of Pittsburgh as corresponding secretary. Delany was to study medicine with both men and both were to be instrumental in gaining his admission to the Harvard Medical School in 1850. Seventeen other physicians in Pittsburgh and Allegheny City joined them in this endeavor.

Over the years still another doctor, Dr. William Elder, originally from Chambersburg and then Pittsburgh, was to be one of Delany's personal as well as professional colleagues. Dr. Elder left the practice of medicine to dedicate himself to the anti-slavery cause.

Yet another physician, a remarkable young man, was to enable Delany to repay, in part, the many obligations he owed to John B. Vashon in 1839. This was Dr. Jonas R. McClintock who returned to his native Pittsburgh from the University of Maryland Medical School in 1830 and set up practice. He was the city's health physician in 1834 and also was second in command of the dashing rifle and marching militia, the Duquesne Grays.

In that year there had been an increase in the number of anti-Negro riots and the target appeared to be the growing "ghetto" known as "Hayti." On at least one occasion, Dr. McClintock marched his militia to the scene and dispersed the mob.

Delany was there with the members of his Philanthropic Society, well-muscled young men who resisted the raiders without charity. Later, in his capacity as a member of the City Charity Committee, he came in contact with Dr. McClintock whose duties as health physician included the care of the Negroes against epidemic. In 1836, in the first public election for the office, Dr. McClintock became Pittsburgh's "Boy Mayor." He was re-elected twice more and could have remained in the post indefinitely had he not preferred to return to practice.

Young McClintock's first election had an interesting platform. In addition to anti-Negro riots, the city was a Saturday night saturnalia which lasted well into early church on Sunday. McClintock was for "law and order" and the establishment of a night police force. He forced an ordinance through his first City Council and, as a result, in the year 1839 he became the first local official in any American city to find a formula for the quelling and prevention of race riots. His method could be studied with profit today by mayors of most cities.

The details of the incident on April 27, 1839, were as follows: It was a Saturday and the drinking began early. There was a fight between a white man and two or three Negroes, according to the accounts, and early that afternoon the Negroes in Hayti learned that the white man was gathering some of his friends for an attack that night. The residents of the area prepared for a riot, as usual. Vashon distributed arms to some of Delany's stalwart young members of the Philanthropic Society, and he vowed that there would be dead whites that night if they attacked. It was time to fight back.

This was wholly Martin Delany's belief. However, he too believed in law and order and appointed a delegation of his young men and some of the Negro leaders to accompany him to the court house. There he saw Judge Amos Pentland, a highly respected jurist. Delany, as spokesman for the Negroes of Pittsburgh, served notice on the white authorities that his people were beyond their patience. They were law-abiding and law-respecting, he pointed out, as the records of the judge's own court would attest. But, Delany added, if the law could not protect the Negroes from the white rioters, they would protect themselves. Coldly he laid before the judge the facts that the night police force was too small and too unwilling to have prevented riots in the past. There was no reason to expect them to intervene with any effectiveness that night.

Having delivered his ultimatum, Delany and his men returned to their defense preparations. A few hours later, Mayor McClintock sent for him and proposed a plan. He suggested that they test it that night and utilize it in the future, if successful.

His plan was simple. He now had the authority, in time of emergency, to appoint special police. He wished Delany to name among his young men the most responsible blacks who would accept the prevention of the riot as their duty, not solely defense against the rioters. He, the mayor, would also select a group of responsible young white men to appoint as special police, and each of his men would be paired with one of Delany's black men to patrol, protect, and prevent disorder as a team.

If that failed then of course the blacks would have to defend themselves. However, he would be at the scene, with his Duquesne Grays, because he wished the full impact of the law to be demonstrated on would-be rioters.

There were hundreds of white men in the mob and they were met by the "black and white" police teams, which plucked the ringleaders from the crowd and handed them over to the Duquesne Grays. Two or three houses were torn down and set afire in the battle. (The owner of one of the houses later petitioned the Select Council for damages but the report indicates scant consideration given it. "A petition purporting to be from Aaron Blanchard praying relief from Council for damage to his property on the night of the 27th inst. by a mob was read and laid on the table.")

However, the work of Delany's blacks and the mayor's whites was to have a most salutary effect. The ringleaders of the white mob were brought before Judge Amos Pentland and were punished to the extent of the law. It was the last planned anti-Negro riot in Pittsburgh, though many raids were inspired by the slave catchers.

The earliest record yet found that Martin Delany had been ranked by the blacks and whites alike as a responsible adult leader in the Negro community is a letter to the editors of the *Pittsburgh Gazette* on March 29, 1838.

> Messrs. Craig and Grant:
>
> The undersigned have been credibly informed that a report is in circulation in this city of a contemplated rescue on the part of colored citizens of the unfortunate Gallego who now awaits the infliction of the highest penalty through our laws. From our intimate knowledge of our brethren, and our daily intercourse with them we feel fully warranted in saying that such a report is wholly false, and without a shadow of foundation. We deeply reprobate a resort to violence under any circumstances as being alike disgraceful to ourselves and our country, and feel ourselves bound on all occasions to maintain the peaceful administration of justice and the supremacy of the laws.

The signatures, in the order of their signing, were: Lewis Woodson, John C. Peck, A. (Abraham) D. Lewis, M. R. Delany, and J. B. Vashon.

Young Delany also had private problems from the moment of his arrival in Pittsburgh—food and shelter while he studied. All manner of unskilled jobs were available to him because he was as energetic a worker as an organizer. Jobs were plentiful in the early years since the city was just entering its industrial explosion, and competition with the other unskilled among the Slavs, Irish, Germans, and Welsh who flooded the city had not yet begun.

But such work and competition were not for Delany. All of his speeches called upon his young colleagues to equip themselves for occupations intellectually and economically above those allocated to them by the whites. Quite characteristically, he chose for himself one of the two most difficult professions for any Negro to enter—medicine. The other was law, and white lawyers of the 1830s were already organized sufficiently to prevent any Negro from passing the bar examinations.

There were no trained black doctors in 1833. There had been only one recognized Negro physician, around 1800, Dr. James Derham, but he practiced in civilized New Orleans before it was annexed by the Cotton Kingdom. This ex-slave from Philadelphia had been owned by three successive physicians, each of whom found him a most gifted medical student. His last owner, Dr. Robert Dove of New Orleans, allowed him to purchase his freedom through his earnings as a practicing physician.

There was no Negro doctor in the country until 1837 when Dr. James McCune Smith returned to New York with his medical degree from the University of Glasgow. All of the medical schools in the United States had refused his applications.

Very few white physicians would treat a Negro, unless the patient was property, a slave. If he or she was a valuable slave, a skilled worker, or a promising breeder of other slaves, the masters saw to it that they had the best medical care available. The free Negroes generally were without medical care except from those ex-slaves who had learned some healing skills on the plantations among generations of experts in folk medicine. Some of these practitioners achieved amazing skills in the art, so much so that even whites used their services. It appears that in life-or-death matters, ailing or dying whites conquered their prejudices and belief in Negro inferiority. There is on record in the Tennessee State Legislature a petition from both the female and male whites of Fayette County in 1843 praying that body to exempt "Dr. Jack" from the law prohibiting the practice of medicine by any slave. Dr. Jack was represented as having served suffering humanity so successfully that those services should become public property. They did not ask repeal of the law, only an exception made for Dr. Jack.

The challenge of a medical career may have persuaded Delany to attempt it, or Dr. Andrew N. McDowell may have induced him to begin the study. We do not know the motivation that caused him to begin his medical apprenticeship in 1833.

Dr. McDowell, formerly of Chambersburg and noted in

biographies of Stephen Foster as the composer's father-in-law, was another of the white physicians who "adopted" young Delany. He is the same Dr. McDowell appearing in the correspondence of Charles Dickens, the two having become friends in 1842 when the British novelist became ill on his American tour.

But Delany was to complete his medical studies many struggles and doctors later. In 1836 he left Dr. McDowell and set up an office at No. 2 Diamond as a "cupper, leecher and bleeder." He also practiced dentistry for a time. In his advertisements, Delany offered as references "The physicians of Pittsburg, Allegheny and Birmingham."

Medical practices in those years retained much of the craft characteristics of the first doctors, and "bleeding" was a recommended remedy in a host of symptoms, from broken bones to inexplicable pains. It was an accepted practice, and all cities had their "cuppers and bleeders." Few, however, had Negro bleeders, for a degree of training was required. Some knowledge of the arterial and venal systems was necessary, as well as skill in the two methods of drawing blood—cupping and leeching.

In both methods the usual practice was to "scarify" or break the protective skin layer somewhat and, in leeching, apply the leeches, which did the rest. Cupping involved the use of a small glass container with a wide mouth and a hole at its bottom or a container with no hole. In both cases, the practitioner created a suction, through indrawn sucking at the container or by burning a bit of wool, then quickly applying the cup to the prepared skin area after the heat had created a suction.

The greatest skill required was in judging the amount of blood to be taken in each treatment. One early British physician, a devotee of bleeding, recommended it for pneumonia and the amount of blood to be taken to be decided by the patient. When he fainted, that was enough.

The achievement of a practitioner's status in the medical field was not only a service to Delany's ego. It was to take another ten years before he could resume his medical studies, but meanwhile he had made possible a continuation of his dedication to his race. His practice as a bleeder solved the economic problem and left him free to continue his studies in history, politics, and ethnology, to continue his community work, to accept the responsibilities his abilities attracted to him, and to travel in behalf of his people.

At the age of 24, Martin Delany had attained an independence of thought, action, and planning that is enviable at any age.

CHAPTER FOUR

The Organizer

The year 1838 was a bitter one for the Negroes of Pennsylvania. It was not only the revival of violence that spread in recurring waves from east to west. Schools, homes, orphanages, and the meeting place of the white abolitionists—Pennsylvania Hall in Philadelphia—were burned, and black men were not safe on any streets.

But white violence was something with which Negroes had always lived. They knew it would persist until they, as citizens, received equal protection of the laws. Each right they held under those laws was a precious foundation for the achievement of further rights. But to lose the most precious right of all—their suffrage—was a catastrophic blow. It happened in 1838, and the circumstances were the first revelation to Martin Delany that he might be living in a dream world to "stay and fight."

The loss of the vote, held since 1780 by Negroes fulfilling the property qualifications, began with a State Supreme Court decision. One William Fogg, a Negro in Luzerne County, had brought suit in Common Pleas Court against the election officials who had refused his ballot. This lower court ruled in Fogg's favor and it was appealed to the State Supreme Court.

The opinion, written by Chief Justice C. J. Gibson, reversed the Common Pleas Court and destroyed the foundation of any hope for future rights at the same time. The very article of the Constitution on which those hopes were based was declared by Judge Gibson "an obstacle to the political freedom of the negro (*sic*) which seems to be insuperable."

In effect, Judge C. J. Gibson preceded by twenty years and for the jurisdiction of the State of Pennsylvania alone, what U.S. Chief Justice C. J. Taney in 1857 declared applied to the country in the Dred Scott decision: that "the plaintiff in error is not a citizen of Missouri."

Yet it was upon the Second Section of the Fourth Article of the U.S. Constitution that the free Negroes rested their faith in a possible future. "The Citizens of each State shall be entitled to all the Privileges and Immunities of Citizens in the several States."

What Judge Gibson decided was that William Fogg could not vote because he was not a citizen of the State of Pennsylvania, since Negroes in the other states—and he cited North Carolina—were not able to vote.

> It is to be remembered that citizenship, as well as freedom, is a constitutional qualification; and how it could be conferred so as to overbear the laws imposing countless disabilities on him in other states is a problem of difficult solution. In this aspect the question becomes one not of intention, *but of power, and of power so doubtful as to forbid the exercise of it.* Every man must lament the necessity of these disabilities, but slavery is to be dealt with by those whose existence depends on the skill with which it is treated. Considerations of mere humanity however belong to a class which, as judges, we have not to do; and interpreting the Constitution in the spirit of our own institutions we are bound to pronounce that men of colour are destitute of title to the elective franchise.

Based on this decision a Constitutional Convention went into immediate action to amend the Pennsylvania constitution in conformity. Negroes of the state gathered hurriedly in Philadelphia on March 14, 1839, and issued an appeal to the whites to stop this legislative murder of their rights. Their memorial declared:

> When you have taken from an individual his right to vote, you have made the government, in regard to him, a mere despotism; and you have taken a step toward making it a despotism to all. . . . Firm upon our old Pennsylvania Bill of Rights, and trusting in a God of Truth and Justice, we lay our claim before you, with the *warning* that no

> amendments to the present Constitution can compensate for the loss of its foundation principle of equal rights, for the *conversion into enemies of 40,000 friends.*

It was useless. The amendment was adopted and its purpose was served merely by the addition of the word "white" to the section relating to eligibility to vote. "*White* freemen of the age of 21 years and upwards who have resided . . . ," etc.

It was a serious step backward. Whether or not the forty thousand free Negroes of Pennsylvania were converted into "enemies" is not known. But it is known that Martin Delany's conversion into the ranks and then leadership of the black emigrationists began in that year. If the first state to end slavery was to be the first state to end the meager suffrage among the Free States, it being a question "but of power" and no enjoyment of Article 4, then what was to prevent Pennsylvania from becoming the first state to *restore slavery?* That would be the logic of it for, as a president was to declare much later, no nation can endure "half slave and half free."

Other "Free" States followed Pennsylvania's lead in adopting more oppressive black laws, notably neighboring Ohio. There were no moral or democratic considerations involved in such legislation. The only determining factor was the extent to which each state reacted against northern abolitionists and to southern pressures. There had been many threats from the South. A typical example, that grew even more pointed with each crisis, is from the *Richmond* (Va.) *Enquirer* in September 1835:

> The South then, warns the North. The crisis may increase. The interests of the North may soon suffer as well as those of the South. The intercourse of her citizens, with the Southern States, will be submitted to unpleasant restrictions, from the effects of the suspicion which is now excited. The public Mail will be fettered. Our own safety will compel us to drive off the most obnoxious People of Color, who will become nuisances in the northern cities. Commerce will be gradually fettered. It will first be prohibited with all the Abolitionists, and who knows but the indignant spirit of an incensed people may extend the restriction to all the merchants of the North?

In all northern state capitols and in Washington there was fear, trembling, and more political compromise to assure the South that American materialism would not be hampered by any humane attitudes toward the black people.

In the winter of 1839 Martin Delany took his first action in investigating emigration possibilities. He went South to see for himself if the still-independent Republic of Texas might be a haven for the free Negroes. All that summer white abolitionists had been agitating against annexation of the new republic. It was a major reason for the split among them, dividing the harassed ranks into those seeking political action, the moderates, and the Garrisonians, who would make no compromise with absolute emancipation, by revolution if necessary. The Liberty party was formed that summer and later nominated Birney for president. A major plank in the platform was opposition to the southern pressure to annex Texas. However, Birney got approximately 7,000 votes and eventually Texas was annexed.

It required personal courage to venture down the Mississippi, visiting the cotton state, and particularly Louisiana. Delany had his "free papers" of course but in visiting the slaves, which was Delany's purpose, he could have been picked up by any of the Parish patrols and brought before a Parish jury which observed no juridical rules for free Negroes particularly. From there he could have disappeared, as so many blacks did. Even white Yankees feared travel down the river during that period of mass hysteria in the South.

However, it was characteristic that Delany weighed the dangers and the need, and decided that his own observation of slavery and particularly of Texas was more important. He spent several months on the journey and returned with at least one conclusion.

Texas would have been ideal for emigration of free blacks if not for the inevitability of annexation by the South, not by the United States, but by the slaveholding South. The whole sorry record of the Texas annexation throes, the final southern victory in Washington, and the war with Mexico was coupled with the southern retention of political control of the United States. That was being challenged by the admission of the northern non-slave states and was to reach a climax in the Kansas-Nebraska war fifteen years later.

But Texas would have been ideal for the free Negroes. It

even had a precedent of freedom for blacks. On April 8, 1830, a Mexican Congress had prohibited slavery in the territory, though it did not interfere with the peonage system among the Indians established in the sixteenth century by the Spanish settlers. The emancipation, of course, was rescinded by succeeding revolutionary governments in Mexico and by the victory of the white settlers at the battle of San Jacinto in 1836. But the land was there, beautiful land for growing both an economy and a culture separate from all the white United States. Only a few years later, German immigrants were to prove this by transplanting their own civilization into Texas and thriving there as an independent culture.

During the course of these travels, Delany fell in with one of the earliest of many military adventurers who utilized the protection of Louisiana and Arkansas as staging areas for their forays against the Mexicans in Texas. It was the encampment of the handsome lawyer from Natchez, Felix Huston, who had recruited and fought as a Texan. Gen. Huston was one of many picaresque amateur soldiers who wanted to march right to the walls of Montezuma without regard for the diplomatic niceties.

While Delany was visiting in the camp, he was asked to tend a wounded soldier. He did so and his skill astounded the white officers to such an extent that Gen. Huston offered Delany the post of surgeon. Though flattered, Delany refused. Nor could he explain to Huston that his "Army's" objectives were opposed to his own.

Unfortunately, none of Delany's reports on his journey in 1839 has been discovered. Yet we have his complete itinerary through Mississippi, Louisiana, Texas, and Arkansas. It is possible to glean from his observations and discussions with both slaves and whites the tempers of the people and the appearance of the terrain. For instance, he went north from Texas into Arkansas, to the Choctaw Indian Nation near Fort Towson to determine why the Indians held blacks as slaves. His interview with the elderly chief included a reply to his statement: "I can't well understand how a man like you can reconcile your principles with the holding of slaves. . . ."

In the novel *Blake*, Delany wrote that the chief's answer was: "Now you see . . . the difference between a white man and an Indian holding slaves. Indian work side by side with black man, eat with him, drink with him, rest with him and both lay down in shade together; white man won't even let you talk. In our Nation Indian and black all marry together. Indian like black man very much, only he don't fight 'nough."

"You make, Sir, a slight mistake about my people. They would fight if they were in their own country, and united as the Indians here, and not scattered thousands of miles apart as they are. . . ."

This dialogue and some seventy-odd chapters of a story that traces Delany's journey and such debates, comes from a novel, *Blake: or The Huts of America, A Tale of the Mississippi Valley, the Southern United States, and Cuba,* written by him twenty years later. The hero of the novel, Henry, is Delany himself in a fictional flight of his own dreams, for his protagonist journeys and talks to people in pursuit of a planned insurrection of slaves that would wipe out the plantations of the South. The entire plot of *Blake* was a dream of vengeance in 1859, just before leaving for Africa and after deciding that emigration was his people's only solution. Henry constitutes a self-revelation. The last sentence of the novel reads: "Woe be unto those devils of whites, I say."

With Texas rejected as a lost cause, Delany returned to the wars at home. Almost immediately he was elected to the Board of Managers of the Pittsburgh Anti-Slavery Society, now comprising the separate groups in the city and in Allegheny Town.

This anti-slavery group was probably the first integrated abolitionist society in the country. It was formed on October 4, 1833, with Rev. Lewis Woodson as its recording secretary. In 1840 the Society actively entered politics, and Delany received his baptism in the frustration of electioneering without being able to cast a ballot. In that election, the Liberty party candidate received only 343 votes among the whites of Allegheny County; but the following year, when Dr. LeMoyne ran for governor on an abolitionist ticket, the county gave him 793 votes. Once more, Delany's hopes soared. Maybe the democratic process did work!

It was in 1841 too that the free Negroes of Western Pennsylvania assumed the leadership of their people in the state, so long held by the Philadelphia group. The immediate cause was a total resignation to the loss of the vote. Three years had passed and nowhere in the state was there even the thought of a concerted effort to launch a campaign in Harrisburg for the restoration of suffrage to the free blacks. The same black men of Pittsburgh who had taken the initiative in the Negro awakening once more took action. They organized a State Convention of the Colored Freemen of Pennsylvania held in Pittsburgh on August 23, 24, and 25, 1841, and Martin Delany assumed his place among the adult leaders in that effort.

At the initial organizational meeting, held on January 12, a committee was appointed to draft a statement justifying the one and only problem to be placed on the agenda of a state gathering—restoration of suffrage to the free blacks. Martin Delany served on this committee with John B. Vashon, Lewis Woodson, and four others. A week later, John Peck, acting president, called for and obtained a unanimous vote on the following:

> *Whereas,* among all the rights of the Republic, none are so sacred and among all the safeguards of the liberties of free men, none are so powerful as the right of suffrage—a right, indeed, which gives political existence to those who possess it, and political annihilation to those who are deprived of it —a right paramount in vitality and importance to all political rights, and to obtain which, when deprived of it, no labor should be counted too severe, no sacrifice too great, and
>
> *Whereas,* the colored citizens of the Commonwealth of Pennsylvania are, by her present Constitution, deprived of this sacred right, for no other cause than it has pleased the Almighty Creator to clothe them with a dark hue—a circumstance over which they had no control, and for which no just Tribunal can or will hold them accountable and to punish them for which with the highest political privation is not only doing violence to nature itself, but is offering insult and mockery to the Almighty Creator of all things and judge of all men, and
>
> *Whereas,* in opposition to this just and wholesome maxim, the colored people of the Commonwealth of Pennsylvania have hitherto maintained an apathy and indifference not only to the exercise of the elective franchise but to other collateral rights of high importance to them as free men; an apathy and indifference highly criminal and for which it is feared they are not prepared to give a satisfactory account, neither to God, their own consciences, nor posterity, and to maintain which apathy and indifference longer would

degrade them still lower in the eyes of all enlightened and good men,

"Therefore . . ." a meeting of all free colored in the state was called. A thirteen-man corresponding committee, including Delany, was elected, and the work of organization began. The committee drew up the call to the convention and all of its seven points were as forthright as the first justification for the meeting. They reveal a practical brand of political activity placing the Pittsburgh men far in advance of the many lofty pleaders for justice and good will among their people. The Pittsburgh blacks were realists.

> 1. It is hardly to be expected that the Constitution will be altered and the right of voting granted to colored persons unless at least a majority of them in the whole State desire it.
>
> 2. If a majority in the whole State desire this right, they must in some way or other show it.
>
> 3. The general way of showing the popular will in the United States in favor of any individual or of any great measure is holding a Convention.
>
> 4. If the white citizens cannot succeed without submitting to the expense and trouble of holding Conventions, we cannot see upon what ground the colored citizens expect to succeed by easier and cheaper means.
>
> 5. Conventions possess a double advantage: 1—of showing the popular will; 2—by arousing the sympathies, they inspire confidence and impart life and energy to the actions of men in a manner superior to all other means. This is the chief reason why they are so often resorted to for carrying great and important measures. So essential are popular assemblies to the liberties of man that he cannot obtain or preserve them without their aid. The whole history of the past is but one continued confirmation of the fact that when there are no popular assemblies there is no Republican government.
>
> 6. We owe it to ourselves, our friends, and our posterity to make at least some effort to silence the charge that has long been preferred against us of indifference to our rights,

> and we can conceive of no way of doing it which promises more success than the one now presented.
>
> 7. A further consideration why we should hold a Convention and, if possible, interest the majority of the citizens in our favor is that after the desired alteration in the Constitution is made and concurred in by two successive Legislatures, it must then be submitted to a vote of the whole State for adoption.

This primer in political science was distributed throughout the state in March, and in July the site of the convention was switched to Pittsburgh from Harrisburg because of the sheer effectiveness of the blacks in the former city. Delany was on the agenda committee and the arrangements committee.

This was an *all-black* convention. Not a single white man, not even the proven friends among the abolitionists, was invited to participate. Not even the "token" whites of the Philadelphia and New York meetings were in attendance. The reasons were given publicly by Lewis Woodson a week before the meetings, when ugly rumors spread through the city that the blacks were going to gather to plot and defy the whites. They were even planning an ostentatious and provocative march through the streets of the Diamond. And these were followed by further rumors that the whites were mobilizing to attack any such parade or meetings.

Rev. Woodson announced in the *Pittsburgh Gazette*:

> Such a thing as marching through the streets was never dreamed of. The days of such childish parade are long since past for us, nor will any other than colored persons participate in the doings of the Convention. The participation of others is not rejected out of any disrespect to them but because it is natural and right. Every man knows his own affairs best, and naturally feels a deeper interest in them than anyone else, and therefore on that account ought to attend to them.

He further pleaded that Pittsburgh not disgrace herself "by any lawless or violent exhibition toward us." There was not a single incident to mar the proceedings.

The gathering in August represented twenty counties in the state, and its major decision was to begin a campaign on the county level. To assure continuity to the program, John C. Peck was elected permanent president; other officers included Woodson and John Templeton. Martin Delany was continued on the publishing committee after he made several speeches at the meetings.

But the entire effort was destined to fail. Restoration of the vote lay only in the power of the whites and they were not in the least concerned. There was no time for such considerations. The whole country had fully recovered from the economic panic of 1837 and it was a time to make materialistic hay rather than trifle with any illusory ideals potentially dangerous to that recovery. It was a time to placate the South and to make still further concessions. This was particularly true in Pittsburgh. Natural gas had been discovered and was in full exploitation. There was coal and iron ore, and there was the Ohio River to start the fabricated metals southward where they had nothing but cotton.

And so, all the strenuous preparation and planning for the convention was for no purpose. The decision to meet again in 1842 was never implemented. It was another futile effort for Martin Delany to evaluate. Stay and fight? Emigrate?

However, the convention did have one concrete result and Delany himself brought it about. Among the many resolutions discussed and adopted (No. 11) was the following:

> Resolved, that in the opinion of this Convention a newspaper conducted by the colored people and adapted to their wants is much needed in this State, and that we request their general cooperation, especially in the East, in establishing such a paper.

The discussion concluded that a newspaper of their own was entirely feasible.

> To purchase a press and its accompanying apparatus costs from five to seven hundred dollars, and to print an ordinary sheet as our case would require, would cost perhaps a little upwards of $35. a week, amounting in a year, say, to $2,000. And what are our resources for sustaining this expense? Our population is near 50,000, and although the statistical

> returns to our Convention were very imperfect, yet they were sufficient to show that we own at least two million dollars worth of property, and will anyone presume that one thousand subscribers able to pay two dollars a year each for a good paper cannot be found? In all those numbers and all this wealth?

Apparently the answer was negative, for two years passed before Delany lost his patience, and tossing all cost calculations aside, began *The Mystery*, for a time the only Negro newspaper published in the United States.

Launching *The Mystery* in September 1843 was an illustration of Delany's propensity to attempt the impossible. Being a journalist, editor, and publisher would be an entirely new experience for him, for he had not yet discovered his own abilities as a writer. In addition, there were personal reasons against taking the step. It would not only reduce his income from cupping and leeching since so much of his time would be taken by the newspaper, but it would further delay the resumption of his medical studies—for now Dr. Joseph P. Gazzam was ready to take him into his office. Finally, there was a personal reason—he was now a family man.

On March 15 of that eventful year he and Catherine A. Richards were married and began a union tested more by his dedication to his people than by the ordinary perils of marriage. It was a strange choice of bride for Delany who paraded his pure black ancestry as a badge of superiority, for Catherine was a product of that dread degeneration known as "amalgamation." Her father, Charles, the son of "Daddy Ben" Richards, had carried on the butcher trade as extensively as his father. Charles had married Felicia Fitzgerald, one of the huge flood of Irish refugees from County Cork, and Katy was one of the offspring.

In addition, Delany had ample evidence of the economic failures in the Negro press ever since John Russwurm and Samuel Cornish founded *Freedom's Journal* in New York in 1827. Perhaps it was true that John B. Vashon and John Peck, among others, were prepared to stand by him as soon as Delany entered the financial morass common to Negro newspapers. All prior experience in all cities indicated inevitable financial loss. The Negro newspapers published hopefully and briefly, just as long as their sponsors had the funds to meet the losses. There was no "Negro market" such as the entrepreneurs have discovered recently, and therefore there was little advertising income. The only revenue was from subscriptions, and the rate of illiteracy among the free Negroes was still understandably high.

Rather than venture into the perilous and arduous career of Negro journalism, it would have been quite natural for Delany to "settle down" to a private life. Many of the pioneers of the Negro awakening had already given up by 1843, had gone to Canada, Haiti, Liberia, or had sunk into hopeless inactivity. Not Delany. By 1843 he was smelted into a rigid pattern by the heat of conflict. Until his mental condition robbed him of decision forty years later, he was to risk his life and remain on the brink of poverty as a result of challenging the odds against his people. He had become an activist.

Delany had need of all his abundant energy during the next four years. It is difficult to conceive of a schedule that could cope with all the responsibilities he assumed. In order to feed both *The Mystery* and his family Delany continued his cupping and leeching practice. Now, however, instead of burying his advertising among the others in the regular Pittsburgh press, which he had often done, Delany was able to place his ads smack on the first column of the first page. No reader could miss it. And he had no difficulty at all in notifying the public of his new equipment or new offices. In the fall of 1846 he inserted, with his regular advertisement, the following:

> *Removal.*
>
> M. R. Delany, would most respectfully inform the Physicians, Families and the public generally, that he has removed his dwelling and office to Hand St. Kerr's Row, between Liberty and Penn, left side going toward Penn, where he will always have on hand, good, active, healthy Leeches and the best of Cupping instruments, and will attend calls at all hours, day and night.
>
> References—The Physicians of Pittsburgh, Allegheny and Birmingham cities generally.

Other advertisers included Negro boardinghouses and merchants, eating houses and the varied beauty ministrations offered to blacks only. One of John Peck's activities, for instance, was an "Ornamental Hair Works." This included the manufacture of "Ladies Wigs, Bands, Curls, Gentlemen's Wigs, Topees (*sic*), Scalps, Guard Chains, Bracelets, all of which is made in the best and most fashionable style."

At the time Peck announced his move into new and more spacious quarters, he advertised for additional help.

Notice—Girls.

> ONE or two young girls to learn the Fancy Hair Manufacturing. Girls from the country or country towns would be prefered (*sic*). None need apply, except they can come well recommended as to reputation, good natural qualities &c."

There was one type of advertising for which Delany threw open his columns of *The Mystery* all the four years he produced it.

$200. REWARD

> ONE Hundred dollars will be paid by the subscribers, a Committee appointed by a public meeting of citizens of Pittsburgh, for the restoration of the two Colored children to the ages of 4 and 7, kidnapped in Beaver co., and
>
> $100 more for the arrest and bringing to punishment the kidnappers.

But there was not enough revenue from advertising to stave off the inevitable. Within nine months, the management of *The Mystery* was turned over to a publishing committee which included John Peck and John Templeton, freeing Delany for purely editorial and promotional duties. The energetic committee went after subscriptions for the newspaper at rates of $1.50 a year "payable in advance." The continued existence of *The Mystery* had become a Negro community responsibility, and that was solely due to its impact first on Pittsburgh, then on Philadelphia and the nation. It had filled a need for a Negro press for a period of about a year and, more than that, *The Mystery* commanded the respect of the white press to such an extent that we know more about its contents from the stories printed in those newspapers than from the paper itself. At this writing, only two copies of *The Mystery* have been found.

The publishing committee sponsored many benefits in behalf of *The Mystery,* and perhaps the most successful became an annual event—the celebration of British Emancipation Day on August 1 of each year. It became the social event of the summer for the blacks in Pittsburgh, and in a few years whites too joined the festivities. The editor of the *Pittsburgh Chronicle* attended the event in 1846 and reported:

> The weather being favorable yesterday, the celebration went off in good style. We paid a visit to the Grove in the afternoon and found collected together a large concourse of the better class of our coloured people, and a good sprinkling of whites. Good order seemed to reign throughout the assemblage and everything moved on harmoniously. The tables fairly groaned under the weight of good things with which they were covered.
>
> The speeches were animated and to the point. We have not listened for many a day to a better address than that delivered by young Peck (the future Dr. David Peck). It was bold, original and at times extremely eloquent, and was received with much approbation. We particularly admired the singing. It was clear, melodious and appropriate to the occasion. The amount of money taken in must have been large. No doubt *The Mystery* will be able to keep on its legs without difficulty hereafter.

The amount was large, for that day and for black people. The committee took in over $500 for their newspaper. Efforts like these freed Delany for both his editorial and promotional duties. For them he almost totally sacrificed his cupping and leeching practice, for he traveled extensively to lecture and sell subscriptions. For a time he concentrated on the large potential among the Negro population of Philadelphia and his success was fully recorded by the organ of the Pennsylvania Anti-Slavery Society, *The Pennsylvania Freeman.* One report is of a meeting in the Bethel AME "Mother Church" which, after Delany and young George B. Vashon talked, elected a committee to draw up a statement.

> *Whereas,* we have been long and are still convinced of the utility and necessity of a newspaper devoted to the interest of the people of color, and
>
> *Whereas,* we believe that the paper called *The Mystery,* published in the city of Pittsburg by Messrs. M. R. Delany and others, as heretofore conducted, meets the decided approbation of our people in regard to the principles it advocates; Therefore
>
> *Resolved,* That we heartily recommend said paper to the confidence and support of the people of color and to the friends of their elevation throughout the country,
>
> *Resolved,* That we entertain the highest regard for the moral and intellectual worth of Dr. Delany and believe him eminently fitted for the post he occupies as editor of *The Mystery.*

There were similar reports in other cities on Delany's promotional tours, and subscriptions grew, placing *The Mystery* in the black. The publishing committee did not report the number but only the fact that circulation had reached a cost-payment basis. Delany's speeches were not the only reason. The committee had recruited a corps of "Agents for *The Mystery*" in eight states and one territory which comprised the past and future leadership of the Negro awakening. Aside from the Pittsburgh area, there were agents in 27 Pennsylvania cities and towns. In Ohio, chiefly in the communities along the Ohio River where there were black concentrations, there were eighteen representatives of *The Mystery* in as many towns. Indiana had five agents and the other states with one or more were: Michigan, Massachusetts, New York, Illinois, and even one brave black, Dr. Jacob Young, in the village of Sisterville, Tyler County, Virginia. There was also one agent in Dubuque, Iowa Territory.

Through all these crowded but rewarding years, Delany did not limit his community activities, and he remained on the City Charity Committee. After the disastrous fire of 1845 he was appointed to the relief committee by Mayor William J. Howard. And his first love remained the work of the Philanthropic Society, for the aid, rescue, and intervention in behalf of the fugitive slaves. His name appears on the court records surviving fire and loss in almost all of the prominent cases to reach legal procedures.

His impact on Pittsburgh with *The Mystery* was immediate. The 1844 *Business Directory* for the city also listed the black self-education groups such as the following:

> The Young men's Anti-Slavery and Literary Society meets every Monday evening, at early gaslight, in the public school room, Multenberger's Alley. . . .
>
> The efforts which are now made for the social elevation of the colored population of our cities are highly commendable and praiseworthy, and there are few more deserving of respect and honor than Mr. Delany, the talented editor of *The Mystery*. The ability and propriety with which this paper is conducted has raised the magnanimous editor high in the good opinion of the whole community.

There were other responsibilities, so many other time-consuming commitments that it is impossible to explain how this human dynamo could cope with them. In a letter dated October 31, 1850, Dr. Joseph P. Gazzam testified:

> M. R. Delany commenced the study of medicine under my direction in October, 1846 and continued until March, 1848. During his pupilage he was industrious and made satisfactory progress.

In still another area, Delany was exceedingly productive. In 1846 there was born the first of eleven children to Katy Delany, of whom seven survived, six boys and one girl. With the birth of the eldest boy the father set a precedent wholly in character with his concept of pride in race. This first-born was baptized Toussaint L'Ouverture Delany after the first black military hero and founder of San Domingo. With one exception, all of the other children were named after the historic great men of the black race. There followed, in Pittsburgh and in Canada, the third son, named Alexander Dumas, for the author; St. Cyprian, for the primitive Christian Church bishop who was sanctified; Faustin Soulouque, for the Emperor of Haiti; Rameses Placido, the ruler of ancient Egypt who so enthralled Delany in his studies, plus the poet and martyred black hero of Cuba; and the only girl, who was named Ethiopia Halle Amelia, for the land of his ancestors.

The exception was the second son, born in 1850 and named Charles Lenox Remond Delany in almost worshipful admiration of the black militant who, in 1840, startled the world with a fiery speech at the World Anti-Slavery Conference in London, England. That speech caused a tremendous outcry in the United States, and he replied before a huge meeting of the British and Foreign Anti-Slavery Society in Exeter Hall, London:

> The system which we wish to see destroyed rolls on unheeded by recreant Americans and, for having spoken the truth, the whole truth, and nothing but the truth, I have been stigmatized as a traitor to my country. . . . I have only to add that if speaking before so large an audience as this on behalf of Freedom constitutes me as a traitor—I am proud of the appellation. I expect to return to my native country soon, and I have said nothing here that I shall not say there, and which I have not already said there again and again. I have been in danger of my life on more occasions than one, and before slavery is abolished, it is probable that I shall again. I believe that there will be more martyrs to the great cause of emancipation than one.

This was the kind of personal commitment that Delany himself had pronounced with his first speech in Pittsburgh. Remond had preceded Frederick Douglass by some ten years as the most eloquent, effective, and most militant black orator. In Delany's admiring eyes, he was the greatest living member of the race, and therefore his second son was so named.

As to *The Mystery* itself, it was Delany's first totally individual effort which brought him national importance among his people and among whites, enemies and friends. It was his initiative that created the newspaper at a time of vital need and it was his intellect that made it distinct and distinguished in the history of the Negro press and a positive force in the division of the United States that was to erupt into the Civil War. It requires examination.

CHAPTER FIVE

The Editor

The Mystery was wholly a reflection of its editor. Aside from its news content, which was concerned chiefly with reports on slave-stealing events, Delany wrote directly to his people on every variety of theme applying to them and exposing every white hypocrisy directed at them. Today, his journalistic colleagues would dismiss him as a propagandist because he thumped a drum rather than pursued the modern course of greater subtlety in general newspaper propaganda. In Pittsburgh, and then throughout the country in Delany's day, his colleagues first were amazed and then admiring—all but the outrightly proslavery editors.

Delany minced no words as his writing on manhood made clear:

> Situated as we are, as mere nonentities in the midst of others—the most deserving, respectable and praiseworthy among us, in the eye of the law and its consequent enactments, being placed far beneath the most vile vagabonds while being denied the privileges granted to the pauper and vagrant—those, by the laws, declared to be nuisance—while privileges are being enjoyed by other men, privileges which from their nature necessarily elevate the female, the wife, mother, sister and daughter, and stimulate the tender youth; we colored male citizens are made the degraded vassals of the most insufferable servility, more intolerable than death itself.
>
> Spurned the right of election as representatives, and peerage as jurors, denied and robbed of the elective franchise and consequently the right of representation; (in

> many of the states) deprived of the right of testimony even against a vagabond; though our hoary headed father or mother may be maltreated, abused or murdered, our wives and sisters ravished before our eyes! Prohibited the right of bearing arms as patriots and soldiers in defence (*sic*) of our Country, thereby precluding us from these *claims* upon our country in common with other inhabitants or citizens; denied the right of *citizenship* in toto, in order thereby to exclude us from the protection of the laws, which of course we are prevented from having any part in making, thereby, disdaining to make us the subject of legislation, except it be for the object of stamping us with still deeper degradation.
>
> This scheme of oppression being complete, as a matter of course, it follows that the forfeiture of every claim to civil and decent respect is fully implied in the base surrender of our manhood, crouching in servility at the feet of insolence and usurpation.

This observation was one of many in *The Mystery* which reached the "guts" of his people's problems. In later writing, Delany was to revert to this theme again and again. He established, as a barometer of a people's social health, the occupations of its women and, therefore, of its men. In doing so, he aroused the ire of the black women, whose status as domestics and children's nurses was considerably higher than that of their fathers and husbands as unskilled laborers. Delany argued that the reverse should be sought, that the women of his race should aim to become ladies themselves, rather than ladies' maids, and that the economic and professional elevation of the male was the true standard of a people's success. Delany's preoccupation with this theme is obvious. He was the son of a free, enterprising, and ambitious woman. His father had been a slave and was now a laborer.

Another recurrent theme written with absolute conviction by Delany was his total rejection of white Christianity and urging on his people of national Negro churches. In *The Mystery*, respect for true faith was extended only to the AME, the AME Zion, and local Negro churches. To the secret plantation churches Delany never failed to shout his praises. His standard approach to the topic appeared to have been a statement that beyond all question it was God's intent to free His black creatures. Someday He would bring holocaust first and conversion to Christianity second to all of the white congregations which had so falsely given Him a duality that both sanctified and forbade slavery.

Yet Delany was ever conscious, in all that he wrote on the theme in *The Mystery,* of the fundamental yearning and absolute need of the black people for a faith. Only in his novel *Blake* did he—and only once—voice another aspect. His protagonist Henry (himself) cried out: "Religion! . . . That's always the cry with the black people. Tell me nothing about religion when the very man who hands you the bread of communion, has sold your daughter away from you."

Delany's concentration on religious discussion in the columns of *The Mystery* was prompted by none other than his former roommate and fellow-student, Molliston M. Clark. One of the earliest issues in 1844 printed a letter from Clark detailing his discussions with the agents for *The Mystery* in Cincinnati where he had the pastorate of the Bethel AME Church. He suggested that "your paper would best promote the general good of our community if you would devote one of its pages exclusively to the subject of religion, provided you would always avoid the quicksands of sectarianism."

Delany printed his reply below the letter and expressed his delight with "the spirit of the above letter."

> We shall most assuredly "run clear of the quicksands of sectarianism," and are proud to hear such an expression from Mr. Clark, a leader in the great Bethel. We wish more of the heads were as he is. We can assure him, as all who are acquainted with our principles will testify, that we never will be grounded on the shoals of sectarianism.

Delany kept that promise throughout the life of *The Mystery.*

There was often an intellectual expression in the columns of *The Mystery* that commanded a place not only in the abolitionist press but also in the pro-slavery white press of Pittsburgh and other cities. Other newspapers often reprinted from *The Mystery* verbatim and sometimes gave credit to this Negro newspaper, a most unusual concession to a press usually mentioned only in mockery. Many of the Pittsburgh newspapers reprinted news stories from *The Mystery*, particularly regarding fugitive slave cases, because their editors knew Delany well and knew too that his honesty derived from self-respect. They agreed and disagreed with him, poked fun at him and rose to his defense. Never, in the four years, did any Pittsburgh editor indulge in journalistic war on Delany as they did among themselves, sometimes to the point of duels. There are numerous examples of the respect expressed for Delany's intellect, such as the effort at humor by John Dunn, the talented editor of the *Pittsburgh Chronicle.*

Which Was the Original Color?

> Spurz Heim (Dr. Spurzheim) admits that it is hard to tell whether man was originally black or white, but tacitly gives it as his opinion that the first man was black, inasmuch as whites will turn dark quicker and oftener than colored people will turn white. This is a very interesting subject, and the question is worthy of the attention of philosophers. The editor of *The Mystery* at this rate may be nothing less than a white man a little tanned. If he would but search into the history of the early inhabitants and let us know how much of Spurz Heim's position is based on good foundation, the colored race may yet stand in the position of masters.

There was a courtroom incident which all of the Pittsburgh press seized with riotous good humor and in which Delany himself delighted. He told it to his biographer with relish.

It was during the trial of a colored man who was being defended by one of the most able lawyers in Pittsburgh, Cornelius Darragh, who was later to be the state's attorney general. He had defended so many blacks in slave stealing that, perhaps automatically, he charged that the prosecution against his client was an obvious fraud and that the charge had been made solely out of prejudice against the man's color.

Unfortunately for Darragh, and more so for his client, the prosecutor was a very nimble-witted opportunist named Samuel V. Black, who was to become one of Pittsburgh's Civil War heroes, a casualty at Manassas. Black turned to the jury and declared:

> They tell you that we have brought on this prosecution through prejudice to color. I deny it; neither does the learned counsel believe it. Look at Martin Delany, of this city, whom everybody knows, and the gentleman knows only to respect him. Would any person in this community make such a charge against him? Could a prosecution be gotten up against him? No, it could not, and the learned counsel knows it could not, and Delany is blacker than a whole generation of the color of the defendant, *boiled down to a quart*.

The *Chronicle* and Dunn maintained a status quo position and for a time feuded with the *Pittsburgh Daily Aurora* which was distinctly pro-slavery. Yet even the *Aurora* showed its attitude toward Delany in reporting its opposition to a visit to Pittsburgh by former President John Quincy Adams in 1843. The newspaper frothed at Adams' visit because in Congress he was the leading force fighting the historic "Gag" law battle against hearing anti-slavery petitions. In most disparaging reports the *Aurora* recorded Adams' speeches and visits in other cities and then, when he was approaching Pittsburgh, inserted the following note:

> VOT A GO—Our papers are disputing among themselves as to which shall be foremost in doing homage to John Quincy Adams. Dr. Delany should head the procession of editors welcoming him to the city.

This was something of an unwelcome recognition of Delany's position in the city, for the *Aurora* had been the most vicious in its attacks on restoration of suffrage to the Negroes. Apparently, Delany had not dropped this issue in *The Mystery*, although there was little public support evident. In 1843 he did manage to gather a small group, confined to Allegheny County representation, which produced still another futile petition to the state legislature.

The *Pittsburgh Aurora* commented at length on this meeting and concluded:

> To the free Negroes it may be said "make yourselves worthy of being freemen before you ask the rights of the free". To those who claim for them equal privileges, make the race

> you wish to befriend socially and morally equal to their white neighbors before you demand for them an equality of political power.

It was Dunn, though, who set a most remarkable journalistic precedent in the *Chronicle* on November 28, 1844, when he actually protested the Jim Crow stage transport of the times. He read *The Mystery* regularly and often noted Delany's participation in events, speeches, and news stories. He really exploded in the following:

> *Contemptible Treatment of a Colored Gentleman*
>
> When M. R. Delany, a talented editor of *The Mystery* of this city we learn by his paper Wednesday, was ordered out of a Stage in Columbus, Ohio, although he had paid his passage money and had a receipt for the same in his pocket. Mr. Delany, although a colored man, is a gentleman of talent and ability, and is doing much to place his brethren on a higher elevation than they have heretofore stood in society in respects education and morals. His name will long be remembered as a benefactor of his race, after the contemptible puppy who refused him a seat in the stagecoach on account of his color shall have gone down "to the base earth from whence he sprung, unhonored and unsung".

It should be noted that Dunn did not protest the general practice of denying passage to people of color, only of a "colored gentleman." Few white editors would attack the discrimination, for doing so would tack the label of "Abolitionist Sheet" on their newspapers and risk destruction of their printing presses. In the Pittsburgh press, printed abolitionism was not to take place until 1847 when Charles Shiras, the white poet who wrote "The Bloodhound's Song," briefly published an anti-slavery newspaper called *The Albatross*. As one of his correspondents, Shiras had one of the most remarkable American women of any era, Mrs. Jane G. Swisshelm. This feminist, married to a Kentucky gentleman, was indestructible. When Shiras went broke, she zoomed into publication of *The Saturday Visiter* (*sic*), a women's liberation and anti-slavery weekly that was second to none in its aggressive editorial policy and vivid writing. It was fortunate for Delany that Jane Swisshelm, from the start of her newspaper, was on his side. Her enemies rued their plight, for how could one reply to a woman's scorn?

In one of the first issues of *The Saturday Visiter*, on Christmas Day 1847 she too took up the story of Delany and his stagecoach travels. This time it was in Buffalo, N.Y.

> The reason for this treatment was that the Doctor was a colored man. We really think it is time that sensible people should cease to manifest upon such occasions prejudices so narrow. What harm could it be to anyone to ride in a coach with a well-dressed, well-behaved and intelligent colored man? For, all of this Dr. Delany undoubtedly is. The most cruel and cowardly thing in this world is a wanton insult to those who are powerless to defend themselves, and whose humility prevents them from giving offense. We have never known a man possessing the education or manners of a gentleman to wantonly insult the feelings of these unfortunate people.

The other Pittsburgh newspapers, which seldom published news of the Negro population, also made an exception in the case of Delany and recorded not only his comings and goings but also his opinions. He had earned their envy and respect as a journalist and editor. All of the newspaper fraternity proved their regard for Delany when, for the first time in any city in the country, a Negro was invited to attend the traditional Ben Franklin birthday anniversary party. Delany received his invitation from the Pittsburgh Typographical Society and the dinner party was held in the Exchange Hotel, which he could not enter under his own auspices. Though a teetotaler, he did break bread with the distinguished guests, all of them white, and considered the event a signal honor to his race for the rest of his life.

The Pittsburgh newspapers also rallied round Delany, when in February 1846 he was sued for libel by a Thomas ("Fiddler") Johnson, a Negro who lived in Cherry Alley and was a well-known character in the Diamond. Delany's campaign against kidnapers, which was prosecuted in every issue of *The Mystery*, had included a story naming "Fiddler" Johnson as a "slavecatcher" who informed the professional kidnapers where their prey was located. The kindly Dunn of the *Chronicle* was reassuring. "The Doctor . . . is not easily scared, as he is aware that editors are frequently sued for libel in this land where the press is free."

However, when the case came up in the Court of Common Sessions, before an all-white jury, Delany was found guilty of libel. In itself, the findings did not rile the public and the press as much as the size of the fine—$150 and costs. It was the highest fine ever assessed any editor in the county on frequent libel charges. Perhaps in self-protection the editors of the city unanimously condemned the fine, but Delany had no alternative but to pay it. He posted bail for its payment and then learned what concern the black and white population of Pittsburgh held for him.

Led by the *Chronicle* and the *Pittsburgh Daily Dispatch,* a call went out for a public subscription to raise the money for the fine. The committee to collect the fund was mixed black and white, among them the most prominent of both races, and they also petitioned Governor Francis R. Shunk for remission of the fine.

They were successful in both efforts. Gov. Shunk remitted the fine, and the committee raised enough money to pay the costs. After it was all over, the *Chronicle* again chided gently: "The Doctor must study the law of libel, and not again permit his praiseworthy efforts in behalf of his race to bring him within its meshes." The warning did not prevent one more libel suit against Delany but in the second one he was quickly found innocent.

The newspaper fraternity throughout the country was interested in the Delany case, probably self-interested. But the Cincinnati *Morning Herald* found virtue in the entire incident.

> The very sentence to which he [Delany] has recently been condemned is, of itself, a testimonial to the value of his labors, and the anti-slavery sentiment of the community. For whatever feelings may have prompted the infliction of a penalty so severe, it amply proves, that in the estimation of the Court, the *reputation* of a colored man was entitled to its protection, and that, in the opinion of the jury, the charge

of being a "Slave Catcher" was slanderous and disgraceful. It will be a brighter day than this, when these two propositions come to be generally admitted.

The unusual aspect of Delany's second libel adventure was the action of Judge William B. McClure, the jurist who achieved national fame in 1848 for his charge to the jury in the notorious George Shaw conviction for slave kidnaping of the equally famous George Harris from Pittsburgh to Alabama. The judge began the charge to the jury with a poem which began: "I would not have a slave to till my land." He went on:

> I am well acquainted with Dr. Delany, and have a very high respect for him. I regard him as a gentleman and a very useful citizen. No Pittsburgher, at least, will believe him capable of willingly doing an injustice to anyone, especially his own race. I cannot, myself, after a careful examination, see in this case anything to justify a verdict against the defendant.

Without leaving the box, the jury acquitted Delany.

Delany's journalistic work in Pittsburgh has achieved a kind of immortality among historians of that city. In almost every account of the Great Fire of 1845 there can be seen, in some cases verbatim, Delany's eyewitness story of the fire in the April 16 issue of *The Mystery*. The paper was printed safely on the other side of the river in Allegheny at the Arthur Anderson print shop, and Delany's story was first throughout the country. It is a most vivid and detailed news story and, in a breathless commentary titled "Pittsburgh in Ruins!!!", Delany reveals his own good fortune. "We just escaped the calamity by removing on Saturday before the fire, from our former residence in 3rd St., to where we now reside in Hand Street."

Delany's imprint on *The Mystery* was evident on its front-page masthead. The first motto came directly from his early studies: AND MOSES WAS LEARNED IN ALL THE WISDOM OF THE EGYPTIANS. He wanted to impress the whites, or more likely, his own people, with their intellectual antecedents. However, some time in 1845 the heat of the struggle dictated the nature of the paper's contents and made Delany more convinced than ever that any improvement at all in the condition of Negroes must be initiated by them. He changed his motto to HEREDITARY BONDSMEN! KNOW YE NOT WHO WOULD BE FREE, THEMSELVES MUST STRIKE THE BLOW!

Consistently throughout the four years of its publication *The Mystery* adhered to its initial prospectus:

> The paper shall be free, independent and untrammeled, and whilst it shall aim at the Moral Elevation of the *Africo-American* and African race, civilly, politically and religiously, yet, it shall support no distinctive principles of race—no sectional distinctions, otherwise than such as may be necessary, for the establishment of true and correct principles pertaining to the universal benefit of man, since whatever is essentially necessary for the promotion and elevation of one class of society to a respectable and honorable standing, is necessary for the promotion and elevation of all classes; therefore our interests are, and should be, one and inseparable.
>
> We shall also aim at the different branches of Literary Sciences, the Mechanic Arts, Agriculture and the elevation of Labor.
>
> We will ever combat error, and repel every species of usurpation and tyranny, and never be found compromising with oppression of any kind, however mild its character.

All Negro newspapers expressed the loftiest of ideals and objectives and some attained them in their columns. There were few, however, like *The Mystery*, which so impressed other editors that they sought out editions of it in order to include Delany's thinking in their own columns. There are numerous examples, but two among the abolition papers of national prominence were most faithful in copying from *The Mystery*. They were the *Pennsylvania Freeman*, edited by Oliver Johnson, and William Lloyd Garrison's *Liberator*.

Johnson early endorsed both the paper and its editor. Under the heading "*The Mystery*" he wrote:

> This singularly named paper, published by a committee of colored friends in Pittsburgh, and edited by M. R. Delany, is quite a spirited and judiciously conducted sheet. Although Mr. Delany is not a man of the highest education,

> he has what is of quite as much importance as an editor, a good deal of tact. We always expect in looking over our exchanges to find something worth notice in his paper.

Whenever Delany was in Philadelphia for lectures, Johnson announced his arrival, as on July 9, 1846:

> The paper is conducted with ability and tact, and deserves the patronage of all interested in its noble objects. Dr. Delany, accompanied by his young friend, Mr. Vashon, a colored student at law of Pittsburg, is now in this city soliciting subscribers, and in other ways laboring to promote the interests of the paper.

Nor did Johnson neglect to let potential subscribers know how to reach them, announcing that they were lodging at 189 South Sixth Street.

Such support from the *Freeman* was frequent. Another type of approval was often given by Garrison in *The Liberator*. Apparently Garrison admired the content of *The Mystery* as much for its objectives, for he quoted Delany's thought and writing more frequently than his news. This began with the first issue of *The Mystery*, and in a single edition of *The Liberator* on October 20, 1843, Garrison reprinted verbatim two short pieces from Delany's pen. The first is a gem of logic.

> *Not Fair*
>
> The question is often asked, why is it that the colored people claim equality with the whites, and so few of them have manifested even a propensity for that equality; that we never have produced authors, writers, professors, not geniuses of any kind, notwithstanding some of us have been free from the formation of this government, up till the present day.
>
> To say nothing about the disadvantage that would naturally arise to the *few*, while the many continued in slavery and degradation; yet when Mr. Jefferson, the "apostle of democracy" was asked by a British statesman: "Why it was that America, with all her boasted greatness, had produced so few great men, and learned authors," the American statesman quickly replied that, when the United States had been an independent government as long as Greece was before

she produced her Homer, Socrates and Demosthenes, and Rome, before she produced her Virgil, Horace, and her Cicero; or when this country had been free as long as England was before she produced her Pope and Dryden, then he would be ready to answer that question.

According to the above sensible position of the American statesman, so characteristic of himself, *we* answer, that more is asked of us, than ever was asked of any other people, and if it is expected that with all the disadvantages with which we are surrounded we should still equal the other citizens, it is giving us more than we claim; it is a tacit acknowledgement, that we are naturally superior to the rest of mankind, and, therefore, are much more susceptible than they.

With this cursory view of the subject, then, all that we have in conclusion to say is that if we produced any equals at all, while we are in the present state, to say the least of it, we have done as much as Greece, Rome, England or America.

The second quote was taken from *The Mystery* for the same issue of *The Liberator.*

Liberty or Death

The following anecdote was related to us on last Monday, by a gentleman recently from Georgia, now in this city:

George, a slave, belonged to the family of —— in the State of Georgia, near the Ochmulgee River whom he served faithfully. He was an excellent *mechanic* (!) and during the life of his owners or claimants (for he never had an *owner*) they would take no money for him, and, in consequence of his faithfulness to them, at their death, George was will (*sic*) a *freeman!*.

Poor George then looked upon himself as one of the lords, even of the accursed soil of Georgia. But George was doomed to disappointment. The unjust heirs broke the will, seized his person, and thrust him into the dark caverns of slavery again! Bound for a new residence, they started down the Ochmulgee. George was on board the steamboat, bound for his destination, but the vicious robbers of his liberty knew not where. George looked sad, and talked but little.

The steamer glided along, with a crowd of guests, unconscious of their weary fellow-passenger. In the night a splash was heard which awakened the attention of boatmen and passengers; all looked with anxiety, but seeing all appeared to be safe, it was just a conclusion, that this must have been the noise occasioned by the falling in of the bank of the river. Morning came, the grindstone of the boat was missed, information was given, and search being made, George was gone, they knew not where.

The river was ordered to be scoured by the eager master, thirsting after the blood of the *mechanic*. It was scoured and George was found with the *grindstone tied to his neck!* Reposing in the depth of the Ochmulgee, preferring as a man, Death before slavery! George had tasted liberty!!!

Pittsburgh's reputation as a trap for fugitive slave stealers and kidnapers of free Negroes is undoubtedly justified. They feared entering the city, and there were so many forced recoveries by Delany's unphilanthropic young men that the slave catchers only operated in groups and at night. They found few officers of the law brave enough or venal enough to place authority on their side.

Delany had hundreds of eyes and ears working for him, and even the rumor that slave catchers were in the area found an immediate warning in *The Mystery*. He not only sounded warnings but reported their successes and failures. It was his story on the Carlisle (Pa.) Riot of 1847, obtained from his own correspondent there, which roused the country and restored the victim, a free Negro, whose wife and child had escaped from the slave catchers during the melee. In defending them, the free black was fiercely beaten and carted off by the slave catchers. He was recovered because Delany insisted, in *The Mystery*, that the judicial and executive powers of the government be exercised in every case. In one of the first issues of the paper he told of a successful kidnaping and concluded: "We understand that a colored boy by the name of Barclay belonging to Pittsburg (sic) is now detained and imprisoned at Clarksville, Tenn., and is to be sold for a slave. Will His Excellency the Executive of this

Commonwealth demand the release of a free citizen of Pennsylvania? We think so." His Excellency did.

Another of Delany's warnings about kidnapers during that "long, hot summer" of 1847 reported two attempts by the same group of Virginians, the first of which failed. He continued:

> On last Saturday night they made a bold attempt to carry their designs into execution, which made the people of the community acquainted with their real character. The four Virginians from Stanton, one of their names Turk, with five of their pimps residing here, making nine in all, left town between ten and eleven o'clock, and at about twelve attacked a colored man named John Finly, living about six or seven miles below town in the mountains, entirely secluded from anyone, and after a spirited battle, in which three of the baby stealers were wounded severely, they retreated, and on Tuesday morning the prime movers of the scheme left for parts unknown. I understand a law suit is to be entered against those who still have the hardihood to sneak around this place. By this attempt against the liberty of a free citizen, they have deservedly called down the execration of all good citizens of every creed.

By his consistent reporting and follow-through on such cases Delany managed to arouse even the anti-abolitionist whites against the repeated defiance of the laws or connivance with law officers necessary in the trade of kidnaping. They too became his eyes and ears. By the beginning of 1845 there was an example of a changed attitude that for those times was astounding.

A free Negro who had stolen his slave wife in Winchester, Va., was being pursued. The couple was caught close to Pittsburgh, and the slave catchers brought them into the city for lodging in the jail while they slept. The jailer refused to accept them without a legal commitment, and the Virginians had to hunt up somebody legally authorized to issue the warrant. An alderman of the second ward flatly refused to act at all. By the time they had found a constable willing to use his authority, for a price, the call to muster had gone out through Hayti, and the Negroes were joined by many whites. There was no violence.

The man and his wife were simply ushered away, and they disappeared.

The incident was one among many similar ones, some accompanied by violence, some quite peaceful. What made it outstanding was the expression by the *Chronicle* of the general feeling among the whites, even among the anti-abolitionists. The changed attitude had little to do with slavery per se, but with a resentment of Southern tactics in perpetuating slavery. The *Chronicle* said:

> We are not political Abolitionists, nor are we in favor of meddling with slavery in the southern states. We are willing to leave the institution with themselves, believing that in time if left alone, their own good sense, judgment, and self-interest, will induce the slaveholders to free their slaves, but we are glad to see the slaves escape from their bondage, and we were pleased when we learned that this woman succeeded in getting clear from the clutches of her master and the constable who was willing to aid in the dirty work. The citizens of the free states are under no obligation, either legal or moral, to send the fugitive back into slavery. If the owners can arrest and succeed in retaining their human chattels we have no right and should not wish to interfere. We regret much that a northern Freeman should so far forget public opinion and his own humanity as to degrade himself as a slavecatcher. We will not utter a word of censure against the public officer who was engaged in this matter. We will leave him to his own conscience and the scorn of those who placed him in the office.

The *Chronicle* went on to name it the duty of the state legislature "to pass a law giving to persons of color who are arrested as fugitive slave, the right of a jury trial." This was nine years, it should be remembered, before that same demand was made of the Massachusetts State Legislature by Rev. Theodore Parker in his heroic defense against charges resulting from the Anthony Burns rescue case. The white citizens of Pittsburgh mobilized their opposition to the Fugitive Slave Act of 1850 a full five years before it was adopted by a subservient Congress and President, aided and abetted by another American hero, Daniel Webster.

The reasoning advanced by the *Chronicle* also pre-dated that of the most fervent Boston Brahmins.

> If a horse should stray from Virginia into our state, and should be taken up by some farmer, any dispute arising in regard to the ownership of the horse would be referred to twelve good men for settlement. We cannot see why the same privilege should not be extended to human beings. If such a law were passed, it would no doubt be the means of preventing many freed persons of color from being kidnapped into hopeless slavery. We think that our fellow colored citizens have a right to demand at the hands of our legislators of the passage of such a law as this as a safeguard to their own liberty, and we believe that three-fourths of all our citizens would be in favor of the measure.

The historic Supreme Court decision in *Prigg* v *Pennsylvania* in 1842 had freed the state and all states from the obligations of assisting in the return of fugitive slaves to their owners in other states, as interpreted in the Fugitive Slave Act of 1793 for some fifty years. A mere provision for a jury trial was entirely within the province of the legislature at that time, but not after the Fugitive Slave Act of 1850.

Of course, wiser and more materialistic heads in Harrisburg prevailed, and Pennsylvania passed no such jury law. But the expression of such sentiment in the *Pittsburgh Chronicle* was a flicker of hope for the remainder of the decade. No small part in the change of attitude was due to Delany and *The Mystery*.

This influence was to be lasting. Another of Delany's converted newspaper editors was J. Herron Foster of the *Dispatch*. He too had to tread carefully to avoid alienating the pro-slavery business world. He too wrote editorials in favor of the justice of freedom but not the rectitude of abolitionists. But in secret, he did much more. He was one of Delany's spies, and when the black man was out of Pittsburgh, he was to turn to just as effective a white man, Dr. F. Julius LeMoyne, Delany's medical mentor and the earliest abolitionist in Western Pennsylvania.

The following letter dated October 30, 1850, and signed by Foster was found among Dr. LeMoyne's effects after his death.

Dear Sir:

Altho. unacquainted with you personally, I feel it my duty to acquaint you (confidentially) of a circumstance which transpired here this morning, trusting my information may save a brother man from slavery.

Mr. McLean, former editor of the *Argus*, of Wheeling, Va., was in my office this (Wednesday) morning, & in conversation enquired who was U.S. Commissioner in Washington, Pa. I did not know— He said, "I suppose if you did you wouldn't tell me, as one of our citizens wants to *seize a slave of his there?*" He wouldn't tell me who the master was, but I feel it my duty to warn you that, if there is no U.S. Com. there the "master" will soon be there himself, in search—

Please put your colored folks on their guard, *especially fugitives from the neighborhood of Wheeling, Va.* The bloodhounds are on the scent.

In still another area, Negro education, Martin Delany's personality and his work on *The Mystery* had a profound and tangible influence on his white colleagues. In 1846, while the campaign for colored public schools from colored tax money was at its height, Delany's friend John Dunn defined the need in the *Chronicle* under the bold head "Education of the Colored People." His observations have amazing pertinence at this writing.

The condition of the blacks is most abject and degraded. Almost every avenue to knowledge and virtue is shut against them. We ask them to obey laws, to be virtuous and good citizens, and at the same time put every obstacle in their way. We will not allow them to pursue respectable occupations—shaving and bootblacking are the only trades we permit them to acquire. We kick them out of our public schools and churches, except in some of the latter where long-faced Elders thrust the colored brethren and sisters into a "nigger pew" away in some dark corner. We exclude them from every means of improving their condition. It is a wonder that under all the circumstances they are not more vicious and criminal. It surprises not that they occupy so much of the time of our courts, but that they do not occupy a great deal more.

Our citizens owe a duty to the colored people among us. We must give them the means of education and self-improvement. It is more economical to do this. It is much better to spend money for schools than for courthouses and jails. Even our Abolition friends in their great love and zeal for the poor slaves, away down in the southern states, forget the poor, downtrodden ones in our own state. Their charity is too much like that of a woman we once knew who drove the deserving beggar from her door, but made large contributions to send missionaries to the South Sea Islands. . . . They need in the whole city several schools. They should also be aided and encouraged in all their efforts to elevate themselves. A helping hand should be extended to them; instead of scorn and contempt, advice and praise should stimulate them in their difficult task of self-elevation. If we do our duty to them, the blacks will be among the most orderly and worthy of our citizens.

The date of this editorial was June 27, 1846, *not 1971!*

The Mystery, and its consistently superior exposition of the work of at least one educated black man, is also credited by contemporaries with influencing a white man, Charles Avery, in the direction of higher education for Negroes. This modest and retiring man was exceptional because he not only professed Christianity but lived it. Born in a large family in Westchester County, N.Y., in 1784, he was apprenticed early to a New York City druggist. In 1812 he moved to Pittsburgh to open his own drugstore. He later moved his home and business to Allegheny. In 1858, Avery was one of the wealthiest businessmen in the county.

The acquisition of wealth apparently meant nothing to him. In his youth he had been torn between the clergy and the economic necessities of his family. He was forced to the pattern of business success but this did not lessen his yearnings to preach. As early as 1818 he is listed as the leader of a class for Methodist Episcopal girls which met every Monday at 2 P.M. in the Old Meeting House. Eventually, he achieved his dream and was ordained by the Methodist Church as a lay preacher.

While he was in a variety of businesses, most of Avery's fortune was made in cotton mills in Allegheny. Therefore he knew the South and slavery. He was one of the first abolitionists in Allegheny County, long before the Negro awakening, and this conviction gave him the spiritual struggle of all sincere Christians, a choice between a church of the North and a church of the South. He chose the North.

There are amply confirmed records that Avery was a life-long philanthropist and that he gave of his mounting fortune in all directions and without regard to race, color, or creed. Such a man could not help but become the most trusted white man in any Negro community. It was not only the money he gave so freely, but the fact that he dined in Negroes' homes and they in his. This unheard of social equality was extremely rare, even among abolitionists. Delany often derided these abolitionists who could justify the practice of prejudice against color while opposing slavery of people of that color.

Avery built a church for the African Methodist Episcopal Zion branch next to his home on Avery Street in Allegheny. In 1849 it was converted into the first institution of higher learning for Negroes in Pittsburgh and one of the few in the country. It was named the Allegheny Institute and Mission Church. Its first Board of Trustees included John Peck, Molliston Clark (Delany's roommate), and others among the blacks. When Avery died in 1858 the name was changed to Avery College, and the institution continued to serve, through all misfortunes, for some fifty years. In the year of Avery's death, George B. Vashon, an instructor, reported an enrollment of 89 boys and 61 girls.

Avery left an estate of $800,000, and his will distributed specific gifts to numerous educational institutions and to his widow. A residue of $150,000 was left in the Avery trust fund with directions that it be used for the "dissemination of the Gospel of Christ among the tribes of Africa"; also another portion in perpetual trust "the interest thereof to be applied to the education and elevation of the colored people of the United States and Canada." As a result, the American Missionary Society became a beneficiary over many years, for the money was invested so wisely by Avery's friends whom he named as trustees that it increased in value. Its benefits have been felt in Pennsylvania, Ohio, Virginia, the Carolinas, Canada, and Africa. One of Martin Delany's most rewarding experiences came twenty years later when the Avery trust fund established the Avery Normal Institute for his people in Charleston, S.C.

Publication of *The Mystery* continued for a full year before the annexation of Texas and through the years of manipulating public opinion toward war with Mexico. It was perhaps the most significant national question during the newspaper's existence.

Martin Delany was not in the least sloganized by Manifest Destiny as were all but the handful of abolitionists who had no chance against the jingoists. He was never taken in by the language describing the biggest land grab in any country's history.

The mass of the American people wanted the land clear to the Pacific. The task of several Congresses was to provide the necessary legislation to legalize the land grabs and appropriate funds, not only for the war, but for purchase of revolution in Mexico. The "snow job" was complete.

Negroes in the Free States were agitated by the annexation of Texas. As an independent republic it at least provided a safer route to free Mexico, if not a haven because of its sparse settlement. Delany was particularly agitated because he had been there and he knew that the annexation was the creation of newer bonds of continued slavery. He agreed with the larger view of Rep. Joshua Giddings of Ohio when, in a House speech on May 21, 1844, he warned: "let us admit Texas and we shall place the balance of power in the hands of the Texans themselves."

> They, with the Southern states, will control the policy and the destiny of this nation. . . . Are the liberty-loving Democrats of Pennsylvania ready to give up our tariff?—to strike off all protection from the articles of iron and coal, and other productions of that state in order to purchase a slave market for their neighbors, who, in the words of Thomas Jefferson Randolph, "breed men for the market like oxen in the shambles"?

But the South won again, in the new Congress, after proper application of the Manifest Destiny slogan had put stars of greatness in the eyes of the least white American. President Polk continued the promotion of mass egomania begun by Tyler's administration and, by blatant conniving, created the border issue so necessary to throw to the world as a cause of war. In the

North the stars blinked out of the befuddled eyes too late to influence events. The armies were marching.

In Boston, the Massachusetts State Legislature, by overwhelming vote, adopted a most treasonous resolution, in view of the country's war status:

> *Resolved*, That such a war of conquest, so hateful in its objects, so wanton, unjust, and unconstitutional in its origin and character, must be regarded as war against freedom, against humanity, against justice, against the Union, against the Constitution, and against the *Free States;* and that a regard for the true interests, and the highest honor of the country, not less than the impulses of Christian duty, should arouse all good citizens to join the efforts to arrest this gigantic crime, by withholding supplies, or other voluntary contributions, for its further prosecution, by calling for the withdrawal of our army . . . aiding the country to retreat from the disgraceful position of aggression which it now occupies toward a weak, distracted neighbor and sister republic.

This expression from the "cradle of liberty" meant nothing to the American people, just as similar pronouncements meant nothing in relation to Viet Nam.

All through those years of moral bankruptcy, Martin Delany was publishing *The Mystery* and exposing the slave-expansion motives of both the annexation of Texas and the war with Mexico. He was understandably bitter:

> *Colored Soldiers*
>
> Will President Polk accept one or more regiments of colored soldiers for the great Southern War? Surely, according to Southern doctrine, they are the only persons adapted to that climate? We should like to have an answer from some of the President's friends, we care not of what politics.

To Delany the entire four years of *The Mystery* were a confirmation of his earlier disillusionments. Stay and fight? Where was the hope? If a people could so discard all morality on an international scale, how could a moral appeal succeed when the needed conversion was within the confines of the country itself? The South still ruled. John C. Calhoun, its voice, had promised the country "political revolution, anarchy, civil war, and widespread disaster" should the North interfere in any way with slave expansion. And his threat cowed the country, in the counting houses of both Washington, D.C., and New York.

Meanwhile, nothing changed. *The Mystery* continued to carry its heartbreaking messages:

> LOST CHILD
>
> Thornton Delany Parker, a small colored boy about 9 years of age, was decoyed from Pittsburgh during the absence of his parents some four months ago— He generally calls himself Thornton Delany.

Nothing had changed in the work of rescuing fugitive slaves. On April 16, 1847, Delany was involved in a tussle with three Virginia slave catchers in an upstairs room of the Monongahela House. Daniel Lockhart, a fugitive from Winchester, Va., disappeared into freedom during the melee. Delany then participated in the prosecution of the slave catchers.

About a week before, Delany had been the principal speaker at a meeting in the Sixth Ward at which T. J. Bigham was presented with an ornate cane and the gratitude of the black people for his leadership in the Pennsylvania State Legislature. He had been successful in getting a memorial in favor of the Wilmot Proviso passed by that body. But the Wilmot Proviso had failed in Washington.

His young friend, George B. Vashon, though refused admission to the Pittsburgh bar had been accepted by the New York bar and that confirmed the closed doors of the professions for the blacks of the city. The discrimination had at least one virtue. It allowed the inimitable Jane Swisshelm to mate her twin crusades. In part, she wrote in the *Saturday Visiter* under the title *Getting Rid of the Nuisances*:

> Many people look upon the expulsion of George B. Vashon from his native State in this light, and think that the refusal of the Pittsburgh bar to admit him was a slight. Now this is not fair. So far from their slighting or insulting him, those

> learned gentlemen elevated him to the same position which they have assigned to their lady-loves, wives and mothers. No one would want to tax the Pittsburgh bar with any want of respect for the fair sex—the angels whom they worship as the stars of destiny and all that sort of thing—yet George B. Vashon and every other colored man in the State stands upon exactly the same platform which the wives and mothers of our judges, lawyers and Governors occupy. There is nothing in our laws or civil regulations to prevent any of them from earning a living by washing, scrubbing, digging, hoeing, reaping, or shoveling in coal—but none of them could be permitted into one of the learned professions.

Other conditions remained the same. The black community of Pittsburgh was still combing its resources to educate its children. They still were not receiving a portion of their tax payments for that purpose. It still was going entirely to the white schools.

Why a man like Delany, who was so intimately immersed in the affairs of his race, and therefore knowing each setback suffered, did not throw up his hands and declare a plague on all houses is difficult to explain. Except that, at the lowest ebb, there were events which still inspired hope. He found it in his own people, for one thing.

In August 1847 an AME preacher, Rev. Fayette Davis, died prematurely at the age of 39. He had been self-taught, born in 1808, the son of free Negroes in a slave state, as Delany was. They were close friends because Rev. Davis was attempting the same program of self-education. While Delany was stubbornly studying medicine with Drs. Gazzam and LeMoyne, Davis was venturing into the philosophies, the histories, the treasures usually buried for all, black or white, until dug out. His last visit with the ailing Davis was three days before his death.

Delany was chosen to deliver the eulogy for the beloved pastor. All of his oratorical ability and his large vocabulary were utilized to bring the mourners to tears. Even today, the eulogy to Fayette Davis, a simple exposition of a man of good will, is a moving document. Delany expressed, among other things, his admiration for any black man who would set himself the tasks that Davis had.

> The wide field of usefulness which he beheld before him when he looked upon his brethren both nominally free and bond, induced him with all his might to hasten the accomplishment of his qualification. To this end he endeavored to embrace within the scope of his studies all the sciences both ancient and modern, and to this great, uncommon exertion do we mainly lay the untimely decline of his body and eventful end of his existence.

Delany's eulogy so affected his audience that it became the first of his writing outside of *The Mystery* to be printed. In a letter dated September 4, 1847, a committee requested a copy of the eulogy for that purpose. They were George B. Vashon, Richard H. Gleaves, and James L. Williams.

These three men were bound to Delany in another way, a tie that was to be a source of hope and aid to him in many states and Canada. The funeral services for Rev. Fayette Davis had been a full Freemason ceremonial. The committee were prominent members of St. Cyprian Lodge No. 13 of Free and Accepted A.Y. Masons (Prince Hall affiliation). Delany was a founding member of this first lodge in colored Masonry west of the Alleghenies. Six years later he was the first Freemason to have published, on request of both the Grand Lodge and St. Cyprian's, a history of Colored Freemasonry in America, *The Origin and Objects of Ancient Freemasonry; Its Introduction into the United States and Legitimacy Among Colored Men,* published in Pittsburg in 1853.

There was, and is, *apartheid* in Freemasonry, and this Delany protested for the remainder of his fraternal life. There also was schism in the colored order against the Prince Hall affiliation. Colored Masonry originated in the United States in 1775 in Boston, making it the oldest continuing organization among Negroes on this continent. There is a decidedly romantic aspect to its history and Delany made the most of it, although his dates are incorrect. Prince Hall, a free Negro from Barbados, with fourteen other colored men, formed African Lodge No. 1 during the British occupation of Boston. They were initiated by white men, something the white Masons of Massachusetts and Pennsylvania had refused to do. There was a lodge in one of the British regiments and the American Negroes were chartered with all the proper ritual, although they were forced to wait until after the

Revolution, until 1787, to receive their charter from the Grand Lodge of England.

Richard H. Gleaves of the Rev. Fayette Davis committee was Deputy Grand Master (and eventually National Grand Master) of the Grand Lodge of Pennsylvania and, in 1846, organized St. Cyprian Lodge with Martin Delany.

To Delany, Freemasonry represented and documented all of his conclusions from ethnological study, that the first flowering of all wisdom was among the blacks of Africa. Besides, its principles matched exactly the high level of behavior and responsibility among his people for which he was pleading weekly in *The Mystery*. Its activities included a tight-knit and secret mutual aid of tremendous importance to members subject to all of the perils of free Negroes at home or abroad. And finally, Delany judged Freemasonry to be a holy bond because of the enemies it made, particularly among white politicians.

Delany was a lifetime Freemason and was to be active in founding still another lodge, in Canada, and in almost all of the states in which he worked for his race. The ritual of Freemasonry delighted his love of ceremony, its secrecy, his deep conviction of being among the chosen, and its true fraternity—an absolute necessity in the dangerous work of the future.

The pendulum swung again with Delany on August 14, 1847, when he was discovered in person by the two greatest men of American Negro history, one black and one white. They knew Delany through correspondence in *The Mystery*, and he was at many of the conventions they had attended. But when Frederick Douglass and William Lloyd Garrison arrived in Pittsburgh on their historic tour of anti-slavery meetings through Pennsylvania and Ohio, they found the man.

From that time onward, though he returned to Pittsburgh again and again, Martin Robison Delany lived and fought in the national arena. Douglass and Garrison, just arrived from being mobbed in Harrisburg, were the epitome of gladiators fully conscious of the odds against them. Yet they fought. And their example induced Delany to "stay and fight" for a time.

CHAPTER SIX

The *North Star*

Delany not only shared the Pittsburgh platforms with Garrison and Douglass but startled the city by rising in their defense in his next issue of *The Mystery*. The *Pittsburgh Gazette*, one of the most pro-slavery newspapers in the country, had attacked the two giants of abolition most viciously as being anti-Christian, anti-democratic, anti-Union, and anti-Constitution.

Delany accused the newspaper of printing things that never were said at the various meetings and of distorting meanings of words actually expressed. The fact that the Constitution was a pro-slavery document by "implication" left little for the *Gazette*'s reply. He declared, on this point:

> Common sense will decide and forever put to rest a decision to the contrary, that among people of sense, an implication is equal to its intentions to an expression. . . . Then, according to this reasoning, which is simple and fair, the Constitution of the United States is a pro-slavery instrument, and no consistent anti-slavery person should either vote or hold office under it.

As for Garrison's attacks on the Christian churches, Delany declared that he had specified "churches," not "true followers of Christ" . . . "but all churches that apologized for or tolerated Slavery, are in direct opposition to the examples of Christ and his precepts, and ought to be either reformed or abolished."

The *Gazette* screamed loudest at some of Frederick Douglass' words that he "welcomed the bolt, whether from heaven or hell, that severed the Union, rather than it should rest on the liberties of three millions of his fellow creatures of whatever origin."

Delany's arguments were destined to define the area of discussion and dissension among the white abolitionists for the next decade, particularly Douglass' warnings against the worth of a Union that is not a democracy. Referring to the above statement he continued:

> Is there aught in this to condemn? Let us suppose that like Mr. Douglass, the editor of the *Gazette* had been piratically robbed for twenty-five years out of his liberty, subjected during which time to all the injury, insult and degradation, concommitant (*sic*) with Slavery, and whose mothers and sisters are still groaning in degradation, all sanctioned by the Constitution and upheld and supported by the Union; would he be less a "fanatic" than Douglass?
>
> Had he, like we, borne the torture of knowing his *father* to have served *fifty-four* years of his life in Virginia Slavery, and was now only free of his own *will*, having walked away and staid—whose head is now hoary with the blighting frosts of his wintry pilgrimage, and whose cheeks deeply furrowed by the sorrows of his toiling pathway—would he, could he, dare he withhold the justly merited rebukes and spontaneous outbursts of his manly indignation against the upholders and abettors of such a system??
>
> Aye, he would welcome the omnipotent arm of Jehovah, stretched forth in terrible projection, holding in his grasp the mighty thunderbolt of vengeance "red with uncommon wrath" ready to dash into eternal nothingness, all and everything that contributed to the perpetuity of such a system!
>
> No union with slaveholders—Perish the Union or any Government rather than to be upheld by the forfeiture of the liberties of the people.

This reply to the *Gazette* was reprinted in full throughout the country where the political theorists among the white abolitionists were raising sham structures based on the Constitutional guarantees which had no bearing whatsoever on the realities. They were to fight among themselves for a decade. Delany's major contribution in his writings was to personalize the Constitution, to examine its application to the individual, not the political theory. He kept alive a moral indignation which was far more potent than the "moral suasion" theory of the white abolitionists.

In 1847 (and today) he would be named a traitor to America "the theory," not America *the fact*. And whenever he was so accused his reply was a question: "In what manner may I be treasonous to a country which I am not allowed to call mine?"

It was at that point, in August 1847, that Delany entered a leadership position among the nation's black nationalists.

"Dear Helen" was William Lloyd Garrison's wife, and he wrote often to her while on his anti-slavery crusades. On August 16, 1847, he wrote from Youngstown, Ohio:

> On Friday we took the steamer for Beaver, on the Ohio River (which commences at Pittsburgh, the Monongahela and Allegheny rivers forming a confluence, and falling into it, just below the city) and from thence rode to New Brighton in an omnibus, some three or four miles, accompanied by several of our coloured Pittsburgh friends—J. B. Vashon and son (George B.), Dr. Peck, Dr. Delaney (*sic*) (editor of the *Mystery*, black as jet, and a fine fellow of great energy and spirit) and others.

There were three on this tour, Garrison, Frederick Douglass, and Stephen S. Foster, the intrepid Worcester, Mass., farmer who was a veteran of the New England mob assaults. Ohio was a forbidding battleground for abolitionists. Its notorious black laws were the most oppressive among the Free States and seemed to provide a license to its population for an open season on abolitionists. The law enforcement authorities almost never interfered. Just the year before, on July 5, in Shaneville, Tuscarawas County, an anti-slavery lecturer named David Officer had had his skull fractured by a brick. There was no murder prosecution.

But those were the occupational hazards of committed men in the America of the day. Garrison's observations to his wife are worth considering due to his wealth of experience. He wrote that despite many anti-slavery lectures in New Brighton (Pa.), "the people generally remain incorrigible."

The secret is, they are much priest-ridden—thus confirming afresh the assertion of the prophet, "like people, like priest". The Hicksite Quakers have a meeting-house there, but they are generally pro-slavery in spirit. No place could be obtained for our meeting excepting the upper room of a large store, which was crowded to excess, afternoon and evening, several hundred persons being present, and many other persons not being able to obtain admittance. In the evening there were some symptoms of pro-slavery rowdyism outside the building, but nothing beyond the yelling of young men and boys. Over our heads in the room, were piled up across the beams many barrels of flour; and while we were speaking, the mice were busy in nibbling at them, causing their contents to whiten some of our dresses, and thinking perchance that our speeches needed to be a little more floury (flowery). The meetings were addressed at considerable length by Douglass and myself, and also by Dr. Delaney (*sic*) who spoke on the subject of prejudice against color in a very witty and energetic manner. Douglass was well nigh run down, and spoke with much physical debility.

The *North Star* was born during that trip and Douglass and Delany probably discussed it then. The circumstances surrounding the genesis of the newspaper are clouded by the separation of Garrison and Douglass that fall, as a result of Douglass' decision to publish. He had returned from his refuge in England in 1847 with financial assurances from the many friends among the British abolitionists he had made there. Garrison, Wendell Phillips, and other Boston anti-slavery adherents had persuaded him to give up the idea, since the only certainty in the Negro press was its financial uncertainty. But that November, Douglass wrote to his British backers, acknowledging the gift of $2,175 for the newspaper and declaring, "I had not decided against the publication of a paper one month before I became satisfied that I had made a mistake, and each subsequent month's experience has confirmed me in the conviction."

Martin Delany's part in the founding of the *North Star* began within a month after the New Brighton trip. On September 20, 1847, John Herron Foster, his friend of the *Pittsburgh Dispatch* reported:

> Dr. M. R. Delany has shown us the Prospectus of a new Anti-slavery paper, to be edited by the celebrated Frederick Douglass and to be published at Cleveland, Ohio, under the title "North Star". The terms of the paper are two dollars per annum in advance. The first number to be issued on the 1st of January, 1848. Dr. Delany is the agent for this city, and is prepared to receive subscriptions.

Soon after, the site of the *North Star* was changed to Rochester, N.Y. due chiefly, according to Douglass, to the existence of an active women's anti-slavery organization in that city. The date of publication was advanced, and the first issue came out on December 3, 1847. Martin Delany's connection with it was changed too. He was named co-editor with Frederick Douglass.

The division between Garrison and Douglass began with the announcement that the black man had not heeded any of the Boston warnings. Of course, the predictions of financial catastrophe were to be proved correct. But there is a curious sidelight on the abolitionist newspapers published by these men. Both the *North Star* and *The Liberator* were always in financial difficulties, and the source of their support were Negro and white abolitionists. But *The Liberator*, published by a white man, had approximately three Negro subscribers to each white subscriber. The *North Star*, published by a black man, consistently had five white subscribers to each black supporter. This raises, not so much a comparison between the two editors, but more a question as to the rationale of the American commitment to emancipation by both groups.

The decision to join one of the then uncompromising leaders of the abolition crusade was one of the most fundamental of Delany's entire career. It signified that he once more had reached the positive peak of that endless cycle of hope and despair for the prospect of his people obtaining a share in American democracy. It meant the sacrifice of a measure of economic security he had built up in a practice now expanding from phlebotomy into actual medicine. It required sacrifice of a most unusual achievement, in which he took so much personal pride, ending his connection with *The Mystery*. And, inevitably, it initiated the vagabond life of an anti-slavery crusader, a sacrifice of home life, and the risk of his own life.

However, Delany was seldom deterred in any of his actions and decisions by any personal considerations. He chose to enter the national anti-slavery movement because it was in a most critical stage. He chose the way of Douglass and Garrison because these two were the leading spirits against a dry rot that had set in among the organized abolitionists. Since the Negro awakening, Delany was to write only five years later, white abolitionists had retreated from immediate to gradual emancipation, and from gradual emancipation to begin at once to a gradualism at more and more distant times. Delany wrote that this process began with the first formation of the white anti-slavery societies, after his people had risen their heads in successive conventions to look each other in the eye and then collectively face the professedly slave-hating whites who had said, in effect, "Leave it to us."

> They earnestly contended, and doubtless honestly meaning what they said, that they (the whites) had been our oppressors and injurers, they had obstructed our progress to the high positions of civilization, and now, it was their bounden duty to make full amends for the injuries thus inflicted on an unoffending people. They exhorted the Convention to cease; as they had laid on the burden, they would also take it off; as they had obstructed our pathway, they would remove the hindrance.

It was Delany's opinion that the free Negroes, at this critical point in their own organizational development, were overawed by the sheer enormity of whites actually donning the hairshirt of penance and leveling the lance of truth against their own brethren. As a result:

> . . . the colored men stopped suddenly, and with their hands thrust deep in their breeches pockets, and their mouths gaping open, stood gazing with astonishment, wonder and surprise at the stupendous moral colossal statues of our Anti-Slavery friends and brethren, who in the heat and zeal of honest hearts, from a desire to make atonement for the many wrongs inflicted, promised a great deal more than they have ever been able half to fulfill, in thrice the period in which they expected it.

Delany hastened to "wish it understood, that we are not laying any thing to their charge as blame since the white abolitionists made those promises in all good faith and remained the truest friends we have among whites in this country."

He did blame the anti-slavery forces, and in no uncertain terms, for one absolute default in their commitments. The complaint has a contemporary tone.

> The cause of dissatisfaction with our former condition was, that we were proscribed, debarred, and shut out from every respectable position, occupying the places of inferiors and menials. It was expected that Anti-Slavery, according to its professions, would extend to colored persons, as far as in the power of its adherents, those advantages nowhere else to be obtained among white men. . . . Thus was the cause espoused, and thus did we expect much. But in all this, we were doomed to disappointment. Instead of realising what we had hoped for, we find ourselves occupying the same position in relation to our Anti-Slavery friends, as we do in relation to the pro-slavery part of the community—a mere secondary, underling position, in all our relations to them, and any thing more than this, is not a matter of course affair—it comes not by established anti-slavery custom or right, but like that which emanates from the pro-slavery portion of the community, by mere sufferance.

That was the stickler, then and now. Delany demanded too much from the white abolitionists—equality, *at least among them*. In today's phraseology, Delany was telling them that they hadn't put their "action where their mouth is." Ideologically, therefore, Delany was ready for the militant abolitionism then personified by Garrison and Douglass.

Delany's public explanation of his move was part of the announcement in the *North Star* on January 21, 1848, that he had given up his connection with *The Mystery* with the completion of Volume IV. It is an interesting exposition of conditions and his own motives. He declared:

> . . . for upwards of four years this paper has been afloat upon the breeze, during which time, except for three months when it was edited by the Committee, we have

stood at the helm of our steady little barque, steering right onward for the continent of Liberty and Equality. If ever we have touched successfully any of her ports, we leave to those who have been the constant observers to decide.

Detailing the early history of *The Mystery*—"we commenced the enterprise alone"—Delany pronounced his own editorial eulogy:

> The position that we assumed was to claim for our oppressed fellow countrymen both bond and free, every right and privilege belonging to man, holding as an indispensable prerequisite, that whatever is necessary for the elevation of the whites, is necessary for the colored. In order the more fully to illustrate the truthfulness of this position, we had frequently to touch subjects that at once affected the pride and interest of our brethren, who often in consequence looked upon us more as an injurer than as a friend.
>
> But our determination being perseverance, and our course onward, we had not long been toiling without the popular tide and current of our people's errors, until the young people, particularly of the West, were aroused to a quickening sense of their condition, and in many cases inexcusable positions in society, and we at one time, had the astonishment as well as the pleasure of seeing ELEVEN papers spring up in different parts of the country, all of which joined issue with us, advocating the very same doctrines, or commending our course.

And he cited six of the eleven new Negro newspapers initiated after *The Mystery* and concluded that there were just too many of them to survive, that some were only begun because their editors saw the success of Delany, "an inexperienced adventurer."

Boastfully, he continued, "And we can safely say, in no period of our modern existence, was the talents of the colored people, male and female, developed to such an extent as since the existence of our paper." Here one must disagree with Delany's sweeping implication. *The Mystery* was one among many evidences of the Negro awakening, by no means an unimportant one, but also not the "be all" his words imply. But there is evidence substantiating his further assertion that "those who before had not the confidence in themselves and would scarce venture a thought, look upon such efforts as a matter of course" due to the example of *The Mystery*. At least, many other Negro papers followed his.

While overstating the beneficent effect of the newspaper, Delany understated his personal difficulties in its continued publication.

> We have ever since gone on steadily and stealthily, until the present date, fulfilling to the letter our promise as editor and assisting the Publishers (Committee) in the fulfillment of theirs; though as we have frequently noticed, gave our services gratuitously to the cause, as well as a portion of our private means, earned by our daily business.
>
> We admit that we have fallen far short of what might have been effected in the same time, the paper frequently appearing quite cold and spiritless, but this could not be avoided, as we had our daily labor to perform to earn our bread. . . . THE MYSTERY is still afloat, with the solemn promise of the Publishers, to keep her tiding on the broad waters of destiny, doing battle in the great struggle for liberty and right, elevation and equality, God and humanity.

He recommended continued support by the readers of *The Mystery*. As for himself, he was entering a "more useful and productive part of the moral vineyard."

> We leave *The Mystery* for a union with the far-famed and world-renowned FREDERICK DOUGLASS, as a co-laborer, in the cause of our oppressed brethren, by the publication of a large and capacious paper, the *NORTH STAR* in Rochester, N.Y., in which our whole time, energy and services will be given, which cannot fail to be productive of signal benefit to the slave and our nominally free brethren when the head and heart of Douglass enters into the combination. We feel loath to leave our *Mystery* but duty calls and we must obey.

After expressing his gratitude to those who worked with him, Delany concluded:

> To our brethren and oppressed fellow men everywhere we give the assurance that so long as reason serves as the dictator of our will we shall never cease to war against slavery and oppression of every kind and defend the cause of the oppressed. Readers and Patrons, as Editor of *The Mystery*, we bid you farewell.

The Mystery continued until the spring of 1848 and it appeared irregularly until the subscription list was taken over by the AME Church in the summer. The AME leadership felt the need for a national organ and they organized the *Christian Herald*, whose first editor was Augustus R. Green. When the name was changed to *Christian Recorder* and the newspaper was moved to Philadelphia, Delany's former roommate, now Rev. Molliston M. Clark, became the editor, and the newspaper has published continuously to this day.

With his usual vigor, Delany took to the abolition circuit and sacrificed his practice. He advertised in the *Dispatch* as well as *The Mystery* whenever the call of the struggle took him away. "M. R. Delany will be absent for several days. Mr. R. Vandevort, Dentist, Smithfield Street, 3 doors below Liberty, will attend to his professional business. Due notice will be given of his return. City dailies please copy, 1 time."

But before he started out, for the second time during their long friendship and cooperative work, Delany and John B. Vashon disagreed on Negro goals. The first time was during the Mexican War agitation.

Vashon believed that citizenship for the Negroes could be achieved by accepting white standards for gaining status, chiefly as a veteran of some war. His own experience as a veteran of the War of 1812 backed up his thesis that white Americans worshiped the man who dons a uniform in defense of his country. Hadn't his success in Pittsburgh, and therefore his ability to help other Negroes, been the result of his acceptance as a veteran by the whites? Since that was true, and it was, if Polk could be persuaded to enlist Negroes for the Mexican War, thousands would be rewarded and would become more useful to their enslaved brethren.

It was not easy to dispute that reasoning, and Delany did not attempt it in *The Mystery*. He printed Vashon's speeches and communications on the subject and, sometimes in the same issue, printed his own belief that all people, white and black, should abhor any war whose purpose was solely the expansion of slavery and the increased domination by the slave South over the legislative and executive councils of the nation. Even if President Polk were to enlist blacks, he expressed no hope that black heroes would ever receive any rewards from whites. Delany began then a lifelong reiteration that there would be no such thing as the voluntary award of citizenship. And it was difficult for Vashon to refute Delany's thesis. For he, too, among the blacks of Pennsylvania, had lost the right to vote.

Vashon and Delany went to the public with their argument. On September 9, 1847, they debated in Temperance Hall on Smithfield St. Vashon took the affirmative and Delany the negative. The question itself was a touchy one to place before the public in early September while General (later President) Zachary Taylor stood at Monterrey with troops readied to send south in support of Gen. Scott's campaign against Mexico City. Yet while the question argued by these two black men—Should Abolitionists Support the Government of the United States?—divided abolitionists, it never came between Delany and Vashon. They remained friends until the latter's death in 1854. In fact, only a few months after the debate, in January 1848, J. B. Vashon sponsored still another benefit for *The Mystery* at Philo Hall.

By the fall, Delany felt once more that it was time to move onto the national scene. Pennsylvania was hopeless. He reported in *The Mystery* the sad news that George B. Vashon had been rejected for admission to the bar of Allegheny County. Just before Christmas this brilliant young protégé of Delany's left for Port Republican, Haiti, to practice law. Delany named Vashon Haitian correspondent for the *North Star*. Foster commented in the *Dispatch*: "There are two things in this that call for special surprise. That a man whose color would not prevent him from being a mechanic, merchant, physician or Divine, should be excluded from practicing law, and the second is that anyone should be so attracted by the profession of law as to abandon country and friends to obtain this coveted privilege." In February 1848 when another of Delany's young men, David Peck, left for Philadelphia to practice medicine and was kicked out of Thomas' Auction Store at a sale of medical books, Foster had the comment: "We presume this gross insult was perpetrated on a young man of education, simply to curry favor with the southern students who were in attendance. Mr. Thomas has doubtless the face of a free man and the disposition of a slave." But, at about the same time, *The Mystery* noted that before sailing for Haiti young Vashon had been admitted to the practice of law in the Supreme Court of New York.

Just as *The Mystery* was a reflection of Martin R. Delany, so the *North Star* was all Frederick Douglass. Eventually, it was to be named just that, *Frederick Douglass' Paper*.

Delany's role for the *North Star* was to be little different from his duties with *The Mystery*—with one exception. He no longer had the responsibility for dealing with printers, making up the paper, and scraping to pay the bills. Douglass assumed these business and production responsibilities in Rochester while Delany traveled in the anti-slavery cause and to obtain subscriptions. He promoted events such as the Charity Fair to benefit the *North Star* and lectured constantly for over a year. In addition, he wrote almost weekly articles on a vast variety of topics. He served as circulation man, promoter, and roving correspondent.

While still in Pittsburgh, arranging his first western tour, Delany's letters reported the meetings and speeches, the personalities and problems of the city. But he did not confine himself at all. Interspersed in his reports during the first few months of 1848 were extended comments on elections everywhere, on Cuba, the Mexican War, Haiti, France, and England, whose ". . . every example is to promote the cause of freedom." His comments and reports reveal an intimate knowledge of and curiosity in international affairs. On February 10, 1848, he contrasted France with England, much to the former's disadvantage, during a spate of rumors of invasion of England:

> But how with France? She is a slaveholding power, deeply engaged in human traffic, favoring and fostering the institution of slavery wherever she holds the power or influence.

As for Pittsburgh, Delany's reports show that his spirit was already winging toward new challenges. It was difficult to arrange meetings in Pittsburgh because "every man is such a real slave to his own business that he has not time to devote to the suffering slave." He again observed that "the Almighty Dollar" interfered with anti-slavery efforts, ". . . being first in thought, first in desire and the first thing grasped at by our fellow countrymen."

There was one encouraging activity, however, one with which he had been so intimately connected for so many years.

> The UGR is doing a fair business here; and while I write, a panting fugitive enters my room, in company with a brother, seeking aid and advice. Of course I immediately sent the brother out for aid. He returns—a ticket is obtained—and another moment and the man is on his way rejoicing. . . .
>
> Ho, the car Emancipation,
> Rides majestic through our Nation!

Delany's plans to begin his western tour were delayed by the illness of an infant daughter, one of the four children he and Katy were to lose. In February 1848 he reported this to Douglass, but there is no indication of his worry until he was already in the midst of his tour. Between meetings in Columbus, Ohio, on April 17, he visited the Blind Asylum there. A young blind girl named Lucinda Shaw was assigned as his guide through the institution. When they came to a music room, she sat down at the piano and played "Rose Bud," whose lyrics lamented the fate of a little girl "nipped in the bud" of life.

> Coming as it did at the instant of the reception of intelligence of the death of my dear little daughter appeared like piercing my heart with a golden spear or riddling my breast with precious stones! It seemed as though that innocent and unconscious young Lucinda selected that song intentionally. It was painfully singular how I enjoyed it. I would that she had sung it again and yet I would that she had not sung it at all.

Actually, Delany had not begun his tour until March 13, and by then Douglass was already approaching the financial crisis that led him to beg for more help from England. He wrote to a most remarkably dedicated woman, Julia Griffiths, the daughter of a close friend of William Wilberforce, the founder of British abolitionists.

> Things have not turned out at all as I expected. The colored people themselves owing to the long night of ignorance which has overshadowed and subdued their spirit. (*sic*) Then again my paper is too free from party dictation to receive much support from any existing anti-slavery party. They have all their own party organs to support and feel only a negative interest in mine. I am also somewhat behind on account of the small assistance in getting subscribers rendered me by my Dear Friend Delany. When I united with him the understanding was that I should remain in Rochester and edit the paper while he traveled and obtained subscribers. This from various causes, he has been able to do to a very limited extent.

Douglass' appeal for money was more than heeded. Miss Griffiths and her sister packed up and moved from England to Rochester, right into his home. She took over his business problems that summer and within a year had him "in the black." One of her methods was to compile and sell a slim volume of writing, a delightful collection of creative work, entitled *Autographs for Freedom.*

Delany's almost weekly reports to Douglass and the *North Star* alternated between jubilation and despair. Beginning with New Lisbon, Ohio, near the shores of the Ohio River about fifty miles from Pittsburgh he had held five weekly meetings by March 22 and found hope only in Salem, the headquarters of the Western Anti-Slavery Society. In New Lisbon he observed that "a respectable looking strange colored man is assailed and assaulted on every side as he passes through the streets with all manner of low and disparaging epithets. . . . So prevalent is this serfdom of prejudice that there is scarcely a child in the place able to lisp a name, but it slips out in disparagement against the colored stranger." He concluded that, unlike Salem only a few miles away, New Lisbon was pro-slavery.

He was to meet much worse, and much better. He shared every experience ever related by that small battalion of heroes who braved the transport and the white people of the day. A white anti-slavery speaker had it much easier—when he was not known. He at least ate at the stage stops and could find a bed at night. Delany went hungry for two days, his longest term of starvation on the road, and thereby equaled Douglass' record.

There were exceptions, of course. The small Ohio towns were no different from New England towns regarding slavery and color prejudice. They were dominated by a person, a group, or a church, and as that dominance dictated, the residents reacted. An example was Cambridge, Ohio, which Delany despised with a relish. An anti-slavery speaker named Hull had been mobbed there eleven times and driven out of town. Delany refused to speak there, even though the white Methodist clergyman invited him to do so right after the Sabbath sermon. "For me to have attempted to expose the hypocrisy of pro-slavery religion by rebuking the infernal system of American slavery before such a congregation, and at such a time, would have been a sin unpardonable." Most of the congregation made up the mob attacking Hull.

And yet, Delany, in Cambridge only to change stages on the national road, found a welcome exception among the whites, a Mr. Carey who ran the only hotel on that part of the road—Temperance House, Delany was quick to add. Carey not only took him in, but fed him in the dining room without fuss or question. Delany fervently recommended to all anti-slavery people, black or white, Mr. Carey's Temperance House in Cambridge, although he warned them against the town.

By the end of April, Delany was an anti-slavery veteran, entitled to several battle stars. He had traveled the national road, about the only east-west highway across mid-Ohio. What is surprising about his reports to the *North Star* was Delany's surprise at such conditions. He had been warned by working abolitionists. He declared that he had never met such

> . . . miserable truckling to the slave power and low servility manifested at most every house upon the road, and in every town through which I passed. Indeed, I cannot permit myself to believe that there is in either Asia or Africa, a tribe, or clan of heathen that can be found among them whom a stranger, of whatever nation or clime, would not meet with more civility, than a colored person—at least than I received from Lloydsville to Zanesville upon this 'National Road'.

But in the larger towns and cities Delany felt that his white audiences left the various halls, homes, and stores in which he lectured at least a bit more receptive to anti-slavery thought.

There is no question that his oratorical abilities were appreciated by his audiences. In a long and complete story on the content of his speech at the sixth Congregational Church, the *Cincinnati Herald* called it "an extraordinary production in more than one respect." Delany delivered a

> well-arranged discourse, a clear, distinct, forcible and manly denunciation of the religious and political hypocrisy of the times. He plunged into the midst of his subject without circumlocution or any labored efforts to do the agreeable. From his earnest, grave and energetic manner, it was evident that he felt the importance of the work he had to perform, and that he had not time to lose in smoothing over sentences made up of soft nothings.

Also in Cincinnati, where he spoke almost without cessation afternoons and evenings on two visits totaling approximately ten days, Delany found hope for his people. The Negro community there had so recovered from the successive riots which began in 1829 when some 2,000 were driven from the city that nearly twenty years later they were restored to stability in the midst of hostility. Their population had risen to about 5,000 and there was even a cultural life among the younger people, much like that of Delany's early years in Pittsburgh. There were a few wealthy colored families and a host of skilled workers. He cited Henry Boyd, a former slave, who was a skilled woodworker and had established his own furniture factory. When Delany met him he had ten employees, including whites. Boyd paid taxes on property later appraised at $26,000, and his bedsteads became famous, selling not only in Ohio but in Kentucky and Indiana as well. There were many other black tradesmen and skilled workers in the city. By 1852 a grocer named Wilcox was taxed on $59,000 in property.

Cincinnati also had one of the two then existing high schools for Negroes in the country, the other being in New York. He met the colored teachers from the East, Mary E. Miles and Caroline Brooks, who became his most successful *North Star* subscription saleswomen. But he was disappointed in the school itself, both in its quarters and curriculum. The school was an addition to the True Wesleyan Church and had only a back entrance. It seemed to Delany a location ". . . as though it were chosen to hide the pupils from the public view." He objected to the lack of teaching the fundamentals of the sciences and the appearance that "the greatest part of the time of the pupils was spent in preparing for exhibitions, which of course make great displays of seeming qualifications."

However, he had the highest praise for one achievement of the combined Negro societies, the United Colored American Association. It was their own cemetery. "This is a most praiseworthy undertaking on the part of colored citizens and how shameful the necessity of a separate burial place for the dead!"

Coincidental with his stay in Cincinnati was the arrival of a slaveowner and fifteen slaves from East Feliciana Parish, Louisiana. This was Rev. William King, a Presbyterian minister who was taking his slaves to Canada for settlement and freedom. Delany, in the *North Star,* mentions his intent to meet Rev. King and discuss the project with him, but there is no further report on it. Eight years later, in Kent County, Canada, they were neighbors and colleagues in behalf of the free blacks and fugitive slaves.

Perhaps Delany's reports from Cincinnati were more frequent and detailed than anywhere else on his trip because it was in the Queen City that he received a signal honor. After his speech before the Friendship Division No. 2 of the Sons of Temperance on May 12, one of the young men, John I. Gaines, rose and delivered a tribute to Delany. "We have been watching for four years the course you have pursued with reference to our rights." He continued:

> Sir, we feel proud that one like you, so well qualified both by nature and education, should report our cause; one who has not a drop of Anglo-Saxon blood. . . . Not that we are prejudiced to color—for this idea we spurn—but for the simple reason that whenever a mind of a higher order is exhibited among us some gossip or goose is ready to attribute it to a little speck of white blood which is said to be coursing through our veins.

From the heights of success in Cincinnati, Delany traveled on through the towns to the depths of Marseilles, Ohio. It was here that he barely escaped the mob. He had been joined by the courageous Charles H. Langston, a brother of the equally famous

John Mercer Langston, who was active in temperance work and was secretary of the Ohio Anti-Slavery Society. Langston was one of those Negroes, like Robert Purvis of Philadelphia, who could easily have "passed," since his features and color did not distinguish him, but he preferred to lead his people. He was later to serve a term in jail for defiance of the Fugitive Slave Act of 1850 in the notorious Oberlin-John Price rescue case.

The two arrived in Marseilles by horse and buggy at sunset. They attracted the attention of the loiterers "pitching quoits" in the center of the main street, but thought nothing of it. In a small town strangers, particularly colored strangers, got attention. To their surprise, the hotelkeeper was a Liberty party man who had been at the Columbus convention Delany had observed and reported on while in that city. He proposed a meeting, since the evening was young and his friends would like to hear an anti-slavery speech. Delany and Langston agreed and the innkeeper set about arranging it for a schoolhouse that night. But one of the innkeeper's friends was a Judas, Delany was convinced.

When they started for the schoolhouse in the dark, they noticed that the streets and alleys were unusually crowded with men and boys, but again they thought nothing of it. Delany had forgotten a copy of his *North Star* and turned back to the hotel while Langston waited on the street. When Delany re-joined his friend, he heard a shocker. The "boys," thinking Langston was white, had talked freely on the streets and planned to break up the meeting, tar and feather Delany, and perhaps commit other "diversions." Langston refused to speak. But Delany insisted that they at least go to the schoolhouse and explain their refusal. The gang fell in behind them. They did find "three or four respectable looking men who appeared as if they came for the sake of the meeting." But the mob poured in too, noisy and threatening.

Delany rose to announce his refusal to speak. "The house, it is true, was quiet and may have remained so, for aught I know, until I had finished a long discourse, at least until some position was taken which displeased them, when from what then really followed it would not then be difficult to determine the consequence."

The Judas-friend of the hotelkeeper rose as soon as Delany declined to speak and made a motion: "I move that we adjourn by considering this a *darkey* burlesque." Delany and Langston were followed back to the hotel by the mob, now armed with "a bass drum, tambourines, clarionet (*sic*), violin, jawbone of a horse, castanets and a number of other instruments."

From their upstairs room Delany and Langston watched the crowd roll the tar barrel into the street in front of the hotel, build the fire, and also build up their excitement to shouts of "Burn them alive— Kill the niggers," etc. The hotelkeeper wanted them to leave by a back door and disappear in the night, but Delany and Langston refused.

> We had done nothing worthy of such treatment and therefore, under no circumstances could submit to personal violence. My friends may censure me—even both of us—for this, but we cannot help it. We are not slaves, nor will we tamely suffer the treatment of slaves, let it come from a high or low source, or from wherever it may.

They watched the white rioters of Marseilles until about 1 A.M. when, no more wood being available, they dispersed, leaving six guards to see that the Negroes did not escape in the night. In the morning the innkeeper had the horse and buggy brought from its hiding place, and Delany and Langston drove off sedately, attacked only by yells and stones. The mob did not respond to the alarm. Delany thought they might have "been ashamed to be seen . . . and identified" in the daylight.

The incident did not seem to affect Delany's nose for news at all. At the end of the Marseilles report to Douglass he said he planned to leave Sandusky City, Ohio, for Detroit City "where there is a very interesting slave case pending before the U.S. Court."

This was the Crosswait fugitive slave case in Detroit, involving a family of six which had escaped from Carroll County, Kentucky, in 1843 and had settled in the fugitive slave center surrounding Marshall, Michigan. There they were informed on, and at daybreak on January 27, 1847, a Kentucky lawyer named Troutman, with a relative of the slaveowner and two other Kentuckians, invaded the home with arms and held the family. But either Crosswait or one of his sons sounded the alarm, which was heard outside, and all of Marshall, both blacks and whites, surrounded the house.

The trouble with the Kentuckians was their arrogance, according to Delany's vivid account. Troutman started to bluster and harangue the crowd, and Charles T. Gorham, a Marshall resident, promptly made it a town meeting and offered a resolution:

> *Resolved*, that these Kentuckians be prevented from taking away the Crosswait family, by moral, legal or physical force and that they leave the state in two hours or be subject to a prosecution for breach of the peace.

The resolution was adopted unanimously. Troutman did some more blustering, enraging the crowd by threatening Dr. Oliver Comstock, Jr., the town's beloved physician.

Marshall was a famous redistribution point for fugitive slaves bound for Canada or elsewhere, and the Underground Railroad, operated by the colored people, was extremely efficient. The blacks tired of the meeting and took the family to Canada, whereupon Troutman brought suit against Gorham, Dr. Comstock, another white man, and three Negroes. Judge John McLean of Ohio was the presiding justice of the U.S. District Court in Detroit. Delany was not dismayed as much by the result of the case as he was by Judge McLean's charge to the jury. The jury disagreed when its foreman, Charles M. Humphrey, held out against eleven fellow jurors who voted for conviction. In the *North Star*, Delany cheered the man but not Judge McLean.

> This extraordinary opinion of Judge McLean, to which I call your particular attention, announced from the Bench as an essential point in civil jurisprudence, is to my mind without precedence in the history of modern—at least enlightened, judicial procedure. . . .
>
> Unexpectedly to everyone, either plaintiffs, defendants or their friends, in his charge to the Jury giving a definition of a criminal in this and all similar cases—the charge being brought for "harboring, concealing, hindering and obstructing" in the language of the Act of Congress "knowing them to be slaves" etc. "shall forfeit and pay for *each slave* the sum of five hundred dollars" etc.; unequivocally asserted, repeatedly, that it was not necessary to the offence that

the person interfering with the rights of slavecatchers should *know* that the person or persons so claimed were slaves. . . .

The merest interference, after this declaration, will suffice to criminate. To make this plain, in reply to an interrogatory by one of the counsel for defence, remarked: "I wish the Jury to understand this. It is not necessary that the person interfering should know that the persons claimed are slaves. If the claimant has made the declaration that they are such, though he should only assert it to the fugitives themselves—indeed, it could not be expected that the claimant would be required the trouble of repeating this to persons who might be disposed to interfere—should anyone interfere at all, after this declaration of the claimant, he is liable and responsible to the provisions of the law in such cases."

Delany fumed over Judge McLean and his court. He warned readers of the *North Star*:

There is not but one important view to be taken of the matter. Previous to this decision, colored persons had some slight semblance of liberty but now every vestige has been wrested from us—each and all of us reduced to the mercy or discretion of any white man in the country, and like the colored man in the South without a "Pass" as it is worded, may at any moment be arrested as the property of another. . . .

So accustomed is the North to Southern rule that it has become second nature. How exceedingly mortifying to see Northern men thus "tamely bowing" their necks to the dark spirit of slavery.

The case became a cause celebre in Kentucky where the state legislature appropriated $2,000 to prosecute further, and there were speeches in the U.S. Senate. Another repercussion affected Judge McLean and blasted his political future forever. That was because of Delany's long report and bitter criticism appearing in the *North Star*, so his biographer claims.

Delany was at the Free Soil party convention in Buffalo, N.Y., a few weeks later to nominate a presidential candidate against the Democrats' Lewis Cass and the Whigs' Zachary Taylor. In the huge Oberlin tent where the delegates and reporters sat, the talk was that the decision lay between Judge McLean and Martin Van Buren.

A gentleman the biography describes as tall and "in the habilments of a clergyman, and of a most attractive, Christian-like countenance" was seen wandering about and asking delegates questions. He finally reached Delany and thrust a copy of the *North Star* before him, pointing to the Detroit story of July 28, 1848.

"Are you Dr. M. R. Delany?"

"I am, sir," replied he.

"Are you one of the editors of the *North Star*, sir?"

"Yes, sir, I am," he answered, feeling, very likely, most uncomfortable by this attention.

"Are these your initials, and did you write this article concerning Justice McLean of the Supreme Court, in the case of Dr. Comstock and others, and the Crosswait family?" continued his interlocutor.

"That is my article, and these are my initials, sir."

"I've but one question more to ask you. Did you hear Judge McLean deliver this decision, or did you receive the information from a third party?" demanded the questioner.

"I sat in the courtroom each day during the entire trial and reported only what I heard, having written down everything as it occurred," returned Dr. Delany.

"That is all, sir; I am satisfied."

And off went the stranger, nor did Delany get his name. But soon after sunset the hero of many a fugitive slave defense, Salmon P. Chase, mounted the platform of the convention to announce that the Committee of Conference had eliminated the name of Judge McLean as the Free Soil candidate for the presidency, at which there was "deafening applause," and Martin Delany took the credit for nominating Martin Van Buren.

The story could have been true. It is recorded that Judge McLean had been considered as a presidential candidate by the party of "free soil, free speech, free labor and free men." He had been proposed and spoken for by Chase himself, in spite of the fact that Judge McLean had rendered verdicts against one of his clients in 1842 to the sum of $1,700 plus legal costs for helping a runaway slave. This was the notorious John Van Zandt case in Cincinnati which went to the Supreme Court. McLean's award of damages was upheld there. Chase's change of attitude toward McLean came about in 1846 when he married his third wife, a niece of the judge's, indicating that even abolitionist politics followed the same patterns now and then. It should be noted that, in 1857, as a member of the U.S. Supreme Court, Judge McLean dissented in the Dred Scott decision.

What is without question is the fact that Martin Delany did recognize in the Detroit charge to the jury a forerunner of the Fugitive Slave Act two years later. Judge McLean's juridical thinking was an ominous shadow over the country, for just as every runaway slave was guilty of the theft of property—himself—so every individual who assisted him, even with a kind word, was guilty of being an accessory in theft. Delany's fears for this precedent, expressed in the *North Star,* were well founded.

From his reports to the *North Star,* Delany had visited and lectured in some forty cities and towns, as well as at numerous crossroad churches, homes, and the like. He could well have delivered hundreds of speeches in addition to enlisting *North Star* agents and subscribers. While Frederick Douglass claimed his own lectures and promotion as responsible for increasing the newspaper's circulation from 2,000 to double that in one year, Delany assuredly was responsible for some of that increase.

By the summer of 1848 Delany was one of a galaxy of black men attempting, through a revival of Negro conventions, to give some point and direction to their own abolition movement. The white abolitionists were hopelessly splintered in varying directions—political, religious, and apathetic. The coterie of Garrison people would not work with the Douglass adherents and vice versa. All of them turned their backs in horror each time a militant like Henry Highland Garnet called for promotion of a slave rebellion sponsored by the abolitionists.

Faithfully for another year Delany promoted the *North Star* and was an active member of convention after convention, in Cleveland, Harrisburg, Philadelphia—wherever there was a state or national meeting of Negroes. He was on countless committees, wrote innumerable resolutions, argued them on the floor, and usually won. But by the spring of 1849 the cancer of despair could be seen in Delany's dispatches to the *North Star.* He saw beauty and humanity here and there but was prone to reverse the coin and show the morbid corpse of both.

On February 24 of that year he reported crossing the mountains from Philadelphia to Pittsburgh for the fourth time in five months, and he gave a graphic description of their beauties. His words pulsate with the wonder of America, then dig savagely into the hidden heart.

> The soul may here expand in the magnitude of its nature, and soar to the extent of human susceptibility. Indeed it is only in the mountains that I can fully appreciate my existence as a man in America, my own native land. It is then and there my soul is lifted up, my bosom caused to swell with emotion, and I am lost in wonder at the dignity of my own nature. I see in the works of nature around me, the wisdom and goodness of God. I contemplate them, and conscious that He has endowed me with faculties to comprehend them, I then perceive the likeness I bear to Him. What a being is man—of how much importance, created in the impress image of his Maker, and how debased is God, and outraged His divinity in the person of the oppressed colored people of America. The thunders of His mighty wrath must sooner or later break forth, with all of the terrible consequences, and scourge this guilty nation for the endless outrages and cruelty committed upon an innocent and unoffending people. I invoke the aid of Jehovah, in this mighty work of chastisement. . . .
>
> I left in Philadelphia on the 5th inst. . . .

Was the above a digression in the midst of his factual report? Far from it. This was a black man asking why? Why? Why? Just as black men do today. It occurs often in his reports, as though Delany, while noting the necessary trivia of his work and observations, tried to block his pen from transcribing their futility.

When he hailed the Liberian Declaration of Independence a week later, Delany declared that he regarded

> Liberia in its present state as having thwarted the design of the original schemers, the slaveholding founders, which evidently was intended, as they frequently proclaimed it, as a receptacle for the freed colored people and superannuated slaves of America; but we view it in the light of a

source of subsequent enterprise, which no colored American should permit himself to lose sight of.

The reverse of the coin? The head of the judicial system in independent Liberia was a Judge Benedict who was "a person of no force of character or fixed moral principles." It seems he had bought his wife out of slavery, and when she objected to his taking some mistresses, tried to sell her back into slavery. "The better feelings of our nature recoil at the idea of the toleration of such a wretch in any capacity wherein pends the responsibility of our destiny, or hope of elevation."

As for John Jenkins Roberts, first President of independent Liberia, his actions raised a question as to the country's actual freedom from slaveholding America. He had been the American Colonization Society's agent for Liberia, and its governor. That was suspicious enough, being "a man whom the Colonizationists and shareholders in the United States extolled to the skies. . . ." But then President Roberts, in seeking the recognition of Liberia's independence and obtaining it from England and France, turned his attention to the United States,

> Like a slave, cap in hand, obedient to the commands of the dons who employ them, bidden on an errand of his master, President Roberts no sooner concludes the business of his mission, a knowledge and official account of which was alone due to his own government, but he writes to A. G. Phelps, a Colonizationist of the United States, giving him an official report of his proceedings as the Minister of Liberia, an independent nation. If ever the curse of slavery were manifest in the character of man, it has fully exhibited itself in this man Roberts.

When Roberts came to America, he reported to Anson Greene Phelps, the pioneer metals industrialist after whom Ansonia, Connecticut, was named. Phelps headed that state's Colonization Society for years and was extremely wealthy.

> Here, faithful to the trust reposed in him by his American white masters, this man Roberts discards the people whom he feigns to represent, considering it a condescension to do so, spurns at the idea of reporting to them the results

> of his mission, but as a serf to his lord, considers it an honor and special privilege to submit his doings first to a white man, hence, that malignant libeller (*sic*) of our race, A. G. Phelps was selected and reported to, over the heads of his country and his people.

Events were to prove that Delany's report and criticism were valid. Liberia remained an American private dependency and Roberts did not even obtain official recognition of its independence. The United States did not recognize its own colonial child until 1862, after the Civil War had begun.

There was bitterness even in his meeting reports that spring. At York, Penn.: "I am sorry to see that a party spirit has crept even into that little place among our brethren and would advise them as soon as possible to do away with it as it has heretofore been the very curse of all our moral efforts."

And when President Taylor was expected to visit Pittsburgh in late February 1849, to Delany he was "Gen. Taylor, of Florida war, Indian-murder, bloodhound and Mexican slaughter notoriety." The plans for the celebration in Pittsburgh, as in all other cities of Taylor's triumphal tour, had a special connotation for Delany.

> The extent to which the American people carry this glorification of military crusaders, is beyond a parallel, except in the days of the Roman extravaganza, which was but a foreboding of the end of her glory and speedy downfall of that haughty, insolvent empire and commonwealth. The extent to which this homage is carried, ceases to be respectful, since it is neither kind nor complimentary, but like the homage of the serf to the noble, or the vassal to his lord, it is ludicrous. It is unfit for freemen, and only worthy of slaves—it is a flagrant outrage upon common sense and propriety.

In July, while hailing the founding of the Allegheny Institute and Mission Church by Charles Avery and giving all the kudos to that philanthropist, Delany still deplored the "moral aspect" of the people of Pittsburgh. He complained about the behavior of the young men while complimenting their fathers who were investing their earnings in real estate. It seems that the young colored men had declined seriously in the eighteen months of his absence. They were earning money on the river "for a season, quit work, dress up and strut about, dangling a gold chain and dandy staves, boarding at considerable expense, gallanting and 'treating the girls' until their funds were exhausted, then to go to work again. . . ." Delany indulged often in the "generation gripe."

From the tone and material in his columns, in the spring and summer of 1849, Delany was reaching a crisis in his thinking. He was beginning to doubt the affirmative of the first question—Stay and fight? And he was not yet ready to accept the alternative—Emigrate?

CHAPTER SEVEN

Metastases of Despair

By 1850 Delany had seen more of America than most whites or blacks, and he had written of the many Americas he had seen with both love and hate. By 1850, at the age of 38, he had absorbed more of ancient and modern social and political philosophies than most whites or blacks, and he could approximate the outlines of that vague American dream far more accurately than the sentimental ballads or the 4th of July orators. America was not beautiful to Delany but it could be. It only needed color blindness. Only welcome the Negro to the land of his birth as were welcomed the Irish, the Scots, the Germans, the Slavs, and all other oppressed of the earth. Why not? Their English speech initially was as unintelligible as a Gullah slave's. Their illiteracy was just as great. Their poverty was quite the same, one of survival. There was proof enough by 1850 that the Negro potential in all endeavors was quite as great as the blondest Scandinavian or the swarthiest Italian immigrant.

That was Delany's American dream and, because he was honest with himself, he turned the coin and saw the reality. America was not beautiful because she had not crowned her "good with brotherhood, from sea to shining sea." She was not beautiful because neither God nor her people had mended "every flaw" nor confirmed "Thy liberty in law." There was every moral, religious, and ethical reason why America was not beautiful to Delany, or to his fellow blacks.

The conflict had its roots, however, in the fact that Delany, like most blacks, loved his native land. Perhaps it was the beauty of the "dream" that effaced the reality.

Delany was not yet ready to leave for another reason. As yet, he saw no method by which he could help his people in doing so. He had not found that solution even by 1852, following one of the severest frustrations of his life. The first full book he ever wrote was published in that year and was:

Sincerely Dedicated
TO THE AMERICAN PEOPLE
North And South
By their Most Devout,
And Patriotic Fellow-Citizen,
The Author.

Delany did not decide to leave America until there was not a shred of possibility of the American dream left to him. The process was to be bitter.

The metastases of despair became more evident in Delany's actions and writing immediately after Frederick Douglass failed in a valiant effort to unify the free Negroes in a National League of Colored People. Douglass sent out the call for such an organization on August 10. On October 26, 1848, he was forced to report in the *North Star* that his proposal for a "*union of the oppressed for the sake of freedom*" met with response from a few—

> . . . the overwhelming mass have remained silent as the grave on the subject. *The Impartial Citizen,* edited by a colored man, did not even notice it. The *Ram's Horn* has been dumb over it. Very few of our public men have, as yet, given to the idea the slightest encouragement. Pittsburgh, that should always be ready to speak, as she always has an opinion, has been silent! Cincinnati, containing a colored population as intelligent, active and wealthy as any in the country, has not lisped a word, *pro or con,* on the subject. New York, as usual, has nothing to say.

Douglass was indomitable so long as he had a platform or a press. But that was not enough for Delany. To him, the speech or the written word was the beginning of an effort, not its goal. While from the platform or in *The Mystery* he could boast of the inevitable victory of the colored people because the world contained so many more of them than whites, there was still the present and the United States, where less than half a million "free" blacks had the task of speaking for more than three million slaves. That was the present reality to be faced—with less than 16 percent of the country's population, where was the hope in 1849?

Political action? The last presidential election had seen the Liberty party expire, the Free Soil party emerge, and its nominee, Martin Van Buren, receive a respectable 291,263 votes. That was enough to upset Cass and elect Taylor, but to Delany it was a choice of pro-slavery Tweedledee and Tweedledum. That might have been a large vote for an anti-slavery party, but Delany made a distinction between anti-South and anti-slavery voters. Most of the Van Buren vote, he believed, was an effort to restore some geographical balance of political power. Yet Delany himself, at the Cleveland, Ohio, convention of colored men on September 6, 1848, had been the delegate to write and offer the resolution calling on all Negroes who still had the vote to support the Free Soil candidates. They, at least, were pledged to halt the expansion of slave territory. He also included a resolution establishing as a test for any candidate or political party in any election a pledge for equality for blacks as deserving the colored vote. But hope for the future through political action? Delany had none. What other hope was there?

Economic independence from whites? He had been in Milton, Ohio, and visited the settlement of a John Randolph, founded as a result of a Virginian's will. John Randolph not only willed his slaves manumitted but also provided them with a legacy so that they could buy land. They found the land about three miles from Milton and, through a white agent, paid for it. Yet the very farmers and townspeople from whom they had bought the land comprised the mob that drove them off the settlement. Delany noted that it was ". . . singular that during all the imposition and outrage on the part of these Ohioans, we see neither executor (of the Randolph estate) nor agent enter litigation in the case, but like peaceful citizens, fold their arms and express their regret at the occurrence." Under the Ohio black laws, Negroes themselves could not bring suit against any white. As for John Randolph's executor, hadn't the money from the estate been paid over for purchase of the land?

He added that the Virginia emigrants were being cheated by the merchants of nearby Troy as well as Milton for their very means of survival, and in addition to the bilking of ignorant ex-slaves, "old horses, old plows, and other farming utensils, worn out and good for nothing, are frequently sold to them at high prices, *all under the name of Abolitionism*, which, when the fraud is discovered, tends very much to their discouragement." Many wished they were back in Virginia. "Have they any security? No, none at all." And the Randolph settlement was only one of many examples of cheating and outright theft from Negroes, solely because they had no recourse to the courts. He found the practice among professed abolitionists as well as avowed pro-slavery men, and concluded that there was no such thing as economic security without citizenship security.

Self-improvement in order to meet and beat the whites on their own economic, social, and political grounds? That state of affairs in his own home town of Pittsburgh depressed Delany.

> Sorry are we that duty enjoins and justice compels us to record the fact, however much we may regret the necessity of so doing, that the *moral* aspect of society among our people is at a very low estimate at present in the city of Pittsburgh and vicinity—indeed, the place does not seem the same.

What was wrong? The youth of the day, that was the trouble.

> The youth now coming up, especially those just emerging into manhood, are fearfully delinquent in that which constitutes decency, civility, politeness, and even good manners —in all of those traits the prerequisites of a good and wholesome state of society. Moral and literary societies are totally neglected by the young people—there not being such a thing in existence as a moral or literary society among the young men and young women of either of the two cities and environs. Gadding and gossiping, bending and gainsaying, occupying doubtless a much higher estimate in their consideration than improvement of the mind and morals. What a fearful state of society is this, and yet there appear to be no influences at work, either temporal, moral nor religious—either in the church or out of the church brought particularly to bear upon it to remedy the evil. That there is a fault lies somewhere there is no doubt. The parents and leaders in society have greatly neglected their duty in many

> particulars we have not a doubt; and call upon them in the name of virtue and morality, to look well to the character of the young people.

Where was the hope for his people if they themselves did not recognize the emergency in their collective needs?

The first public intimation that Delany may have had new plans was announced by Douglass himself in the June 29, 1849, issue of the *North Star*. He announced:

> After the present number, by a mutual understanding with our esteemed friend and coadjutor, Mr. Delany, the whole responsibility of editing and publishing the *North Star* will devolve upon myself. . . . In connection with this arrangement I am happy to state that while the copartnership which has subsisted between myself and M. R. Delany is now terminated, his interest in the success of the enterprise remains unabated; and he will continue to contribute by his pen, as formerly, to the columns of the *North Star*; and do all, consistently with his other duties, toward making the paper prosper to its editor and valuable to its readers. It is proper for me to state that thus far, Mr. Delany has been a loser (as well as myself) by the enterprise; and that he is still willing to make sacrifices that our favorite sheet may be sustained.

And make further sacrifices Delany did. The only difference between the summer of 1849 and the previous year was that he lectured and promoted subscriptions in the East—in Wilmington, in Philadelphia, West Chester, York, and many way stations of Pennsylvania. His letters and articles became impatient, sometimes downright chiding, such as the one in which he scolded both Rev. Samuel Ringgold Ward and Frederick Douglass for feuding, and again when Henry Highland Garnet made it a three-way fight among brilliant and selfless black abolitionists.

In September 1849, Delany returned home, after an absence of six months, but immediately had to hit the abolition trail again. This time it was for meetings in Philadelphia during which he shared the platforms with a man he so much admired, Charles Lenox Remond. The high point of this trip was that "Garnet, Douglass, Remond and myself, all had the pleasure for the first time in our lives of meeting and shaking glad hands together! Truly, the God of Liberty, in this instance, was lavish with favors."

The meetings and resolutions continued, and Delany's reports had all the ups and downs of an active manic depressive. He was suffering a new form of battle fatigue. There was discouragement and a reckless rejection of the fight by his people. It was an attitude of eat, drink, and be merry, for tomorrow ye shall be re-enslaved. In Washington, at the end of 1849, the threats of secession and disunion had the North so cowed that the so-called equal balance of fifteen Free and fifteen Slave States was entirely false. Proof that there was a coalition of Congressmen from the North with the united, aggressive Southern representatives was in the continued failure of all efforts to eliminate slavery from the District of Columbia, under the direct and absolute control of Congress. The inevitability of the Compromise of 1850 engineered by Henry Clay, which included the Fugitive Slave Act, was assured by California's independent action in adopting a constitution forbidding slavery. This audacious act of self-determination really popped the southern cork, and their appeasement included muzzling the abolitionists, both white and black. In fact, the most prominent Boston abolitionists were now singing "Union Forever," and at any price including emancipation.

There was another reason for Delany's temporary departure from the gloom and diffusion of the abolition trail. He realized he had been sacrificing his growing family as well as himself. Fortunately, we have his own words on that.

On October 5, 1849, he replied to an H. H. Burnham of Zanesville, Ohio, on the proposition of founding a newspaper, with Delany as editor, for the colored people of Ohio. After a comprehensive discussion of the financial impossibility of such a paper among the approximately 3,000 literate blacks scattered through Ohio, he recommended support of the *North Star* and then added:

> I have, Sir, other and personal objections to entering into such an enterprise. I have never been sufficiently successful in the cause of our brethren to have a value set upon my efforts. I have labored for naught and received nothing. If I except the use of fifty dollars borrowed from a donation

> of one hundred dollars, presented by the Ladies' Fair to the *North Star*, which sum I still have to pay, the present sum of ten dollars, and various articles of clothing for myself and wife and little children, during my stay in Philadelphia last winter, by several excellent colored ladies, is more than I ever before realized, during seven years as editor of different papers, the last eighteen months of which, thus, were devoted entirely to the cause.
>
> I am fully persuaded that to embark in a new enterprise of this kind, would be heedless in me, and the last precipitous stride and gasping struggle to the certain starvation of my family, whom I am bound by all the ties of consanguinity and self-respect, and what is stronger than self-love—or conjugal and filial affection, to protect and support—protect alike against starvation as well as oppression and personal injury and abuse. . . . My ardent desire for the elevation of our race has caused me to sacrifice more than I was able to bear—more than my share.

Lurking in the pages of this long letter was bitter disappointment at the state of Negro abolitionist affairs. The rivalries and bickerings, the division over the multiplicity of courses sponsored by white abolitionists, and the defeat of all efforts toward unity are the experiences behind the following:

> I have no other desire than to do that which I conceive to be just and right towards God and man—to justify myself without wronging my neighbor. I detest that dog-in-the-manger ambition, which, because I cannot eat the hay myself, will suffer no other one to eat it; and that Pharisaical philanthropy, which because Israel cannot be gathered together, would prevent Jacob from receiving his reward. No, thank God, I have a different object and higher aim in view—the elevation of our race—I care not by whom it be effected so that it be properly done. Let it be Henry Highland Garnet, Samuel R. Ward, W. W. (William Wells) Brown, Henry Bibb, Charles Lenox Remond, Frederick Douglass, or whom. I have no ambition whatever for popular fame and personal distinction in the heaven-decreed pursuit of philanthropy. It admits of no such rivalry. That which

> partakes of the nature of Deity, can possess neither hatred or envy. It is an assumption to force one's services where they are not wanted, especially when they are useless; and he who does it is an intruder, if not a usurper. This being my case, I have determined to remain in the seclusion of obscurity, where I have ever been, wishing God-Speed to our public great men, in every good and laudable undertaking in which they may embark.

The above, no doubt, was an honest declaration of his feelings and circumstances *at that time*. Delany had no need to further prove his dedication to his people, but he did have reason to prove his selflessness. He was an ambitious man and had become accustomed to leadership. Events were to prove that in the fall of 1849 Delany had forsworn only temporarily leadership in the planning of black freedom but never his participation in the effort. Against all of the above protestations, he was again to emerge as a leader.

The country saw to that. The sacrifice of black freedom by concession to the South in the Compromise of 1850 blasted his personal concerns, and his family was again to be sacrificed. The Fugitive Slave Act of 1850 was a more potent recruiting force among black men, bringing them again to unity, than any partial victory toward citizenship or emancipation.

The Fugitive Slave Act of 1850 was the weapon for "law and order" of its day. It was a very simple declaration that property rights were ascendant over the Bill of Rights. To the whites jailed and fined under its all-embracing provisions, it operated much as the "conspiracy" and anti-riot laws of 1968-1969. Just as "aiding" a runaway slave could and did include merely gazing on a chase without obeying a marshal's cry "Stop thief!" so is "inciting to riot" sufficiently vague and all-inclusive to include the innocent bystander swept up in the police net. The inoffensive, mild, and unassuming Quaker, Castner Hanway, was in just such a situation at Christiana, Penn., in 1851 when he made no move to assist the slave catcher, Marshal Kline. He and 33 others were acquitted, but not until they had spent six months in jail.

The law gave supreme authority to U.S. Commissioners whose marshals and deputies became the National Guard of their day. They alone defined the "aid" given a fugitive slave.

They could and did levy fines up to $1,000 plus jail sentences up to six months, plus civil damages to the slaveowner of $1,000 for each slave lost.

For the blacks, of course, the Fugitive Slave Law meant slavery for the free and the slave alike, unless they could get whites to intervene for them. They could neither obtain a jury trial or give evidence as to their status as freemen. It was a declaration of open season for the slave kidnapers.

When the shock of recognition was complete among the Negroes, even before the legislation was adopted on September 18, the exodus from the Free States began. Pittsburgh lost 200 of its Negro community before the bill was adopted and 800 afterwards. Canada West, now the Province of Ontario, was to gain a Negro population estimated at 50,000–60,000 during the next decade.

On September 30, 1850, just twelve days after the Fugitive Slave Act became law, Delany joined whites and blacks in the Market House in Allegheny before the largest crowd ever gathered in the city. When it was his turn to speak, Delany turned to the presiding officer, Mayor Hugh Fleming, and there made his famous speech of defiance:

> Honorable Mayor, whatever ideas of liberty I may have, have been received from reading the lives of your revolutionary fathers. I have therein learned that a man has a right to defend his castle with his life, even unto the taking of life. Sir, my house is my castle; in that castle are none but my wife and my children, as free as the angels of heaven, and whose liberty is as sacred as the pillars of God. If any man approaches that house in search of a slave—I care not who he may be, whether constable, or sheriff, magistrate or even judge of the Supreme Court—nay, let it be he who sanctioned this act to become a law (President Millard Fillmore) surrounded by his cabinet as his bodyguard, with the Declaration of Independence waving above his head as his banner, and the constitution of his country upon his breast as his shield,—if he crosses the threshold of my door, and I do not lay him a lifeless corpse at my feet, I hope the grave may refuse my body a resting place, and righteous Heaven my spirit a home. O, no! He cannot enter that house and we both live.

The cry of "Liberty or Death" resounded wherever there were black men, and both came to pass. In Pittsburgh, the first case under the Fugitive Slave Act won Delany a debate with J. B. Vashon, who finally was convinced that such a government should not be fought for. One of his apprentices, a boy named George White, was recognized by a Virginian and hauled up for a return to slavery. Vashon paid the owner $200 for the boy's freedom.

However, while the outcries of the white abolitionists against the Fugitive Slave Act resound from the pages of historical texts, and undoubtedly there were heroes among them, the black exodus to Canada continued and mounted. Though many northern states passed personal liberty laws, the blacks had no faith in their enforcement, much like today's civil rights laws. They had had such promises before. If Daniel Webster could take from the hands of Henry Clay a capitulation to slavery such as the Compromise of 1850 and assure its passage in his famous March 7 speech, all for a mess of presidential pottage, then what was a white promise worth? Webster denied a public lifetime of antislavery in that speech. What white man was to be trusted after that?

Delany continued to make speeches and to help in fugitive rescue work in defiance of the Fugitive Slave Act, but he also returned to his practice and his studies of medicine with Dr. LeMoyne. He had pursued a plan all through the summer of 1850 which was, to him, most logical. His friend in New York, Dr. James McCune Smith, the Glasgow graduate in medicine, had shown him the example. Dr. Smith not only had a vast practice but was listened to as a black abolitionist by virtue of his medical prestige.

Delany decided to go to a medical school and graduate as the best black physician since the ancient founders of the craft who, he believed, also were black.

To attend medical school was an ambitious undertaking. Only a few Negroes, including young David Peck, had been permitted formal medical study in the United States by 1849. Two had been sponsored by the American Colonization Society and were admitted to Bowdoin College only on the proviso that they practice medicine in Liberia.

During the summer of 1850 Delany was refused admission

to four medical colleges, including the University of Pennsylvania, Jefferson Medical College, and those in Albany and Geneva, N.Y. He was about to apply to a medical college in Pittsfield, Mass., the Berkshire Medical School, when a most extraordinary event took place. No doubt, Delany's medical mentors, Drs. Gazzam and LeMoyne, organized the campaign among the physicians of Pittsburgh and Allegheny.

These white doctors—seventeen in all—signed letters of recommendation for admission of a black man to the medical school in Pittsfield. The doctors of Pittsburgh said that they, "having known Mr. Martin R. Delany for a number of years, take great pleasure in certifying to his upright and honorable conduct while here. . . ." The Allegheny physicians, in another letter, said that Delany was "an upright and intelligent man—one who, despite the depressing influences of caste and color, has always maintained an honorable position in the community."

Dr. Gazzam gave testimony in his recommendation that "Mr. Delany has always deported himself as an excellent member of society—he is much esteemed by the medical men of Allegheny County." Dr. LeMoyne addressed his letter to the Faculty of Pittsfield Medical College:

> Gentlemen:
>
> Permit me to introduce to your favorable notice the bearer, Mr. M. R. Delany—who visits your place with the intention of attending your medical instructions the present term.
>
> He has been reading under my direction for the past twelve months. I have been acquainted with him for several years and can cheerfully vouch for his good morals and gentlemanly conduct. You will subserve the cause of science, justice and humanity if you will accord him the full benefits of Your Institution.

In addition, there were letters from the clergymen of both towns, repeating their endorsements of Delany's character and intelligence. Rev. A. W. Black, pastor of the Reformed Presbyterian Church in Allegheny said that Delany was "a man of considerable intellectual power and of great and persevering energy. He has labored much for the moral and mental elevation of his race. He is entitled to the favorable consideration of good men."

For reasons not yet evident, Delany set out with these letters in November, but somewhere there was a change in his destination. Instead of applying at the Pittsfield school, Delany arrived in Boston and was accepted at the old and prestigious Harvard Medical School, whose Dean was Dr. Oliver Wendell Holmes! With two other black students, Daniel Laing, Jr., and Isaac H. Snowden, both of Boston and both sponsored by the American Colonization Society, Delany was among the first Negroes ever accepted as students by the institution.

It was no small feat to be accepted there. Delany fulfilled the requirements as to age and professional experience which demanded a minimum of three years of study "under the direction of a regular practitioner of medicine" and his letters attested to his "good moral character." For admission he was to "satisfy the Faculty of Medicine in respect to his knowledge of the Latin language and experimental philosophy."

The lectures began on the first Wednesday in November and continued for four months. Two terms were required before the candidate for the medical degree was eligible for examination. All three of the Negro students in that class of 1850–1851 were allowed to complete only one term.

Trouble began almost immediately. On the morning of December 10 the medical students of the school met and adopted a resolution addressed to the faculty asking "to be informed whether colored persons are to be admitted as students at another course of lectures." They sought this information in order to "make arrangements for the future as shall be most agreeable to their feelings in the event of Negroes being allowed again to become members of the school."

That same afternoon, the class met again and adopted another series of resolutions which leave no doubt as to their attitudes.

> Whereas blacks have been admitted to the lectures of medical department of Harvard Uni'ty,
>
> Therefore
>
> *Resolved.* That we deem the admission of blacks to the medical Lectures highly detrimental to the interests, and welfare of the Institution of which we are members, cal-

culated alike to lower its reputation in this and other parts of the country, to lessen the value of a diploma from it, and to diminish the number of its students.

Resolved. That we cannot consent to be identified as fellow students with blacks; whose company we would not keep in the streets, and whose Society as associates we would not tolerate in our houses.

Resolved. That we feel our grievances to be but the beginning of an evil, which, if not checked will increase, and that the number of respectable *white* students will, in future, be in an inverse ratio to that of *blacks.*

Resolved. That we earnestly request the Medical Faculty of the University to listen to this our remonstrance against the presence of such persons, and spare us the necessity of being in such company, or of compelling us to complete our medical studies elsewhere.

Resolved. That a copy of these resolutions be presented to the medical faculty.

Resolved. That we have no objection to the education and elevation of blacks but do decidedly remonstrate against their presence in College with us.

E. P. Abbe (Secretary)

The communication to the medical faculty declared that sixty members of the class were present when these resolutions were adopted. But on the following day another segment of the class met, and 26 out of 27 dissented from the above resolution. Their statement read, in part:

> . . . as students of science, above all, as candidates for the profession of medicine, they would feel it a far greater evil if, in the present state of public feeling, a medical college in Boston could refuse to this unfortunate class any privileges of education, which it is in the power of the profession to bestow . . . and they are deeply grieved that at a moment like the present, any portion of their fellow-students should wish to change a policy dictated alike by considerations of humanity and public right.

Another 22 students also dissented from the resolutions passed on December 10, but did not state their reasons.

The "present state of public feeling" mentioned by those students was Boston's instant reaction to the Fugitive Slave Act. A few weeks before, in Faneuil Hall, some 4,000 persons roared their defiance of the law, and Rev. Theodore Parker had declared the validity of a "higher law." The Boston Vigilance Committee was already posting handbills describing the slave hunters in the city. Undoubtedly, the protests against the presence of the blacks in the Harvard Medical School were not something to make public.

On December 13, the medical faculty met and, among other things, adopted the following:

> That whereas arrangements were made in the beginning of the course, with gentlemen representing the American Colonization Society, for the attendance this year, of certain colored persons destined for Liberia, and whereas all persons who have purchased tickets, have thereby acquired rights, of which they cannot properly be divested—therefore the Faculty does not feel themselves authorized to revoke their arrangement.

But finally, on December 26, the faculty voted to have Dean Holmes notify the Colonization Society that no more blacks would be admitted to the Harvard Medical School. Those presently in the course would be allowed to complete it but could not anticipate the second required term for award of a medical degree. This blasted Martin Delany's hopes and plans most effectively.

Strangely enough, just the day before, on December 25, Joseph Tracy, secretary of the Massachusetts Colonization Society, had written to William McLain, secretary of the American Colonization Society:

> Our colored medical students, Laing and Snowden, are getting along very well, notwithstanding some newspaper nonsense to the contrary. When a third colored student (Delany) who came from Philadelphia (*sic*) was admitted, a Kentuckian made a fuss and induced a few to join him, but the Faculty and a large majority of classes are well disposed.

Tracy appears to have been singularly uninformed, or misled. Three years later, when Snowden attempted to complete the course, his application was rejected. In 1850 both the faculty and the "Autocrat of the Breakfast Table," Dr. Holmes, were determined to placate their students without arousing the public. In other words, they "weaseled" out of the situation.

Yet Dr. Oliver Wendell Holmes, American hero, doctor, poet, essayist, and father of the Supreme Court Justice, was not without moral precedent in this situation. The incident took place at Harvard College the previous year (1849), just before Edward Everett left the presidency of the college to become Secretary of State, and concerned a Negro boy named Beverly Williams. Everett described him, in a speech before the American Colonization Society in 1853, as proof of the Negro intellectual potential.

> When I lived in Cambridge, a few years ago, I used to attend, as one of the Board of Visitors, the examinations of a classical school, in which there was a colored boy, the son of a slave in Mississippi, I think. He appeared to me to be pure African blood. There were at the same time two youths from Georgia, and one of my own sons, attending the same school. I must say that this poor negro (*sic*) boy, Beverly Williams, was one of the best scholars at the school, and in Latin language he was the best scholar in his class.

When Beverly Williams applied to Harvard for admission, the students rose in protest against his admission. President Everett's reply to them was:

> The admission to Harvard College depends upon examinations; and if this boy passes the examinations, he will be admitted; and if the white students choose to withdraw, all the income of the College will be devoted to his education.

But the famous Dr. Holmes did not have the moral stamina for a similar course of action in the Harvard Medical School. Perhaps Delany's disappointment in Oliver Wendell Holmes did not affect him as much as his disappointment in his classmates. There were 116 in the class, out of which just four were from the Slave States—Mississippi, Georgia, Alabama, and Kentucky.

Over 100 were from New England, the historical hotbed of abolition. The chairman of the effectively protesting group was John Randolph Lincoln, whose home was Boston, as was the secretary's, Edward Payson Abbe.

It was true that Delany had two notorious examples of Boston's refusal to accept the Fugitive Slave Act and obey instead Theodore Parker's stricture that "when rulers have inverted their functions and enacted wickedness into a law which treads down the inalienable rights of man to such a degree as this, then I know no ruler but God, no law but natural justice."

Just two weeks before Delany's arrival in Boston, the Vigilance Committee had put William and Ellen Craft, intrepid fugitives from Georgia, aboard a ship for England, after hiding them from the slave hunters sent for them. Just a month before Delany left Boston, a crowd of 150 Negroes had blocked a courtroom while three of their number carried the famous Shadrach bodily to freedom. Prominent in both rescues was a Negro activist named Lewis Hayden, who had fled from Detroit after Judge McLean's decision in the Crosswait case. He was a member of the Boston Vigilance Committee. Shadrach, whose real name was Frederick Wilkins, was to be Delany's neighbor in Canada.

These were heroic deeds in Boston, and they were being duplicated elsewhere. But to Delany they were *reactions*, not actions in behalf of his people. The "higher law" to be obeyed at all costs, including violence, was not applied to slavery. Those 4,000 white throats pulsating their defiance in Faneuil Hall were provoked to it. They did not adopt a "higher law" until the South had stuffed another law down those same throats. Therefore, wasn't the meaning of all the rescues, all the protestations, all the indignation meetings more *against* the provocation by the South, rather than *for* the freedom of the slaves?

But there had been another meeting in Faneuil Hall, after Delany's arrival in Boston, and after the wildly defiant meeting of abolitionists. It took place on November 15, and ironically enough, was called by the same angry abolitionists who had sought to honor the same man fifteen years before, George Thompson, the British abolitionist. Thompson was again the target of Boston anti-abolitionists. The latter were even better organized this time and there was no rioting in the streets. They did not put a noose around William Lloyd Garrison's throat. They just refused to allow him to be heard.

Wendell Phillips took the platform next and the *Boston Post* reported:

> Hissing and Hurraing followed every attempt to speak made by him. . . . Mr. Phillips commenced saying that the people of Boston, by giving Mr. Thompson a proper reception, could make a noble atonement for the mob of 1835 which he styled the deepest stain on our fair and beautiful city. (Cries of louder) They would exhibit the glorious spectacle of the triumph of a repentant people over themselves—(His voice was silenced by yells and cries of "Stop your noise").

Thompson tried to speak and failed. Rev. William E. Channing, Rev. Theodore Parker, Elizur Wright (editor of the *Boston Chronotype*), and Frederick Douglass all were silenced by "clapping, cheering, stamping, hurraing, groans, and calls for 'three cheers for Daniel Webster', 'three cheers for Bunker Hill', 'three groans for John Bull' given with much laughter. . . ."

The meeting was ended at 9:30 P.M., and the gaslights were turned off. No one had made a speech.

Which Faneuil Hall meeting had influenced the Dean of the Harvard Medical School in relation to the three Negro students who were the targets of their classmates? The first meeting had been prompted by a hatred of the slaveholder, not a love of freedom. The second meeting had been the open and organized discard of the vaunted precious rights born in Boston. Delany's classmates, most of them from Boston, were a reflection of both meetings, and no doubt their parents had attended both. But Delany could take no comfort from either meeting.

Back home in Pittsburgh, Jane Swisshelm reported her own version of the Harvard Medical School debacle in the *Saturday Visiter* of January 4, 1851:

> Harvard College is in trouble. Three colored men, among them Dr. Delany of our city, have been admitted into its medical department, and one woman applied for admission. The students held an indignation meeting. The lady withdrew her application and the Professors refused to discharge the men. A colored man speaking of the circumstance, naively remarked, "We are ahead of the women yet, ha ha!"

> Amen, negroes and women, and the negroes ahead! Gallantry, to be sure, and plenty of it; but we rejoice at the reception of these men. Martin Delany will do no discredit to any University in this or any other country. We think female medical students should patronize their own college.

Mrs. Swisshelm was premature. It was the medical degree that Martin Delany wanted. He had had as much training as most practicing physicians of his day and his fellow-students could not prevent his resumption of medical practice. Being denied a chance for that precious degree was the worst blow Delany had ever suffered.

He finished the only term of study allowed him and left Boston at the end of March 1851 embittered by the knowledge that just four months lay between him and the prized medical degree. White men had taken those four months from him. His classmates had said it all in their last resolution and it could be re-phrased to fit the first Faneuil Hall audience of white abolitionists: "*Resolved,* That we have no objection to the (freedom) education and elevation of blacks but do decidedly remonstrate against their presence in (the United States) College with us."

The relation between the "white liberals" of Delany's day and now is illustrated by today's fervent belief in the right of blacks to a choice of residence—"except in my neighborhood."

CHAPTER EIGHT

Hope from Canada

Once more Delany had to chart a new course for himself, and again make a choice between service to his people and the needs of his family.

Actually, it had been Catherine Delany who made possible her husband's years of preoccupation with the freedom and equality wars of the times. Like her mother-in-law, Catherine was a skilled seamstress. It is possible that Pati Delany may have taught her daughter-in-law her own skills, for both she and Samuel were now in Pittsburgh. It had been Catherine's earnings that made possible the gamble in publication of *The Mystery*, the uncertainties of the abolition circuit, the experiment with Frederick Douglass and the *North Star*, and the brief stay at Harvard Medical School. Apparently, whenever Delany settled down to the practice of medicine, his income was quite adequate. But he could no more resist the calls of his people than he could exploit his own skills. Bishop Holly describes his economic situation well, in his In Memoriam.

> Dr. Delany could never descend to the artifices of the selfish trickster, of the mere money-getter or fortune hunter. He raised respectably a large family of children by the faithful aid of the bosom companion (whom he adored) to fill places of honorable usefulness in the community. He maintained his conscience pure and unsullied of all taint of avarice unto the very end, and struggled heroically with honest poverty all his life long!

In March 1851 Delany had little choice, however. Money was needed at home. He had a new son, named for his platform companion and admired militant colleague, Charles Lenox Remond. Toussaint L'Ouverture was now six years old and there was schooling ahead for him. Delany would be denying his own speeches against the system which required the female to be the breadwinner and the male a dependent, if he turned again to the anti-slavery, anti-black law campaigns. Since he would not be returning to Boston to complete the requirements for his medical degree, he should hurry to Pittsburgh and resume his practice.

He did not. Delany took another gamble in serving his people and his family. From Boston he set out westward along the abolition circuit for a series of lectures on the comparative anatomy and physiology of the white and the Negro. The need for such lectures was obvious, and the potential for earnings dependent entirely on the sponsors in each city. For Delany it was a happy combination and a logical course to take.

In the 1850s some of the country's leading scientists were accepting phrenology as a valid method of determining a human's mental powers and even his personality characteristics. The theories of Dr. John K. Spurzheim, the German phrenologist who had died in 1832, were highly popular; and even Dr. Samuel Gridley Howe, the anti-slavery stalwart, studied the "science" as a serious endeavor.

From phrenology came the scientific approach to pro-slavery arguments, that the Caucasian race had a superior cranium and therefore was superior, and the Negro race was inferior because of these and other physical differences. There was a wide choice of "authorities," but perhaps the man most read was Dr. John H. Van Evrie, senior partner in the publishing firm of Van Evrie, Horton & Co., Nassau St., New York City. The firms catalog of "Anti-Abolition and Democratic Publications" indicates that the good doctor wrote most of them. The following are typical extracts from his book *White Supremacy and Negro Subordination.*

> The negro (*sic*) brain in its totality is ten to fifteen per cent less than that of the Caucasian, while in its relations—the relatively large cerebellum and small cerebrum—the inferiority of the mental organism is still more decided; thus, while in mere volume, and therefore in the sum total of mental power, the negro is vastly inferior to the white man.

And another:

> For example: What is there at the same time so charming and so indicative of inner purity and innocence as the blush of maiden modesty? Can anyone suppose such a thing possible to a black face? that these sudden and startling alternations of color, which reflect the moral perceptions and elevated nature of the white woman, are possible in the negress (*sic*)? And if the latter cannot reflect these things in her face—if her features are utterly incapable of expressing emotions so elevated and beautiful, is it not certain that she is without them—that they have no existence in her inner being, are no portion of her moral nature?

According to Van Evrie, the Negro figure when relaxed is that of an orangutang and he does not have "the full, flowing and majestic beard of the Caucasian," which "symbolizes our highest conceptions of manhood," and therefore the Negro is less a man, etc., etc. And Van Evrie was no exception. His ideological descendants write similar white-supremacist literature today, and for the same purpose.

That purpose was to buttress the argument that slavery was "natural." If God and science could be hitched in tandem as ordaining slavery, it provided a most comfortable acceptance of the institution for the whites troubled by consciences. It also gave the pro-slavery northern press new ammunition against the abolitionists who were already labeled heretical. They were able to apply the familiar label of "un-American" to them for flying in the face of Caucasian superiority as the source of the country's greatness. In fact, one of the announcements from Van Evrie's publishing house declared: ". . . our publications are AMERICAN, with *American* ideas, *American* sentiments, and *American* principles, such as were entertained by the great men who founded our government" (emphasis, Van Evrie's).

Such propaganda, eliminating the need for definition, and disseminated in massive proportions, has never failed in America. In the 1850s it not only rallied the anti-abolitionist mobs but had an effect on the Negroes themselves. Why bother with the thoughts expressed by such men as Delany concerning self-improvement if it was organically impossible?

It is interesting that, except for Dr. James McCune Smith,

Delany was the only black man in America equipped to dispute such effusions with the scientific knowledge of the day. His preceptor in anatomy and physiology had been Dr. Oliver Wendell Holmes who, while lacking anti-slavery convictions, was considered the most gifted medical lecturer in the country. In addition, Delany himself had participated in the dissection of cadavers at the Massachusetts General Hospital as part of his course. Those bodies had been both black and white, and the internal organs seemed interchangeable.

Delany's lectures were planned to reassure his black audiences as to their equality with Caucasians, at least in volume of brain matter, and in their equal capacity for the acquisition of knowledge and skills. He was able to draw on his ethnological studies, too, as proof that the ancient black men had had the intellectual achievement of a civilization from which the Caucasians borrowed to assume their hegemony over the world. And from his courses at Harvard Medical School involving chemistry, offered by Dr. Jacob Bigelow, he was able to advance his own theory on skin color. If black was a stamp of inferiority, he argued, then the Caucasian shared that stigma, for the chemical properties of skin pigmentation in both blacks and whites were identical. It was a pigmentation that, in the Caucasian, was more diffused, giving him a "ruddy" complexion. The color black was only a more "concentrated rouge."

Whatever their scientific validity, Delany's lectures filled a need in his black audiences, a rescue from the acceptance of "God-ordained" inferiority. Delany returned to Pittsburgh a happy man. There is no indication whether or not the lecture tour had resulted in financial returns, but Delany himself expressed complete satisfaction with the success of his attack on the white supremacy theory that blacks "are born that way."

He settled down to the practice of medicine, but again the siren call came within a few months. His response was immediate, for that call from Canada opened up entirely new perspectives for the American Negro, both slave and free. Though he was still far from giving up on America, as he was to prove in September 1851, there were stirrings in Canada and in all the world, for that matter, that aroused his intense curiosity.

There were others among the black abolitionists who were just as curious—J. Theodore Holly, later Bishop Holly; Rev.

Samuel Ringgold Ward of Syracuse, N.Y., himself a fugitive slave; the irrepressible Henry Highland Garnet, who had preached insurrection as early as 1843; the forever-angry and militant Charles Lenox Remond; and many others who in 1851 were alienated by the irrevocable divorce between Frederick Douglass and William Lloyd Garrison and were thwarted by the endless conventions which resolved, appealed, and then, hope refreshed, dispersed home to face the futility of their discussions during the dark decade.

The shock of the Fugitive Slave Act forced the vision of these black men toward all points of the compass. Until that measure was passed, emigration had been a dirty word among both black and white abolitionists. For twenty years the awakened Negro had roundly cursed his brethren who deserted their battleground. They were named cowards and traitors for abandoning the enslaved of America. Martin R. Delany was only one among the many black leaders to declare death preferable to submission to the slaveholder. One of his letters to William Lloyd Garrison ended with the lines:

> Were I a slave, I would be free,
> I would not live to live a slave;
> But boldly strike for LIBERTY—
> For FREEDOM or a Martyr's grave.

In one way the situation among the black people of the 1850s differed little from the 1950s. Their internal disunity was created by the perpetual dilemma of all who seek political and economic change—violence or non-violence? There were Martin Luther Kings and Rap Browns in those days, too. There were Urban Leaguers and Black Panthers in their action groupings, with distinct differences of thought and programs.

A primary question rose immediately after passage of the Fugitive Slave Act. If a black man could not obtain democracy in a self-named democracy, then that form of government was a white man's concoction, and another form of government was necessary for the black man. A look at the record up to 1850 would seem to assure the validity of the thesis. In progress toward the elimination of slavery the United States entered the minus column. The rest of the American continent had the following record:

In 1793, the year that the United States enacted its first Fugitive Slave Law, Canada freed its slaves by legislative act. It was a gradual emancipation law, and by 1818 the last of the former slaves had been freed.

In 1829 Mexico banned all slavery from its territory, though it did not interfere with the feudal Spanish serfdom among the Indians introduced by the conquistadors.

In 1833, celebrated thereafter on August 1, Great Britain forbade slavery in all its colonies, and 800,000 slaves were freed seven years later.

In 1845 Sweden ended slavery in its sole West Indian possession, Saint Bartholomew.

In 1848 both France and Denmark emancipated the slaves in all their remaining colonies, including those in the western hemisphere.

In 1850 Brazil struck a vital blow to the Yankee slave trade by declaring that all slaves brought to Brazilian ports would be emancipated and those responsible for bringing them would be punished for piracy.

To a man like Martin Delany, and a few of like mind, well read in history and current affairs, the successive demonstrations of concern for the rights of man shown by these monarchies, empires, and dictatorships raised fundamental questions about American democracy. The contrast would indicate that, for the black man at least, any of the ancient political systems were preferable to so-called democracy, in which an oligarchy of some seventy thousand slaveowners ruled approximately 23 million people, four million of whom were black (1850 Census).

However, neither the fine points of political science nor the world-wide uproar about America's Fugitive Slave Act directed Delany's quest for an answer northward. It was the flood of black men, women, and children—not just fugitive slaves but "free" blacks as well—who crowded the traditional Underground Railroad routes to the North Star, through Pennsylvania, New York, and New England to the bridges at Buffalo and Niagara, along the mud roads and canals of Ohio to the boats at Detroit, Toledo, and Sandusky. It was this vast migration of black families who gave up on America, who did not "stay and fight." They did not stop to argue, as Frederick Douglass and others had, that slavery might or might not be constitutional, that the Fugitive Slave Act was of questionable legal validity. They did not wait for another Sunday and another sermon to the effect that "this too shall pass." They thanked the white abolitionists for their new resolutions and took off for Canada.

Even after Frederick Douglass had exhorted the blacks of Boston to "stay and fight" though the streets of the city would be "running in blood," right in his home town of Rochester, N.Y., the pastor of the Colored Baptist Church, a Kentucky fugitive, fled first and was followed by 112 of his congregation. They fled because they believed that their families were in danger. Nor were they without precedent. Many an American Loyalist had fled to Canada during the American Revolution for the same reason. As far as the blacks were concerned, all of the many schools of opinion personified by the leaders as to the future course of the Negroes went by the boards. Their bodies were at stake and there is nothing theoretical about the transformation from a man to property. While their leaders argued, the black fugitives departed.

Yet the black abolitionists, including Martin Delany, knew well that they would enjoy under the law both freedom and equality in Canada. They had known it for years, at least since Benjamin Lundy reported on his visits to the black fugitives in Canada in 1832. This Ohio Quaker and pioneer in anti-slavery had, since 1821, expressed his belief that emancipation in the United States was a hopeless cause for the foreseeable future. He himself had taken eleven manumitted Negroes to Haiti and settled them there. He not only investigated Canada as a black refuge but went to Texas three times for the same purpose. It was Lundy who inducted William Lloyd Garrison into the anti-slavery cause in Baltimore. If not for Lundy being jailed as a result of a libel suit for condemning, in his newspaper *Genius of Universal Emancipation,* some New Orleans slaveowners, white abolitionism might have had its start in Baltimore instead of Boston where Garrison went to begin *The Liberator.*

But Canada still remained only a "temporary haven" for these black abolitionists. They continued, in 1850, the early belief that Canada would be annexed by the United States at any moment. That belief was buttressed by the events of April 1849 when a mob, inspired by the Montreal mercantile interests who had issued an "Annexation Manifesto," set fire to the Parliament buildings and pelted the Governor General of Canada, Lord Elgin, with eggs and stones.

It is strange that even in 1852 Delany still declared the inevitability of annexation, disregarding the fact that the South itself was the most powerful force preventing it. Southerners knew Canada and the Canadians far better than even the neighboring Yankees, for they escaped the heat of their summers in fashionable watering places in Quebec, on the Rideau lakes, and Thousand Islands shores of Canada West. In this way, they avoided the Yankees and consorted only with the "White Guard" remainders of the United Empire Loyalists who were highly organized to prevent annexation. These were the strange allies too of every black man in Canada who joined the militia to repel invasion from the United States.

The South knew that any annexed Canadian province would be another "free" state and another threat, like the Pacific Northwest, to their political domination of the country. As ever, political realities dictated, not principles. Delany made the same error regarding Canada as his colleagues, for he declared in 1852 that when annexation took place ". . . the fate of the colored man, however free before, is doomed, doomed, forever doomed. Disfranchisement, degradation, and a delivery up to slave catchers and kidnappers, are their only fate, let Canadian annexation take place when it will. The odious, infamous fugitive slave law, will then be in full force with all of its terrors; and we have no doubt that fully in anticipation of this event, was the despicable law created." This was patently true, but annexation was not.

The fundamental error in such a prophecy is obvious through hindsight. The black abolitionists could not know the intense and growing Canadian nationalism that was leading to confederation in 1869. They had never experienced the protection of the law, with its awesome impartiality, such as the colored citizens of Canada know.

Martin Delany's errors regarding Canada as a solution for his people included the belief, often stated, that the Canadian people were in favor of annexation. His mind and observation were clouded by the one dream, expressed as early as 1834, that the black man *must have a country of his own.* Canada was a white man's country and therefore without permanent foundation for the blacks, according to Delany. As he began to examine the realities of emigration, there were many doubts and questions, but Delany never deviated from the belief that only in their own land could Negroes be permanently free and equal. He may have been and may still be correct. In 1851 though, the black people themselves demonstrated to him that temporary freedom in Canada was preferable to permanent enslavement while awaiting the millennium. Most visionaries profit by contact with people and Delany was no exception. In September 1851 he was invited to Canada and there found a formula that was to be the bedrock of his plans to found a free, independent, and self-sufficient black country. There he found the strategy that crystallized his dreaming into substantive action.

The North American Convention of Colored Men held in Toronto on September 11, 12, and 13, 1851, injected a new element into abolitionism in general and black abolitionism in particular. This new element was the proud, independent, self-sufficient, literate, and citizenship-wise Negro whose freedom in Canada had released his potential for leadership. In Canada West particularly (now the Province of Ontario) there were black men who had voted all their adult lives and others who voted though they were only three years away from slavery. There were black men who owned hundreds of productive acres of land and others who owned valuable real estate in the cities. There were black youths attending Trinity and Knox colleges in Toronto. There were black officers in the militia, as well as privates. Black men sat on juries as a matter of course, and in the courts, were witnesses, plaintiffs, defendants, bailiffs, and lawyers. Not one skilled trade was closed to black men, and they plied those trades in all parts of Canada West. Not even unskilled trades were closed to black men in the 1850s despite the flood of Irish and Scottish refugees from the potato famine in the homelands; for this was the era of Canada's railroad expansion, its milling, shipping, building, and timbering expansion, and the government sent agents to Europe to recruit needed labor through immigration. Black labor from the United States was as welcome as white labor from anywhere. Black men married white women and white men married black women without the sun deviating from its course.

Canada was not an unadulterated black Heaven on earth, of course. There was prejudice against color, for there was no "de-propagandized" zone between Canada and the United States, and each day brought new pollution across the border. There were clashes between the Irish and the colored, where there was local competition for jobs. There were a few racists in government, too, both provincial and federal, but their political life appeared comparatively brief.

There was security, citizenship, and opportunity in Canada where none existed in the United States for the black man, in either the North or the South. There was proof of that. In all of Canada's pre-Civil War history only one fugitive slave was returned to the United States through the legal machinery, and the two magistrates involved in that case were immediately dismissed. Henry Clay's negotiations and Daniel Webster's consummation of the Webster-Ashburton Treaty in 1842 did not alter one whit the stubborn Canadian legalism that no man of any color whatsoever could be other than free in Canadian territory. The status of slave simply did not exist. The status of equal citizen did.

It was an exceptional and self-educated fugitive who brought Martin Delany to Canada in 1851 for the first time. Henry Bibb helped hundreds into Canada and only crossed the water himself when the slave catchers came to Detroit looking for him. He had had an adventurous life as a slave, escaping and being caught at least half a dozen times in as many states. When he finally won freedom and completed a process of self-education, Henry Bibb worked for the Michigan Anti-Slavery Society in helping the flood of fugitives across the Detroit River into the refugee towns of Chatham, Malden, Amherstburg, and Sandwich. He himself settled in the last when Detroit became so infested with slave catchers that he could not work openly. From Sandwich he could maintain his contacts with the fugitive slave centers of Michigan.

In 1851 Bibb began his own weekly newspaper in Sandwich, *Voice of the Fugitive,* and one of his earliest correspondents was Martin Delany. The newspaper itself, as well as the North American Convention in September were the result of Bibb's organizing abilities. Through his initiative, the Canadian Negroes were just as quick to react to the Fugitive Slave Act as their brethren in the Free States. But they reacted differently.

A year before, in October 1850, as a result of Henry Bibb's own call for a meeting, there gathered in Sandwich a large group of colored Canadians, each a fugitive or son of fugitives, and they elected the much-sentimentalized Rev. Josiah Henson of "Uncle Tom" fame as their president. But it was Henry Bibb who offered the essential ingredients of the meeting—the entire agenda, wrote all of the resolutions, and defined the objectives of what was to become the Refugee Home Society. There was nothing at all of the "protest and appeal" character of the American Negro conventions. Bibb first stated the conditions:

> Whereas, we have assembled in convention as a union of coloured Americans under protection of Her Majesty (Queen Victoria), discarding all sectarian prejudice and selfishness, resolve to arise from degradation and poverty by honesty, industry and self-respect, putting our trust in God for the final success of our cause.

The further "whereas" statements alluded to the Fugitive Slave Act and:

> According to that hellish law there is no spot in the United States upon which coloured persons can stand and not be liable to be seized and dragged back into perpetual bondage, without trial by jury or the privilege of showing their Free Papers if they have any.

Then followed the resolutions which were most concrete as a program. They did not neglect, however, to give further thanks to God and pledge to Queen Victoria the "discharge of the duty of good, peaceable, loyal subjects of Her Majesty, the Queen of Great Britain."

Briefed to their essentials, the Bibb program adopted by this initial convention was as follows:

1. The immediate problem was the care of refugees, who were crossing the Detroit River without clothing, food, or funds. They were like the terror-stricken fugitives from any war and needed help. Bibb proposed that this be organized. (Almost immediately refugee reception centers were established at each

of the river towns on the Canadian side, the major center in Amherstburg.)

2. That these fugitives almost without exception came from the land and knew only "agricultural pursuits" which, Bibb said, was the "most certain road to independence and self-elevation." Therefore the convention should form a society to purchase 30,000 acres of government land for settlement of the fugitives. But Bibb added a most fundamental condition to the disposition of the acreage, and in this he copied the pattern already set by the immediately successful Buxton Settlement near Chatham, "*that said lands should never be given away but sold to said persons at cost and on such terms as to enable them to pay for it by their own industry.*" (The Refugee Home Society did buy crown and clergy land at approximately $2.50 an acre in the westernmost county of Canada West, Essex, bordering on Lake Erie and the Detroit River, rich farmlands to this day. From not owning even themselves, hundreds of fugitives became landowners almost at once.)

3. Establishment of a vigilance committee, with membership in each of the towns, to oversee the care of the refugees. (At times the flood of fugitives across the Detroit River reached 300 a day.)

4. Founding of a newspaper of their own because "as we struggle against opinions, our warfare lies in the field of thought." (The *Voice of the Fugitive* was the immediate result on January 1, 1851.)

Henry Bibb was an activist and the measures he proposed were concrete. That is what impressed Delany and his colleagues who were becoming dissatisfied with the resounding oratorical generalities of the black abolitionist gatherings in the United States. By the time Delany reached Toronto in September, on Bibb's invitation to be a delegate to the Great North American Convention, the fugitives were being fed and clothed, settled on their own lands, and were sending their children to newly opened schools.

Bibb's next step was to help in the formation of the Canadian Anti-Slavery Society, and here too his efforts were successful. The first meeting was held in the Toronto City Hall on February 24, 1851, with the mayor of the city presiding. This mixed black and white organization began at once to raise funds in

Canada, the United States, England, and Scotland for the care and settlement of fugitives in Canada West. The energetic Rev. Samuel Ringgold Ward, now a refugee himself, was named agent of the Society, whose membership was largely church-oriented.

In less than two months of its existence, the Society advanced to fugitive families the sum of £48 8s. 2½d., most of which was raised at three rousing nights of meetings at St. Lawrence Hall in Toronto. George Thompson, the indestructible British abolitionist again crossed the Atlantic for these meetings, and Frederick Douglass, too, crossed the magic border.

This was action, not just talk; the same was true of the North American Convention in September 1851, at which Martin Delany was the principal speaker. This was a planning convention with delegates from eleven Canadian towns, nine U.S. cities, and one delegate from Jamaica, B.W.I. Henry Bibb was elected chairman, and much of the business was an expansion of his initial Sandwich meeting. Gratitude to the Queen and condemnation of the Fugitive Slave Act were expressed. Once more there was strong urging that fugitives settle the land, *own* it, and sink their roots in the free soil of Canada. Then the discussion came to the meat of the meeting in a conflict over the first resolution! The question was, What could this combined group propose as a course of action for the Negro population of the United States, slave and free? The discussion revealed Delany's still unresolved conflict. The resolution was debated but adopted by the delegates.

> 1. Resolved that the infamous fugitive slave enactment of the American government—whether constitutional or unconstitutional, is an insult to God, and an outrage upon humanity, not to be endured by any people; we therefore earnestly entreat our brethren of the northern and southern states to come out from under the jurisdiction of those wicked laws—from the power of a government whose tender mercies toward the colored people are cruel.

Delany, with three other delegates, two from New York and one from Ohio, objected to the inclusion of "northern" in the resolution, and their arguments were recorded in the minutes as follows:

> Whereas, the convention, in adopting the first resolution, inviting the colored people to leave the northern part of the United States, has done so contrary to the desires and wishes of those of us, from the States, who believe it to be impolitic and contrary to our professed policy in opposing the infamous fugitive slave laws, and schemes of American colonization; therefore we do hereby enter our solemn disapprobation, and protest against this part of the said resolution.

Invite the slaves to Canada, of course, but not the free Negroes! However, the convention did make a concession in a compromise resolution urging the colored people of the United States who wished to emigrate, to come to Canada "instead of going to Africa or the West India Islands, that they may be better able to assist their brethren who are daily flying from American slavery."

A concept voiced at the convention, in the form of a resolution by John T. Fisher of Toronto, was to remain with Delany for years to come. It was the proposal that a committee set about

> the formation of a great league of colored people of the North and South American continents and of the West Indies, for the general abolition of slavery, for the protection of the common rights of their brethren throughout the world, and for their social, political and moral elevation.

How many times Delany had told his colored audiences that they represented two thirds of the world's population and inevitably must win the war with the whites. Here was a proposal to harness this latent strength for a hemispheric attack on slavery!

There was even more from the convention that Delany took home and considered. In fact, a friend of his, James Theodore Holly, then living in Vermont, and not even present at the convention, provided the pattern that was to end Delany's conflict. The delegate from Vermont representing the handful of blacks there brought with him a communication to the assembled delegates in which Holly made an unmistakable break with the organized anti-slavery movements of the past.

> We regard your assembly as the sovereign representatives of the colored people of the United States and the Canadian provinces. You have the supreme right to legislate for their interest, and adopt measures for their advancement *irrespective of any other association* (author's emphasis) so far as wisdom and prudence shall suggest. The organization you shall establish cannot be auxiliary to any other similar organization, but must be sovereign in carrying out its own object. And if other associations have been formed with the same or similar objects, it is to be hoped if they are sincere in the cause, that they will immediately rank under the banners that you will unfurl at Toronto.

This was Holly's declaration of independence from all schools of anti-slavery action, both black and white. He too was disillusioned with the ineffectuality and frustrations of the quarreling groups. He too was tired of the passionate debate on political action, preservation of a union in which the blacks could not participate, or the "moral suasion" approach to emancipation. And he, like Bibb, was concrete on the program he recommended. Because it was the first expression of a pattern on which Holly was to work actively with Delany, it follows in full:

> 1st. Promulgate a constitution for a North American League, of the colored people of the United States and Canada.
>
> 2nd. To embrace as the object of the League: first, to make a comfortable asylum for refugees from slavery; second, to encourage the removal of the free colored people from the United States to Canada; third, to have them engage in the cultivation of the soil, as the basis of all industrial operations—after agriculture becomes well developed, to erect mills and manufactories—after the erection of mills and manufactories to proceed to commercial exportation.
>
> 3rd. As a means to effect this object, let your present convention establish Toronto as the headquarters, or centre of operation for the North American League; and elect a President, Vice Presidents, Secretaries, Treasurer and several Directors, who shall form a Board of Managers or Executive Committee for the League. Two-thirds of whom shall be resident in Toronto, to transact the business of the

League during the interim that will elapse between the annual assemblages of the North American League which should be held every year from now henceforth—to provide for the establishment of associations of the North American League, auxiliary to the Committee at Toronto, throughout the provinces of the Canadas, and in the United States. For this purpose let your convention appoint or authorize the Executive Committee of Toronto to appoint commissioners through the Canadas, and the United States, to superintend the formation of these auxiliary organizations and keep up a correspondence from their various localities with the Toronto Committee—let the North American League keep up traveling agents, under direction of the Toronto Committee, in the United States, Canadas and Great Britain, to present our claims to the philanthropic, and collect donations to carry out the object of the League and oppose the African colonization scheme.

4th. If the laws of Canada will admit of it, to provide for the incorporation of the Toronto Executive Committee as early as practicable, in order to give stability to the organization, and afford security to all contributors for the proper outlay of their money contributed.

This amounted to a proposal that the anti-slavery forces move from the United States to Canada as a base of operations for the continental attack on slavery. It was also a structure for future action. And it was a flat rejection of the situation existing among black abolitionists at that time. Holly, in his concluding remarks, leaves no doubt about the last. "When our people assemble in the majesty of such a noble convention, all portions of them should pay respect and deference to their actions, and all cliques, sections and parties should be hushed into silence, and their animosities should at once cease." As for the white abolitionists: "And all other persons who may be friendly to our race, should remember a people understands their own wants best themselves, and are the most proper to conduct their own affairs in accordance with that sublime sentence . . . (which Delany had used on the masthead of *The Mystery*) . . . hereditary bondsmen, know yet not who would be free, themselves must strike the blow!"

A new direction for black abolitionism, with the establishment of Canada as a base of future operations—not merely for aid to the emigration of the fugitive but also for an international black attack on American slavery—was begun by Delany's participation in the North American Convention.

It was to require another two years for these plans to coalesce, but meanwhile Delany busied himself with a number of activities, one of them a bizarre effort, right out of O. Henry, to establish a new black country in Central America.

Delany spent the winter of 1851-1852 in New York City, his abundant energy dispersed in three directions. First, he obtained the assistance of Dr. James McCune Smith, highly respected in the city's commercial circles. We have none of the details, but it appears that Delany had invented something that would answer the problem of grade hauling freight up and down the rugged Pennsylvania hills with the limited power of the locomotives of the day. It was becoming important to the growing trans-Allegheny traffic to Pittsburgh from the coast. The Pennsylvania Railroad reached Pittsburgh in December 1851 but required another year to eliminate approximately thirty miles of wagon and canal transfers. Its tunnels and grades were not to be completed for another decade.

Delany's gadget allowed the power needed to haul heavy loads up and brake them down without use of a stationary winching engine. He seems to have demonstrated it to a manufacturer and a patent attorney, but without results. He was informed that only a citizen could obtain a patent in Washington. Foreigners could, he was certain, but not native-born Negroes. Delany was bitter at this result but appreciative of Dr. Smith's efforts in his behalf.

Another activity involved Dr. David J. Peck, whom Delany had seen in New York. Like many another young black, then and now, he was asking, "Education—for what?" His difficulties in establishing a medical practice were much like those of young George B. Vashon in practicing law, with all public facilities denied him.

Peck was preparing to head for California when Delany, fresh from the Canadian inspiration, persuaded him to stop at the crossing from the Caribbean to the Pacific shore and investigate the possibilities of creating an independent haven there for blacks. For years there had been turmoil among the United

States, Spanish, and British diplomatic corps concerning the former Spanish empire, now broken into republics of dubious origin or republicanism. The manipulators of political destinies all along the Central American shore were the U.S. State Department and the British Foreign Office. Both quite baldly made and unmade governments. But America's program of Manifest Destiny brought the entire Central American neck into a crisis of international scope after the Mexican War and the U.S. land grab of California. Both countries recognized the inevitability of a canal between the oceans, and at that time, the most logical route appeared to be up the San Juan River from the east, into the string of west-bearing Nicaraguan lakes, and to the Pacific at the Gulf of Fonseca. The eastern outlet became a prize—the storied Mosquito Shore which since 1825 had had a king installed by the British with the imposing paraphernalia of regality.

It was to San Juan del Norte (Greytown) that young David Peck came and found the total absence of a color line. The "Mosquito King" himself was of combined Negro, Spanish, and Indian blood. The ministers of his "court" who had taken the names of Lord Rodney, Lord Nelson, and other British nobility were also of varied mixture. The local government was predominantly black, and some members were fugitives from the states.

Dr. Peck was immediately named Port Physician, and his practice was instantly successful. He was welcomed into the community and soon assumed leadership in the establishment of a black democracy. He was chairman of a convention establishing an elective government in which the mayor would have supreme civic and military authority. The convention then proceeded to nominations and election. Apparently, David Peck's early Pittsburgh schooling in practical American democracy had been effective. A few weeks later, in New York City, Delany reported receipt of the following by special messenger: "Dr. Martin R. Delany was duly chosen and elected Mayor of Greytown (San Juan del Norte), civil governor of the Mosquito Reservation and commander-in-chief of the military forces of the province!"

However, this plan too failed. America could never afford another democracy, and so the Marines landed to prevent "Depredations upon the property of the Accessory Transit Company." This private enterprise was controlled by Cornelius Vanderbilt, and its shares rose in value by $30 each, so everybody except the residents of Greytown was happy.

It was while busy with these two projects, the railroad invention and the free black country of Greytown, that Delany somehow found time to become the country's first black political nationalist with publication of the first comprehensive evaluation of the Negro position in 1852. The book was entitled:

The
CONDITION
Elevation, Emigration and Destiny
of the
COLORED PEOPLE
of the
United States
Politically Considered

The book itself had a curious history. "I wrote not as an author, but as I travelled about from place to place."

Sometimes I sat, sometimes I stood,
Writing when and where I could
A little here, a little there;
'Twas here, and there and everywhere.

"I wrote to obtain subsistence. I had travelled and speculated until I found myself out of means." Delany was to apologize for writing the *Condition and Elevation,* as it came to be called, as a result of the collision course he had taken against the white anti-slavery societies and the Frederick Douglass platform-pounders.

Yet it remains to this day the most significant source of information and thought, of contemplation and activism among the free blacks of the United States in the mid-century.

CHAPTER NINE

Emigrate!

Condition and Elevation has always been a neglected source of information in the study of the American Negro. The reason may be because it violates the American illusion of democratic equality. It sets forth quite clearly and in detail the genesis of one of today's unmentionables—that the American brand of *apartheid* differs little in white attitudes from those of South Africa and Rhodesia.

Delany can be accused—and was—of poor writing in portions of *Condition and Elevation* but never of superficial thinking or compromise with his innate honesty. He declared in his preface that his "sole object has been to place before the public in general, and the colored people of the United States in particular, great truths concerning this class of citizens, which appears to have been heretofore avoided, as well by friends and enemies to their elevation."

Had he too avoided these "great truths," which both white and black abolitionists disregarded in schizophrenic unity, the strange storm that arose among abolitionists after the book's publication would never have occurred. But, then, Delany would merely have written just another recital of wrongs, horror over violation of democratic principles, and appeal to the whites. That had been the formula for twenty years. But Delany had met the free Negroes of Canada and had gained a broader perspective to buttress his studies of ancient black civilizations.

To all but a handful of the abolitionists, Delany's cardinal sin in *Condition and Elevation* was the acceptance of emigration as not only worthy of serious consideration but also of investigation and planning. He stated it without reservation, though he knew full well that emigration and treason were synonymous in the abolitionists' minds.

EMIGRATION OF THE COLORED PEOPLE OF THE UNITED STATES

That there have been people in all ages under certain circumstances that may be benefited by emigration, will be admitted; and that there are circumstances under which emigration is absolutely necessary to their political elevation, cannot be disputed.

This we see in the Exodus of the Jews from Egypt to the land of Judea; in the expedition of Dido and her followers from Tyre to Mauritania; and not to dwell upon the hundreds of modern European examples—also in the ever memorable emigration of the Puritans, in 1620, from Great Britain, the land of their birth, to the wilderness of the New World, at which may be fixed the beginning of emigration to this continent as a permanent residence.

This may be acknowledged; but to advocate the emigration of the colored people of the United States from their native homes, is a new feature in our history, and at first view, may be considered objectionable, as pernicious to our interests. This objection is at once removed, when reflecting on our condition as incontrovertibly shown in a foregoing part of this work. And we shall proceed at once to give the advantages to be derived from emigration, to us as a people, in preference to any other policy that we may adopt. This granted, the question will then be, where shall we go? This we conceive to be all-important—of paramount consideration, and shall endeavor to show the most advantageous locality; and premise the recommendation with the strictest advice against any countenance whatever, to the emigration scheme of the so called Republic of Liberia.

Delany's exposition of the conditions under which blacks, both slave and free, lived in America in 1850, and his long listing of Negro accomplishments in all of man's activities despite these handicaps is worthy of separate study. More important in his book are the details of his pioneering efforts to change American abolitionism from a sterile debating society to an activist group. The contrast between the two sections of the book is startling. The first is a realistic evaluation of the Negro hopes, or lack of them; the second concludes that not until the blacks of all the world unite will the American Negro be free. As for achievement of all the rights and dreams of a democracy, Delany asserted without equivocation that the black man could only succeed in this ultimate of citizenship by creating his own democracy.

This he proposed in his Appendix entitled "A Project for an Expedition of Adventure, to the Eastern Coast of Africa," which followed the chapters exploring all other parts of the world as a site for black refuge and republicanism. Delany revealed that he reached the concept in 1836, when he was 24 years old. If so, he was discussing a "Black Israel" long before the birth of the founder of Jewish Zionism. His proposal for a "Black Israel" was published 46 years before the great Theodor Herzl wrote *Der Judenstat*. Their reasoning was almost identical.

> Every people should be the originators of their own designs, the projector of their own schemes, and creators of the events that lead to their destiny—the consummation of their desires. . . . We have native hearts and virtues, just as other nations; which in their pristine purity are noble, potent and worthy of example. We are a nation within a nation;—as are the Poles in Russia, the Hungarians in Austria, the Welsh, Irish and Scotch in the British dominions.
>
> But we have been, by our oppressors, despoiled of our purity, and corrupted in our native characteristics, so that we have inherited their vices, and but few of their virtues; leaving us in character, really a *broken people*.
>
> Being distinguished by complexion, we are still singled out—although having merged in the habits and customs of our oppressors—as a distinct nation of people; as the Poles, Hungarians, Irish and others, who still retain their native peculiarities, of language, habits and various other traits. *The claims of no people, according to established policy and usage, are respected by any nation, until they are presented in a national capacity* (author's emphasis).

Therefore, declared this Black Zionist, there should be a gathering of the colored people of the United States, "Not what is termed a National Convention . . . but a true representation of the intelligence and wisdom of the colored freemen." He then presented detailed plans for the formation of a National Confidential Council as an executive arm to explore and organize a Black Israel in East Africa.

> The National Council shall appoint one or two Special Commissioners to England and France, to solicit, in the name of the Representatives of a Broken Nation, of four-and-a-half-millions, the necessary outfit and support, for any period not exceeding three years, of such an expedition. Certainly, what England and France would do, for a little nation—mere nominal nation, of five thousand civilized Liberians, they would be willing and ready to do for five millions; if they be but authentically represented, in a national capacity. What was due to Greece, enveloped by Turkey, should be due to US, enveloped by the United States; and we believe would be respected, if properly presented. To England and France, we should look for sustenance, and the people of those two nations—as they would have everything to gain from such an adventure and eventual settlement on the EASTERN COAST OF AFRICA—the opening of an immense trade being the consequence. . . . The Eastern Coast of Africa has long been neglected, and never but little known, even to the ancients; but has ever been our choice part of the Continent. . . . The land is ours—there it lies with inexhaustible resources; let us go and possess it. In Eastern Africa must rise up a nation, to whom all the world must pay commercial tribute.

The condemnation of Delany for his proposals by both blacks and whites was similar to the condemnation of Herzl by both Jews and non-Jews. But none condemned Delany more than he condemned himself years later for the faults of the book, faults not as apparent to the reader of today. True, were Delany intent on seeking support for a Black Israel among sympathizers predisposed to help the Negroes, he could have been more tactful. His trouble was honesty. He alienated the sincere, if ineffectual, white anti-slavery churchmen with one remark during discussion of Central and South America as one of the few ideal havens for people of color. The American Protestant syndrome allowed no considerations of these countries because they were so predominantly Catholic as well as anti-slavery. Delany dismissed this with: "Talk not about religious biases—we have but one reply to make. We had rather be a Heathen *freeman*, than a Christian *slave*."

Such heresy was matched by Delany in other directions. In effect, he denied the doxology of abolitionism, as it had appeared in the anti-slavery catechism for so many years. No matter how the various abolitionist splinter groups disagreed with each other, they shared the same book of the genesis of anti-slavery—that the Israelites must remain in Egypt and attack the Pharaoh and not listen to any Moses like Delany who proposed that his people search out a land of Canaan.

The criticism was inevitable and could have been predicted. What remains puzzling is Delany's own reaction to that criticism. For the first and only time in his life Delany was uncertain, unhappy with his own conclusions because, for a time, he felt isolated from the thinking of men he had always respected. Frederick Douglass ignored his book and did not attack Delany himself until the proposals written in it were implemented in 1853.

On July 10, 1852, Delany wrote a bitter letter to Douglass, complaining that he had sent a copy of *Condition and Elevation* to him in May and it "has never been raised in the columns of your paper. . . . You could have given it a supplemental notice, by saying that such a work had been written by me (saying anything else about or against it that you pleased) and let those who read it pass their own opinion also. But you heaped upon it a cold and deathly silence. . . ."

Perhaps this disregard should not have surprised Delany, for he knew better than most black abolitionists that Frederick Douglass heard only the agreement of the thousands in his audiences and not the deadly hatred of the millions of Americans outside the anti-slavery halls. Douglass was later to summarize his belief:

> The question is: Can the white and colored people of this country be blended into a common nationality, and enjoy together, in the same country, under the same flag, the inestimable blessings of life, liberty and the pursuit of happiness, as neighborly citizens of a common country? I answer most unhesitatingly, I believe they can.

A hundred years later it appears that, for a lifetime, Douglass had been living off "pie in the sky." His beliefs have not been confirmed; Delany's doubts have been.

William Lloyd Garrison, in a lengthy review of *Condition and Elevation* in *The Liberator* expresses kind regard for Delany as a person and a self-sacrificing leader of his people. He even approved of some of the book.

> He is a vigorous writer, an eloquent speaker, and full of energy and enterprise. The sketches he has made of several literary and professional colored men and women are not only authentic and highly interesting but will greatly surprise those who, having been taught to consider the colored population as a very inferior race, are profoundly ignorant as to all such instances of intellectual power, moral worth and scientific attainment. Indeed, says Dr. D. "the colored people are not yet known, even to their most devoted friends among the white Americans"—a remark substantially true, beyond a doubt.

But—Garrison found that Delany was wrong in his criticism of the lack of numbers and zeal among abolitionists; wrong in his history and therefore his conclusions concerning emigration, and absolutely in the gravest error concerning separation of black and white as either permanent or justifiable, for "it would only prove that the people of the United States were past repentance."

> We are sorry to see a tone of despondency, and an exhibition of the spirit of caste, in the concluding portions of this otherwise instructive and encouraging work. Take for example:—"We love our country, dearly love her, but she don't love us. She despises us and bids us begone, driving us from her embraces. But we shall not go where she desires us; but when we do go, whatever love we have for her, we shall love the country nonetheless that receives us as her adopted children". The idea of separatism is not only admitted, but strongly urged, and in a very plausible manner.

Delany replied to Garrison's review on May 14 and he acknowledged the faults of his book, expressed his gratitude to

Garrison for being honest in writing of them. However, he disagreed with the criticism in one fundamental respect.

> I am not in favor of caste, nor a separation of the brotherhood of mankind, and would as willingly live among white men as black, if I had an *equal possession and enjoyment* of privileges; but shall never be reconciled to live among them, subservient to their will—existing by mere *sufferance,* as we, the colored people, do in this country. The majority of white men cannot see why colored men cannot be satisfied with their condition in Massachusetts—what they desire more than the *granted* right of citizenship. Blind selfishness on the one hand, and deep prejudice on the other, will not permit them to understand that we desire the *exercise* and *enjoyment* of these rights, as well as the *name* of their possession. If there were any probability of this, I should be willing to remain in the country, fighting and struggling on, the good fight of faith. But I must admit, that I have no hopes in this country—no confidence in the American people—with a *few* excellent exceptions—therefore, I have written as I have done. Heathenism and Liberty, before Christianity and Slavery.

Delany deplored any differences with Douglass and Garrison, but there was another old friend, Oliver Johnson, editor of the *Pennsylvania Freeman* who appears to have destroyed his customary restraint. Johnson, being white and part of a white anti-slavery organization, its spokesman in fact, understandably opposed the information and proposals of Delany's book. His one-paragraph criticism, appearing in the April 29, 1852, issue, was somewhat snide. He cites Delany's introductory apology for the haste in which the volume was written and then:

> This will probably strike our readers, as it did us, as a very singular reason for publishing a book; but if any better exists, we have not been able to discover it in the book itself. It embodies many facts which are in themselves interesting and valuable, which, if they were less bunglingly and egotistically presented and not mixed up with much that is of questionable propriety and utility, might be available to the reader; but the manner in which the author has

used his materials deprives the work of all value. We could wish that, for his own credit and that of the colored people, it had never been published.

This was the total of Johnson's remarks on the book. Obviously, it was not intended as a review of the contents but only as condemnation without critical justification. In the trade of literary criticism this is known as a "knife job."

Delany lost his restraint and pride the next day. In a letter to Johnson dated April 30, he angrily replied.

That there are a number of palpable errors in this book, is true; which occurred by a neglect to furnish me with a revision proof-sheet—the whole of the present edition being struck off, before I got to revise it—all of which has been ordered to be corrected in the plates, and will stand corrected in the next issue.

But the object of your remarks evidently has been to disparage me, and endeavor to injure the sale of the book, especially among the colored people—upon whose ignorance you presume and take advantage by your position—which but furnishes a striking proof of *your* Negro-hate, in common with many of your less pretending fellows. There is not an intelligent colored man nor woman in the country—except the most miserable, servile and tool—but will indignantly repel this bare-faced insult.

You also charge me with egotism, which is but a prejudicial sneer at a black man, for daring to do anything upon his own responsibility; and is in keeping with Mrs. Stowe's ridicule of Hayti, which you very adroitly avoid in your apology for the objectionable portion of her work, in reply to the manly note of that fearless advocate of his race, Robert Purvis. There is not one word, which to an unprejudiced mind, will be tortured into egotism.

As to your judgment upon my style and taste in composition, I utterly disregard; but under the circumstances, the attack was cowardly. I therefore despise your sneers and defy your influence.

M. R. Delany
Philadelphia, April 30, 1852

Johnson printed this letter verbatim of course, and followed it with lengthy comment of his own, none of it ameliotory. These former friends in a single cause now were enemies in all causes, one of the casualties of slavery never computed.

William Lloyd Garrison recognized this as the real loss of the entire dispute, not the merits or demerits of the book. In his gentle and sincere manner, he chided Delany in the *Liberator*.

CONDITION OF THE COLORED PEOPLE

> Looking at the general merits of the recent work on this subject by Dr. Delany and overlooking what, in its pages seemed like a querulous or censorious spirit, we gave it a friendly notice in a recent number of our paper. Our estimable coadjutor, the editor of the *Pennsylvania Freeman*, not being so favorably impressed by a perusal of it, expressed himself accordingly. This has elicited a letter from Dr. Delany, written in bad taste and an irritated state of mind, which we are sorry to see from his pen. The *Freeman* and its editor have been too long in the anti-slavery field to be suspected of being inimical to anyone wearing a sable complexion. Dr. D. should remember the proverb, "Faithful are the wounds of a friend"; and if he has been wounded by the criticism of the *Freeman* let him not attribute it to an enemy, but endeavor to profit by the blow, as one not meant in the spirit of unkindness, but rather from a sense of duty and with an honest fidelity, though hard to bear.

It was evident that not even Garrison recognized that the squabble between Johnson and Delany was an inevitable detail in what had happened. Something new had been injected into the "anti-slavery" field. He, and Frederick Douglass too, misjudged the potency of the emigration consideration among the unhappy free blacks. They considered the book just another evidence of Delany's vaunting ambitions, which it was, though not exclusively so. Consideration of emigration proved to be a new fertilizer for the arid "anti-slavery field."

Delany's final public word on the entire squabble was expressed in a letter to Frederick Douglass dated July 23, 1852. After it, he occupied himself with implementation of the proposals contained in the book itself.

I desire that our people have light and information upon the available means of bettering their condition; this they must and shall have. We never have, as heretofore, had any settled and established policy of our own—we have always adopted the policies that white men established for themselves, without considering their applicability . . . to us. No people can go on this way. We must have a position, independent of anything pertaining to white men and nations. I weary of our miserable condition, and am heartily sick of whining and sniveling at the feet of white men, begging for their refuse and often existing by mere sufferance."

The next few months were a low ebb for Delany's self-esteem and reliance on his own convictions. He returned to Pittsburgh once more to resume his medical practice and to care for his family. What other choice did he have? Once more he had failed his people. He was alone with his store of knowledge, the product of his studies, even his dreams for his people. The leaders and the spokesmen of the free Negroes scorned him for proposing any change at all in the pattern of the emancipation fight.

Then an amazing development took place. As Oliver Johnson wrote, as Frederick Douglass spoke, as William Lloyd Garrison deplored the straying by Delany from the true path, other free blacks, some of them of local prominence and others totally unknown and inarticulate, read the Delany book. They found a new spirit in it, a new evaluation of their black skins which they could examine. Was it actually a misfortune to be born black—except in America? Delany revealed so much—ancient and modern, and even in America—that men and women of black skin had accomplished. Was there a limit to their capacities? Were they actually a part of America colored black and living only on white sufferance, or were they part of the world majority colored black who ruled countries and fortunes?

Very soon, in Pittsburgh, Delany found that he was far from alone. His book had been a bugle call among his people—heard by the unheard and unknown—and there emerged during 1853 and 1854 new names, new voices, new attitudes, and new leaders among the free blacks.

In 1853 Frederick Douglass was still the actual and acknowledged spokesman for the black abolitionists of America. By the following year, though Douglass continued his beautiful speeches and stirring writing, he remained the Negro spokesman to the whites. The black abolitionists were now working with Martin R. Delany in a new and exciting program.

Other events, as well as Delany, contributed to the disruption of unity among the black abolitionists. *Uncle Tom's Cabin* was published, and millions of Americans wept their way to anti-slavery attitudes momentarily and prayed for poor Uncle Tom in their lily-white churches. In New York they even left the anti-abolitionist riots to attend dramatized productions of *Uncle Tom*. The famous book itself contributed absolutely nothing toward changing American actions toward the blacks—slave or free. It had been expected to.

That is why Delany and other blacks were so puzzled by the presidential elections of that year. Both the Democrats and the Whigs adopted almost identical platform planks concerning the Compromise of 1850—confirmation of its validity, including the Fugitive Slave Act, and opposition to any further anti-slavery agitation. Franklin Pierce was elected, of course, and this Democrat's inaugural address was largely a pledge to the South that the Fugitive Slave Act would be enforced.

The only political party fielding an anti-slavery, anti-Fugitive Slave Act candidate was the Free Soil party, and John P. Hale, the New Hampshire Free Soil candidate, received more than 100,000 *fewer* votes than the anti-slavery candidate of four years before.

Meanwhile, in Washington the political bargains were being struck whereby slavery was assured and the Missouri Compromise of 1820 legislatively buried by the Kansas-Nebraska Act of 1854. In Boston, Rev. Theodore Parker's brave words regarding the Anthony Burns fugitive slave prosecution did not in the least assist any of the whites and blacks being imprisoned and fined in other cities for assisting fugitive slaves.

In February 1852 Frederick Douglass visited Harriet Beecher Stowe in her home in Andover, Mass., and he came away with the earnest belief that she would one day produce a "plan for improving the condition of the free colored people" but that meanwhile *Uncle Tom's Cabin* would cause a moral conversion among Americans because it stripped the slaveholder of all defenses.

To Delany that was the height of wish expression. Only

two months later, on April 18, 1852, he was given proof that the prospect of moral change in America had no basis in reality. The State of Pennsylvania had before its legislature a bill appropriating funds and authorizing the state not only to pay passage of free Negroes willing to colonize in Liberia but also to exile undesirable free Negroes to Africa. Delany was asked to go to Philadelphia and head a movement against this legislation. He was chairman of the meeting and also its envoy to Harrisburg to present the opposition to the bill before the legislature. This was the fact opposed to Douglass' fiction.

Early in 1853 Douglass was able to say: "We have grown up with this Republic and I see nothing in her character or find nothing in the character of the American people as yet which compels the belief that we must leave the United States."

At about that same time Delany was busy in Pittsburgh fighting for the freedom of a colored boy named Alexander Hendrickure who had been kidnaped by a Nashville, Tenn., man from Kingston, Jamaica, B.W.I., and at the same time exposing a new and apparently fertile activity of the slave catchers.

> In our minds there is no doubt but there is now being carried on by unprincipled Americans—Southerners it may be—a regular system of *decoying, kidnapping and selling into hopeless bondage in the United States, the free subjects of Great Britain*.

Delany, with John Peck, Rev. William Webb, and Thomas Burrows, all of Pittsburgh, prosecuted the kidnaper and brought this new slave trade to the attention of the British authorities. This case did not indicate a moral change among the American people either.

Perhaps Delany was closer to the problems of his people. Perhaps his experience with whites had been totally different from those of Frederick Douglass, and therefore he was incapable of the latter's belief and dependence upon them. This does not imply any criticism of Douglass. He was one of the most brilliant romanticists of his race, and his faith in the inevitable conquest of right over wrong was an inspiration to many. He clung to that faith all of his life and it was not shaken even by the storm that rose upon his marriage to a white woman late in life. He still maintained that one day the whites would accept even the dread "amalgamation."

Delany began to lose his illusions concerning freedom by 1838, the year that Douglass escaped from slavery. By 1852 he was an iconoclast, and his search for a solution for his people had left the bounds of standard abolitionism, so long limited in its horizons by hope that America could achieve democracy. Nothing could be clearer than the following:

> Every other than we, have at various periods of necessity, been a migratory people; and all when oppressed, shown a greater abhorrence of oppression, if not a greater love of liberty, than we. We cling to our oppressors as the objects of our love. It is true that our enslaved brethren are here, and we have been led to believe that it is necessary for us to remain, on that account. Is it true, that all should remain in degradation, because a part are degraded? We believe no such thing. We believe it to be the duty of the Free, to elevate themselves in the most speedy and effective manner possible; as the redemption of the bondsman depends entirely upon the elevation of the freeman; therefore, to elevate the free colored people of America, anywhere upon this continent, forbodes the speedy redemption of the slaves. We shall hope to hear no more of so fallacious a doctrine—the necessity of the free remaining in degradation for the sake of the oppressed. Let us apply, first, the lever to ourselves; and the force that elevates us to the position of manhood's consideration and honors, will cleft the manacles of every slave in the land.

In this statement by Delany and in Douglass' affirmation of faith in a future America shared alike by black and white are the seeds of the events following publication of *Condition and Elevation.*

Douglass immediately set about preparations for the last great convention of colored people in the United States after the pattern begun in 1830, which was held in Rochester, N.Y., in July 1853.

Delany immediately set about preparations for an entirely new type of gathering of free colored people in the United States, held in Cleveland, Ohio, in August 1854.

Delany did not attend Douglass' convention, and the latter refused to attend the former's. Both were being honest by refusing to participate in an effort they believed totally wrong. It was not petty rivalry that separated them but rather a forthright difference of conviction. Some of the delegates attended both conventions, and a good many Negro leaders cried for a plague on both houses. Douglass and Delany, however, held to the iron of their convictions.

Students of American history have seldom seen mention of the National Emigration Convention held in Cleveland on August 24, 25, and 26, 1854. All serious students have read the glorious speeches of the Rochester Colored Convention on July 6–8, 1853.

Historians have neglected the Cleveland meetings because they constituted a violation of our national pride. It was frankly announced as a meeting by a minority of Americans in search of escape from oppression. Yet our national ego was even then being fattened on the humanity displayed by a free people in inviting minorities from Europe to flee oppression in their native lands. How could such a contradiction be justified?

Another reason for historical neglect is in the very essence of the Cleveland meetings and fully explained there by Delany himself. Few white Americans are even today willing to face a change of *apartheid* as a solution to the race problem.

The two meetings marked the most important division of thought, personnel, and action in the black history of America; those in Cleveland have been ignored. The Rochester meetings assumed the function of a wake over the prostrate body of the emancipation movement, a happy celebration that the black spirit still lived enough to fight its way while within the gates of purgatory. The Cleveland meetings gave birth to a new concept of black nationalism never before allowed expression in America. By the time Southerners overreached themselves by firing on Fort Sumter, the spirit of the Rochester meetings had disappeared, and the repercussions from the Cleveland meetings were being felt in Congress and by President Lincoln. Delany's lusty infant had achieved maturity in a few short years.

A comparison between the two meetings would not be fair but in one respect it would be valid to judge them, and that is in the one action each shared—their declaration of principles, intent, or call it sentiment. In the Rochester convention it was titled "Claims of Our Common Cause" and was written by a committee headed by Douglass. Others on this committee included two of Delany's close friends and colleagues, his own Pittsburgh protégé George B. Vashon and the poet James M. Whitfield.

The "common causes" are familiar enough, having been defined in every colored convention since the Negro awakening. In the 1854 Cleveland convention they were named "Declaration of Sentiments and Platform of this Convention." While some statements are identical in content, the Rochester resolutions plead, beg, reason, pray. The Cleveland resolutions *demand*. Compare the expression in relation to the Fugitive Slave Act.

> (Rochester 1853): *We ask* that the Fugitive Slave Law of 1850, that legislative monster of modern times, by whose atrocious provisions the writ of "habeas corpus", the "right to trial by jury" have been virtually abolished, shall be repealed.
>
> (Cleveland 1854): That the Act of Congress of 1850, known as the Fugitive Bill, we declare to be a general law, tending to the virtual enslavement of every colored person in the United States; and consequently we abhor its existence, dispute its authority, refuse submission to its provisions, and hold it in a state of the most contemptuous abrogation.

Another resolution concerns political rights.

> (Rochester 1853): *We ask* that (inasmuch as we are, in common with other American citizens, supporters of the State, subject to its laws, interested in its welfare, liable to be called upon to defend it in time of war, contributors to its wealth in time of peace) the complete and unrestricted right of suffrage which is essential to the dignity even of the white man, be extended to the Free Colored man also.
>
> (Cleveland 1854): That, as men and equals, we demand every political right, privilege and position to which the whites are eligible in the United States, and we will either attain to these, or accept of nothing.

Such comparisons could be continued point by point, and all they would prove would be the servility expressed at the Rochester convention and the militancy of the Cleveland meetings. But the omissions are equally important. It is impossible to explain why Frederick Douglass' expressions of beliefs and complaints, why among all the "we asks" there is no mention of opposition to slavery. This was the address "to the people of the United States." Surely there was no doubt of the delegates' condemnation of American slavery. Then was the omission of such expression a further evidence of a basic timidity? In Cleveland, the following year, Delany's statement of principles began:

> We acknowledge the natural equality of the Human Race . . . That man is by nature free, and cannot be enslaved, except by injustice and oppression. . . . That whatever interferes with the natural rights of man, should meet from him with adequate resistance . . . That, under no circumstances, let the consequences be as they may, will we ever submit to enslavement, let the power that attempts it, emanate from whatever source it will.

Yet, even to this day historians consider the Rochester convention of 1853 the most successful in ante-bellum Negro history. That could be because its representation was the largest in the history of the Negro awakening. In attendance were 114 delegates from eight states. They set up a permanent organization consisting of a National Council which would prosecute a program of cooperative purchasing among blacks, an employment office for blacks, a publications committee which would record all statistical information about blacks, and the establishment of a manual labor school. All were laudable.

This program, too, had a familiar ring, and so did the aftermath of the Rochester convention. The first meeting of the National Council, set for January 1854, failed to attract a quorum. The second meeting, six months later, produced eleven delegates, a quorum by just one vote. The third and final meeting scheduled for Philadelphia in 1855 was a total failure. There were no more ante-bellum meetings of councils, committees, or colored conventions—except Delany's.

During the last half of America's darkest decade, the abolitionists of both colors were whipped. The Dred Scott decision of 1857, affirming juridically what existed in fact, the denial of the right of blacks to citizenship, was without real significance to the free blacks. Its only influence was to drive more Negro intellectuals to Delany's world views and to his emigration plans. A pertinent example was William Howard Day, the brilliant Negro journalist from Cleveland, who declared at the Ohio convention in 1851:

> Coming up as I do, in the midst of three millions of men in chains and five hundred thousand only half free, I consider every instrument precious which guarantees to me liberty. I consider the Constitution the foundation of American liberties, and wrapping myself in the flag of the nation, I would plant myself upon that Constitution and using the weapons they have given me, I would appeal to the American people for the rights thus guaranteed.

Day was a vice-president at Douglass' Rochester convention in 1853 and only a few years later it was he who, from the black abolitionist headquarters in Chatham, Canada West (Ontario), issued the orders as head of the organization resulting from the Cleveland convention of 1854. For Day, too, the Constitution of the United States had proved to be "just a scrap of paper." Many others like him reached that same conclusion by 1854, and they joined Delany in the new black abolitionism.

Another prominent participant in the Rochester convention was the adventurous barber-poet from Buffalo, James M. Whitfield. Immediately after the convention he published his first book of poems, *America and Other Poems,* which he dedicated to Delany with the following words: "To Martin R. Delany, M.D., This volume is inscribed as a small tribute of respect for his character, admiration for his talents, and love of his principles by the Author."

Whitfield too was to receive orders from William Howard Day for, like the others who joined Delany, he had lost patience with the past. One of his poems begins with the weariness that brought on the new black nationalism.

> How long, O gracious God! how long
> Shall power lord it over right?

The feeble, trampled by the strong,
Remain in slavery's gloomy night?

The development of Delany's Cleveland emigration convention was marked by a year of dispute, with Delany versus the field. There were old friends against him, men with whom he had worked and would again—Dr. J. McCune Smith of New York, John Jones of Chicago, Robert Purvis of Philadelphia, John I. Gaines of Cincinnati (who had so praised Delany some years before), and many others including Charles Lenox Remond, and his first Pittsburgh friend, John B. Vashon.

In fact, along with his medical practice and many other activities, 1853 was one of Delany's busiest and stormiest years. Somehow he found the time before June 24 to prepare and deliver his treatise on Negro Freemasonry in the United States that became a classic as the first printed historical treatment on the subject in the country. It is a prized document today, and was delivered before his own St. Cyprian Lodge No. 13 by "M. R. Delany, K.M., D.D.G.H.P." Delany assented to its publication, refusing to dodge the furious controversy then going on in Negro Freemasonry.

> We have for years been fraternally outraged, simply for the want of a proper and judicious course being pursued on the part of our Masonic authorities, and the present loudly calls upon us for action in this matter. We are either Masons or not Masons, legitimate or illegitimate; if the affirmative, then we *must* be so *acknowledged* and *accepted*—if the negative, we *should* be *rejected*. We never will relinquish a claim to an everlasting inheritance but by the force of stern necessity; and there is not that Masonic power in existence, with the exception of the Grand Lodge in England, to which we will yield in a decision on this point. Our rights are equal to those of other American Masons, if not better than some; and it comes not with the best grace for *them* to *deny* us.

The substance of the study was to prove the founding of Freemasonry in the earliest dynasties of the Egyptian and Ethiopian civilizations and its purpose: "Masonry was originally intended for the better government of man—for the purpose of restraining him from a breach of the established ordinances." It was entirely natural that Delany should take to Freemasonry so completely as to become immersed in the study of its ancient and modern history.

> Moses, as before mentioned, of whom the highest encomium given, is said to have been *learned* in *all* the *wisdom* of the Egyptians, was not only the descendant of those who had been slaves, but of *slave parents;* and *himself, at the time* that he was so *taught* and *instructed* in this WISDOM, *was a slave!* Will it be denied that the man who appeared before the Pharaoh, and was able to perform *mystically* all that the wisest among the wise men of that mysteriously wise nation were capable of doing, was a Mason? Was not the man who became the *Prime Minister* and *High Priest of Ceremonies* among the wise men of Africa, a *Mason?* If so, will it be disputed that he was *legitimately* such? Are not we as Masons, and the world of mankind, to *him,* the Egyptian *slave*—may I not add, the fugitive slave—indebted for a transmission to us of the Masonic Records—the Holy Bible, the Word of God?

The pamphlet contains some of Delany's most exceptional writing, for it too is based on his early studies of the ancients, and is controversial and philosophical. He declares, for instance, "But to deny to black men the privilege of Masonry, is to deny to a child the lineage of its own parentage. From whence sprung Masonry but from Ethiopia, Egypt and Assyria—as settled and peopled by the children of Ham?"

On the other hand, he does not miss an opportunity of talking to his fellows of the need of the black man—self-elevation.

> To convince man of the importance of his own being, and to impress him with a proper sense of his duty to his Creator, were what was desired, and to effect this, would also impress him with a sense of his duty and obligations to society and the laws intended for government. For this purpose, was the beautiful fabric of Masonry established and illustrated in the structure of man's person.
>
> Man, scientifically developed, is a moral, intellectual and physical being—composed of an osseous, muscular and

vital structure; of solid, flexible and liquid parts. With an intellect—a mind, the constituent principles of which he is incapable of analyzing or comprehending which rises superior to its earthly tenement; with the velocity of lightning, soars to the summit of altitude, descends to the depths of profundity, and flies to the widespread expanse of eternal space. What can be more God-like than this, to understand which is to give man a proper sense of his own importance, and consequently his duty to his fellows, by which alone, he fulfills the mighty mission for which he was sent on his temporary pilgrimage.

But the treatise on Freemasonry was a labor of love during that eventful year 1853. The call to duty—service to his people —was to consume his time and abundant energy from July 1853 through the next ten years. It took him to Canada, Africa, England, and throughout the United States. Eventually, it took him to the White House, too.

Delany began his bold and forthright campaign for the National Emigration Convention in July, even before the minutes of the Rochester convention were printed in Frederick Douglass' shop. It was not the ordinary call issued for colored conventions. It was an announcement that an emigration convention *will* take place. It placed limitations on those eligible to attend. They must agree beforehand to restrict discussion to emigration and to discussion of emigration within the western hemisphere, not "Asia, Africa or Europe." It declared that the convention would be held "specifically by and for the friends of emigration and NONE OTHERS—and no opposition to them will be entertained."

The few blacks who were active in Liberian colonization were warned to stay away, "as we have no sympathy with the enemies of our race." All wishing to attend the convention were first to be approved by Delany and Rev. William Webb as eligible to apply, but would be seated as delegates only by the duly elected credentials committee at the initial meeting.

There was no lofty adornment in Delany's call beyond the statement that

The time has now fully come, when we, as an oppressed people, should do something effectively, and use those

> means adequate to the attainment of the great and long desired end—to do something to meet the actual demands of the present and prospective necessities of the rising generation of our people in this country.

In other words, it was time for action of any kind, and he was proposing emigration as one course.

The furor of opposition began at once, and naturally it was led by Frederick Douglass, who protested the undemocratic nature of the proposed emigration convention. His editorial in *Frederick Douglass' Paper* added a prediction:

> We have no sympathy for the call for this convention which we publish in another column. Whatever may be the motives for sending forth such a call (and we say nothing as to these) we deem it uncalled for, unwise, unfortunate and premature; and we venture to predict that this will be the judgment pronounced upon it by a majority of intelligent thinking colored men. Our enemies will see in this movement a cause for rejoicing; such as they could hardly have anticipated so soon, after the manly position assumed by the Colored National Convention held in this city (Rochester). They will discover in this movement a division of opinion amongst us upon a vital point, and will look upon this Cleveland Convention as opposed in spirit and purpose to the Rochester Convention. Looked at from any point the movement is to be deprecated.

Others joined in the protest against the Cleveland convention. There were anonymous as well as signed letters in all of the Negro press. Delany himself protested to the Canadian *Provincial Freeman* that Frederick Douglass was misleading the colored people by changing the "call" in his paper, ". . . being incorrect in many particulars, even parts of sentences and paragraphs omitted." The only correct version, he wrote, was printed in William Howard Day's Cleveland weekly, *The Aliened American.*

In October 1853 the wealthy merchant of Chicago with whom Delany was to become a close friend, John Jones, introduced in the Illinois State Colored Convention the following resolution: "*Resolved,* That we are opposed to the call for a National Emigration Convention, as put forth by M. R. Delany and we discover in it a spirit of disunion, which, if encouraged, will prove fatal to our hopes and aspirations as a people in this country."

Delany disputed this resolution in a long and intemperate letter which Frederick Douglass printed. Apparently, Delany had been stung by the charge of creating "disunion." "I can submit to any other wrong—as I have been doing all my life—from colored men, except that of charging me with a *design* of *injury* to my race; and this I never shall submit to with indifference from any source, except one too contemptible to merit a notice." The lengthy letter continues a complaint against the "one course laid out by the superiors among us" who allow no diversion from that course, and concludes, "But we have no quarrel with those who love to live among the whites better than the blacks . . . ," and other vitriolic implications.

The controversy continued almost to the opening day of the Cleveland convention and wandered from principles to personalities and back again. A reading of the Negro press of that period would indicate that an emigration convention of any import in attendance or performance was absolutely impossible.

Yet, on Tuesday, August 24, there gathered in the Congregational Church on Prospect Street in Cleveland well over one hundred men and women from ten states and Canada. The representation was almost that of the famous Rochester convention of 1853.

Today all the bickering and divisions resulting from Delany's Cleveland emigration convention of 1854 fade into insignificance when one realizes the new concept he brought to the blacks of America. He preceded by some 115 years the convictions, plans, ideas, hopes, and dreams which divide the black people today and have created the Black Panthers, SNCC, the Muslims, the non-violent, and violent groupings, and the status quo blacks, derisively called "Uncle Toms" by the militants.

What Martin R. Delany initiated in Cleveland in 1854 requires examination. When the delegates gathered on the first day, their first official act was to elect a credentials committee composed of Rev. William Webb of Pittsburgh; James Theodore Holly, then living in New York; Rev. Augustus R. Green, pastor of the Bethel AME Church in Cincinnati; H. Ford Douglass of

Louisiana (not related to Frederick Douglass); and William M. Lambert of Michigan.

The committee asked each aspiring delegate two questions and required a yes reply to each before the delegate was approved.

> 1. Are you in favor of Emigration?
>
> 2. Do you subscribe to the objects and sentiments contained in the Call for a National Emigration Convention, and will you do all in your power to carry out the same?

There were 106 delegates from ten states and Canada who qualified, which possibly indicates the extent to which some of the free blacks had "given up" on America. It also indicates the extent of Frederick Douglass' influence, for 145 people had signified their intention of attending despite all the dire warnings printed in *Frederick Douglass' Paper*. The additional representation unable to attend qualified within a month after the meetings. In fact, Douglass was flatly spurned by the convention.

The report of the publications committee recommended consideration of utilizing *Frederick Douglass' Paper* instead of issuing their own periodical, but this was vehemently rejected

> . . . in consequence of the illiberal and supercilious position assumed by him toward the Convention, from the issue of the Call till its assembling, denouncing those concerned as being "unintelligent", "unwise", etc. and eventually refusing to publish anything in favor of the Movement, but promptly giving publicity to everything against it.

The convention ordered the chairman of the publications committee, none other than James M. Whitfield, to strike the recommendation from its report.

Another peculiarity of the Cleveland representation was the fact that among them were 29 fully accredited and voting women delegates, including Kate Delany. Black women had never before participated so fully in any meeting except their own organizations and never at a national convention of any kind. Delany's first attempt to obtain equal participation for women had also been in Cleveland, at the National Negro Convention of 1848 presided over by Frederick Douglass. The business committee of that convention first refused to take any action on Delany's resolution that women have the right to vote and hold office. When he offered the resolution on the floor, it was voted by the convention to postpone action, and finally there was a compromise allowing women status as "persons invited to attend."

But in Delany's convention of 1854 women debated, voted, served on committees, and were elected to office. Mary E. Bibb of Canada West, whose famous husband had died three weeks before, was elected second vice-president. Four other female delegates were elected to the permanent finance committee.

The three days and evenings of sessions were devoted to business, and there were few speeches. It was an activist convention and its purpose was exclusively to create a permanent organization that would operate daily. In fact, the preface to the minutes of the meetings, written by Delany, declared:

> It is hoped and believed that there will be no necessity for more than one convention, held by the friends of this great movement, which will be to hear the reports of the Foreign Commissioners, who shall have returned from their tour; when the colored people of the whole United States, without restriction, will be summoned to hear and deliberate on the great and effective measures for the anxiously desired Restoration of our once fallen, but now gradually rising race.

With Delany at the helm as chairman of the convention's business committee, there was only one incident interrupting the remarkable work accomplished by the delegates. John Mercer Langston, the young Ohio lawyer who had graduated from Oberlin College in 1849, although not a delegate was permitted to speak. He delivered the only anti-emigrationist speech of the three days, a sincere plea that the delegates persevere in fighting white America. In a way, it was a fortunate incident, for otherwise H. Ford Douglass might never have become as aroused as he was. He demanded the floor in reply to Langston's "bombastic outpouring," and his speech characterized the spirit of the entire convention.

The time has come when the colored men must cease to build their castles of hope upon the ideal sands of a sickly sentimentality, the effect will only be to hush within us the "*Still sad music of Humanity*". The mingled tones of sorrow and woe which come up on every breeze from the deep and damning hell of Negro slavery speaks a common language to each and every individual, no matter how humble he may be, reminding him that he too has a duty to perform in this world as well as the gifted and the great. A truth told by a patrician would be no less the truth when told by a plebeian. Because Mr. (Frederick) Douglass, Mr. J. McCune) Smith or Mr. (J. Mercer) Langston tell me that the principles of emigration are destructive to the best interests of the colored people in this country, am I to act the part of a "young robin," and swallow it down without ever looking into the merits of the principles involved? . . .

I can hate this Government without being disloyal, because it has stricken down my manhood, and treated me as a saleable commodity. I can join a foreign enemy and fight against it, without being a traitor, because it treats me as an ALIEN and a STRANGER, and I am free to avow that should such a contingency arise I should not hesitate to take any advantage in order to procure indemnity for the future. . . .

When I remember that from Maine to Georgia, from the Atlantic waves to the Pacific shores, I am an alien and an outcast, unprotected by law, proscribed and persecuted by cruel prejudice, I am willing to forget the endearing name of home and country, and as an unwilling exile seek on other shores the freedom which has been denied me in the land of my birth.

After that, there was no further dissent expressed against the purpose of the convention.

Delany had prepared a blueprint for a permanent organization, and it was adopted with only minor changes. The convention:

1. Created a central governing body known as the National Board of Commissioners consisting of nine persons "to be chosen

from and located at the place where the President is to reside," plus two additional members from each state.

With Martin Delany elected the first head of the National Board of Commissioners, all of the executive group chosen were from Allegheny County as well. They were known as central commissioners and were allowed a continuity of activity never before possible among the anti-slavery societies which were geographically diffuse. Under them operated four permanent departments—a Committee on Domestic Relations, Financial Relations, Foreign Relations, and a special Foreign Secretary.

All ten states were initially represented by election from the convention. They were Massachusetts, New York, Ohio, Michigan, Kentucky, Missouri, Virginia, Tennessee, Louisiana, and California.

2. Established as the organ of the National Board of Commissioners, a quarterly periodical named the *Africo-American Repository*.

3. Planned and assigned responsibility for exploration of emigration sites. Delany was given Africa; James Theodore Holly, Haiti; and James M. Whitfield, Central America.

Within one month all of these departments were in operation. Within five years the emigrationists had a black-financed organization sponsoring its periodical and three distinct parties of exploration. In April 1861, when Fort Sumter was fired upon, Martin Delany was awaiting a trained nucleus of the first colony to be created in Abeokuta, on the west coast of Africa.

Meanwhile, the free blacks of America were absorbing what H. Ford Douglass called a "Colored Nationality" as a result of one of the most effective contributions made to the convention by its founder, Martin Delany. His report to the delegates, "Political Destiny of the Colored Race on the American Continent," is a classic document of American history and was reprinted many times in many places, including Congressional reports.

"Political Destiny" is a discourse on the American political economy and the black position in it and is of startling applicability today. Any random page displays a cold logic that opens to the eye deeply hidden secrets as incisively as a surgeon's scalpel. It is the first document of black nationalism not clouded by inexpressible emotion. A dispute with the following extract would be difficult.

> It would be duplicity longer to disguise the fact, that the great issue, sooner or later, upon which must be disputed the world's destiny, will be a question of black and white; and every individual will be called upon for his identity with one or the other. The blacks and colored races are four-sixths of all the population of the world; and these people are fast tending to a common cause with each other. . . . And it is notorious that the only progress made in territorial domain, in the last three centuries, by the whites, has been a usurpation and encroachment on the rights and native soil of some of the colored races.

Here Delany lists some of the African, Australian, Indonesian, and Asian colonies of white powers, a list much increased since 1854.

> We regret the necessity of stating the fact, but duty compels us to the task—that for more than two thousand years, the determined aim of the whites has been to crush the colored races wherever found. With a determined will, they have sought and pursued them in every quarter of the globe. The Anglo-Saxon has taken the lead in this work of universal subjugation. But the Anglo-American stands preeminent for deeds of injustice and acts of oppression, unparalleled perhaps in the annals of modern history.
>
> We admit the existence of great and good people in America, England, France, and the rest of Europe, who desire a unity of interests among the whole human family, of whatever origin or race.
>
> But it is neither the moralist, Christian, nor philanthropist whom we now have to meet and combat, but the politician—the civil engineer and skillful economist, who direct and control the machinery which moves forward with mighty impulse, the nations and powers of the earth. We must, therefore, if possible, meet them on vantage ground, or, at least, with adequate means for the conflict.
>
> Should we encounter an enemy with artillery, a prayer will not stay the cannon shot; neither will the kind words nor smiles of philanthropy shield his spear from piercing us through the heart. We must meet mankind, then, as they meet us—prepared for the worst, though we may hope for

> the best. Our submission does not gain for us an increase of friends nor respectability—as the white race will only respect those who oppose their usurpation, and acknowledge as equals those who will not submit to their rule. This may be no new discovery in political economy, but it certainly is a subject worthy of the consideration of the black race.

On still another point Delany supplies both logic and a warning for today. The changing characteristics of America's black population are seldom measured in our desperate maintenance of *apartheid*. On the streets of today's black ghettos are not the youth of Booker T. Washington's or Marcus Garvey's day. Today they are the sons of *their* sons. As Delany pointed out in 1854, a new breed of black man was inevitably developing.

> A half century brings about a mighty change, in the reality of existing things, and events of the world's history. Fifty years ago, our fathers lived: for the most part they were sorely oppressed, debased, ignorant and incapable of comprehending the political relations of mankind, the great machinery and motive power by which the enlightened nations of the earth were impelled forward. They knew but little, and ventured to do nothing to enhance their own interests, beyond that which their oppressors taught them. They lived amidst a continual cloud of moral obscurity—a fog of bewilderment and delusion, by which they were of necessity compelled to confine themselves to a limited space —a *known* locality—lest by one step beyond this, they might have stumbled over a precipice, ruining themselves beyond recovery in the fall.
>
> We are their sons, but not the same individuals; neither do we live in the same period with them. That which suited them, does not suit us; and that with which they may have been contented, will not satisfy us.
>
> Without education, they were ignorant of the world and fearful of adventure. With education, we are conversant with its geography, history and nations, and delight in its enterprises and responsibilities. They once were held as slaves; to such a condition we never could be reduced. They

were content with privileges; we will be satisfied with nothing less than rights. They felt themselves happy to be permitted to beg for rights; we demand them as an innate inheritance. They considered themselves favored to live by sufferance; we reject it as a degradation. A secondary position was all that they asked for; we claim entire equality or nothing. The relation of master and slave was innocently acknowledged by them; we deny the right, as such, and pronounce the relation as the basest injustice that ever scourged the earth and cursed the human family. They admitted themselves to be inferior; we barely acknowledge the whites as equals—perhaps not in every particular. They lamented their irrecoverable fate, and incapacity to redeem themselves and their race. We rejoice, that as their sons, it is our happy lot and high mission, to accomplish that which they desired and would have done, but failed for the want of ability to do.

Let no intelligent man or woman, then, among us, be found at the present day, exulting in the degradation that our enslaved parents would gladly have rid themselves, had they have had the intelligence and qualifications to accomplish their designs. Let none be found to shield themselves behind the plea of our brother bondsmen in ignorance; that we know not *what* to do, nor *where* to go. We are no longer slaves, as were our fathers, but freemen; fully qualified to meet our oppressors in every relation which belongs to the elevation of man, the establishment, sustenance and perpetuity of a nation. And such a position, by the help of God our common Father, we are determined to take and maintain.

There is but one question presents itself for our serious consideration, upon which we *must* give a decisive reply—Will we transmit, as an inheritance to our children, the blessings of unrestricted civil liberty, or shall we entail upon them, as our only political legacy, the degradation and oppression left us by our fathers?

Shall we be persuaded that we can live and prosper nowhere but under the authority and power of our North American white oppressors; that this (the United States) is the country most—if not the only one—favorable to our improvement and progress? Are we willing to admit that we are incapable of self-government, establishing for ourselves such political privileges, and making such internal improvements as we delight to enjoy, after American white men have made them for themselves?

No! Neither is it true that the United States is the country best adapted to *our* improvement. But that country is the best in which our manhood—morally, mentally and physically—can be *best developed* in which we have an untrammeled right to the enjoyment of civil and religious liberty; and the West Indies, Central and South America, present now such advantages, superiorly preferable to all other countries.

In "Political Destiny" Delany continued his fears that Canada would not remain a refuge for his people for long and recommended a southern escape for a permanent home rather than to the North Star. In the course of that argument, he presented one of the most complete and detailed reports on the condition and welfare of blacks in Central and South America yet written.

This report alone, with the 31 defiant points of the convention's platform, constitute the philosophical bedrock on which black nationalism was begun and exists today. It also represents Martin R. Delany's greatest contribution to his people, for the convention itself and all of its consequences were the result of his organizational thinking and the product of his own frustrations in the white world.

He was proud of this accomplishment and spent his next seven years in the prosecution of its program. He drew to the work many of the new leaders of the free blacks, offering them not only a course of action but an individual satisfaction we know now as black pride.

29. That we shall ever cherish our identity of origin and race, as preferable, in our estimation, to any other people.

30. That the relative terms Negro, African, Black, Colored and Mulatto, when applied to us, shall ever be held with the same respect and pride; and synonymous with the terms Caucasian, White, Anglo-Saxon and European, when applied to that class of people.

He offered his people a realization of their own values, not borrowed from the whites or asserted on a bended knee. He gave them an identity with the past and a power for the future not dependent on the calculated subordination under which they had been born in America.

Delany had but one apology for the National Emigration Convention of 1854 and that was for a fortnight's delay in delivery of the minutes of the meetings to the delegates. It was due to the cholera epidemic in Pittsburgh which, he said, "put nearly all business to a stand." He did not explain that this epidemic in September 1854 brought him high public honors for his services as a doctor, and again the kind of recognition he sought. He had all of "Hayti" in Pittsburgh to care for during the epidemic, and his mortality record was the lowest of any group in the city. Again he had served his people well.

The events of the next two busy years were not to change Delany's convictions regarding Canada as only a temporary refuge for his people. But he was driven there by his own creation. He too emigrated in 1856.

The work of the National Board of Commissioners required total freedom from both the whites and the blacks who were opposed to emigration. It required the financial support as well as the active participation of well-to-do blacks scattered through Canada West. True independence of his organization was possible only in a free country. He achieved it in Canada.

CHAPTER TEN

To Canada

The record of Delany's development as America's first and foremost black nationalist is most complete. He was either hated or venerated by both blacks and whites and therefore received attention from both. From the publication of *Condition and Elevation* in 1852 until his move to Canada in February 1856 (and afterward), Delany was a target for frustrated abolitionists of all colors. During these four stormy years Delany matured in his thinking and speaking. He acquired a practicality difficult to dispute, and as a result his removal to Canada became inevitable.

Now, in the 1970s, black militants are reaching Delaney's decisions of the 1850s. They are concluding that American *apartheid* can only be changed by black separatism in the United States and black unity in the world. The extremists among them flee to Cuba, Africa, Europe, and China, not merely to escape jail in the United States, but also to continue their struggles against *apartheid* on an international level. Their experiences with American democracy have been similar to Delany's.

As an example, after the Cleveland Emigration Convention, Delany returned to Pittsburgh and the work of the National Board of Commissioners. He also continued his duties in the Underground Railroad, and 1854 and 1855 were busy years for him. Yet he had none of the illusions of the abolitionists that the Fugitive Slave Act would be repealed as a result of its defiance and the passage of personal liberty laws in each state. He was convinced that his own Underground Railroad activities had no meaning beyond temporary salvation for a handful and, for them, only until Canada was annexed by the United States.

Delany was prophetic in his reasoning. In *Condition and Elevation*, while discussing the Fugitive Slave Act, he wrote:

> This is the law of the land and must be obeyed, and we candidly advise that it is useless for us to contend against it. To suppose its repeal is to anticipate an overthrow of the Confederative Union; and we must be allowed an expression of opinion, when we say, that candidly we believe, the existence of the Fugitive Slave Law is *necessary* to the continuance of the National Compact. . . . but we speak logically and politically, *leaving morality and right out of the question*—taking our position on the acknowledged popular basis of American Policy; arguing from premise to conclusion. We must abandon all vague theory; and look at *facts* as they really are; viewing ourselves in our true political position in the body politic. To imagine ourselves to be included in the body politic, except by express legislation, is at war with common sense and contrary to fact.

The Civil War concluded the dark decade and the rebellion's political motivation, expressed by Delany, are in his words of 1852. When he wrote them, the slaveholding states were ruling more triumphantly and arrogantly over the country. The Yankee skippers joined openly with the South's demand for a repeal of the 1808 ban on importation of slaves from Africa. It would remove the inconveniences caused by the British blockade and transfer of their black cargoes from the West Indies islands to the United States. Disregard of the 1808 law was as flagrant as today's *official* civil disobedience in implementation of the 1954 Supreme Court decision on school desegregation. Conquest of "Bleeding Kansas" by slaveholders totally disregarded the few rights of self-determination left to the settlers by the Kansas-Nebraska Act of 1854, very similar to today's official disregard of the Voting Rights Act of 1965.

Delany saw too that the only blacks "safe" in their status were the slaves. In the Congress there was debate on deportation of the free Negroes as an alternative to their re-enslavement. He himself could be a victim of the slave stealers but more likely as victims of the trade would be his children who, in any circumstances, would have no future in America because they were black. When divested of their lofty expression, in other words "leaving morality and right out of the question," the status of democracy in America was at its lowest ebb. Even the stubborn fighter, Senator Charles Sumner of Massachusetts, grew discouraged. He wrote on January 4, 1854:

> I look around me in the Senate and find all demoralized. Maine, New Hampshire, Connecticut, Rhode Island, Vermont!! All, all in the hands of the slave holders; and even New York ready to howl at my heels, if I were only to name the name of freedom, which once they loved so much.

This was the reality Delany faced and that from which the organized abolitionists of both colors turned. It was the reality of inevitable black separatism first and black nationalism next. In his frenzied administrative activities for the National Board of Commissioners right after the Cleveland convention he shouted his warnings, and his reports to his fellow commissioners constitute to this day the most authoritative sources of information available concerning those crucial years.

Abuse came from all directions and did not abate even after he left Pittsburgh. All of it could be summed up by the statement by Philip A. Bell, the New York Negro publisher who had printed so many of Delany's articles: "I now charge M. R. Delany with being false to his brethren, recreant to the principles he has heretofore espoused." He identified the plans of the National Board of Commissioners with those of the hated American Colonization Society as efforts to accomplish the "exile and expatriation of the entire free colored population and the decrepid (*sic*) helpless slaves."

This was a purposeful and false statement by Bell, an attempt to confuse the free blacks whose leaders had warned them against the American Colonization Society and Liberia for so many years. The minutes of the Cleveland emigration meetings make a clear distinction of the purpose of the National Board of Commissioners and once more condemn the Colonization Society. It was a country Delany wanted to found, not a private colony for black discards.

At just about the same time that Bell made the statement, one William Nesbit returned from Liberia, a disillusioned emigrant. He wrote a scathing pamphlet against both the Society and Liberia, detailing his own experiences. Delany wrote the introduction on June 1, 1855, and congratulated Nesbit for "your graphic portrayal of the infamy of that most pernicious and impudent of all schemes for the perpetuity of the degradation of our race, the AMERICAN COLONIZATION SOCIETY."

> I say most pernicious, because it was originated in the South, by slaveholders, propagated by their aiders and abettors, North and South, and still continues to be carried on under the garb of philanthropic aid and Christianity, through the medium of the basest deception and hypocrisy.

As for Liberia itself:

> The wretches who selected the tide-swamp of the coast of Guinea, instead of a healthful location in Africa, as a colony for the colored people of America, knowingly and designedly established a national Potter's Field, into which the carcass of every emigrant who ventured there, would most assuredly moulder in death.

Bell knew these were Delany's sentiments and so did others among the black abolitionists. They were attempting to separate the militant new emigrationist movement from Delany. They failed, because when Delany did move to Canada, he was followed by the new black leadership which had also been engaged in organizational activity for more than a year.

Right after the Cleveland convention, too, Delany began to question the once-glorious scheme of hemispheric black unity as a plan for both refuge and the abolition of American slavery. He returned more and more, as president of the National Board of Commissioners, to his earliest concept of Africa as the sole hope for a Black Israel. Strangely, his own doubts of the hemispheric plan were reflected in a thoughtful article in the Pittsburgh *Daily Morning Post* on October 18, 1854. Six weeks after the emigration convention this pro-slavery newspaper devoted more than a column to "A Grand Scheme for the Colored Race." It reported on the decisions of the National Board of Commissioners and insisted that Africa should be their goal and inspiration.

> That anyone will be turned aside from so noble a mission by the delusive dream of conquest and empire in the Western Hemisphere is an absurdity too monstrous and mischievous to be believed. Yet the Committee Report (Delany's

> "Political Destiny") was accepted, and adopted and endorsed by a National Convention; and is published and sent forth to the world.
>
> If Dr. D. drafted this report it certainly does him much credit for learning and ability; and cannot fail to establish for him a reputation for vigor and brilliance of imagination never yet surpassed. It is a vast conception of impossible birth. The Committee seems to have entirely overlooked the strength of "powers on earth" that would oppose Africanization of more than half of the Western Hemisphere.

And then the *Post* stated that England, France, Spain, Holland, and Denmark would protect their domains in the western hemisphere, "and where are the armies and navies, the arms and munitions of war, with which these rich possessions are to be wrested from the European powers?"

As for the United States, not even Lord Macaulay's (1854) indictments in the British Parliament ever described American attitudes and purposes more concretely.

> The United States too, with its routes of commerce across Central America, its friendly relations with the doomed republics of the South, its intention to annex Cuba, *and a little more,* will she not bear a part in this grand tragi-comic emeute (riot, disturbance)? We can assure our colored neighbors that Uncle Sam, Johnny Bull, Johnny Crappeau, Queen Christina and the Dutch, will all interpose most formidable obstacles to this splendid project. Nothing but a sudden coup de main could give it any chance of success. And for that there is no adequate preparation. A few years delay, and Cuba will be under the Stars and Stripes; and American railroads and canals will span all the realms of Central America.

This was the mood of white America and no moral considerations were involved. No matter what their number, no blacks would be allowed to interfere with the hemispheric projections of America's Manifest Destiny which included an expansion of slavery as well as the conquest of territory.

That was why Delany had no choice but a removal to Canada. If there was to be any consideration of a hemispheric plan, the National Board of Commissioners could not function anywhere in the United States. The constitution of the organization required that all of its officers reside in the same area as the president. In effect, Delany's move transferred the entire organization to Canada.

For the first annual meeting of the National Board of Commissioners, held in Pittsburgh on August 14, 1855, as dictated by the organization's constitution, he produced a report entitled "Political Aspect of the Colored People of the United States" which was a survey of the United States and other countries' treatment of blacks.

He was able to warn the commissioners that travel in Louisiana, Georgia, Virginia, Delaware, and Maryland by any free black was an invitation to enslavement as a result of new legislation. A special warning, still applicable today, was given—"Mississippi still stands a living reality of American infamy"—and he classed Missouri second in its oppressive measures. Texas, for which a war had been fought, now embodied in her constitution a provision barring emancipation forever. Arkansas too adopted such a law.

The once-free California had shaken off the Spanish influence and allowed, for the past three years, slaveholders to bring their slaves into the state, and had eliminated any legal or court rights for the colored.

Among the northern states he had found that the few which were passing personal liberty laws against the Fugitive Slave Act were not enforcing them. This included Vermont, Massachusetts, and Rhode Island. But that did not matter, since such state action could in no way influence the national legislation. New Jersey, he found, was still a "Slave State" but New York had begun a "Colored" school system following the courageous fight waged successfully by the colored citizens of Boston. In New York, too, in spite of rigid property requirements, blacks were voting. Within a few weeks they would be able to vote for George B. Vashon for State Attorney General under the Free Soil party ticket. In Pennsylvania, as his commissioners well knew, the only change had been a separate school system for colored children.

Ohio, surprisingly and due greatly to the efforts of men like William Howard Day, had begun to relax its vicious Black Code in 1849, and now it too had a separate school system. As for the newer states and territories, Indiana in particular was retrogressing with its new law forbidding entry of any black man. Illinois still denied legal rights while the vast Oregon Territory, with its millions of acres of homesteading land, was forbidden to any Negro. He only mentioned Kansas and Nebraska, since the planned slaveholder invasion, blessed by the Congress, was a familiar story and a continuing one.

These conditions, Delany concluded in the domestic section of his report, endorsed the emigrationist principles adopted by the 1854 convention. But where to go?

Proudly and triumphantly he announced the departure, just six weeks before, of *Commissioner* James T. Holly of New Haven as a duly authorized envoy from the colored people of the United States to Faustin I, Emperor of Haiti. Holly had also been authorized to use discretionary commissioner's powers to negotiate with Jamaica, St. Thomas, Nassau, Martinique, Guadeloupe, and Central America for prospective settlement. He could be expected to report to the board shortly.

He was jubilant also that the "pernicious slavery cabinet in Washington" had been unsuccessful in an attempt to annex the Sandwich Islands solely because King Kamehameha III had once experienced Washington's perfidy as a Minister Plenipotentiary there, and would never be fooled by the tinseled offers of annexation. "The Sandwich Islands, then, for the present, may be regarded as safe."

That was true of Cuba too, by 1855, for the Spanish government had taken a step positively assuring the island's safety from American official and unofficial invasion. It had established an army composed of "colored soldiery" with "an assurance of equal rights." There "is not force enough in the United States to wrest Cuba from the Crown of Spain." Prophetically, he added, "with the aid of the blacks, Cuba is safe, without it she must fall prey to American cupidity."

The filibuster attempts by Walker on Nicaragua, unofficially aided and abetted by Washington, Delany reported, were failures, but that country had already been victimized by the United States in the naval attack on Greytown and therefore could not be considered safe for blacks. The new minister to that country, he added, was a slaveholder from North Carolina.

Then Delany looked northward and concluded:

> The only successful remedy for the evils we endure is to place ourselves in a position of potency, independently of our oppressors. All intelligent political economists and historians know this, and hence their strenuous opposition to our settlement in the Canadas.
>
> The Canadas, from their near proximity and easiness of access, are made the point of emigration by the colored people of the United States; and notwithstanding the studied opposition against it by a class of colored gentlemen known and acknowledged as leaders and great men among their people in various parts of the country, those who prefer this country to going elsewhere; the principles of Emigration are fast becoming the leading policy among our people in this country. We are happy to lay before you the intelligence that the common people generally have entered into this measure with might and main, and whether the "leading and great men" go with us or not, we have fully accomplished our object. We have opened an avenue to the portals of political equality without which man is but a cipher anywhere.

Never in all the 25 years of the Negro awakening had there been a working report, a concrete contribution, a timely posting of the conditions of their problem, as this survey by Delany. Even the language of the report was that of a responsible officer in a national government. He divided it into "Domestic Relations" and "Foreign Relations" and at no time did he mention the black critics of emigration in other than analytical terms such as in discussion of these two divisions which, he said, were

> fraught with considerations of greater magnitude . . . than all others combined; although seldom if ever so considered by those termed the leading Colored Men in the United States, simply because they suffer their interests to be swallowed up in common with those of their oppressors, and content themselves with vociferating the claims that they are part and parcel of the body politic—the sovereign people of this country—and it would seem, judging from their continual acts, desire not to know or acknowledge a difference.

> This most unfortunately is one of those political errors and blunders, so long committed by our political leaders in the different States, especially the free, until it has become the leading established policy among them, though fatal everywhere, in its consequences and results.

Nowhere in his report did Delany mention Africa as a possible goal of the emigrationists, and this was in keeping with the limitations to consideration first of the western hemisphere set by the 1854 convention. However, his own experience with Greytown and Nicaragua led him to include Africa in the resolution, with himself responsible for its eventual exploration. Meanwhile, in his communications with the other commissioners, he did not fail to emphasize the growing political crises in all parts of this continent, particularly in those islands and countries where blacks could settle. In fact, by 1856, he was ready for a second emigration convention, and the call for it, which was issued on April 21 of that year, included a warning:

> I would urge the importance of the forthcoming session upon all concerned, by reminding them that the Kansas issue in this country, the state of affairs in the West Indies islands, the movements in Central America, and the future policies of European nations in regard to their interests in the Western Hemisphere, are all conspiring to precipitate a momentous crisis in Afric-American destiny on this continent.

A month later, on May 29, Delany wrote to the president of the 1854 and the coming 1856 Emigration Convention, Rev. William C. Munroe of Detroit, proposing finally a hemispheric meeting in Kingston, Jamaica, B.W.I. "I shall hold in reserve the plan of calling the proposed Convention and promise you a Report to that effect at our great—and I hope—last Emigration Convention, to meet in Cleveland, Ohio, on the 27th of August next." In the letter he noted the beginnings of a new phase in the minds of the black men of America, which he was in a position to learn from his vast correspondence with other blacks throughout the continent and on other continents. It was a burgeoning realization that blacks are different from whites and could never hope to obtain a hearing from whites without self-recognition of that fact.

> I have said of colored men, because I deem it high time, that the colored races had begun to *love* and *pride* (*sic*) in their origin or classification, as much as the white races. And endeavor to shun it as we may, we cannot ignore the fact, that the world is at present more or less, enquiring into the condition of the colored races, as a distinct people from the white races.

He was beginning to recognize another factor in the perpetuation of American slavery by July of 1856—the economic factor. His Black Israel would mean little in the course of human freedom unless it were economically free from all other nations. Its political freedom, no matter what its internal structure, required economic ascendancy, not dependency. A month before the 1856 Emigration Convention he wrote:

> It is Commerce then that is ruling the world; that is threatening it with fearful devastation, the destruction of the liberties of every nation. It was that which caused the destruction of Tyre, the overthrow of Egypt, the downfall of Carthage, and finally the decline of the Commonwealth of Rome; and fearful is the thought at the rapid strides which this omnipotent and omnipresent invader of human rights is making through the world.

It was this thinking that Delany sent to Cleveland on August 26, 1856, for closed sessions of the National Board of Commissioners. By the end of that day, they had prepared a concrete set of recommendations to place before the convention. Within two days of the meetings, the convention had adopted the following:

1. Creation of a North American and West Indian Trading Association to engage in the West Indies trade exclusively. Its stockholders were to be members of the Association and shares were set at $50 each. These capital funds were to be invested in black dominated and operated ventures and under control of a

Board of Trade elected by the convention. There were six members of this board and all but one were residents of New Haven. The exception was from nearby Hartford. Thus the same principle of geographical concentration of membership would allow the same continuous program of action as the National Board of Commissioners.

2. Establishment of a Board of Publications to issue a quarterly magazine titled the *Afric-American Repository*. This was an ambitious undertaking, an intellectual and cultural effort to provide an outlet for Negro creative genius. "There has never yet been a mature and fair exhibition of the literary and scientific attainments of the Negro race," the prospectus stated. "In the literature of the whites, as well as in white society, the Negro is at a discount, and nothing can raise him in either, but occupying a manly and independent position, attained through his own efforts. It has therefore been maturely resolved to enter the arena of public literature, to exhibit the intellectual capacities of the Negro race, and vindicate them before the world by the publication of a periodical designed to concentrate in one brilliant focus the most cultivated intellects, and the highest order of talents that are or may yet be developed among the descendants of Africa."

James M. Whitfield was named senior editor and he had eight corresponding editors, among them Delany; Holly; Rev. Munroe; Prof. Martin H. Freeman, soon to be president of Avery College in Pittsburgh; Mary Ann Shadd Cary, brilliant editor of the *Provincial Freeman*, the Canadian Negro weekly published in Chatham; Rev. Augustus R. Green of Pittsburgh; and John N. Still, then living in Shrewsbury, N.J.

3. The *Provincial Freeman* was named the official organ of the emigrationists. It was a free and independent news outlet because it was published in Canada by Israel D. Shadd, one of the three fearless Shadd brothers who lived in the Chatham area. H. Ford Douglass of Louisiana was named the traveling agent and lecturer to obtain subscriptions for both the *Provincial Freeman* and the *Afric-American Repository*.

4. The organization of the National Board of Commissioners was revised so that all officers on the Central Board could reside within a sixty-mile radius of its new headquarters in Chatham, Canada West. This allowed continuation of Delany as president, with four of its eight other members from Chatham, two

from Detroit, and one from London, Canada West. Only Rev. James T. Holly, named corresponding secretary, was distant, remaining with his church in New Haven until he was swept up by his new Haiti expeditions. Other members of the National Board, two from each state, lived in Connecticut, New York, Ohio, and New Jersey. However, Delany could always reckon on a quorum of nearby residents on his Central Board and thus continue the daily activity.

This was the machinery with which the emigrationists worked while they prepared for the exploration of the West Indies, Central America and, after 1858, of Africa. These expeditions, publication of the *Repository* and the sale of shares in the Board of Trade all required money. Since the opposition of all the white anti-slavery societies barred their membership as a source, and since the few blacks in the United States who could afford such philanthropy were also opposed to emigration, the sources were limited chiefly to Canada. Delany received neither pay nor even his costs of travel during the succeeding years. The organization's treasurer, William Lambert of Detroit, hoarded all funds for the next two years, until the 1858 meeting of the National Board of Commissioners, held in Chatham, authorized expenditures.

Delany moved to Chatham, Canada West, in February 1856, after 25 years of living in and working out of Pittsburgh. There was every personal reason for remaining there—economic, social, and familial. His medical practice was as lucrative as he permitted it to be and as he allocated time to it, for his reputation as a physician was assured by his work during the cholera epidemic.

Too, he had reached the enviable position, for a black man, of leadership in both the white and the black communities resulting from respect for his intellectual powers and integrity. In position and prestige he was the spokesman for the black population and had taken the responsibilities left by the death of John B. Vashon. In January 1854 Delany was chosen from all of Vashon's friends to preside at two meetings commemorating the man and his deeds, to deliver the eulogies at both, and to formally convey to the Vashon family the condolences of the entire city.

By the end of 1855, too, Catherine Delany was again pregnant and there were to be four children in the family, two of them of school age. By now the separate Negro schools were receiving a small portion of the taxation paid by blacks, and for their higher education there was now the Allegheny Institute and Church, to be re-named Avery College.

But actually Delany had no personal choice. He moved to Canada because he was the key to the only activist plan for his people with any hope of accomplishment. The honored "moral suasion" prayers of his abolitionist colleagues had no effect whatsoever on white America. The alternative was country-wide revolution of the blacks as he proposed in his novel *Blake*, and that, he knew, was a dream born out of desperation. To Delany, only a Black Israel could be realized within his own lifetime and prepared for the benefit of his children.

Besides, he already had friends in Chatham and at nearby Buxton Settlement, by 1856 an extraordinary success as a haven for fugitives. The day after his arrival Delany was hailed by the *Provincial Freeman*.

> We are pleased to state to our readers, the arrival of our esteemed and talented friend, Dr. M. R. Delany, of Pittsburgh, Pa. in this town, yesterday morning, who intends making this his home.
>
> It would be useless for us to attempt to acquaint many of our readers of the character of the Doctor, as a physician, having been long in practice and thoroughly known by all the professional men of the States and the inhabitants generally; and as a writer, and orator, is distinguished among the numbers that now occupy the field, in the distribution of knowledge for the elevation and improvement of mankind, which is certainly commendatory to all friends of progress here and elsewhere. The Doctor proposes to resume the practice of medicine immediately, when he will doubtless be at the service of all who may call at his office on William Street, east of King.

Almost immediately, Delany was swept up by a tide of friends, strangers, public and private figures, by the busy, happy, grateful colored people who had been, almost without exception, fugitives from the states. It was another kind of colored community—different from any in which he had lived or visited.

All of its residents reflected the breathless sentiments of one Mary Jane Robinson written to a friend back home in Weeksville, N.Y.

> Come to a land of liberty and freedom, where the coloured man is not despised nor a deaf ear turned to them. This is the place to live in peace and enjoy the comforts of life. . . . O, we are just beginning to live well enough without the white man's foot on our necks. Away with your King Fillmore. I am for Queen Victoria. GOD SAVE THE QUEEN.

Delany was to learn much from these people, particularly regarding his fears of annexation by the United States. The 24th Kent County Militia was composed largely of young (and old) colored men, not because they were segregated but solely because of the large colored population in Chatham and the surrounding areas in Kent County. They joined, drilled, and served the military in order to repel any invasion from the United States. They were to prove themselves later, after the Civil War, when the Sinn Fein raiders came. They did not fear annexation by force of arms because they were prepared to die in the course of its prevention. These new Canadians feared only a diplomatic invasion, the secret connivance for annexation they remembered when Texas was taken.

Chatham, Canada West, was the fugitive slave capital of Canada. In 1856 it had approximately 2,400 colored within its city limits and thousands of others throughout Essex and Kent counties. Estimates vary considerably concerning the colored population of Canada West but those estimates are the only evidence available. The Canadian census never designated color. As a result of the Fugitive Slave Act, most estimates agree, the colored population of what is now the Province of Ontario grew to 50,000–60,000 by 1860.

The westernmost portion of Canada West was most attractive to the new Canadians because it was virgin country only recently secured from the Indians. There were hundreds of thousands of acres of timbered and watered land available at an average of $2.50 per acre from the government, for this country was held in Crown and Clergy reserves, never raided by the Canadian counterparts of the Astors, Vanderbilts, and railroad conglomerates. In fact, the first east-west railroad reached Chatham in 1855, and it was allowed to purchase only the right-of-way. It was not given a land empire as an inducement to private investment in construction, as in the United States.

There was skilled and unskilled work to be had from Windsor on the west to London toward the east, from the refugee settlements along the shore of Lake Erie on the south to Wallaceburg on the north. In between were colored farmers, singly or in groups, and colored settlements such as the older Dawn Settlement at Dresden founded by Rev. Josiah Henson ("Uncle Tom") only thirty miles from Chatham.

Thirteen miles along the road to Windsor was the unique Buxton Settlement, sometimes called the Elgin Settlement, which had been founded by Rev. William King. In 1848 Delany had mentioned, in a dispatch to the *North Star*, the arrival of this white Presbyterian preacher in Cincinnati with the fifteen slaves he had owned in Louisiana. They had reached the site of the settlement the following year, and by 1856 Buxton had nearly one thousand men, women, and children living on land that they themselves *owned*. William Howard Day settled there, as did Abram W. Shadd with whom Delany had attended many a convention when the Shadds lived in West Chester, Penn. The famous fugitive slaves Shadrach (Frederick Wilkins), whose rescue from the slave hunters in Boston had aroused the entire South in 1851, and William Parker, the leader of the "battle" of Christiana, Penn., in 1852, were settlers in Buxton, too.

Delany was surrounded by a breed of colored man he had never really known, citizens of a white man's country with equal legal and suffrage rights; families with a lower illiteracy content except among the new arrivals, for they had their own schools; and only the vestiges of slavery's matriarchal family structure because the man was the breadwinner. He had met Canadian colored before, of course, but only their leaders in the abolitionist crusade, not the farmers, stonemasons, blacksmiths, teachers, and housewives among whom he now lived.

Very quickly Delany was absorbed into their lives and almost immediately was given the responsibility of leadership. We find him delivering a lecture at "Rev. H. J. Young's Church" on March 19, less than a month after his arrival. In the social news fulsomely reported by the *Provincial Freeman*, on April 12 Delany acted as host introducing Amelia Freeman, daughter of his fellow commissioner and Pittsburgh friend Martin H. Freeman, to Chatham colored society. She had taught music, drawing, painting, and other arts at Allegheny Institute where her father was president and now was opening her own school in Chatham. The story continues:

> Whilst making statements of the qualifications of Miss Freeman, we will mention the following pleasing circumstances which took place on Monday evening, at the Villa Mansion, in the apartment of Dr. M. R. Delany. Miss F. was greeted with some welcome tunes from the Union Brass Band, leader Mr. Robert Francis, a celebrated musician, a pupil of the well-known Frank Johnson; the Band played several beautiful pieces and were responded to by some choice pieces from Miss F. on the Melodian (*sic*).

On May 10, Israel D. Shadd himself, publisher of the *Provincial Freeman*, proudly announced that Delany would be an editorial contributor to his newspaper "over his widely known signature." A special series of articles would begin soon, the announcement promised. On July 5 of that same year, Mary Ann Shadd, niece of Israel D. and daughter of Abram W. who settled in the Buxton Settlement with his brother Absolom in 1851, announced the beginning of a series by Delany in the most extravagant terms.

> With the head of a great statesman and the heart of a Howard, the Doctor combines the practical views of one intimately versed in all minor details. He is *the* man for the high position of President of the Board of Commissioners. As a physician his skill is not excelled by any in this town—charges moderately, and should always be well-patronized. His literary reputation is of the highest order; and, as we have the promise of a continuation of the subject, our readers may anticipate a rare treat.

Mary Ann Shadd, who soon married Thomas Cary, one of Delany's emigrationist colleagues, was the Jane Swisshelm of her race. She reported, edited, and lectured for the *Provincial Freeman* at least ten years, practically for the life of the newspaper. Delany delighted in introducing her at lectures and in writing about her, for she personified all that he had expressed concerning the intellectual potential of his people, both female and male. In one of his earliest *Freeman* columns, on July 12, 1856, he is merciless toward Frederick Douglass who wrote an article on the new leadership in Canada, even approving emigration there. "Surely Emigration must be safe, now that Frederick Douglass has spoken in favor of it." Delany then proceeded to blast Douglass:

> Whence comes all at once, all this pretended friendly feeling: Does anyone believe the writer to be sincere? For our part, we frankly admit we have no confidence in it.
>
> Miss Mary Ann Shadd (now Mrs. Cary) is made the special subject of compliment, with traits of talents and literary acquirements, which places her without an equal among the colored ladies of the United States. Is this a recent discovery? Are the talents and acquired ability of Miss Shadd just beginning to develop themselves that this great keen eyed expositor of our "awakened mental abilities" has just discovered them?

Delany paid less and less attention to his critics during the year 1856. He was too busy tasting the fruits of freedom of movement, freedom of speech, and legal equality. He became occupied with the problems of his adopted community and country and attempted to be of service to both. Out of his own successful medical experience in Pittsburgh he offered a four-point program for prevention of an epidemic in June 1856 when a few cases of cholera were discovered. His suggestions were printed in the *Kent Advertiser* and comprise a surprisingly modern individual and community sanitation program.

Almost from the day of arrival, he was swept up by the first victorious assertion of "black political power" on the North American continent. This was the election of the Reform party candidate for Canada West's provincial parliament from Kent County, Archie McKellar.

It was a clear-cut campaign between proponents and opponents of equality for the black fugitives of Canada, for McKellar was a white man who had stepped forward in 1849 to aid Rev. William King against an organized anti-Negro effort to prevent the founding of Buxton Settlement. His opponent was the organizer and fomenter of prejudice among the whites of Kent County, Edwin Larwill, a Chatham politician, tinsmith, and bon vivant. He was the only racist demagogue of consequence in Canadian history and his defeat in the Buxton Settlement dispute was proof to every black man in the country that emancipation in 1793 also meant equal rights of citizenship. Unlike American emancipation of 1863 and the civil rights legislation of the 1960s, the Canadian legislation ending slavery included mandatory enforcement of political and legal equality. King was able to defeat Larwill only because he had the active support of the government headed by the Governor General, Lord Elgin. The organization financing purchase of the Buxton Settlement lands was named the Elgin Association as a result.

But Larwill was a clever politician and represented the Tories in Parliament for several terms. He defeated McKellar, a last-ditch candidate made necessary by a new political subdivision of Kent County, on the basis of an anti-Negro campaign in the 1854 election. His speeches and newspaper articles would qualify him as a most promising candidate for governor of Mississippi, Alabama, or Georgia. He had a large following of voters because color prejudice was strong in Canada West in those years. It came across the border with every white visitor from the United States and every newspaper. It entered Canada through the commercial ties built by new railroads. Larwill had an audience when he preached against the dread "amalgamation" of the races, against the economic burden represented by hungry black fugitives pouring into the province, even the familiar "depreciation of property values" utilized today in opposition to integrated housing in the United States.

However, when Delany arrived in Chatham in 1856, a new voting element had been added, the black men themselves. The first six years of the Fugitive Slave Act had sent so many thousands of black men to Canada West and to Kent County that many had fulfilled the three-year residency requirement for citizenship by 1856. Black men who had been slaves three years before, now had all political as well as legal rights. In the Larwill-McKellar campaign, the Buxton Settlement alone was able to supply 300 votes, all for their friend, of course.

Immediately on his arrival Delany was recruited to organize the black vote for McKellar. Before he himself could vote, he was speaking and writing in behalf of the black man's candidate. His efforts were credited as second only to those of Rev. King in McKellar's decisive victory over Larwill, by 778 votes, a majority that was not exceeded by any candidate for provincial parliament for the next fifty years.

Some of the black leaders with whom Delany worked were, in later years, to assume distinct roles in American history. They all gathered in Canada West for the same reason, to raise their families and continue their particular abolition work. Delany became involved with them as a matter of course, and they joined him in support of his own firm plans for a Black Israel.

William Howard Day, who had fled Cleveland and lived in St. Catherines and London for a time, was now in the Buxton Settlement and active in all of its affairs as well as in the National Board of Commissioners. He too had been alienated by Frederick Douglass and shared with Delany an active dispute with Douglass in the columns of the *Provincial Freeman* while lecturing and raising money for the emigrationist plans. Delany had first met Day in 1848, at the Ohio Colored Convention where he had been chairman of the business committee and Day the convention secretary. They worked together closely and harmoniously, just as they did in Chatham ten years later at a meeting of the National Board of Commissioners.

At approximately the same time that Delany left for Africa, William Howard Day accompanied Rev. King to the British Isles to lecture in behalf of the Buxton Settlement schools. After a most distinguished career with the Freedmen's Aid Association of the Methodist Church and secretary of the AME Zion Church in Maryland and the District of Columbia, Day settled in Harrisburg, Penn., where he died in 1900, an elected member of the city's school board and employee of the state government. Some years after his death, a commemorative service dedicating a gravestone was held in Harrisburg, and W. E. B. DuBois, the controversial black historian, delivered the eulogy. His final words still remain pertinent:

> It is our duty as men and women living in this new day to understand and understand thoroughly what has taken place since the death of William Howard Day and the closing of the 19th century and what is before us in the last half of the 20th century. But doing this, we cannot forget

the full life and real service of this intelligent, busy and unselfish servant of man.

In Canada, Day was one of the many black men who, like Delany, helped John Brown but was out of the country at the time of Harper's Ferry.

Another of the early black activists with whom Delany worked was Thomas W. Stringer, also a settler in Buxton, who had escaped from Mississippi to Ohio and then to Canada. He returned to Mississippi after the Civil War and was the black "whip" of the famous "Black and Tan" Constitutional Convention of 1868. He was active in the AME Church and became general superintendent of all the churches of that Negro sect in the state. He was also a powerful force in Negro Freemasonry, and the Most Worshipful Stringer Grand Lodge in Vicksburg, Miss., was named for him in 1876.

Stringer was not only a good farmer, but a fighter, and his colleagues in Mississippi declared that he had "a genius for organization." In Canada he used that ability in the founding of the British Methodist Episcopal Church in Chatham in 1855 and its expansion throughout Canada West. He too helped John Brown and was a prominent member of the Constitutional Convention in Chatham in May 1858, which preceded Harper's Ferry.

Delany worked with the only Canadian black to join John Brown at Harper's Ferry when he served on a committee, of which Osborne Perry Anderson was secretary. Anderson was one of the few to escape capture in Virginia. He was a printer employed by Israel D. Shadd on the *Provincial Freeman.*

With Thomas F. Cary, Delany served on a committee to rescue the Dawn Institute from the financial morass which closed it. This manual training school begun so hopefully by the Quakers in connection with the colony founded by Rev. Henson ("Uncle Tom") in Dresden, was to be moved to Chatham and financed initially by sale of the lands deeded to it when it was established. Until he left to join John Brown in August 1859, Anderson was active in this effort. However, title to the land was disputed by the British agent sent to unravel the financial mess, and the move was not successful until 1872 when it was renamed the Wilberforce Educational Institute and it flourished for the colored people of Chatham well into the twentieth century.

Another member of this committee and John Brown's Constitutional Convention was the plasterer-poet James Madison Bell, who sought refuge in Chatham in 1854. While Bell's vocation was plastering, which he learned in Cincinnati as a boy, he worked at it only in the summer and autumn. All winter and spring he traveled the northern states to declaim his anti-slavery poetry at abolition meetings. That was how he met John Brown, for Bell eventually traveled from coast to coast plastering and declaiming.

While Bell had no pretensions as to his poetry, he lived to see the publication of his collected works in 1901, with a foreword by Bishop B. W. Arnett of the AME Church. He lived in Toledo, Ohio, until his death in 1902 and was known as the "Bard of Maumee." However poor his poetry has been judged as to technical virtues, its strength was in its unequivocal anti-slavery protests at first and, after the Civil War, in his effort to perpetuate the memory of John Brown.

From his long poem *Triumph of Liberty*, published in 1870, Bell asserted his own analysis of John Brown's motivation, refreshingly simple among the many psychological analyses:

At length he grew to feel inspired
To what his heart had long desired,
To strike one blow for Liberty,
Where it should end in victory;
Though he should perish in the deed,
He felt that he could plant the seed
From which the harvest would arise,
And shrank not from the sacrifice;
Him call enthusiast, if you will,
Fanatic, or something wilder still,
It will not blur his deathless name,
Nor bar his onward march to fame.

In Chatham, Bell joined Delany in almost every one of his efforts for his people, but he had given his greatest dedication to John Brown. The great martyr lived with Bell during his stays in Chatham, at his home on King Street just around the corner from the Villa Mansion where his white comrades stayed.

There were many other men with whom Delany worked—all three of the Shadd brothers; Rev. William G. Munroe, who was president of John Brown's convention; James C. Grant, the schoolteacher; his own treasurer of the National Board of Commissioners, William Lambert; James H. Harris; Alfred Whipple; Matisen F. Bailey; and others recruited by Delany for Brown's cause.

Most of these black men had another strong tie. They, with Delany, were the founding members of St. John's Lodge No. 10 of the Colored Freemasons in Chatham in 1856. As in Pittsburgh, Delany found this fraternal bond a source of strength and comradeship in behalf of the black people. They were men whose personalities were allowed to flower in the atmosphere of Canadian freedom, whose intellectual potential, allowed outlets, was able to develop. They were a close-knit group and, at one time or another, all of them had a part in Delany's emigration program.

During his first year in Chatham, Delany lived and had his office in the Villa Mansion, an early hotel patronized by the colored. It was located in the "downtown" area on William Street opposite the new Great Western Railroad station. Here he transacted the business of the National Board of Commissioners and kept his medical practice, although he also treated patients in the countryside surrounding the bustling town. He was as busy as ever but must have paid more attention to his practice for by February 2, 1857, he was able to pay $1,800 outright for a home.

Known by the schoolchildren nearby as "The Hut," the new Delany home was located high above the north bank of the Thames River, on Murray Street. It was a cottage with approximately an acre of ground and received its name from an addition, a large section with a low-sloping roof. He may have derived the subtitle of *Blake* here where most of it was written. "The Huts of America" pointed emphasis on the living conditions in most slave quarters as contrasted with the comparative luxury of his Canadian "Hut." The low addition served ideally as medical offices, and the family occupied the cottage itself.

The area was favored by the colored for its Negro Baptist Church and, even more, for the excellent colored school taught by the able James C. Grant. The Delany children attended this school and had plenty of playmates among the neighbors. The last three Delany children were born in "The Hut"—Faustin Soulouque, Rameses Placido, and Halle Ethiope.

The eight years in Chatham were to contain the longest stretches of family life that Delany allowed himself. He was busy, but he was home for three full years until his departure for Africa in 1859. He did not hit the abolition trail again, and although he still lectured, his farthest trip on record was to Ingersoll, near London, for an overnight speaking engagement.

Yet Delany did not leave the struggle. His correspondence for the National Board of Commissioners kept him well informed concerning the ferment to the south resulting from the Dred Scott decision. He could see the repercussions himself, on King Street in Chatham, where he met new fugitives, men who had opposed him three years before because they had had faith in America.

In 1857 and 1858 came the events that made John Brown and Harper's Ferry inevitable. President Buchanan salvaged Kansas for the slaveholders after its settlers attempted to adopt a Free State constitution. After that, in late April 1858, John Brown knocked at the door of "The Hut" in search of Martin Delany.

CHAPTER ELEVEN

Insurrection or Africa?

Poets have sung the praises of John Brown; historians have quarreled about him. Particularly, they have brushed aside Delany's own statements concerning Brown's initial plans, as dictated to his biographer.

Harper's Ferry was a culmination of the entire dark decade as well as a prelude to the Civil War. Abolitionists, both black and white, had seen the slaveholders win territory, laws, court decisions, and the self-interest of the masses of American whites while they pursued their course of non-violence. It simply did not work. The prospect of ending slavery receded further and further and, with the Dred Scott decision in 1857, a few among the abolitionists, though very few, were forced to thoughts of a violent attack on slavery. By 1858 the lid blew off the boiling pot and violence was blueprinted by some abolitionists. Harper's Ferry so closely followed one of these plans that John Brown may have adopted it the following year.

Delany's report of John Brown's plans in Canada would be unimportant today, except to historians penetrating a maze, if not for the fact that black nationalists of the 1960s have followed in the paths of their ideological ancestor, Martin Delany. They too have grouped into a separatism envisioned as a black republic within the borders of the United States, as well as international separatism. The first separatism is all that Delany reports as John Brown's intentions when he left Chatham in May 1858 after the Constitutional Convention. Entirely quoted by the biographer is the following, after Delany recognized John Brown on King Street, from Catherine's description of the impressive man who had twice called at "The Hut" for him:

Delany relates that he asked the man if he were "Captain

John Brown of Ossawatomie," scene of the Kansas battle with the slaveholders.

> "I am, sir," was the reply; "and I have come to Chatham expressly to see you, this being my third visit on the errand. I must see you at once, sir," he continued, with emphasis, "and that, too, in private, as I have much to do and but little time before me. If I am to do nothing here, I want to know it at once". "Going directly to the private parlor of a hotel nearby," says Major Delany, "he at once revealed to me that he desired to carry out a great project in his scheme of Kansas emigration, which, to be successful, must be aided and countenanced by the influence of a general convention or council. *That* he was unable to effect in the United States, but had been advised by distinguished friends of his and mine, that, if he could but see me, his object would be attained at once. On my expressing astonishment at the conclusion to which my friends and himself had arrived, with a nervous impatience he exclaimed, 'Why should you be surprised? Sir, the people of the Northern States are cowards; slavery has made cowards of them all. The whites are afraid of each other, and the blacks are afraid of the whites. You can effect nothing among such people,' he added with decided emphasis. On assuring him if a council were all that was desired, he could readily obtain it, he replied, 'That is all; but that is a great deal to me. It is men I want, and not money; money I can get plentiful enough, but no men. Money can come without being seen, but men are afraid of identification with me, though they favor my measure. They are cowards, sir! Cowards!' he reiterated. He then fully revealed his designs. With these I found no fault, but fully favored and aided in getting up the convention."

What were these plans, in addition to their location in Kansas? After calling on his co-workers, Delany gathered a distinguished group and the Constitutional Convention opened at 10 A.M. on May 8, 1858, in the separate colored school on Princess Street Delany told his biographer:

> His plans were made known to them as soon as he was satisfied that the assemblage could be confided in, which

> conclusion he was not long in finding, for with few exceptions, the whole of them were fugitive slaves, refugees in her Britannic Majesty's dominion. His scheme was nothing more than this: To make Kansas, instead of Canada, the terminus of the Underground Railroad; instead of passing off the slave to Canada, to send him to Kansas, and there test, on the soil of the United States territory, whether or not the right to freedom would be maintained where no municipal power had authorized.

This account was dictated nine or ten years later and printed in 1868, and while errors of memory could include dates and numbers, Delany's accuracy concerning the objectives of anything with which he was connected and against slavery cannot be challenged. In his account of the Constitutional Convention Delany says that he gathered up "probably sixty or seventy colored men" although when the constitution was finally adopted on May 10, only 34 colored men signed their names to it with Brown's 11 white men. Others could and did participate in advance meetings. William Howard Day was one such.

Another discrepancy in Delany's account may have been his claim of credit for naming this plan for escaped slaves the "Subterranean Passage Way" (S.P.W.). There exists an old daguerreotype, apparently taken before Chatham, of John Brown with one of his colored stalwarts, John A. Thomas of Springfield, holding a flag with the lettering SPW on it.

Otherwise, Delany's report must be considered valid. Except for the bare minutes of the Constitutional Convention found in John Brown's effects, there is no complete eyewitness report of what was discussed at the meetings. All were sworn to secrecy and, after Harper's Ferry, the question was academic, in a literal sense. The historical dilemma was summarized by the leading authority on John Brown, Boyd B. Stutler of Charleston, W. Va., as a case of Delany telling only half the story.

> I have no doubt that Kansas was discussed as a possible area of settlement by Negroes freed by the movement led by John Brown and that the old S.P.W. of Springfield, Massachusetts days was revived. John Brown was a non-conformist; he could not work under direction; he was always

an individualist and it seems in character that when he took up the cause of the escaped slaves after removing to Springfield that he would attempt organization of his own system, his Underground Railroad was called the Subterranean Pass Way. Whether it ever got into operation in New England has not been established by documentary evidence—in fact, we have only two or three references to the SPW. John Brown may have convinced Delany that he had no violent purpose in mind, but intended to take his men South to run off slaves. A considerable number spirited away would tend to make slavery insecure, but it is questionable how it would serve to bring freedom to the great mass of blacks.

Delany, it is agreed, did recruit and organize the colored men of the convention. Its president was the same presiding officer at both of Delany's emigration conventions in Cleveland in 1854 and 1856, Rev. Munroe. He, with William Howard Day, James Madison Bell, and no doubt others, did serve as recruiters and correspondents for John Brown after the latter's meeting in Revere House, Boston, with the white backers of the Kansas emigration effort, known as the "Secret Six," had delayed all action.

In fact, the *Chatham Tri-Weekly Planet* of October 25, 1859, commented, in its report on Harper's Ferry:

> The most interesting item at least so far as the people of this section are concerned is the fact that Dr. M. R. Delaney (*sic*), well known in Chatham,—as a physician amongst the coloured people, and who a couple of months ago left this place in command of an exploring expedition to Africa—is somewhat implicated in the uprising. It does not appear however that he was intimately associated with old Brown; but from the letter published below—which was taken from a trunk found in the house shortly before being deserted by Brown and his confederates—it would seem that the Doctor is upon pretty good understanding with those who well knew what was going on. Mr. Delany's letter bears date Chatham, C.W., August 16 (1858) and is addressed to J. (John) H. Kagi.

The full letter indicates that Delany was serving in the role of corresponding secretary long after the Constitutional Convention and long before Harper's Ferry.

The SPW plan for Kansas has retained its significance for over a century. Its logic then was as difficult to dispute as the logic of black self-government today. If whites cannot live equitably with blacks in the United States, why not such a separation instead of our *apartheid* into ghettos and rural exploitation? The slaveholders of 1858 could not be defeated in Kansas without a declaration of defiance to the slaveholders and the establishment of black self-government behind the walls of John Brown's special fortifications.

But if John Brown's entire plan was to bring the escaped slaves to Kansas and build a "fortification so simple, that twenty men, without the aid of teams or ordnance, could build in a day" and spot them strategically in the Territory, why all the folderol of a convention and a constitution? There was precedent for that, as Delany revealed to his biographer:

> The whole matter had been well considered and, at first a state government had been proposed, and in accordance a constitution prepared. This was presented to the convention; and here a difficulty presented itself to the minds of some present, that according to American jurisprudence, negroes (*sic*), having no rights respected by white men, consequently could have no right to petition, and none to sovereignty.
>
> Therefore it would be mere mockery to set up a claim as a fundamental right, which in itself was null and void.
>
> To obviate this, and avoid the charge against them as lawless and unorganized, existing without government, it was proposed that an independent community be established within and under the government of the United States, but without the state sovereignty of the compact, similar to the Cherokee nation of Indians, or the Mormons. To these last named, references were made, as parallel cases, at the time. The necessary changes and modifications were made in the constitution, and with such it was printed. (The printing was arranged by William Howard Day in St. Catherines.)

The biographer continues: "This, he (Delany) says, was the plan and purpose of the Canada Convention. Whatever changed them to Harper's Ferry was known only to Captain Brown, and perhaps to Kagi, who had the honor of being deeper in his confidence than anyone else."

There is small doubt that such a plan, rather than a Harper's Ferry, would meet with Delany's entire approval. Self-government and self-determination for the blacks were what he himself had sought since his first wide-eyed exposure to black self-expression in the early 1830s. Now, approximately 25 years later, a white man was proposing a method whereby the blacks would seize upon a battleground not yet a part of the Union and govern themselves. He could even accept the controversial Article 46 and its compromise language, for America had been founded in the triumphant call for liberty and equality for all, though it had been diverted from that lofty ideal as a nation.

> Article XLVI. *These Articles not for the Overthrow of Government*—The foregoing articles shall not be construed so as in any way to encourage the overthrow of any State Government, or of the General Government of the United States, and look to no dissolution of the Union, but simply to amendment and repeal, and our flag shall be the same that our fathers fought under in the Revolution.

This was the sum total of Delany's ideological commitment to John Brown in that fateful year of 1858. He could not agree to a Harper's Ferry, but there is proof in his novel *Blake,* which he was then beginning to write, that Delany knew all the ramifications of slave insurrection, perhaps better than John Brown did.

Delany was one of those intensely interested in a rising of the slaves and, before the end of 1858, he had ready for publication the first chapters of *Blake: or Huts of America,* A *Tale of the Mississippi Valley, the Southern United States and Cuba.* This was a tale of insurrection, planned and organized. It was not a noble gesture like Harper's Ferry.

Until 1970 *Blake* was never published as a book, despite its real contributions, not to literature, but to a knowledge of the slaves. As Dr. Floyd J. Miller expresses in his Foreword:

"But *Blake* is more than merely a socio-historical account of Southern slavery and Cuban society in the 1850's. It serves, as Delany obviously intended it to do, as the vehicle for the expression of a racial philosophy as radical today as when originally conceived."

That is true, and more. *Blake* has great value in the hero's many lectures—which were Delany's of course—on the characteristics individuals acquired under slavery and the practical methodology of escaping to freedom. In each of the lectures Henry was speaking to the slaves themselves, explaining their fears to them, outlining the stratagems by which the slaveowner could be outwitted and, above all, giving them the revelation that they too represented a piece of society worthy of self-pride. Like *Condition and Elevation, Blake* is an invaluable source of the conditions and thinking of his times, dressed up in literary form.

Originally, it was serialized in the *Anglo-African Magazine* from January to July 1859 and halted after thirty chapters while Delany went to Africa. The balance of nearly eighty chapters was serialized in 1861 and 1862 in the new *Weekly Anglo-African.* After a century of belief that they did not exist they were found by Dr. Miller who expresses the belief that about eight more chapters exist in unfound issues of the *Weekly Anglo-African.*

Delany's valuable observations, presented in dramatic form concern not only the sometimes strange habits of the slave but the equally strange practices of the slaveowners. And he contributes some revelations concerning the accustomed white hypocrisy as shown in their institutions such as churches.

As an example, Delany has Henry stress to each and every slave he names as the key man of the plantation to lead the insurrection, that liberty had its price in hard cash. "Money alone will carry you through the *White* mountains or across the *White* rivers to liberty," and he provides enough incidents during escapes to prove that bribery opens the "White gap" to the North Star among the most ardent pro-slavery men. But how does a slave obtain hard cash?

> The money is within all of their reach if they only knew it was right to take it. God told the Egyptian slaves to "borrow from their neighbors"—meaning their oppressors "all

> their jewels"—meaning to take their money and wealth wherever they could lay hands upon it, and depart from Egypt. So you must teach them to take all the money they can get from their masters, to enable them to make the strike without a failure. I'll show you when we leave for the North; what money will do for you, right here in Mississippi. Bear this in mind; it is your *certain* passport through the *white gap* as I term it.

As for John Brown, the Lysander Spooners, and the few others who hoped for a slave insurrection, in 1858 while writing *Blake*, Delany had decided opinions regarding the slave potential for an uprising. When Henry's party is captured by whites in Indiana due to betrayal by a black man, the latter declares: "We make our livin' by da white folks, an' mus' do what da tell us." Of course, their providential escape is engineered by Henry's ingenuity and bravery.

Delany also believed that the slaves were deluded by their masters in many ways: " 'Tis this confounded good treatment and expectation of getting freed by their oppressors, that has been the curse of the slave. All shrewd masters, to keep their slaves in check, promise them their freedom at their, the master's death, as though they were certain to die first. This contents the slave, and makes him obedient and willing to serve and toil on, looking forward to the promised redemption." And when his fellow-plotters expressed their lack of sympathy for such naive docility, Henry warns them: "As you know, I'll do anything not morally wrong, to gain our freedom; and to effect this, we must take the slaves, not as we wish them to be but as we really find them to be."

Organized religion (as a church, not a faith) Delany writes in *Blake* is still another deception practiced upon the slave to keep him docile. In New Orleans, when his inspired listeners asked him to lead them in prayer, his response was: "If I ever were a Christian, slavery has made me a sinner; if I had been an angel, it would have made me a devil. I feel more like cursing than praying—may God forgive me. Pray for me, brethren."

In Havana, the ladies among his insurrectionists ask a question: "As a Catholic, can I enter this work of emancipation?" Henry's reply was an honest one by Delany, for he was a man of faith, in favor of a religion shared equally by blacks.

I, first a Catholic, and my wife bred as such, are both Baptists. Abyssa Sondan once a pagan was in her town in her own native land, converted to the Methodist or Weslyan (*sic*) belief. Madame Sebastian and family are Episcopalians. Camina from long residence out of the colony is a Presbyterian and Placido a believer in the Swedenborgian doctrines. We have all agreed to know no sect, no denomination and but one religion for the sake of our redemption from bondage and degradation—a faith in a common Saviour as an intercessor for our sins, but one God who is and must be an acknowledged common Father. No religion but that which brings us liberty will we know, no God but He who owns us as His children will we serve. The whites accept of nothing but that which promotes their interests and happiness, socially, politically and religiously. They would discard a religion, tear down the church, overthrow a government or desert a country which did not enhance their freedom. In God's great and righteous name, are we not willing to do the same?

Our ceremonies are borrowed from no denomination, creed or church, no existing organization, secret, secular or religious, but originated by ourselves, adapted to our own conditions, circumstances and wants, founded upon the eternal word of God our Creator as impressed upon the tablet of each of our hearts. Will this explanation suffice, women of Cuba, sisters in oppression with us? Are you satisfied to act and go our own way regardless of aping our oppressors indiscriminately?

With this argument, Delany gives Placido the recitation of a prayer:

O Great Jehovah, God of Love
Thou monarch of the earth and sky,
Canst thou, from thy great throne above
Look down with an unpitying eye!
See Africa's sons and daughters toil
Day after day, year after year
Upon this blood bemoistened soil
And to their cries turn a deaf ear?
Canst thou the white oppressor bless

With verdant hills and fruitful plains,
Regardless of the slave's distress—
Unmindful of the black man's chains?

How long, Oh Lord, ere thou wilt speak
In thy Almighty thundering voice
To bid the oppressors fetters break,
And Ethiopia's sons rejoice?
How long shall slavery's iron grip
And prejudice's guilty hand
Send forth like bloodhounds from the ship
Foul persecutions o'er the land?
How long shall puny mortals dare
To violate Thy just decree
And force Thy fellow men to wear
The galling chains by land and sea?

Hasten, Oh Lord! the glorious time
When everywhere beneath the skies
From every land and every clime
Paeans to Liberty shall rise!
When the bright sun of Liberty
Shall shine o'er each despotic land
And all mankind from bondage free
Adore the wonders of Thy hand!

Still another of the evidences he presented which would militate against wide participation by slaves in an insurrection was the extermination of all rebellious spirit by use of the "professional whipper." As one slaveowner describes the result of turning his slave over to a "whipper": "He's completely broken, sir, and as humble as a dog. The last chastisement that Goodman gave, completely reduced him, taking out the last remnant of his manhood, so that he's as spiritless as a kitten."

The reasons for use of the professional slave trainer stems from one of the concomitants of a slaveholding prosperity. That "gracious" Southern way of life still sung in aristocratic circles had its aura of horror, and Delany described it well in *Blake*.

Few people in the world lead such a life as the white inhabitants of Cuba, and those of the South now comprising the

Southern Confederacy of America. A dreamy existence of the most fearful apprehensions of dread, horror and dismay; suspicion and distrust, jealousy and envy continually pervade the community; and Havana, New Orleans, Charleston or Richmond may be thrown into consternation by an idle expression of the most trifling or ordinary ignorant black. A sleeping wake, or waking sleep, a living death or tormented life is that of the Cuban and American slaveholder. For them there is no safety. A criminal in the midst of a powder bin with a red hot pigot of iron in his hand, which he is compelled to hold and char the living flesh to save his life, or let it fall to relieve him from torture, and thereby incur instantaneous destruction, nor the inhabitants of a house on the brow of a volcano could not exist in greater torment than these most unhappy people.

Of the two classes of these communities, the master and slave, the blacks have everything to hope for and nothing to fear, since let what may take place, their redemption from bondage is inevitable. They must and will be free; whilst the whites have everything to fear and nothing to hope for. "God is just, and his justice will not sleep forever."

Among the many aspects of Delany revealed by *Blake* is his kinship with so many other of the black nationalists whose emotional outlet was poetry. Here and there through a lifetime of writing, Delany injected verse to make his point, but in *Blake* he joins so many others among his colleagues, James Whitfield, James Madison Bell, George Boyer Vashon, Mary Ann Shadd Cary, and others whose verse was the most effective means of release from frustration. Perhaps they did not write great poetry, or maybe they did. The literary pundits have paid them no mind, having in hand the Paul Lawrence Dunbars, Phillis Wheatleys, and others of the past, as well as today's great black poets. That the black man must sing his woes and his joys differs in no way from the early Jew or the early Christian singing his incantation against persecution.

The prayers in *Blake* are only one kind of poetry Delany wrote. He also wrote verse when he wanted to evoke the strongest passions of the reader. An example is the discussion of America as the world's best slave market and the slave trade's illegal entry via Key West, quite without hindrance by the forces of law and order. Key West is described as

A place where demons daring land—
Fiends in bright noonday—and sit
A hellish conclave band to barter
The sons and daughters of our land away.

When Henry sails for Africa on the slave ship *Vulture,* he is the natural leader of the black crew, and of course any clipper must have a chanteyman or two in a novel of that day. The crew sings, in defiance of the white skipper and slave traders:

I'm a goin' to Afrika
Where de white man dare not stay;
I ketch him by de collar,
Den de white man holler;
I hit 'im on de pate
Den I make him blate!
I seize 'im by de throat—
Land!—he beller like a goat.

A love of country, too, caused Delany pain through all of his emigrationist activities, which he shared with the free and fugitive blacks who decided to leave America for freedom. When he wrote *Blake* he wrote the following for himself too:

My country, the land of my birth,
  Farewell to thy fetters and thee!
The by-word of tyrants—the scorn of the earth,
  A mockery to all thou shalt be!
Hurra, for the sea and its waves!
  Ye billows and surges, all hail!
My brothers henceforth—for ye scorn to be slaves
  As ye toss up your crests to the gale.
Farewell to the land of the blood-hound and chain,
  My path is away o'er the fetterless main!

Delany told also of love and loved ones. And how else but in poetry? Few romanticists equaled the words of the young and "Unhappy Cornelia," dated March 14, 1853, in the story.

How sweet at close of silent eve
The harp's responsive sound;
How sweet the vows that ne'er deceive,
And deeds by virtue crowned!
How sweet to sit beneath a tree
In some delightful grove;
But oh! more soft, more sweet to me,
The voice of him I love!

Delany wrote many poems of protest for *Blake*, short, pithy, descriptive poems, as well as long denunciatory pieces. Perhaps the song of Placido commemorating the completed plans for insurrection and their mood while awaiting their D-day should be selected as the essence of Delany's own impatience. He too was tired of waiting for the millennium. In Cuba as well as the United States he claimed a moral justification for an uprising.

All of his past hopes, frustrations, fears, and his own doubts of the future are in the poem:

If thou will soothe my burning brain
  Sing not to me of joy and gladness;
'Twill but increase the raging pain
  And turn the fever into madness!
Sing not to me of landscapes bright
  Of fragrant flowers and fruited trees,
Of azure skies and mellow light,
  Or whispering of the gentle breeze.
But tell me of the tempest roaring
  Across the angry foaming deep,
Of torrents from the mountain pouring,
  Down precipices dark and deep.
Sing of the lightning's lurid flash,
  The ocean's road, the howling storm,
The earthquake's shock, the thunder's crash,
  Where ghastly terrors teeming swarm.

Sing of the battle's deadly strife,
  The ruthless march of war and pillage;
The awful waste of human life,
  The plunder'd town, the burning village;
Of streets with human gore made red,

Of priests upon the altar slain,
The scenes of rapine, woe and dread,
That fill the warrior's horrid train.
The song may then an echo wake,
Deep in the soul, long crush'd and sad,
The direful impression shake,
Which threatens now to drive me mad.

But by the time this poem was in print, Delany had dedicated himself to Africa. By 1859, Harper's Ferry, the first threats of secession, and the cries of both black and white abolitionists of "Union Forever" at whatever cost to the black man, he was convinced that this would be a white man's fight, not for emancipation but for political hegemony. And so Henry bows out of the conflict with his final words, "Woe be unto those devils of whites, I say!"

This was printed on April 26, 1862, after the start of the Civil War, after the bloody forecast made in his poem. But it was still a white man's war, and Martin Delany was among many blacks who were turned away from the white man's door, including Abraham Lincoln's, when they begged a chance to strike a blow against the slaveholders. It would have been the time for the slave insurrection, for the free black men of the North to lead their brethren of the South.

But by then Martin Delany was a new man. He had been to Africa. He had led the first party of scientific exploration to Africa from the American continent, all black manned and black financed. He preceded a white army of anthropologists, ethnologists, and entrepreneurs who were to pour into Africa from all continents. When Delany found Abeokuta, David Livingston was finding Lake Nyasa.

The question arises: Was Delany sufficiently knowledgeable as a scientist in 1857 to lead an expedition? The probability was that his curiosity in the natural sciences was as all-embracing as that of any investigator of his day, white or black. Students of philosophy sought answers in the earth, waters, and skies around them, and there were few "specialists" in any of the sciences—medical, chemical, or physical.

Delany never lost his fascination with the unexplained mysteries of electricity. In Pittsburgh, during the latter part of his years as a "bleeder" he advertised himself as a "Galvanizer," and used electrical energy to scarify the flesh of his patients before bleeding them. It may have been a novelty, a "sales" gadget, or in Delany's belief a valid technique. However, his interest in electricity began then and is evidenced in the February and August 1859 issues of the *Anglo-African Magazine,* which not only contained installments of *Blake* but also speculation on the almost unknown cosmic theories. This was perhaps the strangest diversity of any author publishing in those years and it poses a curious contrast. The fiction in *Blake* is founded in absolute knowledge and was probably less fictional than his scientific sorties. For instance, in the February issue Delany writes on "Comets." He asks what they are and states that "as yet there has not been a plausible theory adduced upon which to settle an opinion."

His own theory is that electricity was responsible. "A comet must be a great sphere of electric fire in a constant state of action, which, like the nucleus termed a 'thunder bolt' flies darting, blazing and sparkling through space, leaving far behind streams of electricity similar to lurid flashes of lightning amidst the darkness of clouds." He cited a comet of the prior year which was "calculated by some learned men at 65 million miles in length. . . . No other force than that of electricity could possibly be the motive power which impels them on with such speed. . . . The purpose of comets would seem to be to distribute electricity throughout universal space . . . and thereby giving life, action, health, and vigor to both animate and inanimate creation. Thus then are comets, the source and fountain from which come supplies of electricity:

> Giving motion to the seas—
> Power to the breeze,
> Excitement to vegetation,
> And stimulus to animation . . .

His theories on the orderly management of the planetary system are presented less poetically in "The Attraction of the Planets," another article that ran concurrently with the last of the thirty chapters of *Blake* in the *Anglo-African Magazine.* He found that the solar system is nicely arranged as a result of the action and interaction of the electrical negativity and positivity alternately possessed by the planets in relationship with each other. His article explains this at length and possibly in the scientific jargon of the day. He concludes: "Doubtless this theory will be disputed like all new discoveries, provided those who are competent deign to notice it; but should it receive a verdict of a 'bill of ignoramus', that will not prevent intelligent minds from reflection."

Apparently, few "deigned" to notice except Delany's old rival Frederick Douglass who wrote in his *Monthly* that the *Anglo-African Magazine* was a most praiseworthy effort to present the intellectual efforts of the colored people. "Martin R. Delany has chosen a lofty subject. He has given a peculiar theory, ascribing to electricity the office of keeping the heavenly bodies in order which other very able men have ascribed to the law of gravitation. Mr. Delany dismisses all our fears that this firm old earth of ours is to be smashed one of these coming days by a collision with any other body in space."

But by then Martin Delany was too busy preparing for a scientific exploration of Africa to bother with Douglass. In that uncertain year, 1858, he was the outstanding example among the black leadership of a man who knew where he was going.

CHAPTER TWELVE

Mission to Africa

There were two major reasons why Delany was one of the few black leaders not confused by the turmoil of 1858. He was, perhaps, the best informed of all black leaders in either the United States or Canada. His correspondence, begun in 1853, was now international in scope, and voluminous. In addition, he had arrived at his convictions over five years before. He had assayed the black chances for a future in the United States and found none.

That is why the Dred Scott decision did not unsettle him. In the United States it had created a mixed havoc of dismay, despair, fighting rage, and resigned hopelessness among the abolitionists. To Delany, the Supreme Court action merely stamped an obvious fact with the white man's rationale that all violations of professed ideals must have legal approval. The decision changed nothing except the self-delusion of the abolitionists, white and black. To Delany, the appeal by Frederick Douglass was a patented gesture of futility. "Abolitionists! return to your principles! Come back, and do your first work over again. Make the slave first, midst and last. Follow no longer the partial and side issues; strike for the abolition of slavery." As ever, Douglass preached his truisms beautifully and neglected methodology.

But black leadership in the United States was too shocked and confused to heed any single voice, and they scrambled in all directions. That was understandable, for the whites now held a whip over every black in the land, free or slave. If no black could be a citizen, then all blacks were subject to any disposition the whites chose—enslavement, deportation, confinement to reservations like the Indians, confiscation of hard-won property, forced labor, or any variations of these suited to legislative whim. There could be no appeal, for now they were aliens in the land of their birth. Small wonder that they found no single path. In New Bedford, Mass., it was desperation instead of his proven courage that caused Charles Lenox Remond to call again for anti-slavery help in fomenting insurrection among the slaves. It was fear of even greater reprisals than legalized loss of citizenship that caused the Massachusetts convention of colored men to vote him down.

In New Haven, Rev. James Theodore Holly once more pleaded for an immediate exodus to Haiti, a black man's country. In Cleveland, O., J. D. Harris led formation of the Central America Land Company in order to purchase a refuge, because "We believe it to be the destiny of the colored race to occupy the tropics of America." As for Canada: "The government drives us to Canada," Harris said, "where we are indeed free, but where it is plain we cannot become a very great people. We want more room, where it is not quite so cold—we want to be identified with the ruling power of a nation; and unless this be obtained, Canada must be looked to as a strong military post for future use, in the very vitals of America."

But that kind of action and that kind of talk was disputed by Harris' fellow black Ohioans. In a state convention in Cincinnati a majority clung to the "right is might" slogans and adopted the following resolution:

> *Resolved,* (4) That we say to those who would induce us to emigrate to Africa or elsewhere, that the amount of labor and self-sacrifice required to establish a home in a foreign land, would if exercised here, redeem our native land from the grasp of slavery; therefore we are resolved to remain where we are, confident that "truth is mighty and will prevail."

In Washington, and later speeches outside of Congress, Rep. Francis P. Blair of Missouri led a fractional House group in a move for Federal support, financial and otherwise, for voluntary Negro settlement in Central America or the West Indies. Holly and Whitfield reacted immediately and begged Blair for the government largesse. Delany sent the Congressman a copy of his "Political Destiny," but pursued it no further because it was the worst kind of "white" money offered, governmental. This would signify a colony, not a Black Israel to Delany.

For the same reason, Delany refused to join Henry Highland Garnet, another tested and true black fighter, in the African Civilization Society, founded that year. Garnet had come the full cycle, like so many others. In 1848 he declared, in opposition to emigration: "We are now colonized. We are planted here and we cannot as a whole be colonized back to the fatherland." Ten years later, before an organizing meeting of the African Civilization Society, Garnet said: "Let those who wish to stay, stay here, and let those who have enterprise and wish to go, go and found a nation, of which the colored American can be proud."

Neither Delany nor Garnet ever considered a mass migration of American Negroes possible. Their plans for sending an elite corps of skilled black men and women to Africa in order to lead the natives into economic ascendancy, political independence, and international importance by capture of the cotton markets were, in substance, the same. Both considered this a path toward abolition by ending the slave trade and its U.S. market.

But the essential difference that kept these two sincere men of identical convictions apart for years was the fact that Garnet willingly accepted the benefactions of whites for his African Civilization Society. His most prominent supporter was Benjamin Coates of Philadelphia, the colonizationist. Eventually, several whites were to assume offices in the African Civilization Society.

Delany's suspicions of white domination as the price of white financial support apparently were justified in the case of Benjamin Coates. As a result of his influence, any colonization scheme through the African Civilization Society would be another Liberia. Delany may not have known it at the time and his opposition to Coates may have stemmed only from his distrust of all whites, but there is evidence that the wealthy Philadelphian had plans not known to Garnet.

When the scandal of the slave ship *Regina Coeli* broke in the summer of 1858, it was to Benjamin Coates that former President Roberts of Liberia reported. He denied both the French and British assertions that the French slaver had picked up 271 native Africans in Liberia through bribery of then President

Benson. It came to world attention when the natives mutinied and took the ship into a British port. This report to Coates is dated from Monrovia on October 9, 1858, at the very time the latter was lending all his influence to assist Garnet. There is still another letter from Coates to Rev. R. R. Gurley, secretary of the American Colonization Society, dated January 13, 1859, at the height of opposition to Delany's own African plans. Coates wrote:

> Africa is at present attracting considerable attention from our Colored people. It is very difficult for them to get over their old and deep prejudices against the "Colonization Society" so that the very word "colonization" gives umbrage but they are gradually getting over it—the Civilization movements based on anti-slavery principles has taken so well that there are numbers now wishing to go to Gouraba (Yoruba) at once— But as this cannot be I have advised them to go to Liberia and I am inclined to think that a great many in the spring will conclude to do so. . . . If any of your friends have had any doubts in regard to the good results of this new civilization movement, you may assure them that it has already created more interest in Liberia as well as in Gouraba than has ever been entertained before. . . . Many consider the African Civilization Society only African Colonization under another name which it really is, except that it professes to be anti-slavery.

As for the Garrisonian clique of abolitionists, chiefly white, their actual anti-slavery bankruptcy was jabbed into their consciousness by a new black voice, that of Dr. John S. Rock of Boston, the brilliant physician and lawyer, the first black attorney to be admitted to practice before the U.S. Supreme Court. On the same platform with him on March 5, 1858, were William Lloyd Garrison himself, Wendell Phillips, Theodore Parker, and Charles Lenox Remond. While at one and the same time the Garrisonians were advocating political action in the new Republican party they were subscribing to a "preserve the Union at any cost" campaign, a cost inevitably borne by the Negro. Dr. Rock must have bled them a bit with his analysis of their values.

> In this country, where money is the great sympathetic nerve which ramifies society, and has a ganglia in every

> man's pocket, a man is respected in proportion to his success in business. When the avenues of wealth are opened to us, we will then become educated and wealthy, and then the roughest looking colored man that you ever saw, or ever will see, will be pleasanter than the harmonies of Orpheus, and black will be a very pretty color. It will make our jargon, wit—or words, oracles; flattery will then take the place of slander, and you will find no prejudice in the Yankee whatever. . . . Then, and not till then, will we be able to enjoy true equality, which can exist only among peers.

And while all of these divisions among blacks and whites were being articulated, there was still another speech, among the many made by Abraham Lincoln in 1858 when he was debating Stephen A. Douglas in Illinois. His "House Divided" speech of June 16 is quoted in textbooks but without questioning a personal preference left unanswered in the words: "I do not expect the Union to be dissolved; I do not expect the house to be divided. It will become all one thing, or all the other." Such lack of commitment was scant comfort to abolitionists of both complexions, but they soon forgot their brave cries of "No Union with slaveholders" and accepted the Republicans as the least of all evils.

In Canada, the only question dividing the colored was not whether, but where to establish a black country. Delany had not changed his convictions. He was still for his Black Israel in Africa, and his plans were now concrete. Once again, as in 1853, when he made his plans public, he called down upon himself the wrath of many black leaders and the unforeseen support of hitherto inarticulate individuals and groups. The artist Robert Douglass of Philadelphia was one of the first to volunteer for the exploration of Africa. There was a black group in Madison, Wisconsin, headed by the well-to-do grocer Jonathan J. Myers, which subscribed both allegiance and finances to Delany.

He himself reports, in outlining the genesis of the Niger Valley expedition, that his correspondence with individuals throughout the United States, specifically on African emigration, had begun in 1856. He wrote:

> The Convention (at Cleveland, 1854) in its Secret Sessions made Africa, with its rich, inexhaustible productions, and

> great facilities for checking the abominable Slave Trade, its most important point of independence, though each individual was left to take the direction which in his judgment best suited him. . . . *Africa was held in reserve.*

In 1858 Delany took Africa out of reserve and began a black odyssey. Characteristically, he first set up the authority for the enterprise and then its machinery. As usual too he demanded, and was given, supreme authority as well as sole responsibility for the entire African program, including financial. All of this was accomplished at successive meetings with the leaders of the National Board of Commissioners in Chatham.

On August 4–7, 1858, he called the third emigration convention and, at the election of officers of the National Board of Commissioners, had himself replaced as president by William Howard Day. He assumed the post of Foreign Secretary which had been held by Rev. Martin H. Freeman of Allegheny City since the 1856 Emigration Convention. There was no conflict at all over the change. Rev. Freeman was then the first head of Avery College and was too much involved for Africa. He wrote to Delany in April of that year:

> I am more and more convinced that Africa is the country to which all colored men who wish to attain the full stature of manhood, and bring up their children to be men and not creeping things, should turn their steps; and I feel more and more every day, that I made a great mistake in not going there, when I was untrammelled by family ties, and had the opportunity.

At the 1858 convention, all commissioners from the ten states were re-elected and all officers of the Central Board were from Chatham or nearby Canadian points. Less than a month later, on August 30, there was an executive council meeting of the Central Board which accomplished Delany's next step. It was a resolution "That Dr. Martin R. Delany, of Chatham, Kent County, Canada West, be a Commissioner to explore in Africa, with full power to choose his own colleagues." He was in command of the African Commission.

Once this was adopted, Delany then presented the council

with his selection of personnel, which also was adopted, and with his statement of the purpose of the African mission. He named his group a Scientific Corps under the name of "The Niger Valley Exploring Party."

> The object of this Expedition is to make a Topographical, Geological and Geographical Examination of the Valley of the River Niger, in Africa, and an inquiry into the state and condition of the people of that Valley, and other parts of Africa, together with such other scientific inquiries as may by them be deemed expedient, for the purposes of science and for general information; and without any reference to, and with the Board being entirely opposed to any Emigration there as such. Provided, however, that nothing in this instrument be so construed as to interfere with the right of the Commissioners to negotiate in their own behalf, or that of any other parties, or organization, for territory.
>
> The Chief-Commissioner is hereby authorized to add one or more competent Commissioners to their number; it being agreed and understood that this organization is, and is to be exempted from the pecuniary responsibility of sending out this Expedition.
>
> Dated, at the Office of the Executive Council, Chatham, county of Kent, Province of Canada, this Thirtieth day of August, in the year of our Lord, One Thousand Eight Hundred and Fifty-eight.
>
> By the President,
> William Howard Day
> Isaac D. Shadd, Vice-President
> George W. Brodie, Secretary

The entire procedure was quite in keeping with Delany's orderly methods, but it did not relieve him from a multitude of problems. He had the delegated authority of his organization, it is true, but in the United States both the organization and Delany's qualifications for such an expedition were challenged. He had the authority to select his own colleagues for the exploration, and those selections were severely criticized. He was, as usual, without funds for such an ambitious undertaking and would accept no money from whites. That left him with a handful of wealthy blacks and his own fund-raising abilities as resources.

In his official report to the National Board of Commissioners dated in Chatham on February 15, 1861, Delany comments on these early organizing difficulties, but with little animus. His attitude seems to have been "I did it in spite of them," and he resorts to derision. For instance, when the project and its personnel were made public

> There arose at once from mistaken persons (white) in Philadelphia, a torrent of opposition, who presuming to know more about us (the blacks) and our own business than we did ourselves, went so far as to speak to one of our party, and tell him that we were *not ready* for any such *important* undertaking, nor could be in *three years yet to come*. Of course, as necessary to sustain this, it was followed up with a dissertation on the *disqualification* of the Chief of the Party, mentally and physically, *external* appearances and all.

The "one of our party" suborned by the Philadelphians was Robert Campbell, the highly capable chemist and head of the science department of the Institute for Colored Youth in Philadelphia. He had agreed to go with Delany, but the monetary prospects were none too bright. Campbell, therefore, accepted African Civilization Society money to leave early for England in order to raise money for the expedition. Campbell issued a circular from Manchester, England, on May 15, 1859, asking for monetary gifts for the exploration. On this, Delany had no restraint.

> Grant, for charity's sake, that it was done with the best of motives, it was flagrantly and fatally at variance with every principle of intelligent—to say nothing of enlightened—organizations among civilized men, and in perfect harmony with that mischievous interference by which the enemies of our race have ever sought to sow discord among us, to prove a natural contempt for the Negro and repugnance to his leadership, then taunt us with incapacity for self-government. . . . I drop every reflection and feeling of un-

> pleasantness toward my young brother Campbell, who, being a West Indian, probably did not understand those *white Americans*, and formed his opinion of American *blacks* and their capacity to "lead", from the estimate they set upon them.

It could be that Delany's charitable words for Campbell were written before he saw the dedication of the latter's report of the expedition entitled "A Pilgrimage to My Motherland." The original edition expressed gratitude to the contributors in America and England, "but particularly to BENJAMIN COATES of Philadelphia, whose unremitting efforts contributed in no small degree to the success of the enterprise." He also selected Henry Christy, the famous London hat maker, for special gratitude.

Nor could Delany have known that in the midst of his own discouraging efforts in New York to raise money for the expedition among blacks that both Campbell and another of the commissioners he had chosen, James W. Purnell, sought help directly from the American Colonization Society.

Over their signatures there is a letter dated February 17, 1859, and addressed to Dr. Harvey Lindsly of Washington, D.C., chairman of the Executive Committee of the American Colonization Society. After describing their plans to "avail themselves of the advice and experience of the authorities of Liberia before they enter upon their work" they conclude:

> This measure has the hearty endorsement of the friends of African Colonization both in Philadelphia and New York, and the Board of Directors of the Society at Philadelphia has made an appropriation toward it. The object which brings us to Washington is to solicit pecuniary and other aid for this enterprise, and it is with the same end we also address you, knowing too that your endorsement will greatly facilitate our work here.

Delany could not have known of this letter, which did not mention his name, or else he was quite a hypocrite in his *Official Report* when he wrote:

> And of Mr. Jas. W. Purnell—who met me in New York two weeks after my arrival, and through the whole eight months of adversity and doubtful progress, stood by me, performing the duty of Secretary, writing in every direction, copying and from dictation for hours at a time, I cannot say too much.

All of the preliminary and behind-the-scenes conflict did have a serious effect on Delany's plans. "Our preparatory progress was not only seriously retarded (I having to spend eight months in New York city to counteract the influence, where six weeks only would have been required) but three years originally intended to be spent in exploring had to be reduced to one, and the number of Commissioners from five to two." At no time does Delany blame Henry Highland Garnet, who was nominal head of the African Civilization Society and, by the end of 1859, its only black officer. Delany blamed only the white colonizationists who were part of the American Colonization Society and would battle any black effort in that area.

He went to Africa anyway, sailing from New York on May 24, 1859, aboard the bark *Mendi*, owned by three Liberian blacks, all formerly from New York City.

Delany's expedition—poverty-stricken and undermanned as it was—still was the first exploration of any part of Africa to set out from American shores. There had been American missionaries and travelers, all of them whites financed by churches or by their own wealth. There had been emigrants sent by the American Colonization Society and other blacks who financed their own removal from the United States, but most went to Liberia. None had Delany's purpose of founding a country as a part of a *weltpolitik* of, by, and for blacks, and none had his ability to observe, analyze, and report scientifically concerning his findings. None, of course, was as free as Delany to pursue his objectives, for all of his commitments were made to black men in the United States and Canada. His *Official Report*, despite its infrequent lapses into Delany's personality and the chip on his shoulder, is a solid and comprehensive survey of what he found in a year of travel in Liberia and the western portion of the Niger River Valley, the Yoruba country. The last words of his report summarize his personal reaction to the wonder of what he calls his "Fatherland." "I return of course, to Africa, with my family."

These personal references in the *Official Report* are far more important today than Delany's factual summaries of the economics, mores, and problems he found. The latter were important for the emigrationists of his day, but Delany's major conclusion, that "Africa for the Africans" should be the first and last commandment for any black has contemporary meaning. The very slogan itself, coined by Delany, was adopted by succeeding generations of disillusioned American blacks who watched the colonization and exploitation of Africa. Marcus Garvey, leader of the "back to Africa" movement among American Negroes in the 1920s, was to center his efforts on that same slogan and it has been the key motivation for recent explosive events on the continent.

But Delany was there in 1859–1860, before Africa's natural wealth and easily exploited labor drew the conquering white armies of colonization from Europe. He was the first to suggest that Christianization of the continent was not enough. After giving full credit to the white missionaries he met, for instance, Delany suggests that "missionary duty has reached its *ultimatum*."

> Religion has done its work, and now requires temporal and secular aid to give it another impulse. The improved arts of civilized life must now be brought to bear, and go hand in hand in aid of the missionary efforts which are purely religious in character and teaching. . . . But it is very evident that the social must keep pace with the religious, and the political with the social relations of society, to carry out the great measures of the higher civilization.

Delany had every opportunity to meet the people of Western Africa, from the most primitive to the most enlightened. He was made welcome not only by the rulers but by the residents of the jungle villages through which he passed. The reason was his blackness, as deep in hue as that of any African. Campbell, a light mulatto, did not receive the same acceptance. The West Africans related him to the darker-colored Portuguese and Arabic slave hunters and traders, and distrusted whites generally.

Such distrust arose, according to Delany, as a result of the black African experience in adopting the white man's civilizing influences and discarding his ancient tribal customs. What had happened to those who followed the missionary leadership?

> And so the African *reasonably* reasons when he sees that despite his having yielded up old-established customs, the laws of his fathers, and almost his entire social authority, and the rule of his household to the care and guardianship of the missionary, for the sake of acquiring his knowledge and power—when, after having learned all that his children can, he is doomed to see them sink right back into their old habits, the country continue in the same condition, without the beautiful improvements of the white man—and if a change take place at all, he is doomed to witness what he never expected to see and dies regretting—himself and his people entangled in the meshes of the government of a people foreign in kith, kin and sympathy, when he and his are entirely shoved aside and compelled to take subordinate and inferior positions, if not, indeed, reduced to menialism and bondage.

In other words, in "civilized" Africa, the position of the blacks was no different from that in "civilized" America where the free blacks were allowed to educate themselves, only to arrive at the same stone wall—for what purpose? Because of this experience, to the educated African, "All seem dark and gloomy for the future, and he has his doubts and fears as to whether or not he has committed a fatal error in leaving his native social relations for those of foreigners whom he cannot hope to emulate, and who, he thinks, will not assimilate themselves to him."

This observation confirmed Delany's life-long preachments of "do it yourself" to his fellow blacks. He follows his diagnosis with a pertinent declaration of intent:

> It is clear, then, that essential to the success of civilization, is the establishment of all those social relations and organizations, without which enlightened communities cannot exist. To be successful, these must be carried out by proper agencies, and these agencies must be a *new element* introduced into their midst, possessing all the attain-

ments, socially and politically, morally and religiously, adequate to so important an end. This element must be *homogeneous* in all the *natural* characteristics, claims, sentiments and sympathies—the *descendants of Africa* being the only element that can effect it. To this end, then, a part of the most enlightened of that race in America design to carry out these most desirable measures by the establishment of social and industrial settlements among them, in order at once to introduce, in an effective manner, all the well-regulated pursuits of civilized life.

That no mis-step be taken and fatal error committed at the commencement, we have determined that the persons to compose this new element to be introduced into Africa, shall be well and most carefully selected in regard to moral integrity, intelligence, acquired attainments, fitness, adaptation, and, as far as practicable, religious sentiments and professions. We are serious in this; and so far as we are concerned as an individual, it shall be restricted to the letter, and we will most strenuously oppose and set our face against any attempt from any quarter to infringe upon this arrangement and design. Africa is our Fatherland and we its legitimate descendants, and we will never agree nor consent to see this—the first voluntary step that has ever been taken for her regeneration by her own descendants—blasted by a disinterested or renegade set, whose only object might be in the one case to get rid of a portion of the colored population, and in the other, make money, though it be done upon the destruction of every hope entertained and measure introduced for the accomplishment of this great and prospectively glorious undertaking. We cannot and will not permit or agree that the result of years of labor and anxiety shall be blasted at one reckless blow, by those who have never spent a day in the cause of our race, or know nothing about our wants and requirements. The descendants of Africa in North America will doubtless, by the census of 1860, reach five millions; those of Africa may number two hundred millions. I have outgrown, long since, the boundaries of North America, and with them have also outgrown the boundaries of their claims. I, therefore, cannot consent to sacrifice the prospects of two hundred millions, that a fraction of five millions may be bene-

> fitted, especially since the measures adopted for the many must necessarily benefit the few.
>
> Africa, to become regenerated, must have a national character, and her position among the existing nations of the earth will depend mainly upon the high standard she may gain compared with them in all her relations, morally, religiously, socially, politically, and commercially.
>
> I have determined to leave to my children the inheritance of a country, the possession of territorial domain, the blessings of a national education, and the indisputable right of self-government; that they may not succeed to the servility and degradation bequeathed to us by our fathers. If we have not been born to fortunes, we should impart the seeds which shall germinate and give birth to fortunes for them.

The economic feasibility of Africa's "regeneration," Delany found, lay in that continent's superior potential in the cultivation of cotton, in its abundance of food produce, and in its virtually untapped sugar and palm oil industries. But in Africa, too, cotton could be "king" and depose the monarch in the United States. Delany is most specific about it, and he uses the possessive "we in Africa" frequently.

> Firstly, landed tenure in Africa is free, the occupant selecting as much as he can cultivate, holding it so long as he uses it, but cannot convey it to another; secondly, the people all being free, can be hired at a price less than the *interest* of the capital invested in land and people to work it—they finding their own food, which is the custom of the country; thirdly, there are no contingencies of frost or irregular weather to mar or blight the crop, and fourthly, we have two regular crops a year, or rather one continuous crop, as while the trees are full of pods of ripe cotton, they are at the same time blooming with fresh flowers. And African cotton is planted only every seven years, whilst the American is replanted every season. Lastly, the average product per acre on the best Mississippi and Louisiana cotton plantations in America, is three hundred and fifty pounds; the average per acre in Africa, a hundred percent more, or seven hundred pounds. As the African soil pro-

duces two crops a year to one in America, then we in Africa produce fourteen hundred pounds to three hundred and fifty in America; the cost of labor a hand being one dollar or four shillings a day to produce it; whilst in Africa at present it is nine hundred per cent less, being only ten cents or five pence a day for adult labor. At this price the native lives better on the abundance of produce in the country, and has more money left at the end of a week than the European or free American laborer at one dollar a day.

To help bring about this modernization of the African economy, with its accompanying social and political benefits, Delany confirmed his original plan in the *Official Report*. He would bring to Africa from among the free blacks of America the skills, teachers, medical men, businessmen, transportation, and cotton and oil specialists to instruct the natives so that they themselves would own and command Africa's great potential. But there was one intent he emphasized repeatedly.

> Our policy must be—and I hazard nothing in promulgin (*sic*) it; nay, without this design and feeling, there would be a great deficiency of self-respect, pride of race, and love of country, and we might never expect to challenge the respect of nations—*Africa for the African race and black men to rule them*. By black men I mean, men of African descent who claim an identity with the race. . . . With such prospects as these, with such a people as the Yorubas and others of the best type, as a constituent industrial, social and political element upon which to establish a national edifice, what is there to prevent success? Nothing in the world.

Delany was jubilant over this prospect when he sailed from Lagos for England on April 10, 1860, his mission completed. He had with him a treaty signed by eight of the most powerful chiefs and tribal officials of the Yoruba, Egba, and Ijebu peoples in Abeokuta, whose domain stretched chiefly between the largely navigable Ogun and Oba rivers. The natural outlet for this rich and populous country was the port of Lagos on the Bight of Benim, east of the Liberian coast, into which the Ogun emptied. The achievement of this agreement was a personal triumph for Delany for it guaranteed the conditions upon which his Black Israel would be founded. It has none of the convolutions of diplomatic treaties granting foreigners certain rights but is, rather, a simple and forthright document.

> This treaty, made between His Majesty Okukenu, Alake, Somoye, Ibashorun, Sokenu, Oguabonna, and Atambala, Chiefs, and Balaguns of Abbeokuta, on the first part, and Martin Robison Delany, and Robert Campbell, of the Niger Valley Exploring party, Commissioners from the African race of the United States and the Canadas, in America, on the second part, convenants:
>
> Art. 1. That the king and chiefs, on their part, agree to grant and assign unto the said Commissioners, on behalf of the African race in America, the right and privilege of settling, in common with the Egba people, on any part of the territory belonging to Abbeokuta not otherwise occupied.
>
> Art. 2. That all matters requiring legal investigation among settlers be left to themselves, to be disposed of according to their own customs.
>
> Art. 3. That the Commissioners, on their part, also agree that the settlers shall bring with them, as an equivalent for the privileges above accorded, intelligence, education, a knowledge of the arts and sciences, agriculture, and other mechanical and industrial occupations, which they shall put into immediate operation, by improving the lands, and in other useful vocations.
>
> Art. 4. That the laws of the Egba people shall be strictly respected by the settlers; and in all matters in which both parties are concerned, an equal number of commissioners, mutually agreed upon, shall be appointed, who shall have power to settle such matters.
>
> As a pledge of our faith, and sincerity of our hearts, we each of us hereunto affix our hands and seals, this twenty-seventh day of December, Anno Domini one thousand eight hundred and fifty-nine.

With this treaty and the wealth of information he had gathered Delany was ready and eager to begin what he considered his life work. He worked on his *Official Report* while en route to England but, invaluable as the document proved to be in London, Canada, and the United States, it does not tell the full story of Delany's experiences in Africa. He says nothing, for example, of his narrow escape from Ilerin, far to the north of Abeokuta, during the initial raids and unrest which began the tribal war of 1860–1862 known as the Ibadan-Ijaiye War. He and Campbell were in somewhat desperate straits, for their funds were running out and they had to reach the port of Lagos. Campbell has a highly dramatic account of this last journey back to the coast in his *Pilgrimage to My Motherland.*

In fact, Campbell's book is a highly readable, if less useful, report of the journey itself. Delany does not mention it, but Campbell gives a horrendous account of being lost all night in a violent and long-lasting thunder storm typical of the Abeokuta regions. When he finally found the city on return from a visit in the country, Campbell relates,

> . . . the Doctor spent half the night wandering over the least inhabited portions of the city, wet to the skin, and rain all the time pouring. He had been but a few days at Abbeokuta, and of course knew nothing of the language. Coming to a native compound, he essayed to attract attention by the use of the two or three words, the pronunciation (not the meaning) of which he knew indifferently. With a loud voice (the Doctor is a second Stentor) he cried *acushe!* (a term of salutation to the industrious). The natives were astonished and instantly extinguishing their lights, they fled to the recesses of their dwelling, and although the Doctor exhausted his whole vocabulary to the effort, he could not induce them to stir.

Delany also was stricken by what he called the "acclimatizing fever," and he writes learnedly of its treatment in the *Official Report*. But we find from Campbell and from Delany's correspondence home that severe attacks of fever disabled him for long periods. In a letter to the *Chatham Planet*, dated from Lagos on October 8, 1859, he tells of an exploratory voyage some fifty miles up the Cavalla River from Mound Vaughan in Liberia.

> During the whole of this adventure I was laboring under the depressing effects of the fever, and the day I walked

> 14 miles over the mountains I had during the whole time a scorching fever. . . . One of the theories in Africa for treatment of the fever is to keep active—so you will see that I practiced the old woman's course. "If a little be good, a great deal is much better." But I paid dearly for my temerity, as it cost me a week's confinement to my room since my arrival here, in consequence of the severe fatigue I underwent.

This was one of the few lapses into personal problems in any of Delany's messages back to the United States and Canada. In that lengthy letter of October 8 he devotes most of it to a description of the country and of the harbor at Lagos during which his worship of the land is revealed. "Thus we had two great bays hugging the island on either side like the embrace of two great persons, whilst those large and widespread streams both east and west, independent of the ocean, are stretched forth like 'the arms of Ethiopia unto God.' "

Very proudly he reported that the port of Lagos, with a population of about 35,000, had the year before handled over $5 million in trade, "the business being all done by black men as there are not over a dozen whites doing business in the place. These black men are all natives, too, many of them from Sierra Leone, and I don't know of one in the place whose business talents equal those of the colored gentlemen doing business in Chatham."

Perhaps the most intriguing episodes of the entire African experience took place at the beginning. Again, Delany only duplicated the correspondence and expressed his gratitude to individuals in the *Official Report*, but he revealed none of the details of the remarkable reception given him in Liberia. Despite his years of articulate opposition to Liberian emigration on the lecture platform, and in *The Mystery* and the *North Star*, Delany was greeted with greater honors in Monrovia than anywhere in the United States and Canada. The account in the *Liberian Herald* reflects some of the public response:

> MARTIN R. DELANY IN LIBERIA
>
> The arrival of Martin Robinson (*sic*) Delany in Liberia is an era in the history of African emigration—an event, doubt-

> less, that will long be remembered by hundreds and thousands of Africa's exiled children. The news of the advent to these shores of this far-famed champion for the elevation of colored men in the United States and the great antagonist to the American Colonization Society spread throughout the county of Monserrado with astonishing rapidity, and persons from all parts of the country came to Monrovia to see this great man. . . .
>
> Dr. Delany is on his way to Yoruba. The citizens of Monrovia, knowing well the position which Dr. Delany has held for the last twenty-five years with reference to African colonization, thought it might be well to invite him to deliver a public lecture in order that the people generally might hear some of the reasons which induced this gentleman to turn his face Africa-wards; also to tender him a formal and public welcome.

Delany received the invitation to speak the day after his arrival in Monrovia. The letter was signed by the most prominent Liberians in the city, including the former Governor of Liberia, Urias A. McGill; the District Attorney, H. A. Johnson; several businessmen and members of the clergy; as well as from one of the country's outstanding intellects, Edward W. Blyden, then only 27 years old but already recognized as a scholar. He was born in St. Thomas, Virgin Islands, and emigrated to Liberia in 1850 after finding it impossible to obtain entrance to any American college because of his color. He was to become Professor of Greek and Latin Languages and Literature at the College of Liberia the year after Delany's visit. With another emigrant, from New York, the Episcopalian priest Rev. Alexander Crummell, Blyden was to be the spokesman for Africa in the United States for many years. Rev. Crummell was ordained in 1842 and, ten years later, emigrated to Africa when his Bishop refused him a parish due to his color. He became Professor of Intellectual and Moral Philosophy and English Literature at the College of Liberia, which Delany named as "a grand stride in the march of African Regeneration and Negro nationality."

The first invitation to speak posed quite a question for Delany. His anti-American Colonization Society attitudes and his earlier concentration on the western hemisphere, rather than Africa, as a site of refuge, were all a matter of record. Yet the invitation recognized this only in passing, and in the midst of much praise.

> The undersigned, citizens of the city of Monrovia, having long heard of you and your efforts in the United States to elevate our downtrodden race, though these efforts were not unfrequently directed against Liberia, are glad to welcome you, in behalf of the community, to these shores; recognizing as they do in you, an ardent and devoted lover of the African race, and an industrious agent in promoting their interests. And they take this opportunity of expressing to you their most cordial sympathy with the enterprise which has brought you to these shores, sincerely praying that your endeavors may be crowned with complete success.

In both his acceptance and in his speech on July 19, Delany denied having spoken "against Liberia" but rather against emigration. The process of change in him was a long one, according to the *Liberian Herald.*

> He avowed that his thoughts had been from early youth, ever set on Africa, and that in turning his attention toward her, he had embraced no new convictions nor changed his principles, but simply his policy in the line of duty and course of action. "I will therefore say to you, Sir, as Ruth said to Naomi," exclaimed he, "that your people shall be my people, your God shall be my God, yea, more sir, *your country shall be my country.*" To this point the Doctor said he had come, and to this point every free colored man in the United States must come before he would consent to leave the land of oppression.

Delany summarized the course of his own experiences and thinking before the Monrovia audience by dividing the Negro awakening into four historic steps.

> 1st. The period of *letter-writing*—when the writing of letters by colored men gave indications to their white fellow-citizens of African intelligence; when letters written by men of color were sent to the city of London as a literary curiosity. He referred especially to the letters of James

> Forten. —2nd. The period of *newspaper publishing* when colored men directed their attention to the proving to white men that they were as capable as the whites of editing newspapers and scattering their thoughts, expressed in proper shape and form, all over the country, sending their ideas into the parlors and bedchambers, into the studies and offices of their oppressors. —3rd. The period of *lecturing* when colored men felt it not only their duty to send their thoughts to their oppressors on paper, but to meet them face to face, and prove to them that they had equally with them the ability to advocate *orally* their own cause. —4th. The period of *conventions* when colored men met to discuss the great question of an African nationality. "We are now in this period," said the Dr. "and it is the desire of an African nationality that has brought me to these shores."

It was a lengthy speech on the subject of the "Political Destiny of the African Race" and Delany received the congratulations of many in the crowded Methodist Episcopal Church. In a strange twist of circumstances, the man Delany had blasted in the *North Star* in 1848 for catering to whites rather than his own people, the first President of Liberia, John J. Roberts, was the man who offered the motion of thanks for the speech. The chairman of the meeting, Dr. Samuel F. McGill, then asked Delany to continue his speech at another date, which he did, on July 29, again before a capacity audience. Before leaving Monrovia he was to speak again, on August 3, this time on "Physiology," as requested.

The repercussions from his welcome to Liberia were to assure Delany the assistance of every missionary, white or black, and most of the native chiefs. The treaty with the chiefs of Abeokuta was witnessed by Rev. Samuel A. Crowther, the native African who, in 1864, was to be named the first Bishop of the Niger by the Church of England. Rev. Crowther and his family were to assist both Delany and Campbell many times, not only in negotiating the treaty but assuring them assistance from the natives in their travels through the primitive country.

Similarly, Delany lived with Rev. Crummell in his home at Mound Vaughan in Maryland, Liberia, for a month and used it both as a base of operations and a site of convalescence from the fever. From this brilliant black scholar Delany received his first indoctrination into black African attitudes with which he would have to deal in founding his Black Israel.

He was to find similar help in the British Isles, too, for by now his reputation and his mission had preceded him. With Campbell, he boarded the British Royal Mail Steamship *Athenian* at Lagos and reached London on May 16 after stops along the West Africa coast and Liverpool.

Delany went to the British Isles instead of starting homeward for one purpose—to complete the framework of his new country's economy.

In a letter to the *Weekly Anglo-African* dated February 1, he had stated that he planned to "sail in March for America" after the ninety-mile journey northward from Idjaye to Illonin in the interior of Central Africa. It was to be the last exploratory trip through the Yoruba country he and Campbell planned to make.

But Delany was convinced by then, from what he had seen, from the black Africans he had met, and from his treaty with the Alake (king) and chiefs in Abeokuta that his plan for economic advancement was entirely practicable. Now, just one problem remained.

Many years before, he had devoted an entire column in the *Provincial Freeman* to the thesis that world commerce was the circulatory system that tied nationalities together and sustained their mutual respect as well as welfare. He maintained that no people or country could remain self-sustaining or progress without international commercial ties. This would be particularly true of his Black Israel in the Yoruba country for, if King Cotton was to be deposed from the United States, thereby rendering slavery economically impossible, a British market for African cotton must be organized. This he accomplished, in Scotland.

> The commercial relations entered into in Scotland are with the first business men in the United Kingdom, among whom are Henry Dunlop, Esq., ex-Lord Provost of Glasgow, one of the largest proprietors in Scotland; Andrew Stevenson, Esq., one of the greatest cotton dealers; and Messrs. Crum, Graham & Co., 111 Virginia Place, Glasgow, one of the heaviest firms in that part of the old world, which is the house with which I have negotiated for an immediate, active

> and practical prosecution of the enterprise, and whose agency in Europe for any or all of our produce, may be fully relied on. I speak from personal acquaintance with these extensively-known, high-standing gentlemen.

But how did this black man, erudite and persuasive as he might be, persuade these hard-nosed Scots businessmen that a commercial agreement with his non-existent country might be profitable or even possible? The news from Africa by November 1860 was that Abeokuta was involved in the spreading tribal war and now the armies of the neighboring king of Dahomey were on the march. Delany's treaty might be no asset at all, and he had nothing else. That proved to be the case.

A year later, the misfortune of war caused the Alake to repudiate this treaty, according to the British Consul at Lagos, William McCoskry. He wrote: "The Republic of Liberia was held out as the result of a similar system of emigration from America; it was represented that the emigrants would erect forts and, opportunity offered, they would drive the natives from the country, and take possession of the soil." However, through the efforts once more of Rev. Samuel Crowther and the British Consul, the treaty was restored, and the end of the war confirmed it. Meanwhile, Delany had a most tenuous asset with which to bargain with businessmen in the British Isles.

In view of the later doubts, whether or not Delany actually had such a treaty in his pocket, in a letter to Lord John Russell dated June 5, 1861, McCoskry wrote at length confirming it.

> In conclusion I would observe that whatever the treaty may be worth, there can be no doubt it was signed by the Alake and the chiefs, with the knowledge of all who could claim any right to know, and that a copy of that Treaty was left with the Alake—that there was no secrecy in the matter, and that it was not until a powerful opposition influence had been brought to bear on the Alake and chiefs that the Treaty was denied.

Delany might have obtained his commercial agreements anyway but events in London immediately after his arrival there from Lagos began a progression of circumstances that could only lead to success. It is a fantastic tale involving the "greats" of all

Europe and America, almost a farce in British-American relations and a most fortuitous meeting in London of Delany's friends and neighbors from Chatham, William Howard Day and Rev. William King. The first act of the London drama of June 1860 began in Chatham in June 1859 right after Delany had left for Africa.

Rev. William King, founder of the Buxton Settlement and the man with whom Delany had worked in electing McKellar in 1856, had decided to go to the British Isles to raise money for new school buildings in Buxton. William Howard Day, president of the National Board of Commissioners, had taken up land in Buxton and was an elder in Rev. King's congregation, St. Andrews Presbyterian Church. He had watched the progress of the Buxton schools, the first integrated schools on the North American continent (1850), and knew their physical needs and importance. They were classical schools and already had students at Trinity and Knox College in Toronto. Day, an orator, newspaper editor, and man of conviction and pride was to be invaluable to King in their tour of the British Isles. Beginning in Ireland, then to Scotland, by the time they reached London they had the money for the Buxton schools.

King and Day had another purpose in extending their successful trip into England. It was the same purpose that sent Delany to Africa. In his autobiography King tells of it.

> In December (1859) I proceeded to London to mature a plan which I, with some of my anti-slavery friends in London had in view, namely to plant Christian colonies on the west coast of Africa as a barrier against the slave trade, which was still carried on on the west coast of Africa notwithstanding the vigilance of the British cruisers that were kept there at expense of half a million pounds sterling for the purpose of suppressing the slave trade. Yet, according to the last anti-slavery report, 40,000 slaves were taken from the west coast of Africa and sold in Havana and Brazil. The proposal was to plant Christian colonies on the western coast of Africa, under British protection. These colonies would teach the chiefs that it was more profitable for them to raise sugar and cotton than to sell their slaves.

By the time Delany and Campbell reached London, in fact, the day after their arrival, they were invited to an informal meeting of the group initiated by King and Day, which later adopted the name of the African Aid Society, with Lord Alfred Churchill as chairman. There were several preliminary meetings before the organization and its purposes were announced. These were for the purpose of reaching an understanding with both Rev. King and Dr. Delany on the part they would play in a program as finally outlined in a public statement:

> I. That the name of the Society be the "African Aid Society"
>
> II. That its chief objects shall be to develop the material resources of Africa, Madagascar, and the adjacent Islands; and to promote the Christian civilization of the African races; as by these means the Society believes that the annihilation of the Slave Trade will ultimately be accomplished.

The program evolved during the many meetings extending for two months, from May 17 until the final private meeting on July 19, reflected Delany's own concrete conclusions as to a course of action for Africa, from the introduction of skills into the production of cotton, silk, indigo, sugar, palm oil, and other products to the promotion of such products in the British Isles. In addition, the African Aid Society decided to raise funds to help emigration to Africa by Canadian blacks with such skills as were needed, through loans and supply of tools and implements. It was an entirely practical program to which Delany could subscribe. However, he reported that he made his position clear early in the meetings

> when I then and there, fully, openly, and candidly stated to the noblemen and gentlemen present what was desired and what we did not; that we desired to be dealt with as men, and not children. That we did not desire gratuities as such in the apportioning of their benevolence—nothing eleemosynary but means *loaned* to our people upon *their personal obligations, to be paid in produce or otherwise.* That we did not approve of *restriction* as to *where* such per-

> sons went (so that it was to some country where the population was mainly colored, as that was our policy) letting each choose and decide *for himself*, that which was *best for him.*

Another thing Delany made most clear to the gentlemen was his complete right of self-determination, "imparting to the first of their knowledge, our true position as independent of all other societies and organizations then in existence." He had both William Howard Day, his own chief officer, as well as the highly respected Rev. King there to confirm this boast.

> To these sentiments, the noblemen and gentlemen all cordially and heartily agreed, establishing their Society, as we understand it, expressly to aid the *voluntary* emigration of colored people from America in general and our movement as originated by colored people in particular. Indeed, I here now say, as I did then and there, that I would give nothing for it, were it not a self-reliant project, originating with ourselves.

They did not conclude these meetings until there was a clear understanding of the relationship of each individual to the African Aid Society and its obligations to them. Rev. King wrote of his part: "I was to furnish the men from the Elgin (Buxton) Settlement who were to act as the pioneers of the Christian colonies to be formed, and the London Society was to furnish the means and protection to the colonists."

Delany was to take the specially trained group supplied him by Rev. King to Abeokuta to make a start, and a target date for the first industrial and agricultural team to sail for Africa was set for approximately a year later, in June 1861. Two thirds of their costs, to cover a year in Africa, were to be advanced by the Society.

With such a complete understanding of both the independence of Delany's group and all obligations, Lord Churchill announced:

> In furtherance of the objects of this Society, the Executive Committee, with the generous aid of friends to this movement, have already assisted Dr. Delany and Professor Camp-

bell (two colored gentlemen from America) with funds to enable them to continue their labors and to lay before the colored people of America the reports of the Pioneer Exploration Expedition into Abbeokuta, in West Africa, from which they have lately returned.

Such financial help permitted Delany to continue his tour of England and Scotland in search of the commercial houses he needed for the new enterprise. It was to become a triumphal tour as a result of events in London which made him the catalyst for an international incident that had all Europe chuckling and the United States "viewing with alarm."

The circumstances of the incident are clear but their interpretations are not. During all of his negotiations with the highly placed noblemen and public figures sponsoring the African Aid Society, Delany was much sought after as a lecturer on his findings in Central Africa. It was not merely the novelty that he was the first black explorer to report; there was genuine public curiosity in the continent. Livingstone had made his first report and, while Delany was in Abeokuta, the British explorer was discovering Lake Nyasa. In addition, anyone with a plan for ending the slave trade received a welcome in Britain because, as Rev. King pointed out, the fruitless effort to stop the illicit trade without the cooperation of its chief market, the United States, was an annual cost to British taxpayers. Finally, public interest was high also in any or all new sources of cotton, for the textile industry in the British Isles now included some three million employees. One circular headlined the comparison: "Cotton is KING! in America"—"Cotton is BREAD! in England."

Delany made many speeches in and around London. He and Campbell were to set a precedent by being the first black Americans honored by the prestigious Royal Geographic Society. Delany, on June 11, delivered a paper titled "Geographical Observations on Western Africa" at the regular meeting of the Society. He surveyed the lands, plants, animals, and diseases of the Niger Valley similar to his presentation of the same material in the *Official Report* and again did not fail to score his point. The Proceedings of the Society, summarizing the paper, concluded: "Dr. Delany finally mentioned that the adventure originated from a large portion of the intelligent and educated descendants of the Africans in the United States and the Canadas, who are anxiously desirous by their own efforts and self-reliance to regenerate their father-land." The report on Delany's paper also expresses amazement that Delany's expedition was made at a cost of £100, "a striking contrast with our expensive expeditions."

Delany also was invited to many social functions attended by the British and European aristocracy throughout his stay in London, and he stresses his reception at each as equal to that of other distinguished guests such as foreign ambassadors. He had special delight in being invited to participate in an annual "Reform Festival," a charity affair sponsored by the astronomer Dr. John Lee at his Hartwell Palace. The custom at this three-day affair was to choose an honorary president to whom was extended the hospitality of the ornate apartments in the Palace once occupied by the exiled Louis XVIII and his queen. Their choice was Delany and he apparently relished every moment of the festival.

The high point of the busy months in London was reached on July 16 when Delany took his seat in Somerset House as a duly qualified delegate to the royally sponsored International Statistical Congress, which was to continue for five days and at which he was to present a paper on his West African explorations.

This Congress was considered the leading scientific gathering of the times and its delegates came from Europe, as well as North and South America. They were appointed by their respective governments, and from the nature of the papers delivered by the scientists, its purpose was an exchange of information as well as methods of fact-finding in the sciences and vital statistics. Delany could not represent a country since he had not been in Canada long enough to meet its citizenship requirements, and no black had citizenship in the United States, nor would any black be chosen to represent the United States abroad. Delany was a delegate by royal commission from His Royal Highness, Albert, Prince Consort of England, who acted for Queen Victoria in welcoming the international delegates. No doubt Delany's appointment was engineered by his highly connected friends of the new African Aid Society.

The chairman of the Congress was the famous fighting Lord Chancellor of England, Lord Brougham and Vaux, then in his

82d year but still filled with the fire that had lasted him for sixty years of leadership in judicial, suffrage, and anti-slavery reforms. In both Houses, in Commons and in Lords, after a baronetcy was bestowed upon him by Queen Victoria, Henry Peter Brougham was an almost vindictive foe of slavery, particularly of American slavery. In the same year, 1860, Queen Victoria had conferred another peerage on him, and the patent clearly stated that it was in recognition of his services in promoting the abolition of slavery and the emancipation of Britain's slaves. Lord Brougham, not a popular figure among Americans at any time, had by the end of the afternoon of July 16 applied an explosive to that smoldering hatred.

In his report to the National Association for the Promotion of Social Science on the meetings of the Congress, Lord Brougham explained the representation at the sessions as including "distinguished foreigners" whom he had invited.

> Among others was a negro gentleman of great respectability and talents, Dr. Delany, who had attended different departments, and in his able addresses had communicated useful information and suggestions. When inviting him to this Congress, I informed him that he would have the satisfaction of visiting the country which first declared a slave free the instant he touches British ground. Dr. Delany's forefathers were African slaves; he is himself a native of Canada (an error which Delany corrected). It is truly painful to reflect that, although his family have been free for generations, his origin being traced to one whom the crimes of white men and Christians had enslaved, he would be, in the land of trans-Atlantic liberty, incapable of enjoying any civil rights whatever, and would be treated in all respects as an alien, the iniquity of the fathers being inexorably visited, not upon their children but upon the children of their victims, to all generations,—children whose only offense is the sufferings of their parents, whose wrongs they inherit with their hue.

Seated on the floor of the Congress assembly room with the other delegates was the official group from the United States headed by Augustus Baldwin Longstreet, the jurist, author, and, at that time, president of the University of South Carolina. Longstreet was a tried and true expositor of the South and had fought in its political battles.

On the dais was seated, with the ambassadors and ministers to the Court of St. James from nearly two dozen countries, the minister plenipotentiary from the United States, George Mifflin Dallas of Pennsylvania, well known to Delany through his slave-expansionist activity as Vice-President of the United States during the Mexican War. This diplomatic corps were all honorary officers of the Congress. They surrounded Prince Albert who, at 4 o'clock, opened the proceedings with a very proper speech.

When the Prince had concluded, Lord Brougham took over as chairman and invited acknowledgment of the royal speech, which was graciously given. There are many versions of what followed—Delany's, Dallas', Longstreet's, and the various newspaper accounts. What Brougham did was to direct a remark to Dallas, calling his attention to the presence of a black man in the Congress.

Delany version: "I would remind my friend, Mr. Dallas, that there is a negro (*sic*) member of this Congress." Dallas version: "I beg my friend Mr. Dallas to observe that there is in the assemblage before us a Negro, and hope the fact will not offend his scruples." Longstreet version: "I call the attention of Mr. Dallas to the fact that there is a *negro* present, and I hope he will feel no scruples on that account."

But it was more than the phraseology that Dallas resented. The entire assembly applauded both Lord Brougham's words and his act of calling attention to Delany. It was this reaction that caused international repercussions, and prompted Delany's response:

> While I fully comprehended his lordship's interest, meaning and its extent, the thought flashed instantly across my mind, How will this assemblage take it? May it not be mistaken by some, at least, as a want of genuine respect for my presence, by the manner in which the remarks were made? . . . These thoughts passed through my mind as soon as his lordship concluded his remarks, and as soon as the minister from Spain was seated, I rose in my place and said,—
>
> "I rise, your Royal Highness, to thank his lordship, the unflinching friend of the negro, for the remarks he has

> made in reference to myself, and to assure your royal highness and his lordship *that I am a man.*"
>
> I then resumed my seat. The clapping of hands commenced on the stage, followed by what the *London Times* was pleased to call "the wildest shouts ever manifested in so grave an assemblage."

Apparently, the unanimous approval of the delegates irked Longstreet, whereupon he led the American delegation in a walkout. Dallas however remained seated and said nothing. The initial session closed abruptly, and as next morning's *London Chronicle* phrased it, "with this small contribution to statistical and ethnological science, the proceedings of the day terminated." But the repercussions began immediately.

Longstreet formally withdrew from the Congress, and the only member of the American delegation to deliver his paper at the sessions (unless Delany might be called American) was Dr. Edward Jarvis from Boston, Massachusetts, a state delegate. The London newspapers chose sides, the *London Times* for Brougham and Delany, the *Chronicle* for Dallas and Longstreet.

It was fruitless for Lord Brougham to try to explain his intent in calling attention to Delany. He did make an attempt on the following day, when introducing Dr. Jarvis.

> This reminds me of a statement made in the papers this morning, that I had designedly wounded the feelings of the American minister at this court, which I deny as farthest from my intention, as all who know me (and I appeal to the American minister himself, Mr. Dallas being a friend of mine) whether I have not uniformly stood forth as the friend of that government and people? Now, what is this "*offence*" complained of? Why, on the opening of this august assemblage (possibly the largest in number, the most learned, that the world ever saw together from different nations, to be among whom any man might feel proud, as an evidence of his advanced civilization and attainments) what is the fact? Why, here we see, even in this unequalled council, a son of Africa, one of that race whom we have been taught to look upon as inferior. I only alluded to this as one of the most gratifying as well as extraordinary facts of the age.

Having thus further enraged Longstreet, Lord Brougham quickly found out that Dallas was not as friendly as he had thought. The minister refused to see Brougham when he called at his residence, ostensibly to present an apology. In his diary, under date of July 18, Dallas notes, "There is no telling to what this outrage may lead. Brougham is already feeling the weight of a unanimous public opinion. . . . Is he, on this question of slavery, deranged?" And on July 20 he made a full entry of Brougham's visit.

> Lord Brougham called at ten A.M. I had just time to tell my servant to refuse me. He is so old, and has been so remarkable a man in his day and generation, that I have to remind myself of his offence and of his aggravating it by the form and manner of his pretended explanation, or I could scarcely screw my mind up to the point of turning him from the door. He came a second time, between twelve and one. I was then at the Kensington Museum, and my secretary, receiving him with the utmost deference, was, nevertheless, silent. He said once or twice, "You know who I am? Lord Brougham, Lord Brougham!" He went to the front door and then returned to the front office, and remarked "You know you don't treat your negroes as well as they are treated in the Brazils!"

The matter became, in Dallas' opinion, a crisis requiring advice from his government and his report to Secretary of State Lewis Cass declared, "You will, of course, perceive the extremely unpleasant position in which this matter places me socially here, and I shall therefore anxiously wait the sentiments of the President."

President Buchanan and his cabinet actually did have a session on Dallas' report of the "insult" to the United States, and Cass' reply stated that the President was pretty unhappy about the whole thing and, in fact, believed that the British government should have apologized officially. The Secretary of State regretted telling Dallas that

> there is one point upon which the opinion of the President and of the Cabinet does not concur with that which guided your decision, and this regards retaining your seat after Lord

> Brougham had made his appeal to you. You were right in preserving silence towards him and his sable associate. To have been led into a controversial discussion with them, as was probably hoped and anticipated, would have been equally unprofitable and undignified, incompatible indeed, with your official character.

But, Cass repeated, Dallas should have joined Longstreet and walked out. Cass, and apparently the entire cabinet as well as the President agreed with Longstreet as to the character of the incident. In his long reply to Dallas he declares

> that the apostrophe to you was intended and received as an insult to that country, no one can reasonably doubt. It was designed as a reproach upon a large portion of the American people, among whom slavery is an established institution and upon a still larger portion of them, of whom I am one, who consider the negro race as an inferior one and who repudiate all political equality and social connection with its descendants.

But as far as the British public was concerned, it was not Dallas who amused them and enlisted more aid for Delany and for the anti-slavery movement than either could accomplish for themselves. Dallas was discreetly silent in public. But Longstreet rushed into print on July 21 with one of the longest letters ever published in the *London Chronicle*. He attacked the International Statistical Congress as being faulty in all the applause given Lord Brougham, upheld slavery as a "heritage" borne by the American people, defended Georgia as his native state, and bade "farewell to Europe forever and forever!" He was heading for Liverpool and home.

Having been appointed to head the American delegation by Secretary of the Treasury, Howell Cobb, Longstreet reported to him at once:

> I regarded this an ill-timed assault upon our country, a wanton indignity offered to our minister, and a pointed insult offered to me. I immediately withdrew from the body. The propriety of my course is respectfully submitted to my government.

> What England can promise herself from exciting the ire of the United States, I cannot divine. Surely there is nothing in the past history of the two countries which offers to her the least encouragement to seek contests with the great republic, either national or individual. Will not her championship of the slave against his master be in full time when the slave shall complain of his lot and solicit her interference?

The newspapers picked up Longstreet's arguments and so did *Punch* (which called it "The London Charivari"). The affair had its repercussions in the American press where the kindest words expressed in the pro-slavery papers were that Lord Brougham must be senile. But Frederick Douglass rose to the heights in his *Monthly*.

> The startling offense of the venerable and learned Lord Brougham was that he ventured to call the attention of Mr. Dallas, the American Minister Plenipotentiary, to the fact that a "*negro*" was an acting member of the meeting of the International Statistical Society. This was the offense. There was no mistaking the point. It struck home at once. Mr. Dallas felt it. It choked him speechless. He could say nothing. It was like calling the attention of a man, vain of his personal beauty, to his nose or to any other deformity. Delany, determined that the nail should hold fast, rose, with all his blackness, right up, as quick and graceful as an African lion, and received the curious gaze of the scientific world. It was complete. Sermons in stone are nothing to this. Never was there a more telling rebuke administered to the pride, prejudice and hypocrisy of a nation. It was saying, Mr. Dallas, we make members of the International Statistical Society out of the sort of men you make merchandise out of in America. Delany, in Washington, is a *thing!* Delany in London is a *man*.

And in London, with Longstreet on his way home and Dallas silent, Delany had the last word. In the closing session of the International Statistical Congress he was asked to comment.

> I should be insensible, indeed, if I should permit this Congress to adjourn without expressing my gratitude for the

cordial manner in which I have been received, from the time when I landed in this kingdom to the present moment, and in particular to the Earl of Shaftesbury, the president of the section to which I belong, as well as to every individual gentleman of that section, it matters not from what part of the world he came. I say, my lord, if I did permit this Congress to adjourn without expressing my gratitude, I should be an ingrate indeed. I am not foolish enough to suppose that it was from any individual merit of mine, but it was that outburst of expression for sympathy for my race (African), whom I represent, and who have gone the road of that singular providence of degeneration, that all other races in some time of the world's history have gone, but from which, thank God, they are now fast being regenerated. I again tender my most sincere thanks and heartfelt gratitude to those distinguished gentlemen with whom I have been privileged to associate, and by whom I have been received on terms of the most perfect equality.

As a result of the Brougham incident, Delany lectured to capacity audiences from London to Glasgow. At some of the lectures he shared the platform with William Howard Day, and the two black men impressed the English and Scotsmen not only with their information but with the fact that they had originated and led a going organization which could have a profound effect on the British economy. Together they made a most effective team.

In Leeds, one of the industrial centers at which the two men spoke, Delany dwelt on the development of the African idea and Day on the importance of the plan to Britain. The *Leeds Mercury* quotes Day's speech as follows:

By the production of cotton, slavery began to be a power. So that as the cotton interest increased the testimony of the Church decreased. Cotton now is three-fifths of the production of the South. So that the Hon. Amasa Walker, formerly Republic Secretary of State for the State of Massachusetts, at the meeting held in London, August 1, 1859, and presided over by Lord Brougham, really expressed the whole truth when he said—"While cotton is fourteen cents per pound slavery will never end." Now we propose to break the back of this monopoly in America by raising in Africa—in the African's own home—as well as in the West Indies, cotton of the same quality as the American, and at a cheaper rate. It had been demonstrated by Mr. Clegg, of Manchester, that cotton of superior quality could be laid down at Liverpool cheaper from Africa than from America. We have sent my friend, Mr. Delany, to see what Africa is, and he will tell you the results—so very favorable—of his exploration. Then we feel that we have in Canada the colored men to pioneer the way—men reared among the cotton of the United States, and who have found an asylum among us. The bone and sinew is in Africa—we wish to give it direction. We wish thereby to save to England millions of pounds by the difference in price between the two cottons; we wish to ward off the blow to England which must be felt by four millions of people interested in the article to be produced if an untimely frost or an insurrection should take place—and, above all, to lift up Africa by the means of her own children.

The entire British press, wherever Day and Delany spoke or whenever Delany occupied the platform alone, spread glowing and optimistic accounts of this new attack on slavery through Africa itself. It was a new, exciting, and seemingly practical plan to the anti-slavery stalwarts of the British Isles. To the general public it had the appeal of economic self-interest. The results proved that the African Aid Society had made a very wise investment in financing Delany's stay in England for five months after the Congress in London. After completing his commercial agreements in Glasgow, Delany sailed from Liverpool on December 13, arriving home in Chatham on the 29th.

CHAPTER THIRTEEN

Return to Chaos

Once home in Chatham, before the fateful New Year of 1861, Delany tried to isolate himself while he prepared his *Official Report* for the printer. It was useless. Within a week he was on the lecture platform in Chatham for two successive nights, and within a few weeks he was embroiled in a dispute, in print, with his old friend and colleague, Rev. James Theodore Holly. After he had finished the *Official Report* and it was printed in New York and London simultaneously, he was the recipient of numerous invitations to speak throughout the northern states.

Delany found himself in a most unaccustomed role. Instead of having to seek out audiences for his message of black pride, he was sought. Both whites and blacks wanted to hear his first-hand report on Africa, the former because Delany was the celebrated black who had caused the diplomatic crisis in London; the latter because, finally, the blacks of America were giving up on the land of their birth. Too much had happened to them while Delany was away and each development seemed to underscore his emigration messages since 1853. Even as he worked in "The Hut" in Chatham during that January 1861, the crises continued.

He had been in Scotland when Abraham Lincoln was elected president. Before his arrival home, South Carolina had seceded. The day after, the secessionists took over the Federal Arsenal at Charleston, S.C. On January 9 the shore batteries in Charleston drove off the *Star of the West* with its provisions for Fort Sumter. Federal military supplies and installations were taken over in Georgia, Alabama, Florida, Louisiana, Arkansas, and Texas. Each day brought new gestures of defiance from the South and new pleas to "Save the Union" from the North. Yet both sides awaited Abraham Lincoln and his inauguration on March 4. It was the climax that had been in the making since the elections. For the blacks, it was the climax of almost exactly four years of tortured suspense, since the Dred Scott decision on March 6, 1857, had discarded all legal bounds in disposition of the 600,000 free Negroes.

Delany had had nineteen months away from these tensions, and his welcome from all he encountered in his travels seems to have given him a self-confidence missing while he was on the defensive in the early emigration wars. It was something Frederick Douglass noted a year later when he gave grudging praise to Delany.

> Rochester has recently heard from Africa. Dr. DELANY has given us three very interesting lectures made up of his travels and observations in that somewhat mysterious country. The most fashionable churches of this city were flung open to him, and the most intelligent audiences assembled to hear him. The black man however shunned and detested when his face is turned towards America, becomes at once an object of interest and regard when his face and his steps are turned towards Africa. But let that pass. Dr. Delany has been among us, and has given us the results of his discoveries. An outside view of Africa, we have long had, but the Doctor gave us an inside view showing us very plainly what Africa is and does, and what she can do and be. —No cant, but much warmth, much enthusiasm, a little hyperbole, but generally a truthful spirit, the Doctor exhibits. His lectures though terribly African, had nevertheless an important American bearing. Dr. Delany himself has this bearing and cannot well divest himself of it. He cannot speak or write without speaking and writing up the race to which he belongs, whether they be found in Africa or in America. His coming here to Rochester has been of great advantage to us all. It has given our white fellow citizens the opportunity of seeing a brave self conscious black man, one who does not cringe and cower at the thought of his hated color, but one who if he betrays any concern about his complexion at all, errs in the opposite direction. "I speak (said he) only of the pure black uncorrupted by Caucasian blood". In his lectures he passed all others in silence. This feature of his discourses is so marked and decided as sometimes to make the impression upon those who do not know Mr. Delany,

that he has gone about the same length in favor of black, as the whites have in favor of the doctrine of white superiority. He stands up so straight that he leans back a little. Nevertheless, we can say we have been deeply interested in Dr. Delany's lectures, and filled with admiration of the man. He himself, is one of the very best arguments that Africa has to offer. Fine looking, broad chested, full of life and energy, shining like polished black Italian marble, and possessing a voice which when exerted to the full capacity might cause a whole troop of African Tigers to stand and tremble, he is just the man for the great mission of African civilization to which he is devoting his life and powers. We gather from his lectures and conversation that he is fully determined to emigrate in the course of the present year with a company of chosen spirits to settle in Africa, upon territory duly ceded to him by treaty during his stay in Abbeokuta, one of the finest cotton and coffee growing countries in the world. Health, long life, and success to M. R. Delany. If we were going to Africa we should unhesitatingly enroll ourselves under his leadership for we should know, that the race would receive no detriment in his presence. —He is the intensest embodiment of black Nationality to be met with outside the valley of the Niger.

—Douglass' *Monthly*, August, 1862

Delany was "terribly African" in everything he said or did after returning to Chatham. In his very first lecture there, shortly after his arrival, the distinguished whites of Kent County gave him both a vote of thanks and a request to continue his lectures. Rev. William King was there to confirm everything he said and, in fact, to second the motion of thanks. Even before the *Official Report* was in print and Delany was to start out on the lecture trail through most of the northern states, he stated his position in the public print.

This came as a result of Rev. Holly's insistence that Delany take a public position on the growing Haitian emigration movement which was now in the hands of James Redpath. The latter, a white man and confidant of John Brown, was an effective organizer. He had been one of Horace Greeley's star reporters on the *New York Tribune* and covered the South as well as emigration stories until his appointment in 1859 as Commissioner of Emigration by the Haitian president. Astutely, he had appointed Holly, Henry Highland Garnet, and John Brown, Jr., as agents for Haitian emigration from the United States and Canada.

But obviously the most influential catch of all the black men in the year 1861 would be Delany and his active, public, and unequivocal approval of Haiti as the destination of emigrants. Redpath did not urge Delany to speak out. Holly either was delegated to the project or assumed the responsibility. Delany replied in the public print, in the *Chatham Planet* of January 15, 1861, knowing full well that the newspaper exchanges would spread his position throughout the northern states. He leaves not a single doubt about his own commitment:

> My duty and destiny are in Africa, the great and glorious, even with its defects, land of your and my ancestors. I cannot, I will not desert her for all things else in this world, save that of my own household, and that does not require it. It will thereby be enhanced. . . . Do not misunderstand me as objecting to your movement as conflicting with mine or ours. This is not the case, as we desire no promiscuous or general emigration to Africa (as the country needs no laborers, these everywhere abounding, industriously employed in various occupations). But select and intelligent people to guide and direct the industry and promote civilization with the establishment of higher social organization, and the legitimate development of our inexhaustible commerce which promises not only certain wealth to us, but all the rest of the world, besides the certainty of thereby putting a stop to the infamous slave trade with a reflex influence upon the—if possible—more infamous American slave trade. In this we desire not to shed their (the southern monsters) blood but make them shed their tears.

As to Haitian emigration, Delany was just as forthright and just as "terribly African."

> I have nothing to say against Haitian emigration, but I am surprised that in the face of the intelligent black men who favor it, two of whom have been to that country and one to Jamaica (yourself, Mr. (J. D.) Harris and Mr. Garnet)

the government would appoint over them to encourage black immigration, a white man, thereby acknowledging your inferiority, and the charge recently made against them by Dr. J. McCune Smith that according to their estimate "next to God is the white man" . . . I cannot, I say, be charged with prejudice when I object to a black government appointing over black men a white when blacks were competent to act and no policy requires the appointment of a white. I object to white men in such cases getting all the positions of honor and emoluments, while the blacks receive only the subordinate, with little or no pay. I maintain this position is necessary to self-respect, and treat with contempt the idea that it makes no difference in such cases whether the person be white or black, where black men are still occupying inferior positions in the midst of the people who deny their equality in all the relations of life.

His only other objection to Haitian emigration, and Delany did not expand on it was that "this movement is too precipitous, not sufficiently matured." And he returns to his familiar theme that the destiny of the colored people must be decided by themselves, not by whites. Otherwise, the "boasted equality" does not exist and the blacks "should be under white masters."

While his letter in the *Planet* left no doubt as to his position in regard to Haiti, that independence he asserted also placed him in the midst of an internecine squabble that had been going on all the time he was in Africa and England. He found himself on the side of his good friend Dr. James McCune Smith of New York and against his good friend Rev. James Theodore Holly of New Haven, in a debate as stridently abusive as his own public fights with Frederick Douglass. Holly's reply was in the *Chatham Planet* a month later, on February 15, 1861, and its chief indictment was that Delany had taken up with "your New York confrere" to distort the Haitian story "with all the malignity of a fiendish slave-holder."

How could you, Dr. Delany, the recognized expounder of the doctrines of Negro Nationality join hands with the old opponent of our cause in this cold-blooded assault on Haiti? If learned colored doctors in America can only point their

> pens to vilify and detract from the fair fame of Haiti while white men like Wendell Phillips and James Redpath are at deep pains to exalt and glorify her noble deeds and heroic people, how can you wonder that the Haitian government should appoint one of such white men as its general agent and not one of such Negro doctors?

Redpath was appointed, Holly explained bitterly, because the National Board of Commissioners, in 1856 and 1858, did not keep its commitments to Haiti after he himself had reported on his negotiations there in 1855. Instead, William Howard Day and Delany himself had directed a change in policy and a violation of the "platform of 1854 which discountenanced emigration to the eastern world" and by concentrating on Central Africa had deserted the Haiti scheme. "I feel therefore that the National Convention broke its plighted faith with American emigrationists." In concluding his lengthy reply, Holly, like Douglass, finds Delany "terribly African."

> But Doctor, did you really mean to convey the idea that black men should place black men first in everything they do in respect to our race, without any exceptions? (This was exactly Delany's intent.) If so, why did you not send your letter to which this is a reply to the *Anglo-African*, *Fred Douglass' Monthly*, for publication first, instead of inserting it in that white man's paper, the *Chatham Planet*, a paper whose editor, past and present, was one of the most bitter opponents of the Negro race in Canada?
>
> Really, your inconsistency in this whole matter is so glaring and so unlike my old friend Dr. Delany that I am almost tempted to believe that you are practicing upon me some fetish trick, learned perhaps from some savage tribe in the jungles of Central Africa.

This was only one of the many squabbles among black intellectuals that these tense years produced, and which Delany found himself embroiled in immediately upon his return home. In another dispute between Dr. Smith and Garnet on the African Civilization Society, Delany sided with the former even before he himself had said a word. In the January 12, 1861, issue of the *Weekly Anglo-African*, which contained an installment of a long-standing debate between Smith and Garnet, Smith, citing a speech by Campbell and declaring that the aims of the African Civilization Society and the hated American Colonization Society were identical, called attention to the treaty of Abeokuta which, he said, included an agreement to "respect the domestic institutions of the country."

> One of these institutions—I have it from Mr. Campbell's own lips—is THE INSTITUTION OF SLAVERY. Mr. Campbell mildly interposes the statement that the slavery of Abbeokuta is of the mildest form, etc. Did you ever hear a slaveholder or his apologist admit of any other kind of slavery? But I forget. You have recently sent out pioneers into the land of Abbeokuta. They may change the face of the matters. Yet they must be mighty men to do so, being themselves, all told two barbers and a poet! In the meantime you owe it to your own fair fame to wash your hands of a treaty which commits your association to respect the institution of domestic slavery.

There was no need for Delany to set Dr. Smith straight. In the next issue of the *Anglo-African* Garnet replied to Dr. Smith's criticism and informed the Negro world that Delany and Campbell were *not* sent to Africa by the African Civilization Society and therefore the treaty of Abeokuta was none of the Society's business.

> Those enterprising, learned and intelligent gentlemen never were, are not now and probably never will be commissioners of the African Civilization Society. They went out and returned and published their papers and books as Commissioners of the Niger Valley Exploring Party, a company which originated in Canada.

In February, Garnet also took it upon himself to reply to Delany's original letter in the *Chatham Planet* addressed to Holly, which had been reprinted in the *Anglo-African*. He addressed himself to Smith and another doctor identified only as "D. D." Each one is taken to task for "opposing" Haitian emigration. To Delany he wrote:

You are indignant at the acknowledgement of the leadership of a *white man* (Redpath) in any work that particularly concerns *black men.* Now, sir, notwithstanding you are alopathic (an alopescist supposedly cures baldness) in your practice, nevertheless I must give you a homeopathic prescription. I see by the newspapers that in the convention held in 1848 (1858) in Chatham, C.W. one *John Brown* was appointed leader—commander-in-chief—of the Harper's Ferry invasion. There were several black men there, able and brave; and yet John Brown was appointed leader. The unfortunate Stevens moved for the appointment and *one Dr. Martin R. Delany seconded the motion.* Now, sir, tell me where I shall find your consistency, as John Brown was a *very* white man —his face and glorious hairs were all white. I am done with you on that point, Dr. Delany. You ought to have accepted the office of surgeon under that great white leader, as a surgeon's place is in the rear, out of harm's way.

There is no record of Delany having replied to Garnet and, in fact, they were destined to work quite amicably together. Delany involved himself in no further emigration disputes until that fall. He was too busy preparing for Africa. All that he asked the *Anglo-African* and other newspapers to print was the following:

King Street Hut, Chatham, C.W.
Jan. 12, 1861

Will you do me the favor to publish this note as the announcement that I have arrived in America and am busily engaged preparing my official report as "Chief of the Niger Valley Exploring Party", preparatory to a hasty return to Africa where duty calls me.

I desire it to be particularly understood that no general nor promiscuous, but simply and especially a select emigration of intelligent persons (male and female) of various vocations, among whom mechanics and cotton cultivators are acceptable. My address during my residence in America will be Chatham, Canada West. All letters must be postpaid to ensure their being taken out of the office.

Mr. Delany

P.S. A limited number of cotton cultivators (I mean

such as can direct and manage the planting) and mechanics such as described, by sending me their names, age, occupations, and the recommendation of the pastor of their standing, can have aid secured to them at once to go out with myself and party in the first adventure.

M.R.D.

Only once did Delany resort to a printed reply to criticism from a friend and that was to William Wells Brown, the first Negro novelist and playwright, with whom he had shared many a platform. Brown, now a Haitian emigrationist, wrote even more scornfully in a series titled "The Colored People of Canada" which was printed in Redpath's new paper *Pine and Palm*. Writing from Chatham, Brown poured thick satire on Delany's pretensions, his treaty with the Abeokuta chiefs and his good fortune to be singled out by Lord Brougham at the International Statistical Congress and predicted that he soon would be "permitted to return to the practice of his profession" because there would be no settlement in Africa. It was a long and extravagant piece to which Delany replied on the day he read it, September 28, 1861. But he sent his reply to the *Weekly Anglo-African*:

> I simply notice the letter of Mr. W. Wells Brown in the "Pine and Palm" of the 28th inst. written from Chatham, Canada, to correct a most flagrant and designedly mischievous misrepresentation therein stated: that I in a speech in London (Canada) had declared that the "first thing" I intended to do after going to Lagos, was to "take off the King's head!"
>
> It is merely necessary for me to pronounce this as false in toto, which I do; as aside from the intimate friendship which exists between me and all the native authorities at Lagos (as my Report just out will show), but no rational person could be capable of such folly as I am here charged with by Mr. Brown, all glaringly to promote for his employer, Haytian emigration.
>
> I have always treated Mr. Brown as a gentleman, and heretofore regarded him as a friend, and would not now notice his uncouth (and certainly unwarranted) attack, only to correct this shameless misrepresentation.
>
> It is not necessary for me to state that my destiny is

> fixed in Africa, where my family and myself, by God's protection, will soon be happily situated.

Delany did not allow himself to be further involved in the dissension and despair among the blacks which had begun while he was abroad. He had one purpose and he pursued it indomitably through the troubled years. The review of his *Official Report* in the *Anglo-African* illustrates the attention and admiration this single-minded course elicited in the United States.

> It is refreshing to turn from the myriad shames of today towards a man of mettle in downright earnest. Such a man is betrayed in every page of the interesting little brochure before us. It is the only book that has the power to withdraw our strained attention from eager watching for every rumor or breath from the seat of war. And if our readers would like to be relieved for an hour or two from the absorbing topic which is driving the nation mad, they would do well to invest the small sum named above (25 cents), and—shades of Colonization avaunt! —Follow Dr. Delany to Africa.

Delany initiated his "terribly African" tour of lectures in response to invitations from New York and New Jersey and quickly learned from his audiences that his message was manna to them. His people had suffered all the uncertainties of those years while he had been away because they had retained some hope in American democracy, a luxury he himself had discarded in 1853. They had been wandering, with no Moses to lead them. It was a totally new vision of Africa that Delany presented to his audiences. They had heard the missionaries and slave traders speak of their barbaric brethren, both of them plying their trades with the arguments that Christianization and importation of the blacks was a resurrection of both their souls and bodies. Delany had a different tale to tell. One of his speeches was on the civilization he found, not the lack of it. We are indebted to *The Liberator* of May 1, 1863, for a full report on one of his Chicago lectures. (Black orators of today who might be style conscious should note that Delany was the first to wear a "dashiki" on the public platform.)

The Liberator, speaking of the rarity of colored lecturers like Delany, remarks:

> We ought not, perhaps, to be surprised at any unusual manifestation of talent in a negro (*sic*), since Touissant (*sic*) L'Ouverture was proof of the abilities.
>
> We do not mean to say that Dr. Delany is a Touissant (*sic*) L'Ouverture, but we do say that he is a better specimen of his race than any we, for our part, have seen before, and that he is by no means a bad lecturer.
>
> He was not ashamed, he said, to be called a negro. If curly hair and a black face helped to make a negro, then he was a negro, and a full-blooded one at that. He had no need to be ashamed of his type or origin. He has a good head and intelligent face—just the kind of a head which a phrenologist would tell you a man ought to have who makes natural observations and accumulates scientific facts.
>
> The dress which the Doctor wore on the platform was a long dark-colored robe, with curious scrolls upon the neck as a collar. He said it was the wedding dress of a Chief, and that the embroidery was insignia, and had a significance well understood in African high circles. He wore it because he thought it becoming, and fitting the occasion.
>
> He wanted to say what he knew of the negro race, not on the coast of Africa, but of the interior Africans, of whom so little is known—the Africans of the Niger Valley. The audience would be surprised to hear that even the Liberians had never until lately been ten miles beyond their territory; and so nothing could be expected from them. He was sorry to say, too, that American school-books inculcated, notwithstanding recent discoveries, very erroneous notions of the country, describing it as sandy and barren, the soil unproductive, the air full of pestilence, the vegetation poisonous, the very animals unusually ferocious. All this is more or less false, so far as the interior of Africa is concerned. He had traveled three thousand miles in the country, and had seen it in all its phases of social and moral life.

Delany dealt with the languages of the African people, their poetry, morals, homes, the high position of their women, their industrious application to craft industries and agriculture; and he spoke with pride of the highly civilized people in the interior. It commanded both the interest and the amazement of his audiences, for an eyewitness account was new and different. For the first time whites and blacks alike learned that Africa, like America, had its "wild Indians," but it also had the American version of prim, pure, and progressive "New England" villages. Delany spoke of Africa's potential for American blacks and its commercial and agricultural promise, and he showed samples of Yoruba crafts to his audiences.

What Delany offered was his old recipe of exhorting his fellow blacks to have pride in themselves and in their ancestry. Even if the new Republican party succeeded in containing slavery, living under its sword was unbearable. The free blacks, even those clinging to their birth in the land of liberty as a guarantee of some rights, wanted to hear about Africa from one of their own. Their avid curiosity was prompted by the eviction notices served on them nationally as well as state by state. It was not only an awakening of pride in the continent of their forefathers, or even an examination of Delany's grand scheme for a Black Israel that filled the halls in which he spoke for the next two years. They had heard about Haiti, Jamaica, and other places from black proponents. But what about Africa, which was far enough from the United States to escape the grasping slave imperialism? The islands of the Caribbean and the havens of Central America were much too close to slavery.

The demand to hear the first black man to investigate living possibilities in Africa kept Delany busy and he became the most authoritative voice among the blacks during those years. It was not due to a change in his personality or convictions that Delany commanded attention. He merely knew where he was headed, and he did not share the confusion of his people, because he was confident of his analysis of their position. It was typical of Delany, not arrogance, that dictated his words to his biographer:

> I thought I could see differently from my friends, those truly talented men, and unswerving friends of their race. Not that I know more than they, for I may not know as much. But we, like white men, have our faculties and propensities and are likely to develop them in the prosecution of our course. In this I think it may not be regarded as an unwarranted as-

> sumption or egotism to say that in national affairs and in fundamental principles of government, I claim to be at least not far rearward of my friends whose counsels I sought. . . . This is not said for invidious comparison with my friends, because as an orator (which I am not), anti-slavery historian, and portrayer of black men's wrongs, I would sink into insignificance in comparison with Frederick Douglass, and would render myself ridiculous were I capable of assuming to be equally learned with James McCune Smith.

Briefed to its essential, Delany believed that "when thieves fall out" their victims are bound to profit. He lectured to both white and black audiences, from Newark to Chicago, and seldom was he allowed to deliver only one speech in each city. And audiences bought his *Official Report,* thus providing him with funds to continue.

He learned that the white abolitionists, in concentrating their efforts on the lesser evil of the Republican party and the preservation of the Union, had relegated abolition of slavery to an unforeseeable and unmentionable future. Not until they were needed did blacks play any part in the considerations of either side in the Civil War. Abraham Lincoln confirmed this in his Inaugural Address on March 4: "I have no purpose directly or indirectly to interfere with the institution of slavery in the States where it exists."

There has been debate ad nauseum over the "moral issues" of the Civil War, and sufficient unto the Sunday is the sermon thereof. If such issues existed, the blacks, slave or free, had no part in them. In the North the free Negroes were of no concern, and in the South the slaves were a simple problem of "law and order." In the sectional rivalry for a share in the country's wealth the slaves were just one item in the total inventory of the riches at stake. American hypocrisy concerning its perpetual materialism has clouded the actual cause of the conflict.

Frederick Douglass, who had expected Lincoln to call on the blacks immediately, by August 1861 had reached the bitter depths.

> Self-deception is a chronic disease of the American mind and character. The crooked way is ever preferred to the straight in all our mental processes, and in all our studied actions.

> We are masters in the art of substituting a pleasant falsehood for an ugly and disagreeable truth, and of clinging to a fascinating delusion while rejecting a palpable reality. Every reflecting man knows, and knows full well, that the real source and centre of the treason, rebellion and bloodshed under which the country is now staggering as if to its fall, is slavery. Every one knows that this is a slaveholder's rebellion, and nothing else. . . . Nobody doubts it, and everybody believes it; and yet the Government and people, owing to their chronic self-deception, their cowardly spirit and want of fixed principle, are practically rejecting what they know to be true, and accepting what they know to be false. . . . The impression which our Government seeks to make upon the slaveholders seems to be that slavery is safer in, than out of the Union.

But it was too soon for even Douglass to perceive the self-deception practiced by the American people in fighting the Civil War. The South not only demanded but was adamant on hegemony over the country because the slaveholders who ruled the Slave States were dependent on Yankee bottoms to carry their money crops, Yankee dollars to finance their operations, Yankee high prices for the finished goods, and Yankee low prices for their harvests. To them the expansion of slavery was but one among many concomitants of political control, such as the use of the fat lands to the west from which the Indians were being driven. Southern pride, States Rights, God-given inferiority of the blacks, and superiority of the whites was the pap fed the numerically preponderant non-slaveowners to keep them ready to use ballot or bullet on the "right" side.

In the North there were the same motivations among all classes. Keep the status quo, demanded the money merchants, the Yankee skippers and textile industrialists, the mine owners and steel fabricators. And to their exploited, the "free" labor of the day, they fed the pap of "Union Forever," with the blacks kept where they "belonged," in the fields down south, while they kept the labor cheap by importations from Europe.

All else were pious mutterings by the whites, rationalizations customary in combat between nations. It became a holy war in the North to preserve the Union founded by our forefathers. It became a holy war in the South to preserve the free institutions, such as local self-determination, established by our forefathers. The Negroes, free or slave, were only a problem in military logistics after Fort Sumter surrendered on the morning of April 13. In only one aspect of black involvement during the first disastrous year of the Civil War were the North and the South in agreement. Get rid of the blacks, a policy to which both Abraham Lincoln and Jefferson Davis subscribed. Send them somewhere, anywhere, beyond the country's limits and out of sight. It was agreed by both sides that a race, as well as a nation, cannot continue "half-slave and half free."

That was why Delany had so many enthusiastic white audiences. He was proposing an emigration scheme. Any and all blacks engaged in such activity were heard and honored because, then as now, American whites wished the "black problem" would go away.

Delany was in such demand in the East that he took up residence in Brooklyn in the area known as Columbia Heights. From there he carried on the work of the first African "adventure" as well as his lectures. Rev. King had reported to Lord Churchill that he had a "team" ready to join Delany in New York whenever a sailing date was set; the British Consul at Lagos, with the help of Rev. Samuel Crowther, had reported encouraging news that the treaty of Abeokuta would be restored as soon as the king of Dahomey withdrew his threat to the Yoruba country; Delany had forwarded his list of emigrants, those he had recruited as well as the families from Buxton Settlement, to the secretary of the African Aid Society—in fact, everything was ready, in the summer of 1861, to launch the experiment. Lord Churchill wrote to McCoskry, the British Consul at Lagos, to expect the emigrants.

> We venture therefore to recommend them to your good offices, and beg your cooperation with us for their advantage. We have made it known to them that those who wish to avail themselves of our assistance should defray the cost of their own passage to Lagos. On their arrival there the Society desires to commence its assistance in their aid, and for this purpose the Committee has reserved the sum of £100. The Committee will feel indebted to you if you will kindly consent to disembark and forward to Abbeokuta with the least delay possible, such of those Immigrants as may wish

to proceed there, and you are hereby authorized to draw upon the African Aid Society for any sum not exceeding the above mentioned.

The Committee have felt some difficulty in determining the proportions in which this sum should be expended, but they consider that a loan of £5 for each adult and £2.10.0 for each individual under 15 years of age, should be sufficient. If the actual cost of landing and transit from Lagos to Abbeokuta does not amount to so large a sum, the surplus of the respective £5 and £2.10.0 might be lent to the Immigrants to assist them in Abbeokuta. In any case the sum advanced to every immigrant is to be considered as a loan. And you are requested to take their note of hand for the advance, in default of better security.

Dr. Delany has already received ample funds to enable him to settle with his family in Abbeokuta. This proposed loan in aid will not therefore apply to him, but only to the first batch of Emigrants arriving at Lagos by the same vessel that brings Dr. Delany to your port.

Everything, therefore, was ready in Africa—and it was ready in Canada and New York. In the Buxton Settlement were two dozen men and their families who knew cotton and sugar culture. There were millwrights, carpenters, masons, and others skilled in plantation needs. Among them, too, were a few teachers chosen by Rev. King for their experience as administrative workers in the settlement.

In New York, Delany had three families waiting, each with commercial experience in cotton and sugar brokerage. The entire group in Canada and New York awaited the arrival of the *Mendi* which was to take them to Lagos. From that port they would take the river passages east into Yoruba country.

But then came Sumter and full-fledged war in America. Immediately upon the outbreak of the Civil War all of the country's plans came to a halt and were converted to a wartime purpose. That is what happened to the blacks and the abolitionists.

No colonists were sent to Liberia because the South would no longer send any kind of manpower. The American Colonization Society became moribund and remained so. The African Civilization Society halted all operations except those helping the Union cause. The white abolitionists and their black supporters fully adopted the one slogan—Save the Union—over which they had been arguing since 1858.

Was this the time to emigrate or the time to stay and fight? It was the same old question in a new context. If Lincoln's policy toward the blacks during that first year of the Civil War were considered, it was high time for the free blacks to emigrate before they were deported. Not only that, Lincoln repeatedly told the blacks that this was a white man's war and to stay out of the way.

On the other hand, Delany believed and had predicted in his lectures that Lincoln's policy *must* change, that, as he told his biographer six years later, "He thought he could discern, in the course then being pursued by Mr. Lincoln, a logical conclusion, and which, if not at first intended, would ultimately result in accomplishing the desires of the friends of freedom—emancipation to the slaves of the South, and the freedmen's rights as an inevitable consequence."

This too could have been wish expression, an afterthought. But it is true that as early as October 1861 Delany had hopes of black participation in the war effort. En route to Chicago, he stopped in Adrian, Michigan, to propose a plan to Asa Mahan, first president of Oberlin College (1835), which had opened its doors to black students. Now president of the new Adrian College, Mahan, originally a Congregationalist minister, had long proved his belief in the capacity of Negroes to live and learn equally with whites. That is why Delany selected him and proposed the formation of a corps d'Afrique patterned after the French Zouaves, organized in 1831 from a Berber tribe in Algeria. Their pattern of guerrilla fighting, Delany explained to Mahan, was peculiarly African and was highly successful in the Haitian revolution.

In their conferences, President Mahan agreed that he would apply to Lincoln for a commission as a major-general, with authority to raise an entire division of colored troops to be trained as "Zouaves" and that he would appoint Delany as his aide, "medical advisor and confidential bearer of dispatches."

Nothing came of this because Lincoln's policy toward the blacks at this time not only barred them from military service but actually planned their deportation from America in the name of "colonization." It took some time for events and individuals, such as Senator Charles Sumner of Massachusetts and

Congressman Thaddeus Stevens, to mold Lincoln into the "Great Emancipator" of schoolbook fame.

In November 1861 Delany was invited back into the fold of organized black leadership and even aligned himself with the African Civilization Society after he had won every change in its constitution he demanded. By then Henry Highland Garnet had been temporarily lost to Haitian emigration, and the Society's officers were now chiefly pastors of Negro congregations in and around New York. The headquarters of the Society was now at the Bible House there and all of the white Philadelphia influence seems to have been purged from the organization.

The *Weekly Anglo-African* reported the event at considerable length, beginning with the initial meeting on Nov. 4 "to hold a conference with Dr. Martin R. Delany, as the representative and exponent of the African movement, as understood by the Emigrationists and others, among the colored people of America, to effect and complete a oneness and harmony of sentiment and action, that their white friends, as aiders and assistants, may have a true and definite point as data before them."

At this meeting a committee was elected, which included Delany, "to draw up a basis as a fundamental principle by which the African Civilization Society shall be governed, and its objects and designs defined." With Rev. Richard H. Cain, pastor of the Bridge Street Church in Brooklyn as chairman, the committee added three articles to the Society's constitution, each of them written by Delany.

> Article I—The Society is not designed to encourage general emigration, but will aid only such persons as may be practically qualified and suited to promote the development of Christianity, morality, education, mechanical arts, agriculture, commerce, and general improvement, who must always be carefully selected and well recommended, that the progress of civilization may not be obstructed.
>
> Article II—The basis of the Society, and ulterior objects in encouraging emigration shall be—Self-reliance and Self-government, on the principle of an African Nationality, the African race being the ruling element of the nation, controlling and directing their own affairs.
>
> Article III—All Agents employed by this Society must

> act under instructions, and consistently with the fundamental principles of the Constitution.

The sum and substance of these meetings and additions of all that Delany had been preaching for nearly a year, was that he now became the spokesman for the organization. His colleagues, among them men like Rev. R. H. Cain with whom he was to work most intimately in South Carolina, assigned to him the task of bringing unity to the free blacks whose stake in the Civil War was so great and who were barred from any action in their own behalf or that of the slaves.

Delany set about his new work with his usual vigor. He appealed to Dr. James McCune Smith to join him and "a great Council of the leading men among us" to come to some policy agreement concerning their race.

> The point to be considered is not whether we are emigrationists or anti-emigrationists, in favor of or opposed to emigration; but whether we cannot agree upon and endorse a general policy which whilst it admits my right to go when and where I think best, admits yours to stay wherever you may think best; and at the same time, secures and defends a reciprocal interest in each other's welfare. . . .
>
> In God's name, must we ever be subordinate to those of another race both in as well as out of Africa? Is subordination our normal condition? Must we either be abject slaves, the property personal of the Caucasian, or the submissive drudges of their social industrial element, ever ministering as domestics to their pride and arrogance? Is it true that we are not to be permitted anywhere to govern ourselves, but must have white rulers? Have we no other destiny—no other social and political relations in prospect as an inheritance for our children? It is for us to determine whether or not this shall be so; therefore, I suggest to you, sir, to join with me in calling upon our educated men, to assemble at some convenient time and in Council, and determine on a settled policy as a rule of action, by which we shall be guided.

Delany made a similar appeal to his old friend in Pittsburgh, Rev. Martin H. Freeman, president of Avery College, in response to a second letter seeking his current opinion of Haitian emigration. Delany explained that he had been reluctant to answer due to the reaction he received a year before "when I met with such unexpected and unmerited severities." As a result: "I had concluded never to touch the subject again."

> Abstractly considered I have no objection to Haitian Emigration. Regarding it in the light of choosing one's own rulers, seeking self-government, aiding our self-emancipated brethren to sustain a Black Nationality, (or Colored, if that adjective be preferred) I agree with it; it is my favorite theme and policy, and you and I endorsed it long before the gentleman conducting that enterprise ever saw America, or Haiti, or probably a black person at all. And if it be to enter into the more elevated and profitable industrial pursuits, and thereby become contributors to the social and commercial relations of society and the world, as well as recipients of the benefits arising from these relations; to this I cheerfully subscribe. To none of these things do I object. My objection is to the fearful manner in which our people are being misled into the belief that Haiti presents the material advantages and facilities of a great and powerful nation.

By then the Haiti scheme was expiring. And by February 1862 so was Delany's own African plan, although he protested the rumor that he had given it up. On January 22 he declared, "I, and all those who originally intended to go to Africa, are making vigorous preparations for the consummation of our designs."

The war, then almost a year old, could no longer be kept out of his considerations. Little by little, President Lincoln was revealing his own plans for the blacks as pawns in the Union strategy, and they did not include black manpower or participation in any respect. They amounted to enforced colonization of a special character. When, on January 17 in the Shiloh Church in New York, Delany "brought down the house" with his promise that, should Great Britain attempt to raise the blockade of the South, the blacks' war cry would be "Insurrection!" and the government would not dare interfere, he was crying in the dark. All black efforts for their own betterment or for aid to the government in the war were stifled. There was every indication of the correctness of Frederick Douglass' statement in March 1862:

> The purpose of the Lincoln Administration, so far as it reveals a purpose at all, is simply to restore the country to precisely the same condition it was in before this terrible slaveholding rebellion broke out, leaving every root and fibre of the old cancerous political and moral sore again to grow and strengthen, till better able than now to destroy the nation's life.

Delany had never allowed himself to live in a dream world and Haiti, Africa, his Council of learned blacks—all these were dreams. It was time the blacks entered the Civil War.

CHAPTER FOURTEEN

The Black Committee

Much has been read into the Emancipation Proclamation by orators who have not read it. And much has been written into the long, puzzling, and painful course toward emancipation to interpret it as the will of the American people. It was not. It was the result of Abraham Lincoln's honest admission that his policy during the initial eighteen months of the Civil War had accomplished nothing toward achievement of peace, that barring the blacks from any consideration or participation in the war had been a failure.

Meanwhile, that policy had laid a pall upon all blacks, including Martin Delany, and actually dictated their continued despair in ever sharing American democracy. Delany was more fortunate than most black leaders. His home was in Chatham and so was his family. None of them need be exposed to the wave of white abuse that rolled over every northern city as defeat on the battlefields created resentment against the blacks who were the "whipping boy" for white frustrations.

Delany did not remain in Canada's shelter, however. He saw in Africa the only certainty for his people. During 1861 and most of 1862 he was to travel to almost every northern state telling blacks that, but he also was so involved in the dreams and hopes of his race that Lincoln's every act had a personal application. It was Lincoln's change of course that was to change Delany's, and it is necessary to examine the President's effect on the blacks throughout those difficult years.

The Emancipation Proclamation was *not* issued in recognition of a principle. It was an act of military necessity taken by Lincoln after many months of disastrous warfare and frankly stated as such by him. At no time did he dissemble or justify his puzzling policy in terms other than the utmost frankness. That policy, or conviction, was most clearly expressed in a letter to Horace Greeley, exactly one month before the September 22, 1862, preliminary proclamation of emancipation. In answer to the criticism of the editor of the *New York Tribune*, the President wrote, on August 22:

> My paramount object in this struggle is to save the Union, and is not either to save or destroy slavery. If I could save the Union without freeing any slave, I would do it; and if I could save it by freeing all the slaves, I would do it; and if I could do it by freeing some and leaving others alone, I would also do that.

The last was the course he had fostered all along in the belief that the Border States were the key to early ending of the rebellion. That is why the Emancipation Proclamation excepted these states and applied only to those which remained in rebellion on January 1, 1863. Slavery was not abolished in the United States until the 13th Amendment was adopted in 1865.

That was Lincoln's policy and judging it has provided fascinating historical speculation, though little enlightenment. He kept it a white man's war for the same reason, until forced to accept blacks because there were too few white volunteers and his draft was resisted by the whites. In debating emancipation with his cabinet, the Congress, and the public, he proposed gradual emancipation, selective emancipation, compensated emancipation. Above all, he attempted to develop, as a concomitant of emancipation, colonization of the freedmen beyond the country's borders through either voluntary or enforced deportation.

Though he did not mention the circumstances, Martin Delany must have been confounded to find his own words utilized in favor of the Lincoln colonization policy, particularly in the business of the 37th Congress. A governmental colony was exactly what he had warned against repeatedly over the years. Yet his report to the 1854 Cleveland Emigration Convention—*Political Destiny of the Colored Race On the American Continent*—was included in a propaganda pamphlet issued by the House of Representatives in behalf of Lincoln's colonization plan. On July 16, 1862, the House authorized printing of ten thousand copies of "Report of the Select Committee on Emancipation and Colonization" and an appendix. This was to be Lincoln's last effort to free some of the slaves and get rid of them through colonization in Central America. When this plan failed, he was forced into adopting the Emancipation Proclamation.

The very problem of slaves freed by military fortune or misfortune early in the war forced Lincoln's consideration of emancipation in the first place. When Congress authorized the confiscation of property utilized by the rebels in fighting, and the President signed it on August 6, 1861, that "property" included slaves. The questions not answered by the legislation were: When the Union forces did capture slaves, what was to be done with them? When families of slaves quite naturally fled to the protection of the enemies of their masters, were they covered by the legislation? What was the Army to do with them?

Having no policy, some fugitives reaching the Union forces were restored to their owners, others were told to go away, still others were put to work on camps and fortifications—all dependent on the attitude of the individual commanding officer toward slavery.

Lincoln asked Congress for legislation defining the obligations of the government toward these refugees and for any blacks the state governments might emancipate. This was in his message to Congress on December 3, 1861, and he added a significant consideration in proposing subsidized colonization for these blacks: "It might be well, too, to consider whether the free colored people already in the United States could not, so far as individuals may desire, be included in such colonization."

On March 6, 1862, Lincoln asked both the Senate and the House for a joint resolution "which shall be substantially as follows":

> *Resolved,* That the United States ought to cooperate with any State which may adopt gradual abolishment of slavery, giving to such State pecuniary aid, to be used by such State in its discretion, to compensate for the inconvenience, public and private, produced by such change in system.

In the message to Congress accompanying the proposed resolution, Lincoln's reasoning was explained as assuring the Border States loyal to the Union that they would be paid for voluntary emancipation, should any of these Slave States decide on it. It was something the Confederacy would never offer in order to buy them away. "While it is true that the adoption of the proposed resolution would be merely initiatory, and not within itself a practical measure, it is recommended in the hope that it would soon lead to important practical results."

The proposal was also to be a sop thrown to the radical Republicans in Congress who continued to demand emancipation, not only as a war measure, but as the final eradication of an evil. It was adopted on March 10 by a vote of 89–31, and not a word of the resolution was changed. That was because, in and of itself, the resolution had no meaning. When there was a motion in the House to postpone action, it was laughed away after the remarks made by Thaddeus Stevens, the firebrand from Pennsylvania.

> I think it is about the most diluted milk-and-water gruel proposition that was ever given to the American nation. The only reason I can discover why any gentleman should wish to postpone this measure is for the purpose of having a chemical analysis to see whether there is any poison in it.

Lincoln's next political step was to define a few things, such as "gradual abolishment" and "pecuniary aid." That was done on April 7 by the House in appointing its "Select Committee" of nine members to look into "the gradual emancipation of all the African slaves, and the extinction of slavery in the States of Delaware, Maryland, Virginia, Kentucky, Tennessee and Missouri." Equally important was the committee's opinion "whether colonization of such emancipated slaves on this continent or elsewhere is a necessary concomitant of their freedom, and how, and in what manner, provision may be made therefor . . ." and how far the U.S. government should go in compensating the masters.

It was a hand-picked committee, resulting from astute political maneuvering by Lincoln, with six of the nine members from the Border States themselves, and they produced exactly the recommendations desired by the President. Their timing was excellent too. On July 14 Lincoln sent to both the House and the Senate a proposed bill giving the President and the Secretary of the Treasury the authority to pay "at $—— per head, of all the slaves within such State as reported by the census of the year one thousand eight hundred and sixty" should they adopt immediate or gradual abolition of slavery.

Two days later, on July 16, the House authorized printing of the Select Committee *Report* with an appendix consisting chiefly of Delany's *Political Destiny* which followed immediately after President Lincoln's two brief messages to Congress. Not a word was deleted, and all of Delany's bitter analysis of the chances for black freedom in the United States—equality, too, not solely freedom—are presented as well as his exhaustive discussion of emigration to the havens of the western hemisphere. Obviously, that was why *Political Destiny* was included, for the Select Committee had come up with the plan Lincoln wanted, along with a lusty appeal to the greed of the northern merchants. The *Report* was a propaganda weapon since it also included the sentiments of the country's leading black emigrationist and his recommendation for black settlement to the south. That is why so many copies were printed—ten thousand —to counter the demands by radical Republicans for unconditional emancipation of all blacks.

The substance of the bill recommended by the committee was the appropriation of $180 million as compensation for the emancipation of the estimated 600 thousand slaves in the six Border States, figured "at the rate of three hundred dollars for each slave." There was a further appropriation in the measure:

> Sec. 3. *And be it further enacted by the authority aforesaid*, That for the purpose of deporting, colonizing, and settling the slaves so emancipated, as aforesaid, in some state, territory, or dominion beyond the limits of the United States, the sum of twenty millions of dollars is hereby appropriated, out of any moneys in the treasury not otherwise appropriated, to be expended for the purposes aforesaid, at the discretion of the President.

Each state was allowed five years from passage of the bill to enact its emancipation legislation and twenty years thereafter "for the complete and entire emancipation of the slaves therein."

The committee's reasoning in proposing the colonization clause entirely reflected Lincoln's thinking and actions almost to the day of issuance of the preliminary emancipation proclamation. It was a conviction that blacks and whites could never live in amity in the same country, under any circumstances. He did not hesitate to state that belief to a group of blacks invited to the White House on August 14, 1862, as well as in speeches and correspondence. In this, he and Delany were in agreement.

The *Report* argued in 1862:

> Much of the objection to emancipation arises from the opposition of a large portion of our people to the intermixture of the races, and from the association of white and black labor. The committee would do nothing to favor such a policy; apart from the antipathy which nature has ordained, the presence of a race among us who cannot, and ought not to, be admitted to our social and political privileges, will be a perpetual source of injury and inquietude to both. This is a question of color, and is unaffected by the relation of master and slave. The introduction of the negro (*sic*) whether bond or free, into the same field of labor with the white man, is the opprobrium of the latter; and we cannot believe that the thousands of non-slaveholding citizens in the rebellious States who live by industry are fighting to continue the negro within our limits, even in a state of vassalage, but more probably from a vague apprehension that he is to become their competitor in his own right. We wish to disabuse our laboring countrymen, and the whole Caucasian race who may seek a home here, of this error. We are satisfied that the labor of our cotton fields, as well as of our corn fields, may be performed by the white man, and we would offer to these sons of labor the emoluments of both. There is no sounder maxim in political economy than that the cultivators of the soil should be the owners of the soil. The committee conclude that the highest interests of the white race, whether Anglo-Saxon, Celt, or Scandinavian, require that the whole country should be held and occupied by those races alone.

There is no equivocation in this expression of future intent in regard to the races. It was no more than what Delany had warned his people of in 1854, when he said, "Let it then be understood, as a great principle of political economy, that no people can be free who themselves do not constitute an essential part of the *ruling element* of the country in which they live." He warned of the hopelessness of ever expecting any change or "cure" of what he called a "disease." "We propose for that disease a remedy. That remedy is emigration." So did the Select Committee. The Lincoln Administration's entire early wartime policy was based on America "for whites only." To implement that policy the blacks must be deported. Merely to ship them out was not possible. Lincoln's feelers, sent out through diplomatic channels to four nations with possessions in the western hemisphere, received a disdainful rejection, in effect stating, "It's your problem." Secret negotiations in Central America also failed. The Central American republics had already seen what had happened to Nicaragua in connection with Vanderbilt's stock speculation deal. None of them trusted the hungry democracy to the north.

Yet some formula to get rid of the blacks must be found, and it was the Select Committee's task to find it. They did. Recognizing the bad odor in which the United States was held in Central and South America the committee frankly presented the reasons:

> We contrived first to cool the ardor of their enthusiasm for the great republic to the north by total neglect and indifference, when perhaps our friendly offices would have served to sustain their struggling people against the intrigues of ambition, fomented by monarchists, to bring republics into disrepute. And finally we succeeded in alienating them by waging war to wrest from them vast provinces, to be planted with slavery, and sent forth our fillibusters (*sic*) to harass and annoy them even when at peace with their governments. Is it surprising that they transferred their good will, and with it their commercial intercourse, to other nations?

To change these attitudes, Central and South America must be warned against European commercial exploitation and "sold" on American commercial and financial ties. First, they must be sold on the advantage of welcoming the American slave to their shores. The following argument was for their consumption:

> Our American Negroes surpass in skill and intelligence all the other colored races of the world as much as the American tropics surpass all other regions in natural wealth and productiveness. They possess that mysterious quality of organism which makes its torrid glare—so fatal to other men—to them the very elixir of life and health. They have been instructed in agriculture and the mechanic arts; they have learned our language, our religion, and have become familiarized with our customs, which form the body of our law and the science of government, by long contact with our people. And when to this is added a natural docility of temper and subordination to authority, no one should doubt their capacity to maintain a free and independent government under the guidance and patronage of our republic; especially should such doubts give way when we have before our eyes such examples of their ability for self-government as they have furnished in Liberia and Hayti.

It should be remembered that the above was for foreign consumption only. It did not lead to recommendation that such ideal citizens be kept at home. For domestic consumption there were other propaganda angles—chief among them, profits. If room cannot be found in Central or South American republics for our blacks, then buy a country for them! It would be a gold mine as an investment. Besides, something should be done to pay off the costs of the war.

> The commercial aspect which the proposed plan of colonization presents claims especial attention at this time beyond that which under ordinary circumstances would attach to it; and instead of being deterred from embracing, by apprehension of entailing additional burdens upon the nation, it can be made to appear that it is essential to the speedy restoration of commercial prosperity, and the only mode of indemnity for the losses and destruction of property inflicted by the war.

It was so "made to appear." Once more an American government attempted to put stars in the eyes of its people with the patented Manifest Destiny approach successful so far.

> It would be difficult, if not impossible, to overstate the productiveness of the tropical regions of America, or to find another spot on earth where labor is so abundantly repaid. The labor of one million rude and barbarous negroes in Cuba may be said, without metaphor, to support the civil, military, and naval establishments of Spain; and yet Cuba is by no means superior to many other portions of our tropics. It may therefore be well imagined what would be the result of planting five millions of American Negroes, far superior in skill and intelligence to those of Cuba, in a country equal to the Queen of the Antilles, protected by our power and directed by our intelligence, and stimulated to exertion by those motives which the wants of civilization, which they have acquired among us, have never failed to supply, and which are higher and more efficient than any other which can animate men. If we add to this the certain result of extending our power and influence, through their instrumentality, over the millions of people who already inhabit these regions, we shall be able to form some conception of the value to our commerce which the foundation of such a colony would confer.

This was not at all what Delany meant in 1854 and expressed in his *Political Destiny*. He had meant no new colony for the United States, only a country for the blacks. He had meant no profits for the New York mercantile houses, only for the blacks. He had meant no government dictated by the United States, only self-government by and for the blacks. His statements are unmistakably clear in the appendix of the Select Committee's *Report*, but the committee gave them the interpretation desired, calling attention to the emigration convention at which

> after deliberation and debate, marked by knowledge and ability, they passed resolutions and issued an address in favor of the colonization in the American tropics, to which their instincts pointed as their future home, and to which their instincts beckoned them to become the founders of empire. Experience, painful and sad, had convinced them that here they would forever remain an inferior caste, denied every right which distinguishes or gives value to personal freedom, while the conviction that the torrid zone, their

> natural organization fitting them to endure its climate, where fervid heat enervates and emasculates all other races, gave the best guarantee against the degradations with which they had been afflicted.

How Delany must have squirmed on reading this, and all of the committee's *Report*! Yet it must be considered in the light of Lincoln's policy. By the year 1900, in accord with that policy, the United States might have been lily white. If not for the continued Confederate victories and the white reluctance to fight in the Union Army, there might never have been an Emancipation Proclamation. That same policy withheld from Delany and many thousands of eager blacks the right to fight in their own behalf. Lincoln allowed no black troops until he needed troops of any color to save the Union. Delany was intimately concerned with that aspect of Lincoln's policy, too, but was as helpless as the rest of the blacks until the Emancipation Proclamation itself allowed him to act. Lincoln declared the slaves in those states in rebellion on January 1, 1863, to be free and specified those Border States and parts of states in which they were to remain in slavery. The Proclamation defined no other aspect of their freedom but did recommend that they "abstain from all violence, unless in necessary self-defense" and that they "labor faithfully for reasonable wages."

But the section that gladdened every black and released Delany for action was the following: "And I further declare and make known that such persons of suitable condition will be received into the armed service of the United States to garrison forts, positions, stations and other places and to man vessels of all sorts in said service."

This too was the result of protest against Lincoln's policy and related to his combined emancipation and colonization efforts. Not a single state made a move toward emancipation of any kind—compensated, gradual, or immediate. He persuaded Congress, later in 1863, to make the state of Missouri a special offer of compensated emancipation, and the Senate appropriated $15 million for the purpose. However, the measure was killed in the House by the Missouri delegation itself. The method of compensation was to be in U.S. bonds at 6 percent interest. What good would U.S. bonds be if the Confederates won the war? they reasoned.

Thereafter, Lincoln changed his policy from political compromise in relation to the blacks to their utilization in winning the war and thus saving the Union.

From just a few days after the outbreak of hostilities blacks, individually and collectively, pleaded continuously for a chance to fight for the Union. Each time, Lincoln refused. As defeat followed upon defeat, as Lincoln quarreled more and more with his generals, each time he canceled a military order utilizing blacks, the free Negroes saw each event as a step closer to extinction of the Union. That would signify slavery for them and no refuge anywhere, for a southern victory would be inevitable purgatory for every black man. That is why they flocked to hear Delany on Africa, for escape might be their last recourse. More than any white man in the North, including Abraham Lincoln, the blacks needed Union victory.

Rejected by Lincoln and unable to join their state militia because of a Federal prohibition of 1792, blacks began to form their own militia in Boston, New York, and Philadelphia. They wrote to the President, to Secretary of War Simon Cameron, to members of Congress. *The Liberator* and *Frederick Douglass' Monthly* with each issue begged, demanded, hailed the black heroes of the Revolution and the War of 1812, and reported "Crispus Attucks" meetings.

Lincoln was adamant. Arming the blacks would anger the rebels, anger the Border States, and anger the white soldiers. In all three, he was correct but evinced no leadership in an effort to change these attitudes. When Cameron, in his December 1861 report to Congress, recommended arming the slaves coming into Union lines in the war zones, Lincoln angrily had him delete it. When General David Hunter, in May 1862 with authority from Cameron, recruited the first black regiment of the war, on the South Carolina Sea Islands, he was forced to disband it. He could get no authorization from Washington for arms, uniforms, and food, to say nothing of pay. However, in Kansas Gen. James H. Lane had small colored units fighting unofficially in his very first engagement of the war. Louisiana had Gen. Benjamin F. Butler recruiting colored troops and finally, on August 25, 1862, the use of blacks to fight as well as labor in the war effort was recognized by the War Department in authorizing Gen. Rufus Saxton in the

Department of the South, to recruit up to five thousand Negro troops.

This official action did not represent a change in Lincoln, only a recognition of a necessity. Early in July Lincoln had asked for 300,000 white volunteers, based on his generals' pleas for soldiers. The response was so scant and the need to hold the deep southern sections of Georgia, South Carolina, and Florida controlled by Gen. Saxton so great, that Lincoln had no choice but to approve the request.

Real recruiting among the northern free Negroes did not begin until after the Emancipation Proclamation had authorized it. But now the blacks did not flock to the colors as readily as they would have a year before. By the early months of 1863 unskilled white labor was receiving competition for war production jobs from the blacks who had never had such job opportunities. There were anti-Negro riots in Brooklyn in August 1862 and in southern Illinois, Indiana, and Ohio the same year as freedmen escaped from the war zones and bid for work. The riots in Boston, New York, Philadelphia, and other eastern cities intensified, but they were traditional, for the hordes of white immigrants from Europe quickly adopted this American custom in relation to the blacks. Delany was living in Brooklyn when a mob of Irish set fire to the Lorillard and Watson tobacco warehouse there, with its approximately 25 colored employees still in it. Fortunately, they were rescued by police. But incidents like this did not induce blacks to fight in what had been a white man's war. And when Lincoln called for a draft, on July 13, 1863, in New York City anti-draft riots occurred beside which the Vietnam demonstrations seem like church socials. They lasted for four days and nights and an estimated 50 to 75 blacks (not all bodies found) were hung, clubbed to death, drowned, or burned. Also consumed by flame was the New York Negro Orphan Asylum.

There were other reasons for initial hesitation by black enlistees. They were discriminated against in the size of the enlistment bounties, an important consideration for the families they left behind; their pay was less and there were War Department regulations, agreed to by Lincoln, that none could hope to become officers.

Finally, there was the widely publicized announcement by Jefferson Davis that the Confederates would not treat blacks in

Union uniform as legitimate prisoners of war. They would be killed or enslaved upon capture.

This warning from Jefferson Davis, widely publicized through the North, naturally raised a question in black minds—what would the President do about that? Again Lincoln procrastinated and it was not until July 30, 1863, that he issued General Order No. 233:

> It is the duty of every Government to give protection to its citizens, of whatever class, color, or condition, and especially to those who are duly organized as soldiers in the public service. The law of nations, and the usages and customs of war, as carried on by civilized powers, permit no distinction as to color in the treatment of prisoners of war as public enemies. To sell or enslave any captured person on account of his color, is a relapse into barbarism, and a crime against the civilization of the age.
>
> The Government of the United States will give the same protection to all of its soldiers, and if the enemy shall sell or enslave any one because of his color, the offense shall be punished by retaliation upon the enemy's prisoners in our possession. It is, therefore ordered, for every soldier of the United States, killed in violation of the laws of war, a rebel soldier shall be executed; and for every one enslaved by the enemy, or sold into slavery, a rebel soldier shall be placed at hard labor on the public works, and continued at such labor until the other shall be released and receive the treatment due to prisoners of war.

Stanton took almost immediate action on this new policy. On August 8 he ordered three South Carolina prisoners held as hostages for the undetermined fate of three colored seamen captured by the rebels aboard the Union gunboat *Isaac Smith* off Charleston Harbor.

What pleased the Negro leaders, and particularly Martin Delany, was the President's terminology in naming black soldiers as "citizens." Whether or not the "eye for an eye" policy deterred the rebels remained to be seen but the blacks of the North were tickled by the first application of General Order No. 233. Three black sailors were held equal to three white rebels! How the South must have frothed at news of that! The Black (Recruiting) Committee immediately utilized both events in recruiting posters, promising "AND RETALIATION WILL BE OUR PRACTICE NOW—MAN FOR MAN—TO THE BITTER END."

Before the war was over, approximately 186,000 black troops had been in the Union Army, all of them enlistees. Their recruitment, in which Martin Delany had a most productive role, was the result of a combined effort by black leadership, and it constitutes a chapter in American history even less known than the remarkable record of fighting ability made by the black troops.

That record was the more remarkable because these black troops had grown up without hope, without future, without all the motivations which, in theory, make national military heroes. Yet, as the abolitionist editor Edmund Quincy expressed it: "If this nation is to be saved, it will be by the assistance of the race which owes us no gratitude and to which the first favor we have granted is the privilege of fighting and dying in our behalf."

All of the military reminiscences of the Civil War attest to the courage of the black troops, and their white officers broke into enthusiastic praise about these "docile" people who were not supposed to be fighters. But few of those generals rallied in their behalf later. The one great exception was Gen. Benjamin F. Butler of Boston, perhaps the most unorthodox commander ever disinherited by any War Department. He had three companies of an "Armee d'Afrique" in New Orleans in 1862 and told Washington not to bother him when he was ordered to disband them. As a result, he was transferred. Ten years later, as a member of Congress from Massachusetts, Butler testified in favor of the Civil Rights Bill of 1875 and recalled the battle of New Market (Va.) Heights in which a 3,000-man division of colored troops allowed the Army of the James to advance by storming a fort. Their casualties were enormous, both dead and wounded. Butler told the House Committee:

> It became my painful duty, sir, to follow in the track of that charging column and there in a space not wider than the clerk's desk and 300 yards long lay the dead bodies of 543 of my colored comrades slain in defense of their country, who had laid down their lives to uphold its flag and its honor as a willing sacrifice and as I rode along among them, guiding my horse this way and that lest he should profane

> with his hoofs what seemed to me the Sacred dead and as I looked on their bronzed faces upturned in the shining sun as if in mute appeal against the wrongs of the country to which they had given their lives and whose flag had only been to them a flag of Stripes upon which no Star of glory had ever shone for them. Feeling I had wronged them in the past and believing what was the future of my country to them, among my dead comrades I swore to myself a solemn oath. May my right hand forget its cunning and my tongue cleave to the roof of my mouth if I ever fail to defend the rights of those men who have given their blood for me and my Country this day and for their race forever and, God helping me, I will keep that oath.

He kept his oath, in 1875 (and until his death in 1893). As a result he was defeated for re-election to Congress by the whites of Massachusetts who, by then, were conceding to the South all that it had rebelled for.

Once more Martin Delany completed the cycle. Once more he turned away from Africa. Once more he turned away from emigration. Here was a concrete and potent reason to "stay and fight." The enemy was quite the same, *all* the whites, but now they were divided—non-slaveholder against slaveholder. Both shared the same attitudes toward his race but there was the truism that the holocaust had converted more sinners into saints than any act of faith. So far, one thing was certain. Approximately 3 million of his people would not be slaves, if the non-slaveholders won. They might not be free, but they would not be slaves. That and that alone would be the greatest advance in the history of American slavery. Delany turned to the new work with his usual aggressive, articulate assurance.

He was lecturing in Chicago when news came that Lincoln had actually signed the Emancipation Proclamation and disclosed that black troops would be enlisted. He was speaking there with the sponsorship of his former opponent to emigration, John Jones, the John B. Vashon of Illinois, a comparatively wealthy tailor and indomitable black abolitionist. Now he and Delany were fast friends, and both forgot the 1854 resolution of the Illinois Colored Convention condemning Delany—and Delany's bitter reply. Both saw in the Emancipation Proclamation an opening door. Now Delany subscribed to Vashon's belief in exploiting the American worship of the uniform to open the door the rest of the way—to citizenship.

His opportunity came in 1862. On January 26 the new Secretary of War, Edwin M. Stanton, just eleven days after he replaced Simon Cameron, issued authorization to Gov. John A. Andrew of Massachusetts to raise a regiment of colored troops. Gov. Andrew had pestered Cameron for such official authorization ever since Gen. Saxton had been given it in August 1862.

Lincoln and Stanton stipulated that the 54th Massachusetts Regiment must have white officers but would have equal pay and bounties with white soldiers, a promise that was not kept. Gov. Andrew set to recruiting work with enthusiasm but soon learned that the thousand volunteers he needed could not be supplied by the small Negro population of his state. In fact, he learned from his superintendent of the census that if all Negro males of military age enlisted he could raise no more than 394 colored troops.

The governor turned to the old-time abolitionist, one of the "Secret Six" who had funded John Brown's Kansas campaigns, George Luther Stearns, the wealthy pipe manufacturer. Stearns organized what came to be known as the "Black Committee" which was to function as a recruiting body among the blacks for nearly two years. He enlisted the services of Frederick Douglass, Martin Delany, John Mercer Langston, Charles Lenox Remond, Henry Highland Garnet, John S. Rock, William Wells Brown, and other black leaders. Delany became a full-time agent and recruited in Illinois and Ohio. By the end of April the roster of the famous 54th, commanded by Robert Gould Shaw, was filled, and the impetus was such that the Black Committee continued to recruit. Soon the Massachusetts 55th Regiment was filled.

Among the first recruits in the 54th Massachusetts and a survivor of its heroic exploits at Fort Wagner, was Toussaint L'Ouverture Delany, who had just turned eighteen and wrote his father from Chatham, asking his permission to enlist. The proud father was delighted and Toussaint was sworn in as a private in Company D on March 27 in Readville, Mass.

Before he had completed his assignment for the Black Committee Delany attempted to join the Army himself. He wrote to apply for a post as Army surgeon, and the War Department replied that his letter had been received and the application was "under consideration." Another black Canadian physician, Major Alexander T. Augusta, then practicing in Toronto, and an honor graduate of Trinity College, Toronto, had written the War Department in February and was invited to Washington for examination. He passed the examination and was appointed surgeon in command at Camp Barker, a refugee and colored soldiers' hospital which he developed into the present Freedmen's Hospital. He was commissioned a major in the 7th U.S. Cavalry.

But the black man in uniform encountered difficulties. When Augusta was granted leave to return to Canada to wind up his affairs, his shoulder straps were torn from him, he was beaten, and the mob carried him out of the Baltimore railroad station and into the streets. He was rescued by a Provost Martial squad, examined for his credentials, and sent back to the depot. In spite of a guard, the mob beat him again, and he had to hide in a store until dark. Yet Augusta returned to duty in Washington, although in civvies, and compiled such a commendable record that several white medical men wrote in complaint to President Lincoln: "When we made application for positions in Colored Service, the understanding was universal that all commissioned officers were to be white men. Judge our surprise and disappointment when upon joining our respective regiments, we found that the Senior Surgeon of the Command was a Negro." Immediately afterward, Maj. Augusta was relieved of his duties and assigned to examine incoming recruits. But his abilities were known to Gen. Saxton and Augusta was transferred south to open a military hospital in Savannah.

But Delany never heard from the War Department, and he returned to recruiting colored troops. Next he worked to raise 2,500 enlistees for Rhode Island and found them in Canada, Michigan, and again in Illinois where John Jones helped so much. But even while he was working as Rhode Island's official agent and without consulting him, the state authorities reduced the enlistee bounty for blacks to $22. Delany wired his protest to Providence and received a reply that he was relieved from recruiting duty. He was summoned to Providence and there, the Rhode Island quota having been filled, Governor Smith recommended him to the Connecticut authorities. Delany went on to New Haven and accepted the task of recruiting that state's quota of 5,000 black men. He went back home to Chatham and there picked up his friend and medical colleague, Dr. Amos

Array, to examine black recruits while he, Delany, found them. To facilitate their work they established offices in Cleveland and Chicago.

This was quite an accomplishment for Delany. He was the first black man to be awarded a recruiting contract by any state. And he had full authority to see that the promises made to enlistees were kept. Those promises and conditions of enlistment were fully spelled out in a handbill he had printed in Chicago on December 1, 1863.

BLACK NATIONAL DEFENDERS!

The State of Connecticut is authorized to raise Colored Troops; and any number of her quota of 5,000 may be colored men. 29th Regiment Connecticut Volunteers, is now being formed at Camp Buckingham, composed entirely of Colored Men, located at the beautiful City of New Haven, the seat of Yale University.

STATE BOUNTY
$200.00 CASH!
on being sworn in.

By an old law of the State, 30 dollars a year are allowed to each soldier for clothing, 10 dollars of which is paid down at the time of entering the service, the other 20 dollars being paid in four month payments each, making 210 dollars Bounty, cash, on joining the Regiment—and 20 dollars more during the year.

An important fact connected with this recruiting is, that the contract for raising the troops has been given to a Colored Man; and Connecticut is the first State since the war commenced, which has been thus liberal and considerate.

This fact alone should be an inducement for COLORED MEN to rally to her standards; all the Recruiting Agents in the West being Colored; and this principle should prevail everywhere. Colored Men should recruit Colored Men, as best adapted to it.

The most liberal compensation will be given to Good Agents, about 50 such being now wanted, and to whom will be paid Cash so soon as service is rendered.

APPLY WITHOUT DELAY TO
DR. M. R. DELANY

State Contractor, Head-Quarters of the West and South-Western States and Territories, 172 Clark Street, Top Story, Chicago, Ill.

JOHN JONES, Assistant

But Connecticut too failed to keep its promises to the recruits. Delany found that in order to assure his men their bounties and allowances he had to accompany them to Camp Buckingham near New Haven and see that the white disbursing officers did pay off. He felt it was right that "Colored Men should recruit Colored Men" but without the proper authority the recruiting officer could offer no guarantees. Delany was to recruit for Ohio too, but by now his heart was not in it. For recruiting Union troops, black or white, by then had become a racket. If the various states kept their promises, their recruiting agents did not. The enlistees of both colors were robbed of their bounties, their traveling allowances to their regiments, their food allowances, their family allowances. Complaints to the state authorities, the War Department, and to Lincoln meant nothing.

Delany was pretty well disgusted with the northern recruiting system. In outlining his clearly fixed conditions of enlistment with Connecticut, Delany told his biographer:

> This I considered justice and so established it as a system of recruiting. If there had not been a dollar, instead of being a hundred, to give as a bounty to a single slave, or to the sons of the distinguished Douglass, and my own, I should have acted as I did—put my own son in the army, endeavor to get the bondsman in, for the purpose of overthrowing the infamous system of slavery and the rebellion.
>
> On returning from Connecticut, I consulted my distinguished friend, the Rev. Mr. Garnet, in regard to the system I had adopted, of which he highly approved, as "*coming from ourselves, concerning ourselves.*"
>
> All this, however, neither covers, defends, nor tolerates in any degree the reprehensible and most shameful impositions continually practiced, by various methods of deceptions under the pretext of recruiting. What I defend is a le-

gitimate system laid down, to be strictly conformed to the letter. Whatever was promised the recruit, he should have received, and this should have been fixed and enforced by the proper authorities, and not left optional with a stolid set of human brokers.

Delany tried once more after the Connecticut endeavor at the request of his friend, John Mercer Langston. The state of Ohio had its quota of colored troops and Delany took on the task but not without demanding and receiving a state commission. Governor Brough had thought that Washington would frown on it but Delany declared that he would not accept the assignment without it. He received the commission while in Nashville, Tenn., where he planned headquarters for the Ohio activity. With that accomplished and without change in the recruiting racket, Delany gave up and returned to Chatham.

But it was while at the height of his Connecticut recruiting in Chicago that Delany renewed his corps d'Afrique plan first suggested to Asa Mahan two years before. He had been into the Border States for recruits and had talked with fugitives from the rebel zones. On December 15, 1863, he wrote the following letter to Secretary of War Stanton:

Sir:

The Subject and policy of Black Troops, have become of much interest in our Country, and the effective means and method of raising them is a matter of much importance.

In consideration of this Sir, I embrace the earliest opportunity of asking the privilege of calling the attention of your Department to the fact, that as a policy in perfect harmony with the cause of the President and your own enlightened views, that the Agency of intelligent black men adapted to the work must be the most effective means of obtaining Black Troops; because knowing and being of that people as a race, they can command such influence as is required to accomplish the object.

I have been successfully engaged as a Recruiting Agent of Black Troops, first as a Recruiting Agent for Massachusetts 54th Rgt. and from the commencement as the Managing Agent in the West and South-West for Rhode Island Heavy Artillery, which is now nearly full, and now have the

Contract from the State Authorities of Connecticut for the entire West and South-West, in raising Colored Troops to fill her quota.

During these engagements, I have had associated with me Mr. John Jones, a very respectable and responsible business colored man of this city, and we have associated ourselves permanently together in an Agency for raising Black Troops for all parts of the Country.

We are able sir, to command all of the effective black men as Agents in the United States, and in the event of an order from your Department giving us the Authority to recruit Colored Troops in any of the Southern or seceded States we will be ready and able to raise a Regiment, or Brigade if required, in a shorter time than can be otherwise effected.

With the belief sir, that this is one of the measures in which the claims of the Black Man may be officially recognized, without seemingly infringing upon those of other citizens, I confidently ask sir, that this humble request, may engage your early notice.

All satisfactory references will be given by both of us.

I have the honor to be sir

Your most obt. Very humble servt.

M. R. Delany

M. M. Wagoner, Secy.

Again Delany waited for a reply. The letter was received by the War Department on December 19, turned over to the Adjutant General's Office on December 23 and, at the same time, it was noted that Cong. Isaac N. Arnold of Chicago had transmitted a message in regard to the letter. The life-long anti-slavery advocate and radical Republican in Congress had added: "I respectfully ask for the consideration of the Secretary of War."

Whether or not it ever was considered by Stanton is not known. At any rate, there was no reply. Twice Delany had attempted to obtain a hearing for his plan for recruitment of the slaves in the rebel states into a corps d'Afrique and twice he had been ignored.

Now he took direct action.

The succeeding months proved that Delany's plan was important. Had it been acted upon early in the war, when he proposed it to Asa Mahan, the Civil War might have been shortened. He foresaw the danger that the Confederates themselves might arm and fight their slaves against the Yankees once it was proved, to their loss, that the black soldier made a mighty good fighting man.

In 1863 Judah P. Benjamin, the Confederate Secretary of State urged arming the slaves and promising them emancipation for fighting. Since the very beginning of the rebellion, he pointed out, slaves had been used, not only to remain on the land and provision the fighting whites, but to build fortifications and perform other labor services. In some Confederate states, they were armed as state militia to keep the domestic peace, and thus freed whites for battle.

During 1864 white soldiers of the Confederacy were growing scarcer, and in his message to the Confederate Congress in November of that year, President Jefferson Davis recognized that slaves might be necessary as soldiers.

> The subject is to be viewed by us, therefore, solely in the light of policy and our social economy. When so regarded, I must dissent from those who advise a general levy and arming of slaves for the duty of soldiers. Until our white population shall prove insufficient for the armies we require and can afford to keep the field, to employ as a soldier the Negro, who has merely been trained to labor, and as a laborer under the white man, accustomed from his youth to the use of firearms, would scarcely be deemed wise or advantageous by any; and this is the question before us. But should the alternative ever be presented of subjugation or of the employment of the slave as a soldier, there seems no reason to doubt what should be our decision.

That point of necessity in utilizing the slave—so similar in expression and content between Jefferson Davis and Abraham Lincoln—was soon reached. In January 1865 the commander in chief of the Confederate Army, Gen. Robert E. Lee, recommended what Delany had feared, arming the slaves. On March 13 the Confederate Congress approved, but it was too late. By then there was no time left in which to train the slaves to be southern soldiers. By then, Delany was doing that for the Union side.

Events proved that his warnings had been correct, that if the Union did not use the slave, the Confederates would. His farsightedness had caused him to sound the first warning in October 1861, more than three years before it was heeded at last.

CHAPTER FIFTEEN

The "Black Major"

In 1864, Delany chose Wilberforce, in southern Ohio, as his family's new home. Wilberforce was a black community and had a black university founded and kept alive by a black church—the African Methodist Episcopal Church. It was founded in 1856, when Delany had moved to Canada, but he had known of its plans because Rev. Lewis Woodson, his teacher and friend in Pittsburgh, was one of the founding trustees of Wilberforce University when the AME Church paid $10,000 for its 152 acres near Xenia, Ohio.

Originally, the community was called Tawawa Springs and was a Negro summer resort in pre-war years. Southern planters who fathered many mulattoes and had a genuine affection for their mothers, sent their dusky families there to educate the children. The mothers usually were set free and remained at Wilberforce at least until their children had completed elementary school. There are on record two examples of white men, legally unable to marry their slaves and loving their families, who settled in Tawawa Springs with them.

It was due to the efforts of one of the AME Church's outstanding scholars, Bishop Daniel A. Payne, that the church organized Wilberforce University, primarily to educate students destined for its ministry. Like all black educational efforts, it suffered the vagaries of poverty, and when the Civil War broke out, lost most of its students since they came from rebel states. The school was closed down until 1863 and reopened with a faculty of two. Through all its vicissitudes, Wilberforce University continued the resolve made at its dedication in October 1856 "that the colored man must, for the most part, be the educator and elevator of his own race."

The Delany family's move to Wilberforce in 1864 was made

shortly after the birth of Halle Ethiope, and the preparatory school there was of primary importance to Delany. Toussaint L'Ouverture was away at war, Charles Lenox Remond was 14, Alexander Dumas was 10, Saint Cyprian was eight, and Faustin Soulouque, six. Only Placido Rameses, two years old, and the newborn were too young for school.

The Delany home was bought from Bishop Payne himself for $670 on November 9, 1864, and had a little over six acres of wooded hillside. The house itself, with eight rooms, was sheltered in a hollow just a few steps from the Wilberforce University campus. Here the family settled in and never moved again. Both Martin and Catherine Delany are buried there with two of their children.

It was an ideal community for a resumption of family life, with an intellectual atmosphere which Delany always craved, a self-governing black community living harmoniously with the surrounding whites of Greene County. It had no doctor, being served by a white physician from Xenia, just three and a half miles away. Catherine's abilities as a seamstress had an immediate demand, and so were Martin's lectures on black nationality, black pride, black Africa. Besides, Delany was now 52 years old and it was time to "settle down."

For Catherine and the children, there could not have been a better choice for them. Their next-door neighbors were the family of Rev. (soon to be Bishop) Benjamin W. Arnett of the AME Church. Soon, the Browns from Chatham moved to Wilberforce in order to educate their children at Wilberforce. Hallie Q. Brown, who graduated from Wilberforce in the same class as Alexander Dumas Delany and was on the faculty, became an admirer of Catherine's, writing about her as one of the "Homespun Heroines." Catherine was popular among the students, too, for every now and then she invited them for a "good, wholesome meal," as one graduate described it. She ran a good home in which Delany could have spent the rest of his life, at peace with all in the world except himself. But the choice was "Stay and *fight*," not "Stay and submit."

Once more the Delany imperative made the decision. He intended to see Abraham Lincoln and propose to the President his plan for the corps d'Afrique. He refused to give up the plan until it was negated by the highest power in the land. He refused an offer to recruit two black regiments for Indiana because his corps d'Afrique was to be commanded by a black and officered by blacks. The only whites with any authority whatsoever over such troops were to be those of superior rank to the black commander. Lincoln and Congress had finally recognized the equality in pay of the enlisted men; now it was time they removed the ban against black commissions. The fight of the past thirty years had now become the struggle for equality, in the military at first.

Two weeks before taking direct action himself by going to Washington, Delany expressed his criticism of the military in a letter to the *Anglo-African* in defense of Gen. Benjamin F. Butler, most independent of all the generals in use of colored troops.

> MR. EDITOR: Does it not strike you and the lovers of liberty, as a most extraordinary proceeding, that the first man who was able to cross the James River, approach Richmond and hold his position, thereby opening the way for the approach of the General-in-Chief, has been removed from his command?
>
> How comes it that *every* popular commander of the *blacks*, in the armies about Richmond, has been removed? I reflect not upon our glorious Chief Magistrate, President Lincoln, nor that great-souled statesman, Secretary Stanton, for these strange things. God bless Gen. Butler!
>
> I would that the government had more silver and gold and less brass and *copper* (Copperheads) to sustain it.

Delany arrived in Washington on February 6, 1865, and was the house guest of his old co-worker, opponent, but always friend, Rev. Henry Highland Garnet. His host was not encouraging.

"I have been abroad," he told Delany, "I have been near the persons of nobility and royalty; but I never saw personages so hard to reach as the heads of government in Washington."

There is no official report of Martin Delany's interview with Abraham Lincoln in the White House two days later, on February 8. Nor is there any inkling as to how he managed to get the appointment, and get it so rapidly. It is possible that Lincoln had heard or read of Delany, for many of his lectures on Africa had been fully reported. Or Lincoln may have heard of the International Statistical Congress incident in London, for that too was widely reported in the American press. Or, he may have read the report of his Select Committee and seen Delany's *Political Destiny* there. We do not know.

But Delany did see Lincoln shortly after 8 o'clock on the morning of February 8 because there is a note about it in Lincoln's handwriting. The note read as follows:

> Feb. 8, 1865
>
> Hon. E. M. Stanton, *Secretary of War*
> Do not fail to have an interview with this most extraordinary and intelligent black man.
>
> A. Lincoln

Delany's account of his interview with President Lincoln, dictated to his biographer, stresses the deep interest and kindliness he was given.

> On entering the executive chamber, and being introduced to his excellency, a generous grasp and shake of the hand brought me to a seat in front of him. No one could mistake the fact that an able and master spirit was before me. Serious without sadness, and pleasant withal, he was soon seated, placing himself at ease, the better to give me a patient audience.

Delany first reconstructed the situation regarding black troops and reminded Lincoln of the threat by the Confederacy to arm the slaves. He told the President that the blacks of the North could "defeat it by complicity with those of the South, through the medium of the *Underground Railroad*—a measure known only to themselves."

Next, he pointed out that the blacks in the Union Army, in spite of the prejudice against them, had accomplished all that they had been called upon to do, and the President agreed. Delany stated that he then discussed the fact that, just as white soldiers would never fight under black officers, slaves in the South would not trust white officers.

> And I propose, as a most effective remedy to prevent enrolment of the blacks in the rebel service, and induce them to

run to, instead of from, the Union forces—the commissioning and promotion of black men now in the army, according to merit.

Looking at me for a moment, earnestly yet anxiously he demanded, "How will you remedy the great difficulty you have just now so justly described about the objections of white soldiers to colored commanders, and officers to colored associates?"

"I propose, sir, an army of blacks, commanded entirely by black officers, except such whites as may volunteer to serve; this army to penetrate through the heart of the South, and make conquests, with the banner of Emancipation unfurled, proclaiming freedom as they go, sustaining and protecting it by arming the emancipated, taking them as fresh troops, and leaving a few veterans among the new freedmen, when occasion requires, keeping this banner unfurled until every slave is free, according to the letter of your proclamation. I would also take from those already in the service all that are competent for commission officers, and establish at once in the South a camp of instructions. By this we could have in about three months an army of forty thousand blacks in motion, the presence of which anywhere would itself be a power irresistible. You should have an army of blacks, President Lincoln, commanded entirely by blacks, the sight of which is required to give confidence to the slaves, and retain them to the Union, stop foreign intervention, and speedily bring the war to a close."

The President's reply, according to Delany, was enthusiastic. "This is the very thing I have been looking and hoping for; but nobody offered it. . . ." They discussed it at length and then suddenly turning, he said, "Will you take command?"

"If there be none better qualified than I am, sir, by that time I will. While it is my desire to serve, as black men we shall have to prepare ourselves, as we have had no opportunities of experience and practice in the service as officers."

The President brushed the objection aside, saying that "the tactics are easily learned, especially among your people. It is the head that we now require most—men of plans and executive ability."

Delany left with Lincoln's enthusiastic good wishes, a glad heart, and a mind already planning. However, his realism soon asserted itself. He had heard many a tale of bureaucratic opposition to any and all of Lincoln's wishes. The incidents included generals as well as his own cabinet members. Secretary of War Stanton had to be convinced too.

He went directly to the War Department where he found hordes of white men waiting to see Stanton. A secretary asked Delany to return another day, and he began to have misgivings. Stanton had never replied to his letter the year before. Without doubt the Secretary of War was assailed with daily plans, served up by self-seeking individuals or groups. He would most likely get the interview, Delany knew, but would he get his armee d'Afrique?

Delany did exactly what is done in Washington to this day. He sought out influence and found it in the person of his old Chambersburg friend, Dr. William Elder, who had loaned him books as a boy. Elder was in Washington as head of the Bureau of Statistics. He had left his medical practice in Pittsburgh to spend all of his time in the anti-slavery fight, and for some years had been editor of the abolitionist *National Era*. He and Delany had corresponded over the years.

Dr. Elder welcomed Delany and listened to his plan. According to Delany, he was as enthusiastic about it as Lincoln and told him to put the whole thing in writing. Delany hurried back to his room and delivered a long letter to Dr. Elder that afternoon, detailing every point in his establishment of an armee d'Afrique. After reading it, Elder turned to Delany: "You *shall* have what you want."

On February 25, Delany had his interview witn Stanton and found that the way had been paved for him. The Secretary of War did not even require a repetition of the plan, according to Delany's report of the interview. "I understand the whole thing, and fully comprehend your design; I have frequently gone over the whole ground, in council with the President. What do you wish? What position?"

Delany's answer was substantially the same as that given Lincoln with the addition "that I am not subject and subordinate to every man who holds a commission, and, with such, chooses to assume authority."

"Will you take the field?" asked the secretary.

"I should like to do so as soon as possible, but not until I have had sufficient discipline and practice in a camp of instruction, and a sufficient number of black officers to command each regiment," was the answer.

"Of course, you must establish your camp of instruction; and as you have a general knowledge of the qualified men of the country, I propose to commission you at once, and send you South to commence raising troops, to be commanded by black officers, on the principles you proposed, of which I most highly approve. . . . I shall assign you to Charleston, with advices and instructions to Major General Saxton. Do you know him? . . . He is an unflinching friend of your race."

Stanton immediately sent for Col. C. W. Foster, Assistant Adjutant General of Volunteers, and ordered him to examine Delany at once. If there were no obvious reasons against it, Delany was to be commissioned a "Major of Infantry, the regiment to be left blank, to be filled by order of Major General Saxton, according to the instructions to be given, and to report the next morning at eleven o'clock."

The next day was a Sunday, but the business of war went on as usual. Delany accompanied Col. Foster to Secretary Stanton's office and handed over the papers. The news that a black man was to be commissioned had apparently spread through the War Department, and they had an audience which included an unnamed major general. Also witnessing the commissioning was the old-time abolitionist who had been responsible in the Ohio State Legislature for easing that state's Black Code, Senator Benjamin F. Wade. Wade was chairman of the Senate Committee on the Conduct of the War and worked closely with Stanton. He was Lincoln's most outspoken critic in Congress, particularly in relation to Reconstruction, and was to sponsor the first legislation for black suffrage that same year, 1865.

Stanton addressed the distinguished audience.

> Gentlemen, I am just now creating a black field officer for the United States service . . . Major Delany, I take great pleasure in handing you this commission of *Major* in the United States army. You are the first of your race who has been thus honored by the government; therefore much depends and will be expected of you. But I feel assured it is safe in your hands.

The commission itself was most explicit as to Major Delany's authority and did not neglect to state that he served "during the pleasure of the President." The full commission read:

The Secretary of War of the United States of America
TO ALL WHO SHALL SEE THESE PRESENTS, GREETING:

Know ye, that, reposing special trust and confidence in the patriotism, valor, fidelity, and abilities of MARTIN R. DELANY, the President does hereby appoint him Major, in the One Hundred and Fourth Regiment of United States Colored Troops, in the service of the United States, to rank as such from the day of his muster into service, by the duly appointed commissary of musters, for the command to which said regiment belongs.

He is therefore carefully and diligently to discharge the duty of Major, by doing and performing all manner of things thereunto belonging. And I do strictly charge, and require, all officers and soldiers under his command to be obedient to his orders as Major. And he is to observe and follow such orders and directions, from time to time, as he shall receive from me or the future Secretary of War, or other superior officers set over him, according to the rules and discipline of war. This appointment to continue in force during the pleasure of the President for the time being.

Given under my hand at the War Department, in the City of Washington, D.C., this twenty-sixth day of February, in the year of our Lord one thousand eight hundred and sixty-five.

By the Secretary of War

EDWIN M. STANTON, *Secretary of War*

C. W. FOSTER, *Assistant Adjutant General Volunteers*

Delany was mustered in on the following day and was handed the orders for Gen. Saxton, to be given to him in person.

WAR DEPARTMENT, A.G. OFFICE
WASHINGTON, Feb. 27, 1865

Brevet Major General R. SAXTON, *Supt. Recruitment and Organization of Colored Troops, Dept. of the South, Hilton Head, S.C.*

General: I am directed by the Secretary of War to inform you that the bearer, *Major M. R. Delany* U.S. Colored Troops, has been appointed for the purpose of aiding and assisting you in recruiting and organizing colored troops, and to carry out this object you will assign him to duty in the city of Charleston, S.C.

You will observe that the regiment to which Major *Delany* is appointed is not designated, although he has been mustered into service. You will cause Major *Delany* to be assigned to, and his name placed upon the rolls of, the first regiment of colored troops you may organize, with his proper rank, not, however, with a view to his duty in such regiment.

I am also directed to say, that Major *Delany* has the entire confidence of the Department.

I have the honor to be, very respectfully,

Your obedient servant

(signed) C. W. FOSTER

Assistant Adjutant General V*olunteers*

Official C. W. FOSTER

Assistant Adjutant General V*olunteers*

The oath of office administered by Stanton was a curiously defensive document in keeping with the times. While it does name Delany a "citizen," just as General Order No. 233 named black soldiers citizens, it, too, like his commission, restricted his service to "Colored Troops."

OATH OF OFFICE

I, Martin R. Delany having been appointed a Major of U.S. Colored Troops in the MILITARY SERVICE *of the* UNITED STATES, *do solemnly swear that I have never voluntarily* BORNE ARMS *against the United States since I have been a citizen thereof; that I have voluntarily given no* AID, COUNTENANCE, COUNSEL *or* ENCOURAGEMENT *to persons engaged in* ARMED HOSTILITY *thereto; that I have neither sought, nor accepted, nor attempted to exercise the functions of* ANY OFFICE WHATEVER, *under any authority, or pretended authority,* IN HOSTILITY *to the United States; that I have not yielded a voluntary* SUPPORT *to any* PRETENDED

GOVERNMENT, AUTHORITY, POWER *or* CONSTITUTION WITHIN *the United States,* HOSTILE *or* INIMICAL *thereto. And I do further swear that, to the best of my knowledge and ability, I will* SUPPORT *and* DEFEND *the* CONSTITUTION OF THE UNITED STATES *against all enemies,* FOREIGN *and* DOMESTIC; *that I will bear true* FAITH *and* ALLEGIANCE *to the same; that I take this obligation freely, without any mental reservation or purpose of evasion; and that I will* WELL *and* FAITHFULLY *discharge the* DUTIES *of the* OFFICE *on which I am about to enter.* SO HELP ME GOD.

(*signed*) *M. R. Delany*

With his commission in hand, Delany realized full well what he had accomplished. So did other black leaders, for none of them had forgotten the slap in their faces when Frederick Douglass was first promised a commission and then the promise was repudiated.

That had happened in August 1863 after Douglass' interview with Lincoln. Douglass too had gone directly to the War Department from the White House. He too had seen Stanton and was promised the post of assistant adjutant on the staff of Adjutant General Lorenzo Thomas who was then in Mississippi preparing for recruiting of twenty colored regiments. On August 13 Douglass received his orders to report to Thomas in Vicksburg and there assist him in recruiting and "in any way his influence with the colored race can be made available." But there was no commission with his orders and Douglass protested. He received a reply from George L. Stearns of the Black Committee, not from Stanton. Douglass would get $100 monthly as pay, with subsistence and transportation, *but no commission.*

This answer came after the last issue of *Douglass' Monthly* in which he wrote his "Valedictory" explaining that he was ending its publication because "I am going South to assist Adjutant General Thomas, in the organization of colored troops, who shall win for the millions in bondage the inestimable blessings of liberty and country." But there was no commission, no recognition of rank in keeping with the military responsibility, nothing but another recruiting job. Douglass returned to the lecture platform where his powers of expression were thrown into the new bid for equality.

Why did Delany succeed where Douglass had failed? One reason might have been the passage of time for Lincoln's timorous policy to develop. Another could have been the fact that between Douglass' disappointment and Delany's appointment, Lincoln had won re-election. The risk of losing the support of Republican anti-Negro votes was no longer a political consideration. Lincoln could now commission a black officer with impunity. The election of 1864 was over.

Still another consideration was the difference in what each black man had to offer to the war effort. Douglass would undoubtedly be the most effective recruiter among all the black men then alive, particularly in Mississippi. He had been a slave, and he had oratorical and writing powers unmatched by any other black man.

But Delany had more to offer—a fighting unit, a "packaged" plan, whereby former slaves would become military units self-sufficient as to training, officers and, in addition, they would be recruiters as well as fighting men. Delany promised a black army within three months, not just black recruits.

That required organizational ability, as well as vigor, and Delany had both. Before the news of his commissioning had spread through the Negro population, Delany was already in motion. He sent word out to almost all of his former co-workers, to William Howard Day, to Rev. J. W. C. Pennington, to Cleveland, Philadelphia, New York, Boston, Cincinnati. He called a meeting in Cleveland to organize the machinery of the Underground Railroad for contacts in the rebel states. He arranged for transportation to Charleston, S.C., of the famous Harriet Tubman, now a scout and spy for the Union Army.

Most of all, Delany wanted black officer candidates, and he began compiling his list. He had the authority, in fact the absolute responsibility, for their selection. There was work to be done and Delany hurried to his Cleveland meeting. He then returned to Wilberforce to await the making of his uniforms and pack away all his treasures from Africa, his correspondence of the past twenty years, as well as the National Board of Commissioners records. He was given a third floor room in the main University building to keep his belongings safe.

But he could not go to war without a speech to his people in Wilberforce and Xenia. This he gave in the Anti-Slavery Church on East Main Street in Xenia and, for the first time, he appeared in public in full uniform. The *Xenia Sentinel* described him.

> Major Delany is a negro, having no "visible admixture" of white blood. He is black—black as the blackest—large, heavy set, vigorous, with a bald, sleek head, which shines like a newly polished boot. And he wears brass buttons and shoulder straps! and is an officer in the army of the Union! These sentences record the history of the progress of the country during the war.

After assuring his audience that there would be no distinction between black and white soldiers and that black men would receive commissions as soon as they qualified, Delany returned to his favorite theme, according to the *Sentinel* account.

> The speaker affirmed that negroes must think more of themselves, that is, have a higher opinion of themselves. They must declare themselves to be the equals of white men, if not their superiors. In no other way could they attain to their proper position in the body politic. The speaker scouted the idea of social equality. Major Delany is a patriotic man, and will undoubtedly do good battle for this our and his country.

The meeting ended in a jubilant celebration for Delany, the *Major*, the black officer who represented an all-important achievement in a hostile white society. In none of his other careers did Delany so completely satisfy the cravings of his race. The "Black Major" shed glory on the humblest black.

The next day, when he left the campus of Wilberforce University for the long journey to South Carolina, the entire student body and faculty, the children from the preparatory school and their teachers, all of the community's residents paraded him to the gates. According to a contemporary account they "sang The Star Spangled Banner after which three cheers were given for the Major, three for General Saxton (who was a trustee of Wilberforce University), six for the President of the United States, and a groan for Jefferson Davis."

Major Martin R. Delany was off to the wars.

CHAPTER SIXTEEN

The Second Civil War

The "Black Major," as Delany soon came to be known in the South, was in active military service for three years and six months, but his role was that of a soldier for only the first few months. The shooting ended in a short while, the Confederates laid down their arms, the slaves were free, and the Union was saved. But this was not the end of the Civil War. It merely entered a new phase in which Delany's role was of greater significance than that of commanding troops. He was to become tribune of his people in the new struggle and refused to capitulate even after 1877 when the South won the Civil War.

The appearance of the new Black Major in military and in racial activities created quite a stir in New York, Beaufort, the Sea Islands, and Charleston during those early months of 1865. Reactions varied. There was bitter scorn on the part of Delany's fellow white officers who were as committed to Negro inferiority as their counterparts in the Confederate Army. As for the blacks, their admiration for this first Negro line officer in the Union Army and for his high rank amounted to adulation.

All through the North the press treated the appointment as an event of national import. One of his old white newspaper colleagues on the *Pittsburgh Dispatch* was delighted and, aside from some sketchy biography of Delany, commented:

> We knew him years ago (twenty or more) in this city—not as a "saucy nigger" but as one who felt himself a MAN, and was determined to overcome the prejudice which crushed himself and his race. . . . We cannot say Delany has ever shown any more military capacity than the average of our Brigadier-Generals—we don't know that he will fight at all —but we do know that he is a self-made and self-educated

> man and we rejoice that, without ever having been selected by a Congressman as a Cadet at West Point, he has attained a fair position in the army, knowing, as we do, that he has more energy and ambition than hundreds who outrank him.

The Negro press, of course, filled its columns with praise of the appointment and, of course, of Delany. The *Anglo-African* not only hailed the Black Major but reported his many speeches in New York, while awaiting transportation South. Its Washington correspondent announced triumphantly that Delany was commissioned "and that, too, as a full-blooded African, a point which he delights to set forth. This is the first regular commission given to a colored man as a full field officer, and viewing it from our standpoint, it could not have fallen in better hands, the country over. The Doctor, as we all know is just at this moment the right man in the right place . . . Who shall say we are not on the onward march?" He also reported that Delany had made quite a stir in Washington with a series of lectures "especially the one entitled, 'The capacity of the African race to the highest civilization.' "

While the black press noted the "furore" the Black Major created when he spoke "before overcrowded and enthusiastic audiences," Delany achieved a kind of immortality in New York. An announcement was made by Robert and Thomas Hamilton, 184 Church Street, New York, publishers of the *Anglo-African*, that at a price of 25¢ per copy a daguerreotype of Delany in full uniform would be available in the form of a "carte de visite" taken by the "celebrated artist, Bogardus of Broadway." This was truly an expression of pride in the "Black Major."

Editorially, too, the *Anglo-African* points out that "Major Delany is a black man, pure and simple, and if he have any white blood in him it is so overwhelmed by the royal African tide as to be entirely invisible. . . . We rejoice, because Major Delany having devoted the whole of a long life to the unselfish advocacy of our people and their cause, he becomes a fit instrument through which to do them honor. So long as we have known the Major by reputation and personally, he has ever sacrificed his private interests in the public good."

The lengthy editorial was written by Robert Hamilton, editor of the paper, who knew Delany well and wrote several paragraphs about him. To him we are indebted for the following:

> The major is on the shady side of fifty, but is younger in mind and body than most men at thirty-five; a little below the middle height, very stout in muscle, large featured and with an eye in which may steadily gleam the "light of battle." His voice—we fell in with many years ago a teacher of elocution who had presided long in Washington, and who was so fascinated with the fine voice of Henry Clay that he would any day walk two miles from his house to the capital, merely to hear Mr. Clay say, "Mr. President, I move that this bill be laid on the table"—well we would travel any three days journey to reach the edge of the battle when Major Delany shall call out "forward, march!"
>
> We do not doubt that the major is thoroughly acquainted with the duties of his office, and of even higher military command; he has made such matters a study, no doubt, among his many acquirements. He has long dreamed and hoped for the present opportunity, under different auspices. A little impatient of control himself, he possesses in a large degree, the magnetism of command.
>
> Congratulate is hardly the term which we would use—it is not strong enough—toward MAJOR DELANY. May God bless him and prosper him a faithful and successful soldier of freedom. May he rise in his new profession until the stars light thickly upon his shoulder-straps. "*Palman qui meruit ferat.*"

Delany apparently made the most of his unique position. According to contemporary accounts he was resplendent in his uniform, on which every possible insignia of his rank shone. Ordinarily assertive and challenging to every white man, in uniform he must have been as arrogant as any "ninety-day wonder" of most American wars. He demanded every prerogative of his rank, as witnesses attest.

But there was self-confidence behind his arrogance, for Delany knew exactly what he planned. In Cleveland and while waiting in New York for a ship south, he had many conferences with his old friend William Howard Day whom he had chosen as his assistant in handling the Underground Railroad contacts in the North and then as his second in command once his all-black regiment was in the field.

From New York he wrote to the Assistant Adjutant General

in the War Department, Col. C. W. Foster, asking for transportation to General Saxton's headquarters in Beaufort, S.C., for two men. One, Anthony Barnwell, he wanted as a scout, for the young slave had escaped from the rebel army nine months before, after serving as orderly to his owner, a Major Rhett. He had been born and raised in Charleston and knew the country. The other, also a young black, Charles Henry Webb, had served as commanding officer and drill master of a Detroit, Mich., volunteer black militia company for some years. "I wish to take them both, and present them to Brev. Major Gen. Saxton, as I know them to be just such persons as we shall want," Delany wrote.

However, he was to be disappointed, for Col. Foster replied that the men would have to be in the Army before transportation could be provided. Delany reported to Gen. Rufus Saxton alone. He found the commanding officer of the Department of the South to be all that he had heard about him, that "among the colored people and poor whites of South Carolina General Rufus Saxton stood as the beloved friend and benefactor, and esteemed among his brother officers generally as a gentleman and soldier."

Gen. Saxton was *the* commanding officer in the field for the Union forces with the most experience with colored people. He was the first to be authorized to raise black troops and he sought out the noted Boston abolitionist, Thomas W. Higginson, to command the regiment. The record made by these black fighters was enthusiastically reported to the War Department by Gen. Saxton.

More than his interview with the general, Delany was impressed by one peculiarity. The headquarters of the Department of the South in Beaufort had a good many officers on duty there and each of them had an orderly. Among them all Gen. Saxton was the only officer with a *white*, rather than a black, orderly. To Delany this signified equality between the races as a personal attitude of the general's, for it was accustomed and accepted military practice that such a menial post should be assigned to a black man.

Saxton gave Delany an entirely free hand. In his orders to the Black Major dated April 5, 1865, Delany was to report immediately to Charleston "for the purpose of aiding in the recruitment of troops. . . . II. Major Delany will visit the freedmen of Charleston and vicinity, and urge them to enlist in the military service of the United States, reporting by letter from time to time to these headquarters the result of his labors."

The fact that Delany was to report directly to Gen. Saxton, rather than to the ranking recruiting officer in Charleston, Lt. Col. R. P. Hutchins, was both unusual and important, for it left him free to follow his own plans without prior permission from anyone. As a result, Delany had the 104th United States Colored Troops recruited and ready for drill in record time.

But first there were duties resulting from both his color and position. Gen. Saxton wanted the Black Major as part of his official entourage at Fort Sumter in Charleston Harbor on the fateful day of April 14. The occasion was the official raising of the Stars and Stripes on the fourth anniversary of Fort Sumter's surrender to the rebels and Lincoln's official recognition of a state of war on the following day. It was more than a military ceremonial, for it touched off a week of triumphal celebration among the black people of Charleston, and gave Delany an opportunity for reunion with some of the veterans of abolition with whom he had worked for thirty years. Many of them were there, including the aging but still aggressive Britisher, George Thompson, Rev. Henry Ward Beecher, and others. Among the military, Delany for the first time met the famous Robert Smalls of the *Planter*, the former slave pilot from Beaufort who had taken the same ship out of Charleston Harbor under Confederate guns. He now commanded the *Planter* which took the official blacks to Fort Sumter for the flag-raising.

But the man Delany was happiest to see and hear, to shake hands with, and to have admire his uniform was William Lloyd Garrison. Obviously, from his own comments, Delany was emotionally affected by the appearance of the most faithful, self-sacrificing, and unswerving abolitionist of them all, the man he called "the immortal Garrison." For the entire week of jubilee, the blacks of Charleston could not hear or see enough of this white man. Thousands followed him to dockside when he and all the distinguished visitors left for the North. The Black Major was delegated to make a farewell speech, but the blacks demanded another speech from Garrison, and the final words were indelible in Delany's memory:

> And now, my friends, I bid you farewell. I have always advocated non-resistance; but this much I say to you, *Come*

> *what will never do you submit again to slavery! Do anything; die first! But don't submit again to them—never again be slaves.* Farewell.

Many things happened to the Black Major during that momentous week. He was reunited with his son, Toussaint L'Ouverture, for the 54th Massachusetts had taken part in the occupation of Charleston after the rebel garrison fled northward to avoid being caught between the siege guns of Morris Island and the inexorable advance of Sherman's army through Georgia.

Toussaint was only a private, but his father was a Major and could issue orders. And so the young soldier accompanied the official entourage to the flag-raising, just as he was to move in with Delany and attend the many events at which the appearance of the Black Major was demanded by the Charleston blacks. Delany was every bit the proud father, for his son was a veteran of the 54th Massachusetts. Among freedmen that had more significance than even the status of a black preacher. To them, every man in that regiment was a hero.

On April 18 the news came belatedly that on the night of the Fort Sumter flag-raising—while the black regiments were marching, bands blaring triumphantly, still giddy from the heady wine of freedom—Lincoln had been assassinated. Grown men and women who had known greater grief than the death of loved ones, cried openly and went to their churches to pray for the soul of their emancipator. They turned to the Black Major for comfort and reassurance, although he needed both himself. The new freedmen wanted to turn on the few remaining white natives of Charleston to avenge Lincoln, but they listened to Delany who sent them to the Zion Presbyterian Church instead. He set them to work putting the church and all public buildings in mourning.

The Black Major was the first to suggest a Lincoln Monument and his proposal was printed in the *Anglo-African* of April 20. He told the blacks of Charleston that they and all the freedmen of America had the greatest right to memorialize Abraham Lincoln.

> I suggest that, as a just and appropriate tribute of respect and lasting gratitude from the colored people of the United States to the memory of President Lincoln, the Father of American Liberty, every individual of our race contribute

> *one cent*, as this will enable each member of every family to contribute, parents paying for every child, allowing all who are able to subscribe any sum they please above this, to such national monument as may hereafter be decided upon by the American people. I hope it may be in Illinois, near his own family residence.

Nor did Delany drop the plan for a monument from the blacks. On May 13 he enlarged on it and then proposed an actual design, suggesting that the colored artist Patrick Reason of New York sketch it. In great detail Delany outlined the monument as chiefly a female figure kneeling over an urn,

> the face with eyes upturned to heaven, with distinct tear-drops passing down the face, falling into the urn, which is represented as being full; distinct tear-drops shall be so arranged as to represent the figures 4,000,000 (four million) which shall be emblematical not only of the number of contributors to the monument, but the number of those who shed tears of sorrow for the great and good deliverer of their race from bondage in the United States; the arms and hands extended—the whole figure to represent "Ethiopia stretching forth her hands unto God." . . . This figure is neither to be Grecian, Caucasian, nor Anglo-Saxon, Mongolian nor Indian, but African—*very African*—an ideal representative *genius* of the race, as Europa, Britannia, America, or the Goddess of Liberty, is to the European race.

There was another calamity that fateful night of April 14 which resulted in more than a personal loss to Delany. Historians, too, were the losers, for the main building of Wilberforce University burned to the ground. Classes could be held in the surrounding homes, in barns, and in the church, but irreplaceable were the early records of both the University and the AME Church, which were not stored in the Philadelphia Mother Church. And Delany's personal records, the years of his voluminous correspondence, and most of the National Board of Commissioners journals were irreplaceable. He also lost, in the third floor storeroom, the artifacts, industrial products, and notes on his African exploration, which would be difficult to replace.

The loss enraged Delany (he learned of it the beginning of

May). He immediately declared it an act of arson, and on May 11 wrote an impassioned appeal to the American people to help restore Wilberforce. It was printed in the AME paper, *Christian Recorder*, but there is little evidence for his charges.

> The destruction of this great structure, the only University of learning among the colored people, as such on the American continent, was an atrocity of vast magnitude and of great importance. . . . It was a deliberate act of an enemy of the colored people, the schools and the Union; and the hand which placed the torch to these magnificent buildings, was leagued in sentiment with the same dastard-villains who, the same day, struck down and deprived the world of the greatest Chief Magistrate of the present age, and aimed at the life of one of the greatest ministers and statesmen of modern times (Secretary of State William H. Seward).

The only evidence of arson that Delany presented, however, was the fact that the campus was deserted. Bishop Daniel W. Payne, president of Wilberforce was away, and all of the students and faculty were in Xenia that night, celebrating the fall of Richmond. But Delany's purpose was an appeal to the wealthy, black and white, to raise $40,000 for restoration of the University.

> Wilberforce University cannot be spared, and must be rebuilt as soon as possible, because no school in existence can take its place, or become a satisfactory substitute for it. . . . The school must go on. A University of their own is as essential to the black race—the colored people with their present *status* and prospective destiny as a part of the great American people—as a *language* is to a race or a literature to a nation. No people can rise except on their own merits and these merits must be inseparable with their identity. . . . As those serving and risking their lives in the National cause, we make an earnest appeal, which we know will not be in vain, to the wealthy of the United States, to aid immediately in helping to rebuild an Institution, essential to our elevation as a part of the American people.

The purely military duties of those early weeks in Charleston were no great problem for Delany because of his organizational abilities and experience in recruiting. He had recruited for so many states that he knew the regimental structure and was able to act with dispatch because he had the nucleus of a black organization right in Charleston with him. The Massachusetts 54th was there and he knew many of its men because he himself had recruited them. He immediately commandeered the services of two of its non-commissioned officers, Sergeant Major Abraham W. Shadd and Sergeant Frederick Johnson, and his son Private Toussaint.

Young Shadd was only 21 years old, but he was from Buxton Settlement near Chatham and had gone to Rev. William King's school there. Before his enlistment, he had been an active member of the Kent County militia. He was a second-generation Shadd, son of Abraham W., Sr., and nephew of Israel D., publisher of the *Provincial Freeman*. Delany gave him an acting commission of Captain and named him as his aide and chief clerk. To assist Capt. Shadd and run the recruiting headquarters, Delany assigned a lieutenancy to Toussaint. Johnson was in charge of the records.

Delany also leaped at the opportunity to have, in actual command of the recruits as they signed up, the newly commissioned Capt. O. S. B. Wall, companion of many an abolition meeting in Ohio and successful black merchant of Oberlin, who was sent to Delany by Stanton.

They found headquarters in a large and elegant abandoned mansion at Calhoun and St. Philip streets, which became not only a recruiting office but something of a black city hall for the Black Major was sought out by all blacks with any kind of problem—personal, domestic, or public.

The recruits began pouring in the very day that the first call for enlistment in the "Charleston Regiment" was sent out as a handbill written by Delany.

ATTENTION, CHARLESTONIANS!

RALLY ROUND THE FLAG!

Charleston, S.C., April 28, 1865

To the Free Colored Men of Charleston:

The free colored men in this city, between the ages of

> eighteen and forty-five, are hereby earnestly called upon to come forward and join the
>
> CHARLESTON REGIMENT,
>
> now to be organized. It is the duty of every colored man to vindicate his manhood by becoming a soldier, and with his own stout arm to battle for the emancipation of his race. I urge you by every hope that is dear to humanity, by every free inspiration which a sense of liberty has kindled in your hearts, to be soldiers, until the freedom of your race is secured. The prospect of your future destiny should be enough to call every man to the ranks. But in addition, you are to have the
>
> PAY, RATIONS AND CLOTHING
>
> our other soldiers receive.
>
> Let a full Regiment of the Colored Freedmen of Charleston be under arms, to protect the heritage which has been promised to your race in this department.

The pay offered ranged from $16 monthly for privates and musicians to $26 for sergeant majors, and there were other benefits:

> In addition to the pay as above stated, one ration per day and an abundant supply of good clothing are allowed to each soldier. Quarters, fuel, and medical attendance are always provided by the government, without deduction from the soldier's pay. If a soldier should become disabled in the line of his duties, the laws provide for him a pension; or he may, if he prefer it, obtain admission into the "Soldiers' Home," which will afford him a comfortable home so long as he may wish to receive its benefits. It is the intention to make this an excelsior regiment. All desired information given at Recruiting Office, No. 64 St. Philip Street, corner Calhoun.
>
> M. R. DELANY,
> *Major 104th United States Colored Troops*
>
> R. P. HUTCHINS, Colonel
> Office No. 123 Calhoun St.

By May 3 the 104th U.S.C.T. was recruited and Delany was ordered to begin recruiting the 105th Regiment. The regimental camp and drill field was established on the extensive grounds once used only for the diversions and duels of Charleston's aristocrats, the race course of the South Carolina Jockey Club. Col. Hutchins took command of this post and left all recruiting activities to Major Delany.

But the "armee d'Afrique" was to have a brief existence. After the fall of Richmond on April 2 and Gen. Lee's surrender at Appomattox Courthouse a week later, the Confederate forces began to crumble. The final capitulation was on May 26 in New Orleans. The bloodiest war in America's history was over and, on June 7, Delany received orders to halt recruiting and report in person to Gen. Saxton at Beaufort for further orders. The 104th had not fired a shot and its only duties as a military unit were that of a security force for the city. The first battalion of the 105th Regiment, already drilling, never saw duty at all. For most of these black soldiers, the fighting war was over and a new kind of battle had begun—the struggle for the freedom they were told they had already won.

For the Black Major, this new war was to be the climax of a lifetime of struggle in behalf of his people. During the few short months of his initial stay in Charleston he too had been drilled in preparation for the coming battles of the next phase of the Civil War. From his first day in Charleston he began to see both the opportunities for his people as well as the dangers, for he was in an almost black city. Not only were the occupation troops black but its population of approximately 20,000, both slave and free, had swollen by an estimated 100,000 fugitives from masters who wished to send them to the hilly north counties, fugitives from the fighting, and deserted black families from the surrounding counties in search of food. Few whites had remained in the city when the rebel troops evacuated it, though they had endured the shelling from Morris Island for some time. Those who did stay, the aged and infirm, the secret Union sympathizers, and the lost women and children joined the blacks in the lines outside the Quartermaster's storehouse, for the Army fed them all.

We have Delany's own impressions of Charleston:

> I entered the city, which, from earliest childhood and through life, I had learned to contemplate with feelings of

the utmost abhorrence—a place of the most insufferable assumption and cruelty to the blacks; where the sound of the lash at the whipping-post, and the hammer of the auctioneer, were coordinate sounds in thrilling harmony; that place which had ever been closed against liberty by an arrogantly assumptuous despotism, such as well might have vied with the infamous King of Dahomey; the place from which had been expelled the envoy of Massachusetts, for daring to present the claims of the commonwealth in behalf of her free citizens, and into which, but a few days before, had proudly entered in triumph the gallant Schemmelfening, leading with wild shouts the Massachusetts Fifty-Fourth Regiment, composed of some of the best blood and finest youths of the colored citizens of the Union. For a moment I paused—then, impelled by the impulse of my mission, I found myself dashing on in unmeasured strides through the city, as if under a forced march to attack the already crushed and fallen enemy. Again I halted to look upon the shattered walls of the once stately but now deserted edifices of the proud and supercilious occupants. A doomed city it appeared to be, with few, or none but soldiers and the colored inhabitants. The haughty Carolinians, who believed their state an empire, this city incomparable, and themselves invincible, had fled in dismay and consternation at the approach of their conquerors, leaving the metropolis to its fate. And but for the vigilance and fidelity of the colored firemen, and other colored inhabitants, there would have been nothing left but a smouldering plain of ruins in the place where Charleston once stood, from the firebrands in the hands of the flying whites. . . . Whatever impressions may have previously been entertained concerning the free colored people of Charleston, their manifestation from my advent till my departure, gave evidence of their pride in identity and appreciation of race that equal in extent the proudest Caucasian.

The pride Delany mentions sprang from hope among the free blacks he met, not from any national identification. Nor did they represent the four million former slaves who had no concept of the word freedom. Most of his dealings had been with the proud free blacks of the city, who, curiously, looked down on the former slaves. Those fugitives were lost in the miasma of slavery and truly had to "begin from scratch."

Strangely enough, a former opponent of Delany's helped them make a start toward education. James Redpath, of Haitian emigration fame, had entered Charleston with the first occupation troops and was immediately named Superintendent of Public Education. By April 30 he was able to report that about 4,000 black students were being taught by thirty teachers sent south by anti-slavery organizations, the new freedmen's relief associations, and the American Missionary Society. But they needed books to read and paper on which to write.

Redpath was also to help Delany on an educational project, just before he was replaced by Reuben Tomlinson, the old-time abolitionist, as superintendent of education. On May 9 the Black Major was the principal speaker at a capacity meeting in the Zion Presbyterian Church in behalf of his own proposal that the colored people of Charleston establish their own press. There was a report on the meeting in the *Charleston Courier* on the following day.

> Major Delany explained the object in view would be the establishment of an organ to advocate the interests of the colored population in this city and State, and the diffusion of intelligence among colored people of the South generally. He spoke of the wide field now open and of the bright futures they might make for themselves and their children by industry and perseverance, and by showing through the medium of a public press, their capacity for education and their fitness to be American citizens. He desired that some distinctive name should be adopted, which would show that the paper was devoted to the benefit of the colored race, and the dissemination of universal intelligence among their people. He wished the conductors of the paper, editor and assistants, to be educated colored men, and men of ability. The Major also stated what qualifications of the editor should be, and what would be the probable cost of the materials of a paper.

As a result of the meeting, a stock company issuing a thousand shares at $10 per share was formed for the purpose of financing the new newspaper. Redpath's office at 281 King Street was designated as headquarters. However, events intervened, and Delany was not to get his newspaper published for some years.

Three days later, Delany was again a speaker in the Zion Presbyterian Church. It was an event, overlooked by historians, of extreme significance, the first mixed black and white meeting to plan definitive action in behalf of the freedmen of South Carolina. It was the first attempt to assert a measure of self-determination in achieving an equal status for the freedmen. Less than three months after the Confederates had evacuated the city and Sherman had destroyed the state's capital of Columbia, there came together a group of white visionaries and black ex-slaves for a common purpose.

Besides Delany, the speakers were Chief Justice of the U.S. Supreme Court Salmon P. Chase, Lincoln's Secretary of the Treasury until June 1864 and now on an inspection trip to report to President Johnson; Reuben Tomlinson, sent to South Carolina by the new Freedmen's Bureau to organize education for the freedmen of the state. But the most important speaker was Gen. Rufus Saxton, one of the most unusual military men of the Civil War. In fact, this meeting on May 12, 1865, *was* Saxton's meeting, initiated by him, called by him, and the speakers invited by him.

Saxton was a humanitarian, an abolitionist, and that rarity among the military, a progressive. He was also dogged in his purpose, which was to make the former slaves useful members of American society. He had been assigned their care in July 1862, a year after the Union forces had captured the cluster of Sea Islands stretching along the Carolina coast from Charleston almost to Savannah, Georgia, with Beaufort as their mainland heart. For nearly three years Gen. Saxton watched and worked to help the blacks make crops on their own, without their masters' orders or overseers' whips. They divided up plantations and worked them, helping to feed the Union Army as well as themselves and raise enough of the hated cotton for military needs. They also formed the First South Carolina Volunteer Regiment while Lincoln was still frowning on enlistment of colored troops. By June 1863 some 5,000 children and adults were in schools founded by northern missionary societies at Saxton's request.

Four months before the Charleston meeting Saxton, in his

annual report to the Secretary of War, declared that the assignment "to which I was entrusted was given with a view to a critical experiment of the capabilities of the Negro for freedom and self-support and self-improvement, to determine whether he is specifically distinct from and inferior to the white race, and normally a slave or dependent, or only inferior by accident of position and circumstances. . . ."

He reported his conclusion that they "have made progress and proved their right to be received into the full communion of freemen."

> They have shown that they can appreciate freedom as the highest boon; that they will be industrious and provident with the same incitement which stimulates the industry of other men in free societies; that they understand the value of property and are eager for its acquisition, especially of land; that they can conduct their private affairs with sagacity, prudence and success . . . that they are intelligent, eager, and apt to acquire knowledge of letters, docile and receptive pupils; that they aspire to and adopt as fast as means and opportunity admit the social forms and habits of civilization; that they quickly get rid of in freedom the faults and vices generated by slavery, and in truthfulness and fidelity and honesty may be compared favorably with men of other color, in conditions as unfavorable for the development of those qualities; that they are remarkably susceptible of religious emotions and the inspirations of music; that in short they are endowed with all the instincts, passions, affections, sensibilities, powers, aspirations and possibilities which are the common attributes of human nature.

Just two weeks before, and the immediate reason for organizing the Zion Church meeting, Saxton had sent out a circular letter to all of his subordinates and agents, on April 23, 1865: "It having been reported to me that unauthorized persons are now settling on lands which have been reserved and set apart for freedmen, the following is published for the information and benefit of all concerned." There followed the pertinent extracts of the famous January 16, 1865, Special Field Order No. 15, issued by General William Tecumseh Sherman from Savannah, Ga., largely through the urging of Gen. Saxton. Field Order No. 15, one of the truly hopeful acts negated by Johnson, declared

> The islands from Charleston south, the abandoned rice fields along the rivers for thirty miles back from the sea . . . reserved and set apart for the settlement of negroes made free by the acts of war and the Proclamation of the President of the United States . . . on the islands and in the settlements to be established, no white persons whatever, unless military officers or soldiers detailed for duty, will be permitted to reside; and the sole and exclusive management of affairs will be left to the freed people themselves, subject only to the United States Military Authority, and the acts of Congress. By the laws of war, and orders of the President of the United States, the negro is free and must be dealt with as such.

Sherman authorized Gen. Saxton, as Inspector of Settlements and Plantations, to pass on sites chosen by freedmen "to establish a peaceable agricultural settlement." Individuals or families could have "a plot of not more than forty (40) acres of tillable ground," with possession of the land guaranteed by the military "until such time as they can protect themselves, or until Congress shall regulate their title." Blacks who had enlisted in the Union forces also had guaranteed and similar homesteading rights, even though duty called them away from their land. Gen. Saxton was authorized to give the freedmen written title to their land "subject to the approval of the President of the United States."

The reason for reissue of the famous Special Order No. 15, which had sent black hearts soaring with hope, was the reappearance of former slaveowners to reclaim their lands, plus the fact that Lincoln was dead and Andrew Johnson was now president. Saxton's circular letter of April 23 was an unmistakable warning:

> Having been detailed by the proper authority, and being held responsible for the enforcement of this order, I hereby warn all persons against violating any of its provisions, as all such will be held to the strictest accountability for trespass, their effects will be seized for the benefit of the Freedmen, and

> themselves sent out of the Department (of the South), or otherwise punished by sentence of a Military Commission.

His subordinates were ordered to post the letter conspicuously and place copies on all islands and plantations.

> Thirty days will be allowed for the proper circulation of its contents and all who fail to vacate premises which are occupied by them, contrary to and in violation of the provisions of General Sherman's Order, No. 15, will be at once arrested. Should it be necessary to employ military force to carry out the provisions of this circular, application will at once be made to me for such force.

General Sherman's order was backed up by Congress on March 3, 1865, when the bill creating the Freedmen's Bureau included Section 4, allowing the Bureau Commissioner the authority to "set apart, for the use of loyal refugees and freedmen, such tracts of land within the insurrectionary states as shall have been abandoned, or to which the United States shall have acquired title by confiscation or sale, or otherwise, and to every male citizen, whether refugee or freedman, as aforesaid, there shall be assigned not more than forty acres of such land."

One would consider the principle a fixed one—that at least Saxton's blacks would keep their land. Saxton was not worried about defiance of his orders nor that the ex-rebels could intimidate his freedmen to the extent of forcing them off the land. But he was concerned about politics—about Washington and Andrew Johnson's policies toward the freedmen, for Congress was not in session and Johnson made no move, after Lincoln's assassination, to call a special session. Saxton had good reason to worry. Just seventeen days after the May 12 meeting, Johnson issued his general amnesty order of May 29 which gave back to the rebels title to the lands confiscated by act of war.

Saxton had hoped to influence a different outcome by his meeting. The Zion Church was crowded to capacity. His colored troops and the black Home Guard occupied the galleries, and on the main floor his own regimental band entertained the audience until the proceedings began. The whites and blacks were mixed on the benches, the first time that had happened in Charleston, in fact the first such meeting ever to be held in Charleston's Negro church.

In his speech, Delany told the audience the old story of the Denmark Vesey insurrection of 1822 in that same city. He did so with a purpose, a call for unity among blacks of all shadings. It was a mulatto who betrayed Denmark Vesey, he said, and the slaveowners utilized the antagonism aroused by nurturing prejudices among Negroes of various hues in the "divide and conquer" technique. He called for absolute and total unity in Gen. Saxton's program.

Tomlinson urged the whites, particularly the "poor whites" to join with the freedmen and "do something towards building up the government of South Carolina."

Chief Justice Chase, veteran of so many racial battles and once named the "Attorney General for the fugitive slaves in Ohio," spoke of the responsibilities of the freedmen: "I have said the victory is won; the armies of rebellion are disbanded; peace returns and peace brings with it its duties. A great race numbering four million is suddenly brought into freedom. All the world is looking to see whether the prophecies of the enemies of that race will be fulfilled or falsified. It rests upon the men of that race to tell." He warned the blacks that all kinds of scurrilous charges would be made against them but that the lies of their enemies could easily be refuted by their industry and thrift. "You will save yourselves and reflect credit upon those who have been your friends."

> Now as to the elective franchise. Major Delany said that he heard me say in the Hall of the House of Representatives at Washington that I know no reason why the hand that laid down the bayonet might not take up the ballot. If he had listened to me twenty years ago in the city of Cincinnati, he might have heard me say substantially the same thing. But the colored man did not get the elective franchise because I said it then; quite possibly he may not now. Certainly, however, events have progressed remarkably in that direction.

All of the speakers won the applause of the audience at that meeting, but Gen. Saxton also won the deep appreciation of all in the church. He proposed action, applied at its point of greatest effect—on the President. He wanted the blacks to have the vote. That would be their security. A beginning would be a petition to the President.

> When I came here soon after the occupation of this city by our forces, by order of the Government, I came here to tell you how to get land. I wished every colored man, every head of a family in this Department to acquire a freehold, a little home that he could call his own. I am happy to say that many of the colored people here availed themselves of that privilege. I suppose there are now thirty thousand colored people located on farms in this Department. At the time I told you the titles were not perfectly secure, but would do all in my power to make them so. It is for that purpose principally that I appear here this afternoon.

The death of Lincoln and an end to the fighting required reorganization of the South and the position of the blacks. "But I would not have the colored men here without a voice in that reorganization. You must ask for that voice." They had earned that right, he told them. "If a nation asks you to help in a time of war, you certainly have a right to call for the help of a nation for your rights in a time of peace."

He cited the Revolutionary slogan, No Taxation Without Representation, and declared:

> If that motto had been our watchword this time, this Civil War through which we have passed never would have happened. If there had been taxation, and equal representation, there would have been no slavery in this country and we should have gone on prospering. . . . I want the colored men in this Department to petition the President of the United States and Congress for the right to exercise the elective franchise, the right to vote for those who are to rule over them.
>
> I want to see 150,000 men voting in South Carolina—I want to see the black men in the future save a nation's honor. I believe measures will shortly be introduced into Congress to pay the Rebel debt—a debt contracted to make you slaves. I believe in that way the black man will have an opportunity to save the nation's honor. There is no telling how much virtue there is in this petition. Wilberforce, the

great English Emancipator, obtained after 21 years ceaseless labor, the emancipation of the blacks of the West Indies. Your petition will have to be sent to President Johnson and to the Congress, and Congress will insure the right of a black man to vote in this country. I cannot see how it can be otherwise.

I want you now to elect and choose a committee to draft this petition, have it clearly, strongly worded, with good reasons why you should vote, and get every colored man to sign it. I can get 3,000 in Beaufort to sign it, but I want it started here in the city of Charleston, the leading city of the Rebellion. I want it to lead in the movement to ensure your political equality. I now propose three cheers for the Union, three cheers for the Ballot, and three for the Elective Franchise for the colored men.

He got those cheers and more—for himself. He had given the blacks frank talk and a course of action. But Gen. Saxton was on the wrong track. Giving blacks the vote definitely would handicap the restoration of the plantation system and that was the basis of the Johnson plans for Reconstruction. It was inevitable that Saxton would run into the President's displeasure for, to the very last, he continued his campaign for land and votes for the blacks. In his last effort, on December 3, 1865, Saxton suggested a daring plan. "Inasmuch as the faith of the government has been pledged to these freedmen to maintain them in the possession of their homes, and as to break its promise in the hour of its triumph is not becoming a just government, I would respectfully suggest that a practical solution of the whole question of lands . . . may be had by the appropriation of money by Congress to purchase the whole tract set apart by this order (of Sherman). . . ." Shortly afterward General Rufus Saxton was transferred into obscurity. He had offended his commander in chief.

Delany had been introduced by Thomas W. Cardozo, superintendent of schools for the American Missionary Association, and Delany's fellow passenger from New York to Hilton Head. Cardozo reported that over 4,000 attended the meeting.

This great meeting, with the seats, aisles, the galleries, the doorways and the yard crowded, will long be remembered

> by the people of this secesh egg. General Saxton's band gave several patriotic airs. Three cheers were proposed for the major, three for Gen. Saxton, and three for Father Abraham! The dear freed people could not leave the house until they made a target of the major's head, by aiming at it boquets (*sic*) and grasping his hand until it was sore. . . .

Aside from such recognition, the meeting on May 12, 1865, was an important one to Delany. He had been the only black spokesman in that pulpit. Three whites, all prominent men, had taken the initiative in urging action by the black audience. Gen. Saxton particularly had outlined the same kind of "do it yourself" program for which Delany had always pleaded with his people.

When Gen. Saxton sent for him, and Major Delany had the choice of mustering out, as so many officers were doing, or going to the Sea Islands for the decisive fight for land, he was delighted. Stay and fight? Of course, so long as there was the faintest hope.

CHAPTER SEVENTEEN

What Is a Freedman?

America's first Federal welfare program was doomed to failure—because it worked. The Freedmen's Bureau was allowed to continue its operations for approximately three and a half years, over President Johnson's veto, solely because the radical Republicans in Congress insisted on it. Johnson was correct in February 1866 when he warned, in his message vetoing a two-year extension of the Freedmen's Bureau, "A system for the support of indigent persons in the United States was never contemplated by the authors of the Constitution." Many a president and Congress have agreed with that interpretation ever since.

There is little variation from Andrew Johnson's opinions today in regard to aid to the races. The Federal food assistance in Sunflower County, Mississippi, Senator James O. Eastland's home empire, spells the difference between survival and starvation for the blacks there. In 1865 that same food assistance issued by both the Freedmen's Bureau and the Army meant survival for millions, and perhaps to everyone's surprise, the Freedmen's Bureau expenditures fed and housed more whites than blacks in the rebel states during its brief lifetime.

The doom of the Freedmen's Bureau (and of current welfare programs) was dictated, almost from its inception, by the economic forces in command, not by the military or political. If the freedmen were to be fed and housed, they would demand more compensation for their labor, thus the profits from restoration of the plantation system would be reduced. That was the sole reason for the expiration of this first Federal welfare agency and not, according to the historians, the existence of corruption and inefficiency within the Bureau.

In South Carolina the Bureau did assist more blacks than

whites, solely because of the preponderance of freedmen in that state. The Census of 1860 counted 402,406 slaves and 9,914 free blacks in the state, in comparison with a total of 291,300 whites. But in the hill counties of the north and northwest parts of the state, thousands of poor whites survived the post-Civil War years due to Federal assistance. The record of accomplishment by the Bureau in South Carolina is astounding.

Approximately 3 million rations were issued to blacks and whites during the Bureau's effective operation. Under a crop-lien plan, whereby many were enabled to regain their self-sufficiency, $300,000 worth of supplies were distributed, such as seed and fertilizer. About 175,000 persons were given medical care, and 5,000 were given free transportation to their homes or families from whom they had been separated by the war. Bureau agents supervised 300,000 work contracts between planters and freedmen, in addition to arbitrating many thousands of disputes. And the Bureau assisted in the maintenance of 85 schools whose student enrollment averaged 100,000 for the three years.

Martin R. Delany was responsible for much of this accomplishment as well as for that all-important intangible—pride and motivation of the blacks among whom he worked. That was General Saxton's reason for requesting the War Department to retain the Black Major in the military instead of mustering him out with his regiment and other officers from other regiments. He was to work in the Sea Islands for the next three years.

There was sorrow in Charleston when Delany informed his new friends of his orders to report to Beaufort. The freedmen did not know why the Black Major was taken from them, and Delany could not explain it either. The colored troops were to be mustered out and that too was disquieting to the blacks. Besides, on the streets of Charleston they could begin to see the familiar white faces, the figures of men and women who had once dictated the life of the city. They were beginning to return and reclaim their abandoned houses. The grapevine from the Sea Islands and from the Combahee River rice country informed the blacks that the old masters were returning, and they were demanding both their lands *and* an owner's share in the crops then in the ground. News came from Washington that President Johnson had given them pardons and that by merely taking an oath of allegiance, the past was forgotten, and they could reclaim their lands. What was to happen to the freedmen? Nobody knew, including Delany.

He requested and was granted a delay in his orders so that he could wind up affairs of the 105th Regiment in Charleston and therefore did not leave for Beaufort until June 26th. There he found Gen. Saxton on the point of departure for Washington where, it later developed, he was appointed Assistant Commissioner of the new Bureau of Refugees, Freedmen and Abandoned Lands by Gen. Oliver O. Howard, head of the Freedmen's Bureau, with the approval of the War Department. While there Gen. Saxton saw to it that the War Department issued special orders, dated July 15, 1865, relieving Delany and Capt. Wall from duty with the 104th Regiment and assigning them to the Freedmen's Bureau under Saxton's command.

Delany had left Charleston in a rage, ready and anxious to speak his mind. The returning whites were taking every possible advantage of the ignorance of their former slaves. Two days before he left the city he received a copy of General Order No. 62 issued by Brevet Major General John P. Hatch, Northern District commander, finally recognizing the fact that the blacks were being victimized.

> It has come to the knowledge of the District Commander that in some of the contracts made between planters and freedmen, a clause has been introduced establishing a system of *peonage*—the freedman binding himself to work out any debt he might hereafter incur to his employer. All contracts made under authority of these Headquarters will be understood as merely temporary arrangements to insure the cultivation of the ground for the present season. Any contract made under the above authority which contains conditions tending to peonage will be considered nul. . . . Contracts will be simply worded, whilst acknowledging the freedom of the colored man, such expressions as "*freed by the acts of military forces of the United States*" will not be permitted. The attempt to introduce anything into the contracts which may have the appearance or the intention at some future date to contest the question of the emancipation of the Negroes will be reported to the commander of the sub-district who will examine into the antecedents of the

person making the attempt, and report upon the case to district headquarters.

The *Charleston Courier* "viewed with alarm" such behavior by the planters and predicted, "Military power will be the order of the day until the time shall have arrived that the people have abandoned the old notion of States' rights and signified their unqualified adherence to the principle of the general government."

Through all rebel states, not just in South Carolina, the returning rebels were attempting to prey on their former slaves by binding them legally to the land and claiming a lion's share of the 1865 crops then growing and soon to be harvested. Most of the freedmen, illiterate and obedient, were to find themselves out of homes, out of crops, and some even in debt to their former masters. The process began with each of the thousands of pardons granted by Johnson.

Meanwhile, Delany was in Beaufort, fretting over the delay in his future orders, bothered by unaccustomed idleness and disturbed by reports flowing into Beaufort from all the Sea Islands that the blacks were restive over the uncertainties of their future. Naturally, this became Delany's concern, since they were his people. Having no duties, he visited some of the islands to speak to them, believing it to be quite non-military business of his own. He soon found himself to be a subversive character.

In Gen. Saxton's absence, the officer in command at Beaufort, Col. C. H. Howard, on July 22 received an unsigned letter as follows:

> I beg to inform you, that I have, from a reliable source, received information that Major M. Delany (Negro) 104th U.S.C.T. has been endeavoring to persuade the col. people on the adjacent islands not to work for the Whites, and has in various other ways stirred up trouble among the negroes, by his speeches and interviews with them.
>
> The gentleman, Mr. Mitchell, Asst. Postmaster at Beaufort, S.C. who has imparted to me this information, tells me that Major Delany purposes to deliver a lecture to the Colored people on St. Helena Island at the Brick Church —tomorrow, Sunday, July 23rd either in the morning or afternoon, and that it has been announced that his subject

> will be of a nature calculated to create disturbance and perhaps serious trouble between the negroes and their employers, for whom they have been quietly and peaceably working up to this time.
>
> I would therefore—in the absence of Genl. Saxton respectfully suggest, that as Major Delany is under your command, an officer be requested to visit the Brick Church at St. Helena Island tomorrow morning at 7 or 9 o'clock A.M. for the purpose of listening to the lecture, and to make report of anything which may be productive of future evils.

This warning caused a military furor whose repercussions were to last for the rest of the Black Major's career in the Sea Islands. Col. Howard sent Lt. Alex Whyte, Jr., to St. Helena Island and also informed the Assistant Adjutant General of the post, Bvt. Maj. S. M. Taylor, who assigned still another observer to hear Delany, Lt. Edward M. Stoeber. The two lieutenants appear to have split up the work, with Whyte making extracts of Delany's speech, while Stoeber's report not only quotes Delany but makes comments at length. Between the two reports it is obvious that Delany was at his fire-eating best before the estimated 500–600 that crowded into the little Brick Church. Since Whyte's report was taken from his notes and Stoeber quoted from memory, the former's report sounds more like Delany typically declaring his defiance of the white man.

He told the freedmen that South Carolina was peopled by Negroes who were "able, intelligent, honorable negroes, *not an inferior race*, mind you, who are ready to protect their liberty." He continued:

> I want to tell you one thing. Do you know that if it was not for the black men this war never would have been brought to a close with success to the Union, and the liberty of your race if it had not been for the Negro? I want you to understand that. Do you know it? Do you know it? Do you know it? (cries of yes, yes, yes). . . . They can't get along without you.

He warned them against the "Yankees from the North who come down here to drive you as much as ever it was before the war. It's slavery over again, northern, universal U.S. slavery. . . ."

Again and again Delany warned them against the Yankees, comparing them with their former masters who got rich on their labors.

> There are good Yankees and when you come across a good Yankee he is smart. . . . But what I don't like, and what I won't have is these fellows from the north, who were nothing at home, and ape the southerner with a big brim hat, he has his overseer too, a chuckle-headed slave driver on the fence or in the crotch of a tree, and say Sam or Jim do this, do that, light my pipe, as lazy as any southerner or overseer was. They promise you a 30¢ task, you are to get ⅓ crop and I will see that you get it. You must not think you are Yankees. You are Negroes the same as I am. . . .
>
> And so it is with these Yankees from the North, they don't pay you enough. I see too many of you dressed in rags, and shoeless. . . . These Yankees talk smooth to you, o yes, their tongue rolls just like a drum (laughter) but it's slavery over again as much as it ever was.

Delany advised his people to wait on future plans, to get their own land.

> I expect Gen. Saxton back soon. He is working with me, when this matter will be settled. I mean about lands when you can plant and work your own farms. Don't be anxious for large places. Forty acres is enough cotton—will bring 30¢ for two years to come. That is putting it at a low estimate (he figured they could earn $900 a year this way). . . . But you must only deal with the Govt. accredited agents, recognize none but authorized cotton agents.

Whyte's conclusion to his extracts from Delany's speech is simple, "There is something rotten in Denmark." There are many points mentioned by Stoeber that are not in Whyte's report and some of them do sound like Delany's thoughts but not his expression. However, in substance, the reports agree that Delany told the freedmen to defy their new masters from the North, get their own lands, and always remember that the whole country depended on their labor for its prosperity. Beware of cheating white men, southerners or northerners. Stoeber does charge Delany with one declaration not mentioned by Whyte. He quoted from memory: "Believe not in these school teachers, Emissaries, Ministers and agents, because they never tell you the truth. . . ."

But Stoeber's comments and conclusions are lengthy and alarming. He viewed the whole speech as a major disaster and concludes his report with:

> In my opinion by this discourse he was trying to encourage them to break the peace of society and force their way by insurrection to a position he is ambitious they should attain to.
>
> The excitement with the congregation was immense; groups were formed talking over what they have heard, and ever and anon cheers were given to some particular sentence of the speech. I afterwards mingled with several groups, to hear their opinions. Some used violent language, "saying they would get rid of their Yankee employers." "That is the only man who ever told them the truth." "That now those men have to work for themselves or starve or leave the country. We will not work for them anymore." Some Whites were present and listened with horror depicted in their faces at the whole performance. Some said "What shall become of us now?" and if such a speech should be again given to those men, there will be open rebellion.
>
> My opinion of the whole affair is that Major Delany is a thorough hater of the white race and excites the colored people unnecessarily. He even tries to injure the magnanimous conduct of the Government toward them, either intentionally or through want of knowledge. . . . He openly acts and speaks contrary to the policy of the Government, advising them not to work for any man, but for themselves. *The intention of our Government, that all the men should be employed by their former masters, as far as possible, and contracts made between them superintended by some officer empowered by the Government.* He says it would be the old slavery over again, if a man should work for an employer, and *that* it must not be.

Finally, Stoeber found a sinister implication in Delany's statement that the 200,000 colored troops had won the Civil

War. "The mention of having two hundred thousand men well drilled in arms—does he not hint to them what to do, if they should be compelled to work for employers?"

The most significant fact about these reports was their submission. Both lieutenants appear to have reported a typical fighting Delany speech which is not expected from a man in uniform. The Black Major certainly should have harnessed his tongue, according to military custom. And, according to custom, these two reports should have gone to Gen. Saxton, Delany's immediate superior and to whose orders he was subject. They were not. The reports were submitted to Major General G. A. Gillmore, commanding the Military Department of South Carolina. This gentleman had been on the platform at Gen. Saxton's meeting in Charleston on May 12. He was Chief Justice Chase's escort throughout his South Carolina inspection trip.

Gillmore sent both St. Helena Island reports directly to Washington with the following transmittal message:

> Respectfully forwarded for the information of the War Department, and the Commissioner of the Bureau of Refugees, Freedmen and Abandoned Lands.
>
> The course pursued by Major Delany, 104th U.S.C.T. since his advent into this Department, has been calculated to do harm, by inciting the colored people to deeds of violence.
>
> The well being of the freed people would be advanced by his removal to some other field of duty.

When Saxton returned from Washington on August 7, he issued his orders to the Black Major. It was somewhat ironic because Delany became a neighbor of Gen. Gillmore on Hilton Head Island, where the military headquarters was located. Saxton appointed Delany a sub-assistant commissioner in the Freedmen's Bureau and the orders requested Gillmore's Quartermaster to find him transportation and quarters.

Saxton also received copies of the lieutenants' reports as well as another report dated Aug. 21 from his agent in St. Helena Village, a W. S. Towne. It commented chiefly on the tension among the blacks on the island and gave a most interesting recital of the formation of a black Union League with the blessing of Bishop Daniel W. Payne of the AME Church then visiting them. It also noted the presence of arms and militia drilling among the blacks, their economic improvement, and reluctance to sign work contracts. Towne did not mention Delany by name but wrote:

> An unwise speech made here a few weeks ago by a northern black man has called out a free expression of the latent spirit of discontent, on the land and cotton questions, and though it was intended, I believe, only to teach the people to be on their guard against all southern white men, and all northern speculators, and to urge them to uphold their own race, yet it had the effect of exciting animosity against all white men. This spirit is confined to a very few, and whether it will grow and give trouble, remains to be seen.
>
> I think the speech could have had nothing to do with the formation of the Society (Union League), as that was organized before the speaker came to the island. Neither can he be responsible for the drilling, as that was to meet a local emergency of which he had no knowledge. His speech was not approved by the more intelligent of the people, and its effect will be counteracted by their influence.

Still another report was made to Gen. Gillmore that August, and this one he did forward to Saxton. It was an inspection report by a Capt. S. H. Hawkins of the 6th U.S. Infantry who was sent out to investigate rumors of unrest among the freedmen in the form of a series of raids led by a Negro with the intriguing name of Double Quick. In the course of the report, Capt. Hawkins referred to Delany's speech:

> The system of contracts seems to be working well on the islands, but upon the main few if any have been entered into. In this regard I regret that it is my duty to report that a Major Delany of the 104th U.S.C.T. has created great dissatisfaction among the evil disposed toward the whites, by a late public address in which he cautioned the colored people to beware of all whites, Northern and Southern, telling them that they owed their liberty to their own strong right arms alone, that they should disregard all contracts made with the whites, that they are entitled to their share of the crops, and that he would see they obtained it.

Many Negroes disposed of their cotton crops of 1864 at one dollar the pound and were to have received an additional sum provided the New York Market remained at its then high rate. The capture of Savannah cotton caused an immediate rapid fall and the additional price could not be paid.

This the Negroes cannot understand and Major Delany's remarks have only heightened their discontent—at a supposed breach of contract, and increased their jealousy of the whites.

All of these reports were read by Saxton and he continued to give Major Delany a totally free hand in his work on Hilton Head. Gen. Saxton had been to Washington and he knew what was to be done to the freedmen. Delany was speaking Saxton's sentiments at St. Helena for the general had learned of President Johnson's intention to take away the plots of land on the Sea Islands given the freedmen under Sherman's Field Order No. 15. Those lands were to be returned to the former masters or sold at open auction to the highest bidders who, he knew, would be northern speculators. It would be Saxton's duty to tell the freedmen this policy. He did not relish the task, and he could not refute any of Delany's warnings on St. Helena. In fact, Gen. Saxton's refusal to use armed force in dispossessing the blacks from land they had cropped for three to five seasons was the reason for his removal from his post on January 15, 1866. President Johnson wanted the land restored to plantation status, not to free and independent, sometimes prosperous, black enterprise.

At no time during his service as a Freedmen's Bureau officer did Delany hesitate to speak his mind—to the military, to the whites, and to the blacks. Therefore, he was despised by his white fellow officers, hated and feared by the white civilians, and almost deified by the blacks. There were many complaints filed against him for what he said and did, but he was never fired by his superiors, as were so many other Bureau officers for one reason or another. He served as long as the Freedmen's Bureau was active, and he survived many a military commander of his District. He was not mustered out of the Army, and therefore out of his post with the Bureau, until August 5, 1868, after almost exactly three years of service.

One reason he was retained after Gen. Saxton's removal was the certainty that the blacks would retaliate with violence if their Black Major was taken from them, and their potential for armed rebellion was always close to the surface. Another reason, perhaps, was Delany's diligence in his work. As usual, when he reached Hilton Head he set about organizing the numerous responsibilities facing every Bureau officer.

He found there, fortunately, that the agent for the Bureau was Josiah W. Pillsbury, brother of Parker, who for many years was an officer in the American Anti-Slavery Society. Josiah had been willing, sympathetic, and energetic in behalf of the freedmen, but he was a civilian. The military had him licked.

Delany proceeded to "pull rank." Pillsbury had been crowding his work, supplies, and applicants into a tiny storeroom. Within a week Delany had the Quartermaster assign to him a spacious building on the road leading to the all-black village of Mitchelville, formerly occupied by a general. He demanded and got military rations for the freedmen on time. He demanded and had his paper work, particularly requisitions for his people, processed in time. He was forced to dogged persistence in every action he took in connection with the white military. An example reported at length by Bishop Alexander W. Wayman of the AME Church in his autobiography illustrates the petty problems Delany encountered in all his duties, as well as his unusual degree of patience. Bishop Wayman was at the wharf at Hilton Head when the Black Major returned from some trip and

> as we were coming from the wharf going to the Quarter Master's office, one of the guards attempted to stop him, and asked where was his pass.
>
> The Major paid no attention to him. One of the gentlemen that was with us said to the guard, "he is an officer," and that was enough. In a moment he saluted the Major.
>
> On reaching the Quarter Master's office the Major drew out his papers, and presenting those said, "Mr. Quarter Master I want transportation for myself and two servants to Beaufort." The officer's Clerk commenced writing, then paused a moment and said, "Major, what Regiment are you attached to?" "None," said the Major, "I am on General Saxton's staff." The Clerk then said, "Major I think you

will have to get a permit from the Provost Marshal for your servants." The Major said, "Is that so?"

The Major ascertained that there was no steamer for Beaufort until next afternoon, so he had to retire to the ship, and I went to my quarters at Mitchellsville, and spent the night with my old friend, Brother Dennegal.

Next morning I started down to see how the Major was faring, and he invited me to go to the Provost-Marshal's office with him to get passes for his two servants, to go from Hilton Head to Mitchellsville. On our way we met a gentleman from Pittsburgh who recognized the Major, and addressed him as Mr. Delaney (*sic*). The Major said to him, "don't you know better than to address an officer as Mr.?" The gentleman said, "I beg your pardon. What shall I call you?" "Major Delaney." "Oh!" said he, "Major Delaney, how are you sir?"

We entered the Provost Marshal's office. The Major said, "Mr. Provost Marshal, I want passes for two servants to go (to) Mitchellsville." He wrote the passes and gave them to the Major.

In the afternoon I went down to the steamer to see the major and servants leave for Beaufort; and when I reached the wharf, there was Capt. O. S. B. Walls sick with the chills, and the Major and his two servants. The guard at the steamboat refused to let the Major's servants pass, which rather excited him, and he turned around and asked some one where was General Littlefield's Headquarters, saying he knew that the General was above any Provost Marshal, and started in that direction, but had not gone far before he met the General coming, and he said to him that the guards at the steamer refused to let his servants pass.

The General then spoke to the guard, saying, "Let Major Delaney's servants pass." It was all right then.

But all this was only an annoyance to Delany, as were the complaints by the planters to the military authorities, to Gen. Saxton, to Gen. Howard, and to President Johnson. He paid no attention to those complaining and a great deal of attention to those white planters who indicated an honest intent to deal fairly with the freedmen. It was just as much an educative process for these whites, he realized, as it was for the freedmen. They must learn that they cannot reimpose the conditions of slavery on their labor just as the blacks must learn the responsibilities as well as the privileges of freedom. Of the latter, he wrote:

> The great social system was to them a novelty, and without proper guidance would have been a curse instead of a blessing. Unaccustomed to self-reliance by the barbarism of the system under which they had lived, liberty was destined to lead them into errors. To prevent this the Bureau was established.

He had no difficulties at all with most of the freedmen on the broad reaches of Hilton Head Island. The only exceptions were those freedmen who had believed all the wild tales of freedom being a way of living as their masters had, in idleness and opulence. As for those freedmen on Hilton Head Island who were ready for violence to retain their plots of land obtained under Sherman's Order No. 15, he was with them all the way and encouraged their resistance throughout the rest of that crucial year of 1865.

As for the planters, he utilized a unique educative process. Early in September there began to appear in the Sea Islands newspaper read by all the whites, *The New South*, a series of anonymous articles under the heading "Prospects of the Freedmen of Hilton Head." They were short pieces, and each made a definite point. All of them had the unmistakably intricate and overwritten style so characteristic of Delany and the newspapers of the day. But in each installment there is a pointed lesson for the white planters who were stubbornly resisting any change in their relationship with blacks and each black who sank back into the slothfulness of slavery.

The question raised in the first insertion was, "Have the blacks become self-sustaining? And will they ever, in a state of freedom, resupply the products which comprised the staples formerly of the old planters?" He admitted that they had not become self-sustaining but asserted unequivocally that they did desire to work. "*But industry alone is not sufficient, nor work available, except these command adequate compensation.*"

Delany followed with his oft-repeated history of the arrival and use of the slave by the Spanish, Portuguese, French, and

English in several installments and again asked the whites a question: "After these centuries of trial and experience, would these people have been continually sought after, had they not proven superior to all others as laborers in the kind of work assigned them?"

As proof of the worth of such labor, Delany then cited the emancipation in the British West Indies and declared that opposition to freedom there for those 800,000 slaves was not a fear of loss of their labor but rather that "capitalists" in London who held the mortgages on West Indian plantations got the 20 million pounds sterling, not the planters there, because Parliament undervalued the compensation. They paid an average of $120 per slave "when men and women were then bringing at the Barracoons in Cuba from five to six hundred dollars apiece in cash."

What about those freedmen who refuse to work? Delany had an answer to that, too, by pointing out that under slavery the entire family worked "from seven years old to decrepit old age. . . ." At Hilton Head, as well as in the British West Indies, perhaps half of the blacks will not work. What of it? he asks, and in answer presents the ideal freedman's family, a hypothetical family.

> Before liberated, Juba had a wife and eight children, from seven to thirty years of age, every one of whom was at labor in the field as a slave. When set free, the mother and all of the younger children (consisting of five) quit the field, leaving the father and three older sons from twenty-five to thirty years of age, who preferred field labor; the five children being sent to school. The mother, now the pride of the recently-elevated freedman, stays in her own house, to take charge, as a housewife, in her new domestic relations—thus permanently withdrawing from the field six-tenths of the service of this family; while the husband and three sons (but four-tenths) are all who remain to do the work formerly performed by ten-tenths, or the whole. Here are more than one half who will not work in the field. Will any one say they should?

The planters, of course, said they should, but Delany's reply was that under slavery they followed the master's choice of occupation. As freedmen, Juba's children "having different tastes and desires" will make their own choice. "Some who were field hands, among the young men and women of mature age, will seek employment at other pursuits, and choose for themselves various trades,—vocations adapted to their tastes. . . . Will this be charged to the worthlessness of the negro, and made an argument against his elevation? Truth stands defiant in the pathway of error."

The final article, before Delany decided to identify himself as the author, is a remarkably clear and valid lesson in political economy. Its sole point is that if land is made available to the freedmen, instead of confining them to the plantation system, the entire country would be served and its economy strengthened.

> In the apportionment of small farms to the freedmen, an immense amount of means is placed at their command, and thereby a great market opened, a new source of consumption of every commodity in demand in free civilized communities. The blacks are great consumers, and four millions of a population, before barefooted, would here make a demand for the single article of shoes. The money heretofore spent in Europe by the old slaveholders would be all disbursed by these new people in their own country.

They would want homes instead of huts, he continued, cotton gins for themselves as well as farming implements, furniture, "genteel apparel," as well as the luxuries. Therefore, it was in the country's best interest to give them land of their own, to create a profitable new market. To the industrialists of the North, the mercantilist, the argument made sense, though not to the former slaveholder of the South. But the 39th Congress was about to convene and, Delany fervently hoped, might put an end to Johnson's restoration policies. It was time to speak out publicly and he did so on December 7 in *The New South.*

> The restoration of the industrial prosperity of the South is *certain,* if fixed upon the basis of a domestic triple alliance, which the new order of things requires, invites, and demands.
>
> Capital, land and labor require a copartnership. The capital can be obtained in the North; the land is in the

South, owned by the old planters; and the blacks have the labor. Let, then, the North supply the capital (which no doubt it will do on demand, when known to be desired on this basis), the South the land (which is ready and waiting), and the blacks will readily bring the labor, if only being assured that their services are wanted in so desirable an association of business relations, the net profits being equally shared between the three,—capital, land, and labor,—each receiving one third, of course. The *net* has reference to the expenses incurred after gathering the crop, such as transportation, storage, and commission on sales.

Upon this basis I propose to act, and make contracts between the capitalist, landholder, and laborer, and earnestly invite, and call upon all colored people,—the recent freedmen,—also capitalists and landholders within the limits of my district, to enter at once into a measure the most reasonable and just to all parties concerned, and the very best that can be adopted to meet the demands of the new order and state of society, as nothing can pay better where the blacks cannot get land for themselves.

He signed this letter with his full title and authority, and declared that the "triple alliance" plan had been endorsed by three widely known planters—and he named them—the military command, and "Of course it receives the approval of Major General Saxton."

One immediate result of the triple alliance slogan was its dissemination throughout South Carolina and then to other states, for it was contract time in the South. Delany himself received an immediate challenge from a Colleton River planter and former Confederate colonel, to provide 260 freedmen and families—"Try to arrange it so that each family will average three field hands as I have house-room to accomodate (*sic*) them on that basis."

Delany's reply was that the colonel could depend on it, with some modifications of the preferred agreement—the freedmen would be there. "I reply most positively that you may confidently rely upon such aid in your business arrangements, as the people are waiting, ready and willing, to consummate such contracts as this plan proposes, alike advantageous to all the parties interested."

The freedmen were there and the labor jam was broken on Hilton Head. Freedmen who had no hopes of land signed up while planters who had held out for better labor terms, now consulted with Delany. He delivered the colonel's help "on the dot," and saw to it himself that every obligation in the agreement he approved was observed by both parties.

But Delany could do nothing for the approximately 40,000 black families in the Sea Islands who held Sherman Order No. 15 land. Nor could Gen. Saxton. He confessed as much to the freedmen during his last inspection tour. Nor could Gen. Howard change President Johnson's determination that the Sea Island land be returned to the original owners or sold in large parcels to the highest bidders before the 39th Congress convened and interfered with his restoration policies.

On July 28 Howard had issued a circular containing orders to sub-assistant commissioners of the Bureau, such as Delany, to keep as many freedmen as possible on their own land. But President Johnson was displeased. In Gen. Howard's own words:

> My circular of instructions did not please President Johnson. Therefore, in order to avoid misunderstandings, now constantly arising among the people in regard to abandoned property, particularly after I had set on foot a systematic method of granting to the former owners a formal pardon, he made me draw up another circular worded better to suit his policy and submit it to him before its issue. But he, still dissatisfied, and with a totally different object in view than mine, had the document redrawn at the White House and instructed me on September 12, 1865, to send to send it out as approved by him, and so with reluctance I did. This document in great part rescinded former land circulars. Besides allowing assistant commissioners to return all land not abandoned, it instructed them to return all abandoned lands to owners who were pardoned by the President, and provided no indemnity whatever for the occupants, refugees, or freedmen, except a right to the growing crops.

Howard suggested that a condition of restoration of property be that each planter grant his former slaves a small homestead on his acres but "President Johnson was amused and gave no heed to this recommendation. My heart ached for our beneficiaries, but I became comparatively helpless to offer them any permanent possession."

To cap Gen. Howard's burden, the President also ordered him south to investigate specifically the problems of the Sherman Field Order No. 15 land grants and find "an agreement mutually satisfactory to the freedmen and the land owners."

"Why did I not resign?" Howard asks in his autobiography. For the same reason Saxton and Delany had not. They all hoped for some way of salvaging a concept—land for the freedmen. Howard set about his hopeless task as ordered, and explained the President's wishes to a large audience of freedmen on Edisto Island. That defeated him. Afterward, he was to rest his hopes on Congress. On that late October afternoon of 1865 Gen. Howard gave up, although, as a soldier, he remained on duty in the Freedmen's Bureau.

> My address, however kind in manner I rendered it, met with no apparent favor. They did not hiss, but their eyes flashed unpleasantly and with one voice they cried, "No, no!" Speeches full of feeling and rough eloquence came back in response. One very black man, thick set and strong, cried out from the gallery: "Why, General Howard, why do you take away our lands? You take them from us who are true, always true to the Government! You give them to our all-time enemies! That is not right!"

One of the best known slaveholders, William Whaley, also spoke, but he found that his former slaves did not trust a word he said. In a petition drawn up by the freedmen in the audience and dated October 25, 1865, they informed President Johnson that "the King of south Carolina as the Privalage to have the stage that he might a Dress the ordenence (audience) of the freedmen"; then followed a devastating description of Whaley's character and customs when he was the "old master." Somebody said, "Here is Plenty Whidow & Fatherles that have serve you as slave now losen a home." All they wanted was "a acres and a ½ to a family as you has the labers and the Profet of there Yearly (early) Youth." But when Gen. Howard asked Whaley at what price he would sell land to the freedmen, the answer was not less than $100 an acre, naturally far beyond any of their resources, and "so then we therefore lose fate (faith) in this southern Gentleman." They begged "the wise President" to give them "a Chance to Recover out of this trubble." There is no recorded reply to their petition.

By the time Congress met and took action, it was too late. Approximately 10 percent of the freedmen were able to retain their lands, but no more. The policy had been made and backed by military force. Gen. Saxton explained what that policy was on February 21, 1866, when he was called to testify in Washington before Congress' Joint Committee on Reconstruction. One of the questions asked him was, "What is their (freedmen's) disposition in regard to purchasing land, and what is the disposition of the landholders in reference to selling land to Negroes?" Gen. Saxton's reply was unmistakably bitter:

> The object which the freedman has most at heart is the purchase of land. They all desire to get small homesteads and to locate themselves upon them, and there is scarcely any sacrifice too great for them to make to accomplish this object. I believe it is the policy of the majority of the farm owners to prevent negroes from becoming landholders. They desire to keep the negroes landless, and as nearly in a condition of slavery as it is possible for them to do.

The failure of those directly involved with the freedmen, in all of the rebel states, to create a proportionate middle class of self-sufficient homesteaders among the Negroes—a group worshiped as the bulwark of American democracy—took place between the assassination of Lincoln and Congress' declaration of war on Johnson. The ascendancy of property rights over all others was asserted during the brief period and proved to be the first nail in the coffin of black equality after the Civil War.

It is difficult to guess whether Delany's eternal realism dictated his course and his conviction that, as always, property rights would win in a white man's country, or whether he was simply pushed by circumstances into his strange position as special pleader for the blacks of South Carolina.

The effectiveness of the Black Major in resolving the conflict over work contracts within his jurisdiction as well as the triple alliance concept which provided a formula for agreement was probably the reason Gen. Daniel E. Sickles, who replaced

Gen. Gillmore as military commander of the Department of South Carolina, summoned Major Delany to Charleston on December 8. Sickles was the colorful individualist who has been branded both a hero and an incompetent—depending on the school of military strategy upheld—for his role at Gettysburg. He was also the first man in the United States to plead successfully temporary insanity after shooting and killing the son of Francis Scott Key for making advances to Mrs. Sickles. This rugged individualist, who had lost a leg at Gettysburg, had little trust in the wisdom of his commander in chief, even though restricted by his orders. Toward the end of 1865 Sickles' headquarters were flooded by complaints about the blacks, all of them emanating from white planters whose contracts for the coming year were rejected by the freedmen. In the near future, the whites reported, there would be black insurrection through all the low country of South Carolina, and the details of the horror and violence wreaked upon the innocent white women and children differed in no way from all the insurrection fears repeated periodically since Denmark Vesey in 1822.

On the other hand, Sickles was informed by the blacks themselves that on Christmas Day 1865 there would be a division of the rich lands, and each black family would have its own acreage to work. Therefore, why sign up with the "old masters" for 1866?

To get at the truth of the situation, Gen. Sickles chose the Black Major, one of the few Freedmen's Bureau officers still under military command, to investigate. His special orders, issued on December 21 were:

> *Major M. R. Delany*, 104th United States Colored Infantry, will proceed at once to the Military District of Port Royal, and the Sea Islands in the Military District of Charleston, South Carolina, and inspect, and report upon the condition of the population therein, according to the instructions received from the major general commanding. Commanding officers will afford Major Delany all necessary facilities. . . . The quartermaster's department will furnish the necessary transportation.

As a result of these orders, Delany became the general's trouble shooter throughout the military district. Within a few days upon his return to Hilton Head to prepare for his trip he went into action. There was rumored to be a plot by the blacks of Port Royal who were to rise on Christmas Eve and celebrate by killing the whites. Informed that the insurrection would begin at Beaufort, Delany requisitioned a detachment of the 21st U.S.C.T. stationed at Hilton Head and the transport *Sampson,* and on Christmas Eve the force set sail for the scene of carnage.

He found that in both Beaufort and Port Royal the blacks had indeed spent a jubilant Christmas Eve—their first as freedmen—while the whites huddled in hiding. It was the most orderly and sober holiday in the many years since white masters had handed out rum for their slaves' celebration. In 1865 there was no rum.

And the only trouble Delany found in Port Royal and on Edisto Island, at Mount Pleasant and on Sullivan's Island, along the Ashley River and elsewhere was an effort by white planters to secure military aid in forcing unjust contracts on the freedmen, sometimes with the connivance of Freedmen's Bureau Officers.

On one of these missions, with a Brigadier General Bennett and two companies of colored troops, Delany steamed up the Ashley River to "quell an insurrection" already in progress. The extent of the disorder was a refusal to accept still another contract returning to the freedmen less food than when they were slaves. The blacks were packing their scant belongings to leave, against the orders of the "old master." That was the extent of their violence!

Delany settled that dispute quickly. He offered the freedmen military rations and transportation away from the plantation, whereupon the planter conveniently found a way to offer his blacks a contract they could accept. Reports of this result markedly reduced the number of insurrection rumors and reports to the military, and Major Delany became poison to those planters trying to exploit their freedmen to the fullest extent.

On the other hand, the Black Major aroused the antagonism of some of the blacks by his insistence on being truthful with them. On Edisto Island, after addressing a large meeting of freedmen on New Year's Day, Delany for the first time was characterized somewhat as a black militant today would attack a black moderate, as an "Uncle Tom." He had first met with a delegation of old slaveholders headed by the largest planter on the island, Jacob J. Mikell, and verified President Johnson's pardon policy legally returning title to their lands to them. He then told the freedmen the facts of life. They could not hope to obtain their own homesteads, not under current policies, and should plan the coming year without this false hope. Understandably, the freedmen did not care for this blasting of their dreams by their own Black Major.

However, he also warned the planters that although the Freedmen's Bureau was perennially without resources, the military was not, and unless a fair division of the profits of the new crop year was offered to the freedmen, they would starve. Delany became a one-man labor relations board in behalf of his ignorant and victimized people.

Most of all, he made it clearly understood to the planters, as well as the freedmen, that he considered himself the final authority on work contracts. He inserted the following notice in the "Business Directory" of *The New South*:

TO PLANTERS

> All persons employing Freedmen to work on Plantations on Hilton Head Island must complete their contracts before the Acting Sub-Assistant Commissioner, Bureau R.F.A. Lands, Port Royal, Hilton Head, otherwise such contracts will be null and void, according to Circular No. 5, Headquarters Assistant Commissioner, Charleston.
>
> M. R. Delany
> Major A.S.A.C. Bureau
> Port Royal, H.H.

This did not endear Delany to the planters, nor did another step he took that fall when cotton was being picked on the lands cropped by freedmen under the Sherman order. They were hopelessly ignorant of the marketing of their cotton and were victimized by the planters, the new Yankee owners, gin mill operators and cotton brokers. Delany recalled, "I found, on assuming duty here, that it was the established system both at Hilton Head and in all the Districts referred to (Edisto, Beaufort, Lady's Island and St. Helena Island) for many traders to buy the cotton of the poor, ignorant country people, at the lowest possible prices, in the seed or before picked, rating at from 6 to 12 cents before and after picked. I have checked this in my District, and challenge a censure."

With the full approval of Gen. Saxton, Delany established a centrally located gin mill and cotton warehouse at Lands End on St. Helena, where the freedmen could by-pass all of the leeches feeding on his crop, have his raw cotton ginned and baled at nominal rates, and sold directly to purchasers at New York market prices. Often this spelled a difference of as much as a 300 percent higher return in a freedman's cotton crop and, for some, allowed them enough cash to bid on small parcels of land sold for taxes.

This too was highly unpopular among the whites, and complaints that the Black Major was putting the government into the cotton business went to all official offices including the White House. Even today, editorials against the subsidization of black enterprises by government agencies use the same arguments.

In all his Bureau work, Delany was under no illusions as to the permanence of each step he took, or of the life of the Freedmen's Bureau itself. The only permanent status among the freedmen, he knew, would be determined by the extent to which they participated in whatever civil government emerged from the coming Congress. President Johnson had made his intent clear. The blacks were to have no participation whatsoever in their local, state, or national governments. They were not to constitute a portion of the body politic. Although they were never to be slaves again, in Johnson's restoration policy, only whites were to determine exactly what their position was to be in American society.

This policy grated on Delany, but theoretically he was helpless. Both as an officer of the Freedmen's Bureau and the Army, he was forbidden to engage in any political activity. He brushed aside both restrictions and utilized every public forum he addressed, in connection with his duties, to once more preach a "do-it-yourself" political program. By November 1865 he was among a small and growing number of black men who were to emerge as the freedmen's political leaders in South Carolina for the next decade.

By then, Johnson's hurried plans to complete the restoration in the ten rebel states before Congress convened were fully consummated. On June 30, 1865, he had appointed provisional governors for the rebel states and his choice for South Carolina was Benjamin F. Perry, who had opposed secession at the Charleston convention in 1860 but, when voted down, served the Confederacy as a district attorney and a judge.

Perry's first act was to do exactly what was expected—restore to public office all who had been serving when hostilities ceased, and to summon the state's rebel leaders to a constitutional convention in September. They were *not* elected, but were handpicked by Perry. Naturally, the result was a replica of the presecession document, with the one exception demanded by Johnson—recognition of the abolition of slavery. There were no other conditions set by Johnson for readmission to the Union, no determination whatsoever of the future status of the blacks. So, quite naturally, the South Carolina Constitutional Convention of 1865 paid no attention to the blacks except to exclude them from voting for the state legislature, which was to convene in December.

The convention did not even discuss, merely tabled, two petitions from blacks addressed to them. The first such expression by the blacks was from the independent and articulate freedmen of St. Helena's Island and was a direct result of Delany's rousing speech of July 22.

They held a large meeting on September 4 and adopted five resolutions addressed to Perry's convention, the key one being:

> 1. *Resolved,* That we, the colored residents of St. Helena's Island, do most respectfully petition the Convention about to be assembled at Columbia, on the 13th instant, to so alter and amend the present Constitution of this State as to give the right of suffrage to every man of the age of twenty-one years, without other qualifications than that required for the white citizens of the State.

The other resolutions underlined this demand for suffrage, one declaring, "We will never cease our efforts to obtain, by all just and legal means, a full recognition of our rights as citizens of the United States and this Commonwealth." The St. Helena freedmen also declared that "the future peace and welfare of this State depends very materially upon the protection of the interests of the colored man."

Later that month 103 blacks in Charleston assembled for a similar petition to the convention. It was far from the positive assertions of the St. Helena freedmen, pleaded rather than demanded, though the objective sought was the same—suffrage. The contrast between the two petitions is strangely similar to that of Frederick Douglass' 1853 colored convention in Rochester and Martin Delany's Emigration Convention the following year.

The Charleston blacks "prayed" that the convention "will not debar any man from exercising the rights or privileges of citizenship because of the color of his skin." They acknowledged the "deplorable ignorance" of the majority of blacks, "But we do ask that if the ignorant white man is allowed to vote, that the ignorant colored man shall be allowed to vote also."

Finally, "If our prayer is not granted, there will doubtless be that same quiet and seemingly patient submission to wrong that there has been in the past. We can bide our time. . . . We fully understand what prejudices and preconceived opinions must be overcome before our prayers can be granted . . . ," etc. This petition was tabled on September 27 by the convention with the notation that it had not been read to the delegates.

This is understandable because of the convention's composition. Twelve of the delegates had been members of the 1860 secession convention, including its president, D. L. Wardlow, and the man who had offered the motion to secede, J. A. Inglis.

Aside from resuscitation of the pre-war Constitution, the convention ordered the election of a state legislature, with the right to vote restricted to those whites eligible to vote in 1860. It also appointed a committee to draw up a Black Code to offer to the new legislature. Once that body was elected and ratified the 13th Amendment abolishing slavery, South Carolina could take its place in the nation's councils. Johnson would be satisfied. It would not matter to him that the Constitution was never ratified by any "popular" vote, even one barring the blacks.

But before the year was ended, an effort was made to influence the new legislature. For the first time in history, the blacks of South Carolina gathered in Charleston, with representation from each of the state's legislative districts. They met for five days, from November 20 through November 25, and thoroughly thrashed out their hopes and aspirations for the future. The Black Major attended most of the sessions, having been elected an honorary member, with five other future black leaders of the state from the North, at the first gathering. He was called on to speak in the evening of the second day but, unfortunately, the minutes of the Colored People's Convention contain only comments on his speech.

> After a stirring interlude from the band, Major Delaney (*sic*) was introduced to the audience. He made one of his happiest efforts, and that is saying a good deal, when they are all happy. He completely charmed and carried away the crowded and eager auditory in one of his powerful and passionate appeals. We will not venture even an attempt at a sketch of the Major's speech. We could not do him justice. Only they who heard and felt it can properly appreciate it. He dwelt on discipline and obedience to the laws, and showed what had been accomplished by it both in the Crimean war and in the late revolution.

The results of the meetings were the formulation of united black demands for full citizenship made to the people of South Carolina, the state legislature, and the U.S. Congress. In addition, the convention drew up and placed before each a "Declaration of Rights and Wrongs" which summarized all that required correction:

> It is said in the Declaration of American Independence, "that all men are created equal; that they are endowed by their Creator with certain inalienable rights; that among those rights are life, liberty, and the pursuit of happiness."
>
> That the phrase "all men" includes the negro no one will attempt to deny. Therefore, we, the colored citizens of South Carolina and of these United States of America, justly claim such rights as are set forth in the above Declaration.
>
> To secure the free enjoyment of these rights is the proper object of civil government.
>
> "Right" is defined to be the just claim, ownership or lawful title which a person has to anything.

"He has a right to own his body and mind," his money or other property, which he has honestly earned, and the right to dispose of the same as he will, provided this is not done to the injury of others and in violation of the laws founded upon the rights of men.

But, in violation of the above principles and of justice and humanity, we have been deprived of our natural rights, which are founded in the laws of our nature, which consists of personal liberty, the right to be free in our persons, and the right of personal security and protection against injuries to our bodies or good name.

These are a portion of our inalienable rights, because we cannot be justly deprived of them.

We have been deprived of the free exercise of political rights, of natural, civil, and political liberty.

The avenues of wealth and education have been closed to us.

The strong wall of prejudice, on the part of the dominant race, has obstructed our pursuit of happiness.

We have been subjected to cruel proscription, and our bodies have been outraged with impunity.

We have been, and still are, deprived of the free choice of those who should govern us, and subjected unjustly to taxation without representation, and have bled and sweat for the elevation of those who have degraded us, and still continue to oppress us.

ZION CHURCH, Charleston

November 24, 1865

The people of South Carolina—meaning the whites—were asked in an address, which was an exceedingly well-phrased expansion on the "wrongs," to recognize the acts of their representatives.

Without any rational cause or provocation on our part, of which we are conscious, as a people, we, by the action of your Convention and Legislature, have been virtually, and with few exceptions excluded from, first, the rights of citizenship, which you cheerfully accord to strangers, but deny to us who have been born and reared in your midst, who were

> faithful while your greatest trials were upon you, and have done nothing since to merit your disapprobation.

In response to this, of course, the whites of South Carolina were silent until 1868 when another Constitutional Convention changed the entire state. Then they showed their approval of the actions of Perry's convention and legislature.

The appeal to the state legislature, asking that "those laws that have been enacted, that apply to us on account of our color, be repealed" received special treatment. The legislature's Committee on the Colored Population, whose chairman was the same as during the entire war, decided that the petition "involves subjects over which the Legislature has no control. It properly belongs to a Convention to consider and act on the prayer of the Petitioners." Thus was the buck passed back to the convention that originally had passed it to the legislature in September.

Congress was memorialized to right the wrongs cited above.

> We protest against any code of black laws the Legislature of this State may enact, and pray to be governed by the same laws that control other men. The right to assemble in peaceful convention, to discuss the political questions of the day; the right to enter upon all the avenues of agriculture, commerce, trade; to amass wealth by thrift and industry; the right to develop our whole being by all the appliances that belong to civilized society, cannot be questioned by any class of intelligent legislators.

But Congress was not yet in session, and its war with Johnson had not yet begun. On December 21, 1865, the South Carolina General Assembly adopted a Black Code so dominating every black life that it was a total restoration of the conditions of slavery, if not of the term itself. It governed relations between black man and black wife; between black man and white man; between white employer and forced black labor; between personal liberty and penal labor. It was, perhaps, the most inept piece of sweeping legislation enacted by any of the ten rebel states and to it must be credited the mobilization of the blacks within the state for armed resistance and the impetus given the radical Republicans in Congress to challenge Johnson.

The vagrancy clauses of the Black Code alone restored slavery to the state, for almost every freedman was made eligible for arrest and assignment to punitive and uncompensated work on the plantations. It was fortunate for the whites that Gen. Sickles was in command of the Department of South Carolina; otherwise bloodshed would have been inevitable. On January 1, 1866, just ten days after the passage of the Black Code, Gen. Sickles issued General Order No. 1, which totally negated every clause of the Black Code. It was an eighteen-point declaration of black rights, all couched in terms of enforcing equality of treatment. "XIII. The vagrant laws of the State of South Carolina applicable to free white persons, will be recognized as the only vagrant laws applicable to freedmen. . . ."

How much Martin Delany had to do with General Order No. 1 we do not know. He was still under Gen. Sickles' special orders as trouble shooter and may have influenced Sickles. However, the Black Code was the immediate cause of Delany's open and overt political activities. He concluded at that time that without the vote there was nothing black people could do to guarantee even their physical safety in South Carolina. He knew that the key to a solution was the new Congress, but meanwhile there was the black man himself. He had been taught how to use a gun.

CHAPTER EIGHTEEN

The Economic War

There could easily have been open and bloody warfare between whites and blacks in South Carolina if it had not been for a handful of moderates of both races, Martin Delany among them, no matter what Gen. Sickles did to keep the peace. For Sickles did not have enough troops to penetrate the remote plantations where die-hard planters attempted to reassert the conditions of slavery.

There were reports of the resumption of floggings, of black recalcitrants disappearing, their bodies never found, as well as black bodies *being* found. Many of these incidents were validated while others may have been rumors. But these were individual, not organized, expressions of the hatred that was to develop between the races.

Martin Delany restrained his people only because the Congressional war against Andrew Johnson had been declared by Senator Charles Sumner of Massachusetts at the opening session of the 39th Congress on December 4, 1865. His classic struggle began with six bills and a number of resolutions against Johnson's policies, and it was to have no concrete victory for fifteen turbulent and uncertain months until the First Reconstruction Act placed the military in control of civil government, canceling out Johnson's provisional governments. But this was not until March 2, 1867.

Sumner had tried to reason with the President before Congress convened and had had an interview with him on December 2. "I left the President that night with the painful conviction that his whole soul was set as flint against the good cause, and that by the assassination of Abraham Lincoln the Rebellion had vaulted into the presidential chair. Jefferson Davis was then in the casemates at Fortress Monroe, but Andrew Johnson was doing his work."

On December 20, on the floor of the Senate, Sumner offered his incontrovertible evidence that the conditions of slavery had been restored in all rebel states by encouragement of the executive branch of the government. When the content of this speech seeped through to the South, Martin Delany once more began to wonder about democracy as the ideal political system for his people, for Sumner preceded his documented report on each rebel state with a reading of Tsar Alexander's emancipation proclamation of 1861 which freed 23 million serfs.

> I have in my hands an official copy of this great act, published at St. Petersburg, by which it is declared that the serfs, after an interval of two years, are "entirely enfranchised." Under this Proclamation a new set of local magistrates was constituted, with "special court" and "justices of the peace" in each district, to superintend the working of the Proclamation and to examine on the spot all questions arising from Emancipation. This provision was not unlike our Bureau of Freedmen, which is thus vindicated by this example.
>
> But the good work did not stop here. The Emperor did not leave the freedmen without protection, handed over to the tender mercies of their former owners. By a careful series of "regulations" accompanying the Proclamation, prepared with infinite care, and divided into chapters and sections, the rights of the freedmen are secured beyond question. . . .

Sumner proceeded to give the Senate chapter and verse from the Russian emancipation proclamation and then summarized:

> Thus does Russia by careful provisions, supplementary to the act of Emancipation, secure her freedmen in all their rights; first, in the right of family and the right of contract; secondly, in the right of property, including a homestead; thirdly, in complete Equality in the courts; fourthly, in Equality in political rights; fifthly, in Equality at schools

> and in Education; and finally, all these safeguards are crowned by declaring that they cannot lose their rights or be punished except after judgment according to fixed rules; thus completely fulfilling that requirement of our fathers, that "government should be a government of laws and not of men."
>
> I trust that this example is none the less worthy of imitation because it is that of an empire, which is not supposed to sympathize with liberal ideas. Surely a republic cannot in this respect lag behind an empire. . . .

In his indictment of each rebel state, Sumner was particularly explicit concerning South Carolina where, he reported, less than two hundred former Confederate military men and public figures controlled every facet of civil life.

> Thus is the freedman, whose liberty the United States are bound to maintain, to be handed over to *compulsory service*, and under no circumstances is land to be rented to him. And yet these people announce that they accept the existing state of things and that it is their honest purpose to abide thereby! Of course they will accept a state of things which leaves them once more "masters" of their former slaves. Of course they will abide by it. Be it our duty to teach them the duty and necessity of Equal Rights.

This was the beginning of the torturous passage toward black suffrage, the long course of one of the most valiant legislative struggles in American history. Not until June 1868 was this battle won, although it did not end the war.

Delany was strangely restrained in his judgment of Andrew Johnson. That would be understandable in his public statements, for Johnson could have "busted" him overnight, and he would be of no further use to his people in South Carolina. But on February 22, 1866, he wrote to his old black abolitionist friends and enemies as a group, to men like George T. Downing of New York, William Whipper of Pennsylvania, Frederick Douglass and his son Lewis, John Jones of Chicago, and others gathered in Washington in an effort to persuade Johnson to change his policies. They had been delegated to do so by a convention of colored men from thirteen states, held in Washington.

The delegation met with President Johnson on February 7 and the only encouragement of any change of policy was on a program of black emigration, a renewal of the Lincoln colonization plan. Otherwise, Johnson was entirely antagonistic. This fact and actually the entire interview was widely reported in the press as a total failure by the blacks. Yet on February 22 Delany wrote to the delegation pledging his active agreement with their stand which "challenges the admiration of the world. At least it challenges mine, and as a brother, you have it."

> Do not misjudge the president, but believe, as I do, that he means to do right; that his intentions are good; that he is interested, among those of others of his fellow-citizens, in the welfare of the black man. . . . Do not expect too much of him—as black men, I mean. Do not forget that you are black and he is white. Make large allowances for this, and take this as the stand-point. Whatever we may think of ourselves, do not forget that we are far in advance of our white American fellow-citizens in that direction.

He even resorted to verse in his plea for temperate attitudes:

> Be patient in your misery;
> Be meek in your despair;
> Be patient, O be patient!
> Suffer on, suffer on!

This was not the fighting Delany of the past or of the immediate future either. Always when he or his fellow blacks had received such a total rejection as was given that delegation, Delany's expressions and recommendations had been extreme. Yet his letter ended in unity with them "in behalf of our common *country*." Before 1866 and after, it would have concluded "in behalf of our common *race*."

Again, in July, he took pen in hand and wrote to President Johnson himself "*simply* as a black man" and proposed enfranchisement of the blacks as a means of preserving the Union. He referred to Great Britain as the menace that held the colonies together; now the menace of rebel attitudes was a similar danger.

> What becomes necessary, then, to secure and perpetuate the integrity of the Union, is simply the *enfranchisement* and recognition of the *political equality* of the power that saved the nation from destruction in a time of imminent peril—a recognition of the *political equality* of the blacks with the whites in all of their relations as American citizens. Therefore, with the elective franchise, and the exercise of suffrage in all of the Southern States recently holding slaves, there is no earthly power able to cope with the United States as a military power; consequently, nothing to endanger the national integrity.

Perhaps that was a valid argument and the letter to Johnson had a purpose, but the latter is not discernible. Delany had never been politically naive. Had his early and consistent success in the Sea Islands led him to believe that a clash with the powers that ruled South Carolina could be avoided? Hadn't he himself in Charleston some six months before warned the blacks that they might have to resort to arms? Hadn't he too been dismayed by President Johnson's veto of the bill extending the life of the Freedmen's Bureau and granting the agency punitive powers against planters who cheated the freedmen?

Nor did Delany restrain himself in the least concerning events directly applicable to his race. Throughout his Freedmen's Bureau career he is copiously quoted in his customary fighting words. At the same time he wrote to President Johnson, in July 1866, the *Christian Recorder* printed his blistering opposition to a public recommendation made by President Warner of Liberia, that all four million former slaves be shipped to his country and financed by the United States—again Lincoln's colonization plan but to another continent.

Delany did not like the suggestion. There was hope for the black man in America. Settlement in Africa must be voluntary, planned, and for the purpose of an ideal society.

> No one who knows me, will doubt my African proclivities—indeed, I believe it will be conceded that I am the most African of all the black men now in this country; so much so,

> that I have possessions in Africa (right to land under the Treaty of Abbeokuta) which I intend and hope to enjoy, and my children to inherit and possess. . . .
>
> Henceforth, let President Warner *think* before he speaks, and look before he leaps—and a most fearful leap was this one—ere he precipitates, not only himself, but the destiny of his country into an abyss, from which there is no recovery.

He expressed sorrow for Warner and for the shades of former presidents of Liberia for

> Recommending (tacitly) the expulsion of a large part of a national population—indeed an important elementary part of the nation, as this has been since civilization began on the continent, the industrial element of the South . . . commencement of such an act of national injustice is itself a barbarity that might lead to *extermination*, a much cheaper and by far easier method of ridding the nation of this people.
>
> Heaven forbid that so monstrous an idea ever again enter the brain of any man occupying a responsible position, much less find expression from the lips of one at the head of a nation, and that nation, the kindred people of those against whom the issue is invited.

His lengthy castigation of President Warner was matched by many another speech and article quoted in the press with his characteristic vigor of expression. He was just as vehement the following year in favor of emigration *to* Africa when a large number of freedmen, completely dispirited by being kept in suspension between Black Codes and total freedom, planned an exodus to that continent. But in July 1866 Delany had the conviction that blacks could win equality. He had proved it within the limited perspective of the Sea Islands, and therefore it was possible nationally. Frequently he told the blacks of Hilton Head to put their faith in their muscles, in their God, and in the righteousness of their cause.

Today, practicing politicians would laugh at Delany's faith that justice would triumph. They know the power of lobbyists in Washington and in every state capital, without exception. The

American people are aware of the existence of lobbying and occasionally, when it is particularly blatant, a story creeps into the news media that some member of Congress or Federal official accepts "campaign contributions." But, fundamentally, few are informed about the direct influence of lobbies on legislation and taxation, either Federal or state.

The black leaders during the Johnson restoration, particularly Delany, appear to have been totally ignorant of the fact that the lobbyist for South Carolina, William Henry Trescot, would render it impossible to obtain even consideration from Johnson, let alone justice. Trescot and Johnson, with assists from Generals Grant and Sherman, made inevitable the return of the Sherman Order lands to their rebel owners within the next two years and the eviction of the freedmen from them. By the end of 1867 and the ending of the whole issue of title to those rich lands, just 1,565 out of some 5,000 Sherman warrants were recognized and even these were whittled down by court proceedings which the freedmen could not afford to contest. The total land granted to freedmen in Sherman lands was 63,000 acres, approximately forty acres per family. That was the extent of the old "forty acres and a mule" fiction that kept hope alive in the freedmen. Of the 400,000 blacks emancipated in South Carolina, less than 2,000 families owned any land at all by 1868, and most of these had such small acreages that few could subsist on them. Thus, they were retained as available labor supply.

What the blacks, including Delany, did not know was that this result had been decided by October 1865—perhaps earlier—after Trescot began his operations as lobbyist from South Carolina. He was employed under the title "State Agent" immediately after President Johnson appointed Perry as provisional Governor, and he left his plantation near Beaufort for a long stay in Washington. Trescot was a brilliant young lawyer and had been active in South Carolina politics for many years, and during the Confederacy had served in its legislature.

Events were to prove that Trescot's reports to successive governors of the state were entirely truthful and his observations penetrating. Those secret reports are in themselves a complete revelation of the methods by which Johnson connived with the former Confederate leaders to wrap up the restoration before the Congressional elections of 1866.

In his first report to Gov. Perry, dated October 24, 1865,

Trescot assured Perry that the Sherman Order No. 15 lands would be restored to their original owners.

> The further Order No. 45 was issued instructing Gen. Howard to make the arrangements and extend the orders necessary to their restoration. At present, therefore, all the lands in the State by the U.S. Government, except lands taken and sold under the Tax act, are to be restored.
>
> It is not necessary that I should report the various conversations which I had the honor to have with the President and Gen. Howard. They were confined chiefly to the discussion of the mode in which the restoration could be effected with reference to the obligations which the Government had assumed toward the Freedmen and to the rights which the Government recognized in the original owners.

Trescot also warned Gov. Perry against antagonistic legislation by the South Carolina General Assembly.

> On that I deem it necessary now to say that whatever may be our own opinions, we ought not to forget that the action of the Administration is watched with jealous hostility, especially on all these subjects, by a large and powerful party in the U.S. and that with our property restored and rights recognized, it is only just that we should afford every assistance to the Government in reconciling this discharge of its duty to us with its obligations to the rest of the country.

He also warned Perry that they had better not get rid of the Freedmen's Bureau just yet, because without some government agency "it would not at this moment be possible in many sections of the state either to re-establish the owners of lands in their rights or to make any arrangement for the renewal of laborers."

As to unfortunate delays in the presidential pardons, Trescot reported

> the action of the President is the fulfillment of his profession "that he would rather pardon twenty than refuse one" and he expressed to me his readiness to give immediate con-

> sideration to any cases which the State deemed of special importance to her industrial interests. The restoration of the lands in the lower part of the state to those who have been pardoned renders the early issue of such pardons a matter of great importance to a large class of our citizens. But with every desire on the part of the President to extend the benefits of Executive clemency . . .

there were just too many applications to speed through the White House. Trescot needed an office and an "efficient clerk" to handle all those pardons. But he had more to report. "I cannot conclude this report without expressing to your Excellency and through you to the Legislature, my profound sense of what this State owes to the wisdom and courage of the President's policy. It has saved us from destruction that would have been as rapid as it was ruthless."

Trescot ended his first of many reports on lobbying President Johnson with an expression of gratitude for "the readiness with which I was permitted to lay before him your Excellency's suggestions. . . ." For over a year, Trescot was highly successful in the restoration. He was to be particularly helpful to Gov. James L. Orr, South Carolina's first "elected" governor during Johnson's restoration of white political as well as economic domination. The likable Orr was even popular among radical Republicans because he was always ready to compromise any issue. He agreed with Trescot's warnings as to the new Black Code, and his personal relationship with the military power in his state, Gen. Sickles, aided in restraining some of the white abuses of the blacks. He and Sickles had served together in the U.S. Congress during the 1850s.

When the new Freedmen's Bureau bill, enlarging the agency's powers over labor and land, was first introduced into Congress, Orr sent north to Washington two influential South Carolinians, William Whaley of Edisto Island and former governor and congressman William Aiken, reputedly the wealthiest man in South Carolina before the war. They diligently served Trescot and South Carolina at this time of crisis and, among other things, settled the Sherman land question then and there. Trescot's February 4, 1866, report to Gov. Orr relates how it was done. After all three appeared before the House committee in opposition to the Freedmen's Bureau bill, they went to the "power-house" where Johnson was acting while Congress was debating.

> Gov. Aiken, Mr. Whaley and myself waited on the President in reference to the Bill. He heard us very attentively but said very little from which we could infer his intention. But as we had learned that Gen. Sherman had arrived in Washington and was not unwilling to say what his own interpretation was, we so informed the President. He said that he thought such an expression would have great weight and that he would advise us to procure it. We went immediately over to Gen. Grant's headquarters where we found Gens. Grant, Sherman, Meade and Thomas in consultation. Gen. Grant however immediately received us and they all participated in the discussion of the real meaning of Gen. Sherman's order. Gen. Sherman expressed himself decidedly and said he would make his statement official upon a reference either from the President, Gen. Grant or the Chairman of the Senate or House Committees. Gen. Grant said that (he) preferred the reference should come from the President. We returned to the President and I addressed him a note stating the importance of this testimony and asking that either by reference of that note to Gen. Sherman or in any other way which he deemed proper he would give us the advantage of it. The next morning he addressed a communication to Gen. Sherman and put his answer in our hands to be used as we deemed advisable. This letter of Gen. Sherman's I enclose. You will find it explicit on the point that he intended his Field Order to serve a temporary military purpose and to terminate with the war.
>
> The publication of this letter has produced considerable effect and I send with this one or two newspaper reports from which you can draw your inferences.

Sherman's letter was such an asset that Trescot was most encouraged and told Gov. Orr, "I think if I had a delay of a fortnight and a fair opportunity, I could secure the defeat of the Bill." For the first time, too, in this same report, he predicted Johnson's veto.

When the Freedmen's Bureau bill was in limbo—it was not passed over Johnson's veto until July 16—Gen. Howard dismayed Trescot with a plan to declare a plague on both houses of Congress and the White House, with an order dated March 8 to distribute the Sherman lands at once and, where they had been restored through presidential pardon, to grant the freedmen forty acres of the same plantation. Trescot wrote directly to the President, warning him that "as far as these lands are affected the action of the Bureau will be precisely that which it would have been if you had not by your veto of the Freedmen's Bureau Bill won the confidence and the gratitude of the whole nation." Trescot found a way for President Johnson to settle the crisis caused by Howard. He reported to Gov. Orr:

> On Thursday night I saw the President. He said that he was anxious to settle the question but that the pending vote on the veto of the Civil Rights Bill, and the canvass going on in Connecticut compelled him to be cautious. I told him that for those reasons I had avoided pressing the subject on his attention but that I was aware that he had decided to send Generals Fullerton and Steadman as a commission to the South, that if he would give them full authority to settle the whole matter, it would be very easy to arrange a restoration quietly and that their action need not be reported until their return from their visit in the South, at which time public opinion would probably have passed beyond that question. . . . This morning Mr. Stanton informed me that the instructions to these gentlemen would be issued on Monday. . . . I am satisfied with the arrangements. The President could doubtless have ordered the immediate restoration but the order would have been telegraphed to every village gathering in Connecticut, it would have been malignantly misrepresented in every stump speech, the radical press would have heralded it everywhere as convincing proof of the President's readiness to trample on the rights of the Freedmen for the benefit of the rebel masters.

That was how the Sherman land question was resolved. By the time Congress passed the Freedmen's Bureau bill over the President's veto, there was little of that land not restored to the "rebel masters" and the Bureau was powerless to challenge the titles.

In other reports, and they were as frequent as the crises,

Trescot commented freely on affairs. On April 15 he advised Gov. Orr not to get too agitated about the passage of the Civil Rights bill on April 9 over Johnson's veto. "It gives, as far as I can see, no further rights to the negro than his freedom gives him." He predicted that it would be found unconstitutional by the Supreme Court (and it was, but not until 1883). He was surprisingly accurate on other predictions, particularly regarding the political future.

Only in one of these reports is it evident that Trescot's composure was disturbed. He told Gov. Orr that one of the President's secretaries, a Major Long, had secretly warned him that the sale of presidential pardons was a little too brisk in South Carolina. The President even believed that Trescot was getting a pay-off on them. "As you may suppose, I lost no time in seeing the President, who told me that he was entirely misunderstood, that he had never associated my name with pardons in his own mind, that he was not aware that any pardons had ever been granted at my request." But the President did tell Trescot that a certain Col. Elford was getting too much of a pay-off for the pardons he was handling. Trescot advised Gov. Orr that a degree of discretion should be asserted. Thus, it should be noted that the famous "pardon racket," on which historians base some of the corruption charges against rebel state governments after 1868, had its inception among "whites only" two years before, and the techniques were well established by the time blacks were allowed to participate in government. The freedmen did not get a "cut" of the profits from presidential pardons when the practice was established in 1865.

Trescot was a highly skilled Washington "operator" and could be a mentor for the many lobbyists haunting the halls and hotels of Congress today. The blacks of South Carolina were completely at the mercy of such political connivance and, by the time they did have some power in the vote, their economic servitude of the future was assured. There was no principle, right, or question of justice involved. The economic aspect of the black future was decided for them by customary American political practices.

As a result, throughout his time in the Sea Islands, Delany was constantly fighting a phantom, an unseen power behind his daily problems as middleman between the freedmen and the planters. Its only evidence was in the arrogant self-assurance of the planters, but that was indigenous to South Carolina whites. Besides, Delany had yet to meet his match in arrogant self-assertion when convinced of his own judgment. It was something of a stand-off of personalities. Officially, however, the planters, who planned from crop year to crop year, feared the power of the Freedmen's Bureau and of the military. It was a temporary authority, they were informed from Columbia, to last until Johnson could restore them to their proper pre-war status. Meanwhile, they were instructed, not to "rock the boat" by defiance.

Delany was a peculiar trial to the Sea Islands planters. He was the official Freedmen's Bureau officer among them, but he was *black;* he was a high-ranking military officer among them, but he was *black;* he was at least as well educated and far better informed than most of the white planters, but he was *black.* He advanced more practical plans for optimum use of the crop year than any of them (since they approached the problem solely from profit motives), yet he was *black.* He had far more command over the freedmen by his powers of persuasion than whites had, even with the threat of the whip, and that was unprecedented in a *black.* Perhaps worst of all, from their viewpoint, was the fact that very early in his Hilton Head career Delany proved to them that he had the national ear through the so-called radical and black press. That was an important political consideration for them, at least until South Carolina was firmly back in their hands in all respects.

In most of his dealings with the whites, therefore, Delany placed himself in a position of personal equality, difficult for the proud South Carolinians to accept, and in a position of official superiority, which also stuck in the Southern craw. In view of the circumstances and personalities, which were not duplicated elsewhere in the rebel states, it is surprising that Delany won not just the forced cooperation of the planters but their admiration as well. The *New South,* written and edited for the planters, by its February 3, 1866, issue evaluated Delany's work as follows:

> Major M. R. Delany, the "black major" of the Freedmen's Bureau, is now on the right track. Comprehending the situation of affairs, he has seized at once upon its difficulties, and is doing a noble work for his race. His sympathies, of course, are with those of his own color; but, being a man of large experience, highly educated, and eminently con-

> scientious, he does not allow prejudice to sway him one way or the other, and, consequently, he has a wonderful influence for good over the freedmen. He tells them to go to work at once; that labor surely brings its own reward; and that after one more good crop is gathered, they will find their condition much better than at present. And he tells the planters they must be kind and just to their laborers, if they would quickly bring order out of chaos, and establish a prosperity far beyond what they ever dreamed of in the dark and dreadful era of slavery.
>
> Our whole community here is taking heart. One obstacle after another, to thorough regeneration, is being removed. As the planters succeed in procuring laborers, their credit is improved, and the merchants of this place come forward to assist the onward movement. Agricultural implements, seed, subsistence, and the various wants of a plantation, are being much more liberally supplied than they were a month ago. We all look forward to a large measure of success the present season.

Actually, in comparison with the other Freedmen's Bureau districts, Delany's—despite the Sherman land issue—was the most advanced, economically, educationally, and in black-white relationships. In the school activities, while Delany won the public gratitude of many of the volunteer teachers sent to the Sea Islands early in the war by the missionary and Freedmen's societies, he merely assisted, not initiated. However, in his many activities in promotion of land-use, of social behavior among the blacks, and of restraint of the whites in their exploitation of the freedmen, Delany was an innovator.

He managed to sell both the freedmen and the planters on his "triple alliance" slogan, in reality a share-cropping formula that in later years degenerated into peonage when the "third party" authority, such as the Freedmen's Bureau, was eliminated. In that time of transition, however, it did succeed in its purpose—getting a crop into the ground. By the end of the planting season in early 1866, on Hilton Head Island alone there was an estimated two fifths more land under cultivation than ever in the island's history, under slavery or the Union military.

Delany, of course, was not responsible for all of this increase but he was credited with most of it. Aside from counseling and granting seed to the thousands of Sherman land freedmen still on their plots, he both supervised and approved 58 labor contracts involving nearly 4,000 freedmen on Hilton Head alone. There were others on other islands, some on Parish, St. Helena, and Port Royal, as well as other areas outside his own jurisdiction on Dawfuskie, Bull, and Pinckney islands. His special mission for Gen. Sickles had involved him in many contract disputes.

In addition, Delany managed to convince most of the freedmen that the one acre per family he insisted on in each contract —for the family's private use, not the plantation's—should be utilized for their own subsistence crops. This was one way of preventing the customary cheating on food rations advanced by the planters. Article VII of Delany's typical contract forbade any sutler stores on the contracted plantation, and that annoyed the planters and merchants of Hilton Head, since the ignorant blacks could keep neither accounts of their own nor verify the bills rendered them. Only necessities "such as good, substantial food, and working clothes, conducive to health and comfort" could be sold on contracted plantations, and that "at cost." Nor could liquor be sold. Finally, the standard contract granted the Bureau officer the authority to see to its enforcement and to act as judge in any dispute arising within its lifetime.

How did Delany manage to get so many planters—"old masters" and "Yankee speculators" among them—to sign up? Solely by his influence over the freedmen, a form of blackmail. If the prospective planter wanted a crop, he signed up or else had no prospect of obtaining labor. The strategic use of Delany's limited supply of rations kept the freedmen from starvation while the planter was forced to make up his mind that an equitable contract was his only choice.

Also on the economic front of his war with the white planters, Delany insisted on supervising freedmen's cotton from the seed to its sale on the open market on the "Row" in Hilton Head where the cotton brokers maintained their quarters, or in Beaufort or Charleston. Every step in the transaction was dominated by him. He had his own weighmaster, baler, ginning facilities, and open bidding for the cotton, thus forcing the highest prices and fullest profits to the freedmen. Instead of owing for rations advanced, by 1866 most of the independent freedmen had cash money with which to buy land, or even shoes.

In other words, Delany closed all the customary avenues of

victimization of the blacks which had made the Sea Islands such a gold mine for Yankee "ingenuity." In doing so, he often was downright dictatorial and interpreted his authority most generously to himself.

Delany offended the whites in still another way. He took from them their old powers as slaveholders over the black communities on their own plantations. It was an extremely interesting and effective social measure best described in his own report of August 1, 1866, to the assistant commissioner.

> On the Plantations throughout my Bureau District, I have adopted Police Regulations. On each place the best man selected by the people, is appointed by me as Head man or Chief of Police, with authority to choose four assistants, each to report their cases to him. His duties are simple and comprehensive, similar to those of "Captain of Civil Police" or Watchman, in a ward or precinct of a City, only reporting such cases to Hd. Quarters of the District, as cannot or may not be settled by themselves, before the Head man. He is to report all his doings once a month to Head Quarters.

This was the freedmen's first venture into self-government on all of Hilton Head except the military village of Mitchelville. And once the planters had become accustomed to the ignominy of placing their complaints before a black "Head man" they found it a distinct asset in the administration of the plantations. As for its effect on the freedmen, Delany had the following observations:

> This simple course has an excellent effect, engenders self-respect, by showing them that the new life which they have entered as freemen requires more of them than simply obedience to the white man, on whose place they may be, or with whose authority they may be threatened. It engenders self-confidence and self-reliance, and induces them each to seek and respect the counsel of the other. It aids in establishing the desires and orders of the Major Gen'l, that all trivial affairs be settled on the places where working, among the people themselves. I have never as yet had occasion to refer to Head Quarters for adjustment, a single case originat-

ing within the limits of my own Bureau District, in which I have jurisdiction.

Generals Saxton and Sickles backed Delany all the way in this measure of self-policing, and soon the complaints by the planters turned to praise of Delany for establishing "law and order" on their plantations, thereby resulting in greater volume of work production.

But Delany was unable to do anything with the largest community of blacks on Hilton Head Island, the village of Mitchelville, which at the end of 1864 had a black population of about 3,000. It had grown around the military headquarters established at Hilton Head when the Sea Islands were captured by Union forces in 1861. But when the military post was shifted to Charleston in 1865 most of the blacks lost their jobs and were destitute. Delany's first efforts to relieve their distress was also his first clash with superior authority in the military. As early as August 21 there was a complaint lodged with the Provost Marshal against Delany's "interference" with the municipal government of Mitchelville by a Rev. A. Murchison, a black preacher who had been the mayor of the village since military days. The complaint reached Gen. Gillmore, the Black Major's commander in the military hegemony, although he was under Gen. Saxton's direct orders in the Bureau. In his reply to Gillmore's assistant adjutant general, Delany disputed Murchison's authority to interfere with *his* work.

> On last Wednesday two weeks after arriving here, I called upon Rev. A. Murchison, advisedly informing him in a friendly manner of his relation to the Bureau for Refugees, Freedmen and Abandoned Lands, and requesting among other things, that the proceedings in regard to turning people out of the houses, be stayed, as the Bureau took these things under its jurisdiction.
>
> I have never talked to the people of Mitchelville as such, and in the several instances in which I have been called upon to inform them about their houses, I have told them that I had consulted with "Squire" Murchison—as I always expressed it to them, simply to engender respect toward him—about staying proceedings till the Office of the Bureau was fully established here.

> I do not think, that any such remarks toward the Provost Marshall was ever made to Mr. Murchison coupled with my name, because there never was an occasion given by me for any such remarks; no person ever having mentioned to me anything about the order, save Murchison himself, when my reply was, that the same order had obtained many other places, and applied to all civilians black and white.
>
> Mr. Murchison is an illiterate man of childish simplicity imagining himself to hold rank, place and power—military and civil—that has no existence in fact with him. Anything in his imagination interfering with his authority, would render him dissatisfied.

Apparently this amounted to disobedience, as far as Gen. Gillmore was concerned. He sent orders that Delany was to stay out of Mitchelville, which drew an immediate reply from the Black Major, placing the dispute nicely within the military hierarchy.

> I have the honor to state that in obedience to the command of Major Genl. Gillmore given me by Lieut. Col. Clitz, Post Commandant, yesterday morning, I have necessarily to disobey the orders of Major General Saxton, to whom I must report. I therefore most respectfully request, that to prevent mistakes and in justice to myself, you will favor me with the order in writing.
>
> I understand the order to be
>
> 1st: That I am not allowed to hold the election for the Village Councilmen in the Methodist Church on Friday next the 2nd proximo, nor have anything to do with the people there whatever, and that no change will be allowed in the affairs of the people of Mitchelville, Mr. Murchison being permitted to go on and do things in his own way.
>
> 2nd: That I am not permitted to hold any public meetings among, make any speech to, lecture, address, or advise the colored people, without orders from Major General Gillmore, through Colonel Clitz.

Gen. Gillmore won the fight with Gen. Saxton, Delany reported later.

> To this order Major Gen. Saxton objected, but the Major Gen. Commanding Dept., discarded his displeasure, and held me in obedience to his command in the matter, until relieved in December (1865) by Major General Sickles. It was not until then, that I had an opportunity of advising the people of Mitchelville.

Advise them he did, and in the spring of 1866 the population of the village was reduced by half. The blacks went "to the fields," and "every one seems now to pride in their knowledge of cultivation; and those who before obtained aid in rations and other favors of government, now bid fair and promise this year to be self-sustaining."

This was only one clash with superior authority. Delany had many, except with Gen. Sickles, who had a high regard for the Black Major's intelligence and integrity. Delany was to dispute with Gen. Saxton's successor, Gen. Robert K. Scott, who became assistant commissioner of the Freedmen's Bureau in mid-January 1866. But Delany soon won his admiration, too, even though Scott was to order a full investigation of Delany's activities quite soon. It was Gen. Sickles, however, who rendered it practically impossible for any of the "brass" to plague Delany too much.

In January 1866, when the War Department ordered another muster-out of troops, particularly colored troops, Gen. Sickles wrote the following to Gen. E. D. Townsend at the War Department:

> General,
>
> I have the honor to invite your attention to the following extract from a recent report of Maj. J. P. Roy, 6th U.S. Infty. and Actg. Insp. Genl. of this Dept. regarding the services of Maj. M. R. Delany, 104th U.S. U.S.C.T.—
>
> "Before closing this report I desire to bear testimony to the efficient and able manner in which Maj. Delany, 104th U.S.C.T., and agent of the Freedmens Bureau is performing his duties. I took occasion several times during my stay to go to his Office and hear him talk & explain matters to the Freedmen. Being of their own color they naturally reposed confidence in him. Upon the labor question he entirely reflected the views of the Maj. Genl. Comdg. and seemed in

all things to give them good and sensible advice. He is doing much good & in the event of his regiment being mustered out I hope he may be retained as an agent of the Freedmens Bureau."

I have also received the same satisfactory reports from other sources and concurring in the foregoing suggestion of Maj. J. P. Roy, I most respectfully recommend that Maj. M. R. Delany be for the present retained in the military service of the United States. I have advised his muster-out to be postponed until a reply is received to this communication.

On February 8 Gen. Sickles received a communication from Delany's old War Department friend, Col. Foster, declaring that the Secretary of War ordered "retention of that officer in the service until further orders from the War Department." This placed Delany in an almost impregnable position among his military enemies. It would require a lot of dirty linen to oust the Black Major since that could now only be done by order of the Secretary of War. That may be why Delany launched his energetic campaign against the cotton cheaters of the "Row" and elsewhere, thereby organizing most of the cotton brokers against him. They directed their campaign through Gen. Scott.

The appointment of Gen. Scott to Saxton's position in the Freedmen's Bureau was made by Gen. Howard. Actually, Scott was recalled to active duty to assume the post, for he had returned to Ohio after three years of active military command. He had led a brigade throughout Sherman's march to the sea and won his rank as a result. He and Delany had a good deal in common, for Scott too had practiced medicine in Henry County, Ohio, and won popular acclaim for his services in the same cholera epidemic of 1854 during which Delany served in Pittsburgh. Scott too found other interests than medicine—money—and was highly successful in both real estate and merchandising.

There is no question that he was a capable administrator and a stickler for detail. He made three inspections of Delany's district during the year and found a high degree of organization each time. But Scott acquired political ambitions as the year advanced, and Congress pledged new constitutions and popular elections for the rebel states before they would be readmitted to the Union. He began to listen to the planters and discover some inefficiency and dishonesty among his agents in the Bureau. As a result of frequent absences, too, for both Bureau and political reasons, he left a good deal to his assistant adjutant general, Bvt. Lt. Col. H. W. Smith.

It is obvious from their correspondence that there was mutual dislike between Delany and Smith. The latter appears to have lost no opportunity to criticize Delany for late and incomplete reports, although the volume of paper work seems to have been enormous. Their feud began almost immediately, and no doubt Delany provoked it.

While consulting with Gen. Scott in Port Royal on February 12, the assistant commissioner ordered some changes in Delany's standard contract between the freedmen and the planters. Delany complied with the orders in the very next contract he negotiated between a Justice Goodman and the freedmen, and he sent a copy to Col. Smith. But before that he had presented it to the public for judgment and his covering letter to Smith concludes, "I also send a copy of the *New South* in which it is published, and simply add, that it is very acceptable so far to the Planters and Freedmen who have seen it or heard it read."

This procedure irked both Col. Smith and Gen. Scott. Two weeks later, Delany received new orders from Col. Smith.

> Major:
>
> Brig. Genl. R. K. Scott, Asst. Comm'r directs me to instruct you that when fair and equitable contracts are entered into between the planters and Freedmen, there will be no interference on the part of the agents of this Bureau. It is entirely impractical to attempt to establish a uniform form of contract, therefore all equitable forms of contracts will be approved, when the freed people enter into them willingly.

Delany appears to have ignored this order for he kept just as tight a control over the 1867 work and land contracts as he did those of 1866. But on that occasion, in March 1866, he told Col. Smith off. He knew the source of the complaint, a planter named James Kuh who leased several plantations and did not care for Delany's contracts. As a partner in the cotton brokerage firm of Kuh and Park, he liked even less Delany's insistence that the freedmen market their crops through their own non-profit organization. And so he had gone to Bureau headquarters in Charleston to see what he could do.

On March 22 Delany received a letter from Smith "severely censuring me and bidding me as '*Agent of this Bureau*' not to 'interfere with them.'" His reply politely blistered Smith. After explaining that his differences with Kuh had taken place after Gen. Saxton had been relieved and Gen. Scott was not yet on hand,

> I advised Mr. Kuh to go to see Major General Sickles, and also advised him to go and see General Scott at the time that he went. . . .
>
> I have the honor to state, Sir, that I have never arrogated nor assumed anything, but all that I have done—though frequently under many disadvantages—I have endeavored in my humble way to do for the best to promote the interests of the Bureau, without complaint or reflection.
>
> I hope it may be well understood, that I have neither the desire nor the disposition, to remain where I am censured for doing the best that I can under the circumstances, denied the right of judgment or discretion when required, or disregarded in my official capacity.

The response to this declaration of independence was a complaint from Smith on April 19 that his March report was late. For a time, Delany had Smith licked. But by early fall the planters and cotton brokers were organized against Delany on two counts. He was hounding them for cheating the freedmen in prices for supplies, and planned once more to have a non-profit cotton ginning, baling, and selling organization that crop year. Delany had reported fully to Scott on both problems.

On August 1 he wrote that the planters and merchants were forcing the freedmen to "pay double and treble what an article is worth, simply because he must have it and cannot get it elsewhere." As examples he cited prices of $10 and $11 per barrel of grits if paid in cash or $14 or $15 if on credit. The cost to the planter, Delany stated, was $5 and $6 per barrel in Savannah. The freedmen were paying up to eight cents a pound for corn meal costing the planter two cents a pound.

"Of course among the traders there are a few honorable

exceptions but very few." The situation would not be corrected, he said, until competition in suppliers is allowed by the planters.

Even more evil, Delany reported, was the sale of their cotton by the freedmen, who were "totally ignorant of trade regulations, or prices current and rates of exchange." They require the "protection of the authorities" before placing their crops on the market, he maintained. "A deep laid scheme and system are at work under the name of legitimate trade, to obtain the produce of these simple minded, uneducated people, for little or nothing." In combating this, he cited the success of the Lands End depot with the 1865 crop and recommended an expansion of it.

> Last year by an arrangement of this kind granted at my request by Major Gen. Saxton, an Agency at Lands End, St. Helena, sold for the Freedmen, one hundred and forty thousand Dollars worth of cotton in cash, the minimum price being, one Dollar a pound, and doubtless the highest price which they could have obtained on an average for the same cotton ginned, and in the seed, would have been forty cents, or a saving to these poor people of Eighty-Four Thousand ($84,000.) Dollars. This year the Planting interest of the Freedmen on Hilton Head Island and Dependencies, call for the same kind of protection under the auspices of the Major General.

Without further discussion or question, Delany went right ahead with his plans for a cotton agency and even planned a larger operation than the prior year since direct purchasers from both New York and Liverpool markets had signified their intention of buying.

The opposition came unexpectedly and directly from Scott on October 16 when the valuable, long-staple Sea Island cotton was in the process of ginning and baling. It was a letter to Delany from the assistant commissioner.

> It is currently reported in this city and has been represented to these Headquarters, that you have established a Depot at Hilton Head where you compel all the Freedmen to store their Cotton and orders are given on a certain Store in payment. I cannot believe this Report to be true, and that the public may be corrected on this subject, I wish a full and

> clear report of the manner and extent to which you exercise control over the cotton of Freedmen. I thought I had been sufficiently explicit in stating that the only object in having a Weigh Master, was to see justice done, and not to act as a factor, or take charge of the Cotton. The people must be left free to sell when they think proper.

It is obvious, again from the correspondence, that Scott and Smith were again listening to Kuh and the other cotton factors. They knew in August that Delany planned to protect the freedmen's cotton for them. As early as August 22 Delany had written Scott for permission to utilize one of the many empty military storehouses being sold off by the Quartermaster at Hilton Head for the purpose of "selling the cotton of the freedmen in this Bu. Dist. at highest market price." Both Scott and Smith would have remembered this request because once again the head of the Freedmen's Bureau of South Carolina tangled with the head of the military forces of South Carolina as a result.

On August 29, Scott had approved the request and Delany was "authorized to take any unoccupied Govt. building to use as specified within"—and this was over Col. Smith's signature "By command of Bvt. Maj. Genl. R. K. Scott."

On September 4, the Chief, Quartermaster Corps, Gen. R. O. Tyler, requested permission by the Headquarters, Department of the South. "I wish to call your attention to the endorsement of Bvt. Lt. Col. Smith. . . ." On September 12, Gen. Sickles himself disapproved the request, to Gen. Scott.

> There is no authority for officers in the public service, acting as Agents or factors for freedmen, in the sale of their cotton. The action of Bvt. Major General R. K. Scott, Asst. Comr. of the Bureau of R.F. & A.L. in authorizing Major M. R. Delaney (*sic*) Act. Sub. Asst. Commissioner to take any unoccupied Government building to use for the purpose is irregular and void.

The next day, September 13, Scott replied to Sickles that there had been an error in the request, that it should have been requisitioning "any building belonging to the Bureau," and that on the approval of Maj. Genl. O. O. Howard "I have issued an order making Depots where cotton can be sold, and an agent appointed to weigh it."

Scott was well aware of Delany's plans a month before his accusations of October 16. He had heard from Delany himself and read in his reports that all his efforts were directed at protection of the freedmen from the cotton parasites in human form. But he did yield to the pressure of the merchants and planters. Even before Delany had replied to his charges, as requested, Scott had an investigation under way. He sent Bvt. Brig. Gen. B. F. Foust to Hilton Head on October 25 and his orders were to conduct "an investigation of the alleged concern of Major M. R. Delany, S.A.C. in buying and shipping cotton and forcing the freedpeople to dispose of their crop to, or through his agent."

Foust talked to six white merchants on the "Row," including James Kuh; to three freedmen, three of the colored police force, J. H. Tonking, black, who was Delany's claims agent for colored troops; Robert S. Houston, black, who was weigh master and issued credits on the freedmen's cotton while it was being processed and sold; and Calvert & McIntyre, white, owners of the store honoring Houston's credits. Foust reported on October 29:

> I visited the warehouse wherein is stored the cotton which Houston proposed to gin, bag and sell for the people at a price of 6 percent upon the sale. I found the lots separate, the books apparently well and fairly kept, and no appearance of anything improper or disadvantageous to the people or the Bureau, so long as Houston acts only for the former, and not as the Agent of the latter. I have to recommend no interference with him in the former capacity.

Kuh and the other merchants told Gen. Foust that Delany positively forbade them from buying cotton from any freedmen until it first had been weighed in at the "Agency." The colored policemen informed him that they had received no orders to arrest anybody in relation to the sale of cotton. The three freedmen said that Delany "*advised*" them to take their cotton to Houston "where they would be more likely to obtain its value, than they would upon the Row."

Foust's conclusions were that Delany was not at all implicated in any "fraudulent transaction" and had received no financial consideration of any kind from anyone connected with the freedmen's cotton.

> I do not think that Major Delany is engaged directly or indirectly in trading or shipping cotton, nor do I think he interfered in the sales of cotton by freed people for his own benefit, or for any ones' but that of the people themselves. . . . I think that Major Delany has been over-zealous, but that his intention has been to benefit the freedmen and not himself, and that while he has sometimes prevented the sale of cotton to the "Row" merchants, that in more cases he has been misunderstood, and his verbose, impulsive conversation been construed as an imperative where he intended only an admonitory style.

However, on the following day he transmitted orders to Delany to fire Houston and hire a white man as weigh master. The orders came from Scott. Also Delany was ordered to "refrain, even by implication, from so directing, as to convey the idea, in your orders or communication, that the freedmen are not allowed to dispose of their cotton to whom they please."

While Delany's integrity was cleared for and by his superiors, his policy was not. The white planters and merchants of Hilton Head and the neighboring islands believed that they had pushed Delany aside and could feast on the freedmen's cotton. Delany obeyed his restrictive orders, but his friends among the plantation police, the teachers, and his black admirers spread the good word and the new Weigh Master was as busy as Houston had been. The freedmen had learned the perils of the "Row" for the cotton factors there handled as little freedmen's cotton as the prior crop year.

The obvious opposition from his superiors did not stop Delany. In 1867 he was back again with his cotton agency plan, except that he began earlier, on March 1, to establish this protection for the freedmen during the crop year. The 1867 work contracts were just as closely scrutinized and commanded by him. He talked, publicly as well as privately, wherever and whenever he had the opportunity, and he did not change what Gen. Foust so charitably described as his "admonitory style." He was downright dictatorial, and the white planters and merchants "took it," for they had no choice.

The political picture was coming into focus during 1867 as a result of the 1866 elections which won two thirds of each branch of Congress for the radical Republicans. Johnson's defeat in the political arena did not correct the damage he had done to the freedmen's hopes for land and equality, but it did warn the white planters that his restoration could be undone. And so they co-operated with Delany, a few willingly but most because they saw no choice.

Because of his peculiarly independent position in South Carolina affairs, Delany outlasted every Freedmen's Bureau field officer and even Scott himself. When the Bureau was allowed to dissolve into the military government established by Congress at the end of 1867, the War Department itself excepted the Black Major from the muster-out. He was asked to remain on duty as disbursing officer for as long as the function was necessary. He was to report to the military, not to the Freedmen's Bureau, for by then even Gen. Howard was out of authority and facing the courts-martial instigated by the search for a political scapegoat.

All of his experiences in the Sea Islands and in the military directed Delany to one inevitable conclusion. If his people were to retain their slight gains as freedmen, the fight was in the political arena—and to that he journeyed for further adventures.

CHAPTER NINETEEN

The Political War

While Delany managed to evade Col. Foust's orders against political activity, such as in the village council election at Mitchelville, for a time he was frustrated. He believed that self-government, wherever it was possible, was second in importance only to food and shelter for his people. The very act of voting—for or against anything or anybody—was to him an essential part of their education, fully as necessary as the reading and writing taught in the adult schools he helped to found.

In short, to Delany black suffrage and black participation in government was the only guarantee of any form of freedom, even the limited emancipation of South Carolina under the Black Code. The 13th Amendment had eliminated slavery in name only. Change was possible only through suffrage. He seized on every opportunity to talk and write black suffrage throughout the three years it hung in the balance. They were tortured years for one who knew the inevitability of black suffrage and expected its inception at any day. He had rejected Chief Justice Salmon P. Chase's warning at the Gen. Saxton meeting in the Zion Church in April 1865 that the blacks might not get the vote for "perhaps a good while hence."

It was a good while, three years for most of the rebel states. Even then suffrage was not a permanent right of the blacks but rather was dependent on the political fortunes and misfortunes of the Republican party. While the 14th Amendment to the U.S. Constitution, ratified on July 28, 1868, had finally recognized blacks as citizens by right of birth and had declared that "No State shall make or enforce any law which shall abridge the privileges or immunities of the citizens of the United States . . ." the northern states continued their hypocrisy by barring the black vote until the 15th Amendment spelled out the right. But this was not until March 30, 1870, and was dependent, as in school desegregation, on the political strategies of the day for enforcement.

As the record shows, nothing relating to the blacks was permanent, and that was particularly true of South Carolina. Johnson had set the precedent when he named Perry provisional governor in his Proclamation of June 30, 1865, and ordered a convention to write a constitution. He defined as qualified electors anyone who had taken his amnesty oath of allegiance "and is a voter qualified and prescribed by the constitution and laws of the State of South Carolina in force immediately before the 17th of November, A.D. 1860, the date of the so-called ordinance of secession. . . ." It was up to the convention of former secessionists to establish qualifications for voters thereafter, and as we have seen that convention substituted the Black Code for suffrage.

The first Civil Rights Act, passed over Johnson's veto on April 9 also conferred citizenship on blacks but held no guarantees against its withdrawal by any state, nor did it specifically grant suffrage to the blacks. The first Reconstruction Act, also passed over Johnson's veto on March 2, 1867, did specify that the military guarantee to the blacks that their new constitutional convention delegates were to be elected by all male citizens over 21 "of whatever race, color or previous condition," but that is as far as the legislation went. Once readmitted to the Union on the basis of the new constitution and withdrawal of military rule the state could take away the right to vote.

Having experienced the loss of the vote in Pennsylvania, Delany's fears were justified. Events since have proved that restoration of the principle of States Rights in the South inevitably resulted in state constitutions, restrictive legislation, and intimidation which destroyed most black suffrage from 1877 until the Voting Rights Act of 1965—at this writing still to be conscientiously enforced. For all those years successive Congresses avoided observance of the last portion of the 14th Amendment, Section 5, "The Congress shall have power to enforce, by appropriate legislation, the provisions of this article."

The history texts fed to schoolchildren picture Johnson as the villain against the massed demand of the American people that black suffrage be granted. There was no such demand, just as there had never been a popular demand for emancipation of the slaves. In the North there were small groups of former abolitionists who talked militantly to each other in favor of black suffrage and formed their inevitable organizations. Frederick Douglass and William Lloyd Garrison wrote. Rev. Henry Ward Beecher and Wendell Phillips did both.

In Boston, a distinguished group including such veterans of abolitionism as Dr. Samuel Gridley Howe, George Luther Stearns, Edward S. Philbrick, and the "token" Negro Lewis Hayden, formed the "Impartial Suffrage League." Its formation, it was announced, was "for the purpose of securing for all men, throughout our entire country, the full enjoyment of EQUAL CIVIL AND POLITICAL RIGHTS without regard to color or race." It was in September 1866 that the organization's program was announced and it beat the New York National Reconstruction Club by just a month. This group had a sixteen-point program, chiefly economic, but including "Representation of all persons residing in the United States, irrespective of race, nationality or condition."

Nothing was heard from or accomplished by either organization thereafter and the interim years certainly refuted the claim of the Impartial Suffrage League that "public opinion at the North" was turning to black suffrage.

> The people are ready for it, but the politicians are timid. The latter need the stimulus of an aroused public opinion which shall force them to accept the issue, tendered even by the Loyal White Men of the South, that IMPARTIAL SUFFRAGE IS THE ONLY SAFE METHOD OF RECONSTRUCTION.

The record indicates that public opinion was aroused, but in *opposition* to black voting. Between 1865 and 1868 the following states voted on and denied suffrage to blacks: Wisconsin, Minnesota, Connecticut, New Jersey, Ohio, Michigan, and Pennsylvania. In only five states, with a handful of blacks in each, could they vote.

That the politicians were "timid" in granting such suffrage was correct. Even Charles Sumner in the Senate and Thaddeus Stevens in the House declared their hesitation about immediate suffrage for the freedmen, Stevens suggesting it "four or five years hence, when the freedmen shall have been made free indeed, when they shall have become intelligent enough, and there are sufficient loyal men there (in the South) to control the representation from those States." But after the radical Republicans won such an impressive Congressional victory in the fall of 1866, even Stevens speeded up his time schedule.

Curiously, the leaders of the South were far ahead of the people of the North and their spokesmen in accepting the strategy of black suffrage. Of them all, Wade Hampton, Confederate general, who was to eliminate the Negro as a political factor in South Carolina, led in the move for black suffrage. He was quite as practical, politically, as Sumner and Stevens, and he was well informed as to conditions in the South, owning plantations in South and North Carolina and in Mississippi. As early as 1865 he had been planning a restoration of the white South, *with the aid of the Negro vote*, and was successful. One of his aides in the famous "Red Shirt" campaign of 1876, the former Confederate general who was in command of the white "rifle clubs" of South Carolina, was James Conner of Charleston. Hampton wrote to Conner from Columbia on March 24, 1867, three weeks after Congress adopted the first Reconstruction Act dividing the rebel states into five military districts with registration and voting for constitutional conventions open to blacks. Hampton said:

> We can control and direct the negroes if we act discreetly, and in my judgment the highest duty of every Southern man is to secure the good will and confidence of the negro. . . . Say to the negroes, we are your friends, and even if the Supreme Court pronounces this Military Bill unconstitutional, we are willing to let the educated and tax paying among them vote. . . . Like you, I am only solicitous about our State government, and if we can protect that from destruction, I am willing to send negroes to Congress. They will be better than anyone who can take the oath and I should rather trust them than renegades or Yankees.

Again in a letter to Gen. Conner, Hampton wrote on April 9 another comment on their common interest with the blacks and against the Yankees.

> My experience has been that when a Yankee can do a bit of rascality the temptation to do it is almost irresistible, but

> when at the same time he can tell a lie, it is not in his nature to resist. . . . We can control the black vote, I believe, but I do not think that any Southern State that does so, will be allowed to send members to Congress. We had better endeavor to compromise with the negroes, allowing them to go to Congress if they will let us have the State.

All of the rebel provisional legislatures received gratuitous advice too as to a new method of countering the inevitable black vote. Henry B. Blackwell, the advocate of woman suffrage, who married one of the most militant suffragettes, Lucy Stone, memorialized the South. He proposed that each state give the women the vote and that would cancel out the black vote.

> Your Southern Legislatures can extend suffrage on equal terms to "all inhabitants" as the New Jersey State Convention did in 1776. Then let the Republicans in Congress refuse to admit your Senators and Representatives, if they dare. If so, they will go under. Upon that issue fairly made up, the men of positive convictions would rally round the new and consistent Democratic party. The very element which has destroyed slavery would side with the victorious South, and "out of the nettle danger you would pick the flower safety."

There were to be other schemes advanced by which the black vote could become an asset to the white South against the white North, and after formation of military governments in the rebel states, none challenged the fact of black suffrage. But it did *not* come about by the democratic will of the American people. Like the emancipation of the blacks, it was a national necessity, a political necessity in this case, for there was no other course for the radical Republicans to take.

If Johnson were to be deposed by the radical Republicans from his absolute authority over military reconstruction it could only be done by taking the Army away from him. This was done at the same time as the First Reconstruction Act, on March 2, 1867, when a rider was attached to the Army appropriation bill. The "Command of the Army" Act demoted the President from commander in chief of the armed forces in fact, if not in name.

Johnson could only issue orders through the commanding general, in this case Ulysses S. Grant (who had his eye and heart on the presidency for himself). Only the Senate could remove the General of the Army, and any who by-passed Grant in obedience to any order by President Johnson was "liable to imprisonment for not less than two nor more than twenty years, upon conviction thereof in any court of competent jurisdiction."

It was only because there was no popular support in the North that black suffrage was easily negated in the South after 1877. Its existence in South Carolina or the other rebel states was in no way caused by any belief in black equality. That did not and does not exist, either North or South, in the minds or hearts of the American people, in their churches, schools, or legislatures. In 1867 blacks of the South voted solely because it was the strategy of the dominant political party for them to do so. Passage of the Voting Rights Act of 1965 had exactly the same political motivation. It is purely fiction that these approaches to black equality had the virtues of democratic conviction, for the American brand of *apartheid* does not initiate black equality, it concedes compromises with it solely as political expediency.

Fortunately for Delany the President named Gen. Sickles commandant of the Second Military District created by the First Reconstruction Act. The area included North as well as South Carolina but headquarters were kept in Charleston. Sickles did not last long. In the very beginning of his new command he issued his famous "Order No. 10" which was his guarantee to the blacks that they were to share equal civil rights in all respects, in the courts, property, police, taxes—in all civil administration. He established a provost court in Aiken to hear capital crimes involving blacks, knowing they could not expect justice in civil courts. He tried and fined a steamboat captain for not allowing a Negro woman to ride first class with the white women. He insisted on the right of blacks to sit as jurors.

Naturally, all this irked the South Carolina whites, and the President intervened in one case, early in August 1867. Sickles appealed to Gen. Grant, as provided by the First Reconstruction Act, was upheld by Grant, and so Johnson fired Sickles.

Gen. Edward R. S. Canby was assigned to command the Second Military District and he proceeded to enforce Order No. 10 quite as meticulously as Sickles had. More important, as far as Delany was concerned, Gen. Canby carried on the work of registration of voters, including blacks, who would decide whether or not to call a new constitutional convention.

In reality, Delany could not have been happier than if he had plotted the whole thing himself, instead of it being a proper creation of the Congress. It was not merely his pleasure to see that his people registered to vote—*it was his duty as an Army officer.* In other words, when he busied himself on his Freedmen's Bureau routine of seeing the freedmen and helping them with their problems, registration to vote definitely was within his realm. He delighted in taking the fullest possible advantage of his position as a catalyst in his people's very first political action. He worked hard all summer and perhaps may have contributed to the imbalance of the registration in his Beaufort election district. By September 30, when registration was completed, his district had 6,278 blacks eligible to vote and 927 whites. The disproportion is not a true one, however, since so many unreconstructed whites refused to consider registering. The importance of the accomplishment is in the total of blacks registered, second highest of all districts in the state.

The year 1866 had been extremely bad economically, for the planters as well as the freedmen. Too much rain and too many insects ruined cotton, which already had taken a painful drop in prices as a result of renewed supplies from the South and the absence of capital with which to hold for a better market. All the hard cash was in the North. Planters had neither seed nor credit for the crop year. Freedmen who had not raised any corn or subsistence crops for themselves either starved or half-starved with the aid of the Freedmen's Bureau. In fact, the monthly reports made by Gen. Scott to Gen. Howard reflect the spread of destitution, growth of crime (theft of livestock and grain), and the organization of white violence into the Ku Klux Klan, the latter due to bad times as well as political purpose.

It was during this period of economic chaos that Delany's early "interference" with both planters and freedmen in their contracts, his disregard of higher authority in renting tax lands to freedmen at $1 an acre provided they grow food as well as cotton, and his annual battle for a cotton agency and annual curbing of cheating planters—it was now that Delany's cavalier approach to his duties "paid off."

An example is Gen. Scott's report for May 1868 on all of

his Bureau districts. All through the state each Bureau officer was deluged with applications for subsistence rations, even though the crops in the ground were coming along well. There just was not enough food left in the planters' storehouses to advance to the freedmen until the crops came in. There was restlessness, uncertainty, and violence against the blacks. The first Negro church in the state (in Graniteville) was burned by the whites because meetings were held there. Tempers were growing short.

In sharp contrast to this is Scott's lengthy excerpt from Delany's report. Without question Hilton Head was suffering from the economic depression of the times—but not as much as the other districts. His freedmen were not totally dependent on the planters for daily rations of corn. Only the aged, the infirm, and the improvident freedmen needed Bureau rations. There was petty crime but no organized violence. Scott reported Delany's comments to Gen. Howard mainly on the problems of schools and teachers on Hilton Head, apparently a repeated complaint by the Black Major. Otherwise:

> There is evidently an advancing improvement in the general social relation of the people in this District, a higher sense of their social status, a better conception of their moral obligations, with a higher sense of their religious claims, consequently a more general knowledge of their duties as members of the body social and politic.

While the other Bureau districts reported a marked increase in disease, Delany reported the reverse:

> The health of the District was very good, there being little sickness, which may be attributed mainly to the ability, professional skill and commendable attention of that excellent young gentleman and Medical Officer, Stephen Van Dyne, M.D., Surgeon Department of the Bureau. I cannot but attribute the absence of much of the disease and mortality common to these localities, to his professional skill and attention because in many other neighboring parts disease and mortality prevails.

The greater part of Delany's comments sent to Gen. Howard were a reminder that he had complained about lack of support for the schools before. He himself had done his utmost to satisfy the freedmen's eagerness for education, but as the land was being restored to the "old masters," so were their houses. In his land-use reports of the year before, Delany commented that with one exception "all the Mansions are either occupied by Teachers or reserved for school purposes." But now the need for schoolhouses was critical. There was not a single schoolhouse in his entire District designed for that purpose, he reported, "the Teachers being obliged to make use of temporary, ill-constructed 'shanties,' or such churches as they may be permitted to occupy for a time." But all this had been "stated in a former report" and there was no action from Washington although "there is not apparent any good reason why there have not been school appropriations made in the District. . . ." Again Delany complained:

> The attention of the Maj. Gen. Asst. Comr. is respectfully invited to the neglect of the schools in the sub-district of Hilton Head; the American Missionary Association, New York, alone having kept up and sustained the schools here, no appropriation of the School Fund of the Bureau ever as yet having been obtained, though requisitions have been several times made from this office.

The only reaction he received from Washington or Charleston, Delany concluded plaintively, was from the Superintending Officer of Schools who deemed his last application "unnecessary."

Delany never did have a chance to get a schoolhouse anywhere on Hilton Head. By 1868 the planters would not have objected to it, for they had learned that a school meant a stable population which also meant an available labor supply. The fact was that the Freedmen's Bureau simply could not build schools out of its two-year appropriation of $7 million. There were too many white and black mouths to feed, and nothing left with which to feed their minds.

All that Delany ever achieved in relation to the schools of Hilton Head was the appreciation of the teachers who wrote home and to their organization publications about the help given them by the Black Major. One teacher in Beaufort, in reporting to the *Christian Recorder* on her school in Beaufort, also noted Delany's speech on ownership of land and commented that "his labors are indispensable to the well being of these people." On Hilton Head a Miss E. P. Breck wrote home, "I am now engaged in teaching adults, who come at those hours in the day when it is most convenient for them to leave their work. After they have finished their day's work in the field, many of both men and women will come to recite their lessons. . . . Major Delany has been on a tour of inspection over this island, and he gives a very favorable report of the doings of the freedmen; says he was perfectly surprised to see the amount of labor they had performed, every foot of land being under cultivation, one woman and her daughter, sixteen years old, were cultivating ten acres. . . ." She too cited Delany's value to his people. Collectively, the teachers thanked him in a letter from Rev. George Whipple, corresponding secretary of the American Missionary Society in New York.

> Dear Major: Several of our teachers have reported your attention to their interests, and many acts of kindness in ministering to their comfort.
>
> In their behalf and at their request, and in the behalf and at the request of my associates in these rooms, I beg of you to accept our and their thanks for your oft-repeated kindnesses to them, and your continued interest in our great work. As you have given them more—"a cup of cold water" in the name of a disciple, may you receive a disciple's reward.

There were many good reasons why Hilton Head was in such better economic and social health than the rest of the state by the spring of 1868. Chief among them was Delany's persistence in accepting or rejecting his orders as he saw fit. Many of the most sincere among the Freedmen's Bureau agents submitted to its bureaucracy or the planters who had the ears of the "right people." Many of the junior officers still in the Army who had fought with the black troops and thereby came to respect them obeyed their superiors who declared that the welfare of the blacks was none of their business. Delany was an outstanding exception.

Throughout 1867 and even after he was mustered out in August 1868, Delany's monthly reports to the assistant commissioner, to Gen. Scott, to the various Bureau departments, to Gen. Howard in Washington, and in the press were all militant demands for correction of evils as he saw them. At no time did he compromise either his convictions or his language. Given a chance, he repeated again and again, the freedmen took care of themselves and their families. It was when they were denied opportunities and cheated that they became dependents. That was why he established his own policy on land-use in 1867 after reporting fully to Gen. Scott, his superior in the Bureau; to Gen. Sickles, his superior in the military; and (a copy) to Gen. Howard in Washington that March.

The situation resulted from Congressional starvation of the Freedmen's Bureau. To obtain some income, Gen. Howard agreed, in 1866, to allow U.S. Tax Commissioners to rent abandoned and confiscated lands to the highest bidders. According to Delany, the result was disastrous.

> It was apparent from observation and experience, that the custom of renting the lands to Speculators (*sic*), who sublet them to or employed the Freedmen to work for them at disadvantageous rates, that these poor people at the end of the planting year, habitually come out with nothing, absolutely nothing, generally; nay, worse than nothing, as those working the lands on shares, having rations supplied from the Stores of the Speculators, or renting the lands and obtaining rations on credit from such stores, when the crops were realized, paid them all away to these Stores for the scanty mouthfull (*sic*) they received on credit, finding themselves with nothing—in rags and in debt for a "balance due" on the books of these first hand lessees and supply speculators.

He could not blame the tax commissioners, Delany continued, since they "had their orders and instructions from the Department at Washington" and those orders "were to rent the Lands at the highest cash offer regardless of domestic surrounding, which they did. This of course threw out the Freedmen and Refugees (poor whites) placing them entirely dependent upon and at the mercy of these speculators." There were a few exceptions among the lessees of the government land, and Delany named them. As for those freedmen he had helped toward raising their own crops, they "were equally the victims of the brokers and petty cotton traders (from their superior knowledge and intelligence) and the almost entire want of the qualifications on the part of the freedmen, their cotton being sacrificed in the market." All who utilized his office's cotton handling facilities sold their crops at the market prices and without the exorbitant commissions.

> It was evident from these facts, that there could be little or no chance for the Freedmen or Refugees, to compete with the bidders or lessees of the land, let at the highest cash price, frequently far above their value in this District, except by the adoption of some measures for their protection, whereby a portion of their scanty earnings could be saved, and the lands let to them at prices suited to their means, in preference to speculators and capitalists.

To cure both evils, Delany suggested to all of his superiors that his example be followed and that the Bureau itself establish a Freedmen's Cotton Agency in Charleston. He detailed the plan of its operation. Then he reported what he had done on government lands under the Sherman titles and recommended that it become a national policy.

The freedmen who had utilized his Hilton Head cotton agency had cash at the end of 1866 and needed more land:

> To this end, interview and correspondence were had with the Tax Commissioners, who being without instructions and awaiting the action of Congress and the Government in relation to the divisions and assignment of lands on the tenure of Lieut. General Sherman's great Field Order, No. 15, after mature consideration, as the season for planting was rapidly approaching and the people clamorously anxious to go to work to prepare for cultivation, concluded to divide the responsibility with the Bureau (at its earnest solicitation, suggestion and representation) and let the lands to the freedmen at *one dollar an acre*, for the year 1867.

While Delany was busily negotiating an arrangement of this kind, he had organized the freedmen in preparation. He instructed them to place \$2 an acre in the hands of one man on each plantation, just in case the tax commissioners might agree to the method but feel forced to show more income from the land. But they approved his recommended rate of \$1 an acre.

> In less than three weeks from the time notice was given to this effect, upwards of three thousand ($3,000.) Dollars in cash and cotton vouchers was deposited in the Bureau to secure the leases, and fourteen plantations were taken, with the extreme satisfaction of paying back to each individual, one half of his money, or one dollar for every acre of land taken by him.

At that time, in March 1867, Delany was to predict what he reported in March 1868. "By care, frugality and proper management, with the requisite protection in their operations, at the end of the planting season, I anticipate in this Bureau District of Hilton Head, better prospects than any preceding year since their emancipation."

The total land thus leased and cultivated approximated 2,434 acres. The surrounding lands sub-let by Delany's hated "speculators" averaged $15 an acre to the freedmen. That saving, plus being protected from such tricks of the cotton brokers as short-weighting, downgrading of quality, and sacrifice prices to the freedmen placed Delany's freedmen on a plane of economic independence.

His next step was diversification of crops.

> Every month in the year but one (December) may be made productive of some vegetable for Provision or family use, whereby the people may be independent in subsistence. It is a settled matter, that in this country, cotton can only be profitably produced by extensive cultivation and large capital under favorable circumstances; consequently, it is a loss of time for the freedmen to plant cotton with their limited means of land and materials, as the ground to them, can be put to a much more useful purpose. I am preparing the people in this Sub District to this end, and believe that against the approaching leasing year, they will be quite ready and willing to enter into the new system of habitation and occupancy.

Every move made by Delany won him the enmity of the planters, for each independent freedman reduced the available labor supply and set an example for the remainder to bid for higher shares or wages. However, in only two cases were they able to hamper his operations, and both of them were minor. In one of these, Bvt. Major Edward L. Deane in Gen. Scott's Bureau headquarters, told Delany in no uncertain terms to "lay off" Col. Benjamin S. Pardee and his dealings with his freedmen. If they wanted to work for the gentleman, "it is no ones business but theirs."

Delany obeyed this order and wrote back to the Bureau that he was withdrawing his charges as instructed. However, he must have been secretly enjoying himself, for he added that he had turned all "charges and specifications" over to the military authorities at Hilton Head, thereby infinitely complicating Col. Pardee's problems.

In August 1867 there seemed to be a plot against Delany as a party in defrauding the freedmen of their cotton proceeds. The charges were made by form of affidavit from a freedman named John Robinson who made his mark on a paper prepared by Provost Judge William Cantwell of Hilton Head. The charges were that he had never been paid for a bale of cotton weighing 330 pounds which he turned over to Major Delany on January 19, 1867, as a result of a meeting in the church at Mitchelville to which the freedmen were "ordered."

> Your deponent attended the meeting, which was very large, 200 or 300 freedmen being present. He made a speech to the people and told them they must not sell their cotton to the merchants or traders of this place, that they would cheat them. He further said they must bring the cotton to him and he would furnish the bagging and that he would sell the same to the best advantage, pay himself for the bagging and pay over to the people the balance in money.

Delany insisted on another military investigation, and again he was completely cleared of any wrong-doing. Five days after Cantwell had made the charges, Robinson took oath, and made his mark on a new affidavit, this time witnessed. It seemed that Delany had offended a planter named Crofut. The statement, dated August 7, 1867, at Port Royal was as follows:

> I, John Robinson, commonly called Jack Robinson, do solemnly testify on oath, that I was requested by Mr. Cantwell, at the suggestion of Mr. Crofut, to go to his office; that I did

> not then know what for; that after I entered the Provost office, he Mr. Cantwell, the Provost Judge, commenced asking me questions about Major Delany, and the loss of my cotton, at the same time writing on a slate; that I never was sworn by him, nor never saw any paper; that he did not write down what I said on paper, neither did I touch a pen to a mark as mine, nor knew what he was writing the statement for.

The Bureau of Civil Affairs of the Military District could find no fault in Delany, in investigating the case, "than to show a possible error of judgment in advising certain Freed people in reference to the selection of an Agent to sell their cotton."

This attack on Delany's integrity was a complete failure. A few months later, on November 26, 1867, Gen. Grant ordered that all volunteer officers in the Army be mustered out as of the first of the year, with the exception of the commissioners and disbursing officers of the Freedmen's Bureau. It was part of the attack on Gen. Howard that was to lead to his court-martial and the dissolution of the Bureau.

Delany was the only volunteer Army officer retained in South Carolina to continue his Bureau work. Gen. Canby simply named him a disbursing officer and added some more islands to his District. Now he was to have the additional duties of handling soldiers' claims against the War Department. In fact, Delany was one of the last officers of the Freedmen's Bureau to be mustered out by the War Department. His honorable discharge was ordered on August 5, and he completed his duties on September 18, 1868, with the commendations of both his military and his Bureau commanding officers.

But meanwhile Delany was in the thick of political adventures. He could take no formal part in the hectic South Carolina political scene while an Army officer, but he could and did propagandize, write for the press, and work avidly, though privately, for his people's political opportunity that year.

To Delany 1867 was a year of jubilee, for his people *voted.* There was starvation and lawlessness in the state, shooting, cutting, flogging, burning, and robbing of the freedmen. The Ku Klux Klan was organizing. Washington was temporizing. The black leaders of the North were being befuddled by the politicians.

All that was unimportant to Delany. His people voted! True, they only voted to determine whether or not they should establish a new government through a constitutional convention, but they cast their ballots!

To many of the new freedmen it was a mystic rite, to others it had religious implications—to Delany it made his black brothers men in America, the equal of any white. When Gen. Canby set November 19 and 20 as the days on which all who registered were to decide whether or not to have a convention, he was jubilant.

The whites, regrouping their ranks into the Democratic party, were not happy. The group coalesced around Gen. Wade Hampton's leadership, and calling themselves the conservative Democrats, met in Columbia and decided to boycott the election. It was merely a gesture since the totals indicated that many whites had boycotted registration, too, and therefore the blacks had nearly a 2–1 majority eligible to vote. A convention would be a certainty. Their public explanation for advocating a boycott on white voting was, in part, a hope that their abstinence might render the convention unconstitutional, plus some most extravagant rhetoric.

> Free negro labor, under the sudden emancipation policy of the government, is a disaster from which, under the most favorable circumstances, it will require years to recover. Add to this the policy which the reconstruction acts propose to enforce and you place the South politically and socially under the heel of the negro; these influences combined will drag to hopeless ruin the most prosperous community in the world. What do these reconstruction acts propose? Not negro *equality* merely, but negro supremacy. In the name, then, of humanity to both races; in the name of citizenship under the constitution; in the name of a common history in the past; in the name of our Anglo-Saxon race and blood; in the name of civilization of the nineteenth century; in the name of magnanimity and the noble instincts of manhood; in the name of God and nature, we protest against these acts as destructive to the peace of society, the pros-

> perity of the country and the greatness and grandeur of our common future. The people of the South are powerless to avert the impending ruin. We have been overborne, and the responsibility to posterity and to the world has passed into other hands.

What was not made public in any terms, simple or verbose, was the planned strategy for the future. At that time it was a two-point program originated by Hampton's friend, Gen. Conner. The first was the control of the black vote by *armed force.* It had been Gen. Conner who founded the first rifle club in South Carolina made up of white men from the "best" families of Charleston. They were named the Hampton Guards, and certified as a state militia by Gov. Orr.

It had been Gen. Conner who, as a delegate to the "lily-white" Constitutional Convention called by Provisional Governor Perry in September 1865, offered an amendment on voting qualifications winning high praise. The *Charleston Courier* editorialized in discussion of the new constitution.

> One of the most noticeable features in the document is in regard to the qualifications of voters of this State, and is the result of a proposition made by Gen. Conner of your city which was agreed to and incorporated in that shape in the Constitution. It bestows the right to vote upon European immigrants who have declared their intention of becoming citizens of the United States two years previous to the day of election, and have resided six months in the election district where he offers to vote. . . . Mr. Conner's amendment is worth thousands of good citizens for us in the future, and is the most valuable auxiliary which your immigration companies will have in their endeavors to populate the State with the yeomanry of Europe.

Thus the Democratic party in South Carolina was reorganized around the dual program of arming the whites and importing other whites, both to reduce the black majority which was Republican. The result of the vote on the constitutional convention in 1867 did not matter to them. As expected, it was heavily weighted by blacks in favor of the convention. Out of a total registration of 125,328, 71,087 ballots were cast. *For* the convention—69,006; *against*—2,081. The composition of the vote was recorded as well, and all *against* the convention were white votes. All except 130 *for* the convention were black votes.

While the Constitutional Convention was in session in Charleston in January and February 1868, Delany seized every opportunity to attend it. Ironically, while it was still framing guarantees of suffrage for the blacks of South Carolina, Delany's own home state of Pennsylvania was once more confirming northern hypocrisy by a vote of 29–13 *against* enfranchisement of the blacks there. It was a particularly painful reminder to Delany and a lesson as well. There was more hope for black equality in backward South Carolina than in progressive Pennsylvania, for the black man was represented in proportion to the population of the state. South Carolina was erecting a new structure, based on a new society. Its people were doing so by military compulsion, a factor not exerted anywhere in the victorious North. In the South racial hatreds were curbed for the time being but in the North one of the fruits of victory was continued white supremacy.

That, basically, is the reason Delany remained in the South after the Freedmen's Bureau faded away, after the Army no longer had need of him. Those 55 days of discussion at the 1868 Constitutional Convention in Charleston convinced him that there was more hope for the achievement of democracy for his people there than in Ohio. The color phobia was the same, but in South Carolina black suffrage and black participation in government was a reality. The state that triggered the bloody and useless Civil War could become the leading stronghold of republicanism and a shining example to all other states of the Union. So long as the possibility remained, so did Delany.

A reader of the *Proceedings* of the South Carolina Constitutional Convention could easily forget the century and think he is reading the most recent issue of the *Congressional Record*. Beyond the legalisms of the actual construction of a civil government, the discussions on taxes, welfare and relief, race and caste, "law and order," the landed (corporate) society versus the laboring (freedmen) society, the differences between liberty and license—all were debated in 1868, almost in the contemporary language as well as the conflict of today.

There was lofty idealism expressed by all who took the floor, and trickery and knavery in committee meetings. There was bombast and sound common sense, self-interest and public interest openly and secretly connived, a profound belief in his own self-importance possessed by each delegate, and a wariness of the reporters busily engaged in noting everything that was said for the usual editorial misinterpretation in their newspapers.

In other words, the South Carolina convention differed from any legislative body only in its color composition. Out of the 124 delegates, 76 were blacks, and the balance of whites were chiefly of the same political persuasion—Republican. The whites were "renegades" and "scalawags" and "carpetbaggers" to the Democrats who had boycotted the convention. Twenty-three of these whites were natives of South Carolina, including the future governor, Franklin J. Moses, Jr., who boasted in the convention that he, personally, had hauled down the United States flag at Fort Sumter. Massachusetts appeared to dominate the white "carpetbaggers." But black leadership emerged from the natives in a fashion unexpected by observers, and the southern newspapers commented on that in frequent amazement. Among them were Robert C. DeLarge, former tailor; Beverly Nash, a former slave, and barber; Francis L. Cardozo, son of a white man who had had him educated abroad to become a teacher; the famous Robert Smalls; and Alonzo J. Ransier, who could have "passed" but preferred to identify with the blacks.

The convention was a typical body, such as is chosen by the people in all elections, and it reflected the composition of the body politic as faithfully as any legislative body in the country. It was the issues before the convention that made it different from other such assemblies. Day after day was spent in debating whether or not to aid debtors in the legal stay of execution of their debts. Conditions were such that whites would lose their lands to "loan sharks" through foreclosures. One of the pressing problems of the state was to get the lands under cultivation, and such lands would be held by "speculators," northern, of course, who would hold the acreage idle for future sale at exorbitant profits or else farm them at the going rate of $5 per month for freedmen and $3 a month for women, slow starvation for them. On the other hand, if the white planters, South Carolinians, were saved from loss of their lands, they would see that the freedmen ate. The argument appeared logical to the convention until the point was raised that almost all of the litigation and debt execution being pressed at that time was the result of the purchase and sale of slaves prior to the war. Should such debts be recognized? Aside from the fact that all whites lost their chattel property by emancipation and without compensation, since they lost the war, should judgments rendered on traffic in human flesh be honored with the status of legal debts?

Some of the arguments were surprisingly contemporary. It was agreed by the convention that freedmen and poor whites in the state were starving. The Freedmen's Bureau did not have the resources to feed them. Only the Federal government had the resources; South Carolina certainly did not.

It was proposed that Congress be memorialized for the loan of a million dollars to the state, protected by its bonds, which would be distributed among the freedmen, *as loans,* in order to buy land and become self-sufficient. The question arose: Since this amount, it was estimated, would allow the purchase of 5 1/7 acres of land per family, where was the hope of self-sufficiency? Besides, cotton required large acreage to be cultivated profitably. A Homestead Act required huge amounts of money to accomplish its purposes, and people were hungry today, right now. Some means of relief was needed at once.

It seemed that the term "relief" was a dirty word then, too, as "welfare" is today, although "charity" seems to remain respectable. The Freedmen's Bureau had spent $876,000 in South Carolina, it was reported, and yet had reached only a tenth of those in need of food. All the familiar charges were voiced. "They don't want to work"; and "Feeding them would rob them of initiative."

Even while these debates were in progress in Charleston, a few streets away, in the Health District No. 3 Dispensary, the physician in charge was writing his report about the health conditions among the freedmen who had flooded the slums of his area. Dr. John L. Ancrum advised enforcement of "the most stringent vagrant laws . . . with a view to driving the unemployed back into the country." He wrote:

> The common dictates of humanity would make it appear to be imperative that ample public provision should be made to meet the misfortunes of those whose greatest crime is poverty; but the question arises, are the worthy, honest and industrious poor commonly the recipients of this charity? In some cases they are; in the majority, they are not; it is

> the worthless, vagabond, idle, dishonest, improvident drones of society, who are either too lazy to earn a living by honest labor, or who squander their daily gains in the pursuit of vice and debauchery, who crowd our dispensary registers. . . . The Freedmen, having been clothed and fed and educated for the last three or four years to the belief that he is the special ward of the Government, very naturally imagines that his color entitles him . . . to the unrestricted services of what he denominates as the "Poor", the "State", or "Spensary" Doctor, and to an unlimited supply of any and every kind of medicine which he desires.

Dr. Ancrum had another solution for these freedmen, aside from driving them into the country. It was that each health officer be given "a severe discriminating power toward the applicants." But his report was typical of all those offered the Constitutional Convention, many from Freedmen's Bureau officers.

Each of the urgent issues debated prior to being written into the new constitution had a racial import. A homestead act would benefit the blacks more than the whites and therefore it was "class and caste" legislation. There were more freedmen destitute than whites and therefore provision of food became color legislation. And when the legislators reached the problem of public education, all of the school desegregation arguments of today are but an echo of 1868. They had no precedent on which to base their thinking, this being the first public school program for the state.

The freedmen's thirst for knowledge was one of the most unexpected developments of the emancipation. It was generally agreed, among the abolitionists too, that the slaves were little more than animals with only primitive, non-intellectual urges. Among the free Negroes of the North, there was an easy explanation for their continued demand for schooling for their children. They were aping the whites. But the slaves were another matter. Never having been allowed to learn, it was assumed that their happy ignorance was a natural state. But, with the capture of Port Royal in 1861, scarcely a reporter or a soldier writing home failed to mention the black cries for schools.

At the end of 1865 Gen. Howard sent John W. Alvord, his new inspector of schools, on a 4,000 mile tour of the rebel states.

Alvord declared in his report, "The desire of the freedmen for knowledge has not been overstated." By the time the Constitutional Convention met, a plan for public schools was second only to the immediate need for food in the expressions of the freedmen.

One of Delany's friends, Benjamin Franklin Randolph, who had taught at Hilton Head for a time, was among the strongest proponents of *compulsory* school attendance reported out by the Committee on Education. He was adamant on the need of compulsion, knowing, as a teacher, that parents are slothful and, as a Freedmen's Bureau agent, that most black parents needed their children's labor.

But the nub of the discussion was the fact that with compulsory school attendance, the whites and the blacks would have to attend the same schools. Some delegates said that this would defeat the constitution because the whites would not stand for it. Others said the constitution would be defeated because the blacks wanted their own schools. For day after day it was argued and finally summed up by the brilliant young Cardozo as the opportune time for the blacks to strike out for what they needed, "as we may not ever have a more propitious time."

> We know when the old aristocracy and ruling power of the State get into power, as they undoubtedly will, because intelligence and wealth will win in the long run, they will never pass such a law as this. Why? Because their power is built on and sustained by ignorance. They will take precious good care that the colored people shall never be enlightened.

One delegate arguing against the compulsion of attendance phrased it almost word for word as it has been since the Supreme Court school desegregation decision of 1954.

> Now, what is likely to be the result of retaining this section, and thereby opening the public schools to all? Simply, that they would be attended only by the colored children. If the attempt is made to enforce a mixture in this way, I have no idea that fifty white children in the State would attend the public schools. . . . Now would it not be far better to have schools entirely impartial in their organization, but separate and all classes attending them, and ac-

> quiring an education, and everything working harmoniously together, than for us to introduce a measure here that would very likely prove injurious to the cause of education, but which we could not change because it is in the Constitution?

Perhaps the only part of this debate not just as valid today is the question raised by young Robert C. DeLarge, native free Negro of Charleston. It would be difficult to enforce, he said. "It is just as impossible to put such a section in practical operation, as it would be for a man to fly to the moon."

The convention called for an election for or against the proffered Constitution, and for state offices, and concluded its sessions on March 9. Gen. Canby set the elections for April 14 through April 16 and laid down the ground rules for voting in General Order No. 41. It was detailed and explicit as to free and peaceful balloting.

Once more the whites railed against the black supremacy that enslaved them with such a document as the new Constitution, and the state Democratic party became divided over the question whether or not they should offer candidates for state office. As a result, they boycotted the election and predicted ruin for the state under such laws. But the black-dominated framers of those laws must have accomplished something worth-while. The Constitution they wrote was not changed by the whites when Wade Hampton and the Democrats took command of the state in 1877. It was to remain their Constitution for 18 more years.

On July 11, 1868, Gen. Canby was able to wire his officers throughout South Carolina as follows:

> The Legislature of South Carolina having ratified the Constitutional Amendments, you will cease the exercise of any authority under the Reconstruction Laws of the United States.

And, on July 22 the first governor to be elected under the new regime, Gen. Robert K. Scott, wrote to Gen. Howard in Washington.

> I have the honor to inform you that after 1st proximo the services of Major M. R. Delany U.S.C.T. (now on duty as

Asst. Sub Asst. Comm. at Hilton Head) will not be required in this district, and would respectfully recommend that he be ordered to report elsewhere for duty.

I make this recommendation not because of any fault to be found with Maj. Delany whose services have always been characterized by zeal, and efficiency, and have resulted in great good to the people on the islands, but after the 1st prox. I do not think that occasion for his presence there will longer exist.

CHAPTER TWENTY

The Race War

By the time the Black Major had concluded his duties as a Freedmen's Bureau officer and as an Army disbursing officer, South Carolina was well launched on its experiment in self-government. The generalities applied to that period from 1868 to 1877 spring from the "Southern School" of historiography in which Gen. Wade Hampton had a part. He wrote Gen. Conner from Mississippi in April 1869 about "the formation of a grand Historical Society, with branches all over the South."

> We wish to put on record in an enduring form the truths regarding our struggle for freedom, and thus preserve untarnished our glorious position and our heroic deeds. If we let the Yankees manufacture a history as they do wooden nutmegs, we shall have of the former about as good an article as they give us of the latter, and as much like the genuine. You can see at once the importance of such a Society as is contemplated, and I hope you will lend your aid zealously.

As a result, one of the most widespread of the historical generalizations relating to the government elected by a black majority is that it was also an era of black corruption. That is utterly false. In no other phase of the state's life was desegregation practiced, not in the public schools, the churches, civic events, agriculture, or commerce. Only in corruption was true equality achieved between black and white. There was no color line drawn by those in elective or appointive public office when it came to thievery. If anything, the Negro electors were amazingly generous in giving the larger share of the "take" to the whites. They could have kept it all.

In June 1866 they elected just one black to state office, Francis L. Cardozo, Secretary of State and head of the black political organization, the Union League of South Carolina. All six of the other state officers, from Gov. Robert K. Scott down, were white.

According to the "black corruption" school of historical texts, all members of the General Assembly, county and school district officials were in on the graft. If that was true, then either the blacks were generous or they were ignorant of the opportunities for corruption. Only in the House of Representatives did they have a black majority. In the state Senate, nine of the 32 elected were black, and the balance was white. Both men sent to the U.S. Senate were white. All eleven judges elected in the state were white. In the area of local graft, all 31 county treasurers appointed were white and among the guardians of the public purse, the county auditors, there was one black appointed and 31 whites. Three fifths of the local magistrates were white; all 31 of the sheriffs elected were white; all 31 clerks of court were white; ten of the 31 school commissioners were blacks. All four of the U.S. Congressmen were white.

Throughout the succeeding elections and appointments until final defeat of the Republicans, these color proportions in public office varied but little. The fact of corruption in public finances cannot be challenged for South Carolina—or other states and the Federal government under President Grant. But it was never a black monopoly, and the former slaves who "lived high on the hog" in Columbia while the General Assembly sat, were too ignorant to steal as skillfully as the whites at first. But they learned fast.

It is extremely difficult to arrive at an exact figure of the total stolen from public funds, and perhaps it is not important. The fact that participation was widespread is important, however, for it influenced Delany's future political action. As recently as 1901, in the *Atlantic Monthly*, Daniel H. Chamberlain of Massachusetts, white attorney general and later the last Republican governor of South Carolina, estimated the state debt at $17,500,000 in 1872, just five years after the Republicans took over when that debt, he wrote, was a million dollars. He did not mention in the article that the state debt increased by another six million while he was governor. Nor did he mention why that debt rose, aside from the legitimate reasons, such as expanded schools and failure by white landowners to pay taxes. From the election of Governor Scott and Chamberlain in 1868 the state's financial agent in New York was Howard H. Kimpton who was recommended by the new attorney general. He and Chamberlain had been roommates at Yale University. By 1877 Kimpton had received approximately $735,000 in commissions for handling the sale of South Carolina, Blue Ridge, and other railroad bonds at from 25 to 75 percent of their debt values. That was his "take" in a legitimate fashion. His pay-offs to successive governors, Scott, Moses, and Chamberlain, are only spottily recorded in his correspondence with them, so a total is unknown.

In actual dollars stolen therefore, a goodly portion was lost on the bond market in New York, as well as in the pockets of Kimpton and the governors. And since so many of the South Carolina bond issues eventually were repudiated, there were more agonized outcries from Wall Street than from the Democrats of South Carolina to sustain the "black corruption" theme.

In reality, the amounts stolen were peanuts compared with New York's "Boss" Tweed raid at the same time, or the pay-offs to Congressmen in the Credit Mobilier scandal of Grant's administration, or the "Whiskey Ring" millions stolen from the Internal Revenue Department during that same period. Corruption in America has never had either a racial or geographical character. It is a national characteristic.

And again, South Carolina's "black corruption" was *not* restricted to radical Republicans. The white Democrats had their cut in the Blue Ridge Railroad bonds, as only one example, just as they did in all graft throughout the country. No single political party ever has cornered the graft in the United States.

The blacks of South Carolina, however, had no place to go politically except to the Republican party. It was the party that had emancipated them, fed them through the Freedmen's Bureau and, in 1868, had troops protecting their right to vote. No matter what the color of the thief, the freedmen supported the Republican label. That is perhaps the major reason Delany's political career was most active and most unsuccessful. He was a political maverick because he advocated the sacrifice of party affiliation in demanding personal integrity.

Delany had managed to maintain comparative peace on his islands, but when he left both whites and blacks adopted the state-wide pattern of political and physical combat preparedness.

The fact that open warfare, except at the polls, never broke out on Hilton Head as it did all over South Carolina was due, at least in part, to his demonstration through three crop years that black and white sharing of the profits of agriculture paid off for both. He left behind him better educated whites, as well as freedmen, for during the coming stormy years the Ku Klux Klan and its later designation as "Hampton's Redshirts" never organized violence there as effectively as in the rest of the state.

While the regulations of his position did not allow Delany to speak out on South Carolina, nothing restrained his expression regarding the problems of his race. He too had learned on Hilton Head. When, in the summer of 1867, the irrepressible Wendell Phillips, enthusiastic over Congress' defiance of the Reconstruction Act vetoes, called for still more aggressive action by the radical Republicans, Delany was forced to differ with him. Phillips had suggested that the coming Republican convention nominate a black man for vice-president in the 1868 elections.

Ordinarily, Delany would be the last to oppose the elevation of one of his race, but apparently he knew the northern whites as well as the southern. A black man on the Republican national ticket would be political suicide, he believed. Only the old-time abolitionists might be fired up with the potential for black equality but not the people. Such a step would split the Republicans and elect a Democrat as president of the United States. Again and again he had warned his people that the whites could be forced to accept black suffrage, but not black rule.

He voiced his opposition to Phillips' proposal and, once again, found himself utilized by the opposition, just as his *Political Destiny* had been used in Lincoln's colonization propaganda. The *New York Times*, the country's leading press opponent of the radical Republicans, named Phillips as an "arch-agitator" and complained: "That Warwick of the blacks would make a negro Vice-President, because we should thus show to the world that his people stand in social equality with our own." That, of course, was not true and could not be true, the *Times* continued. The black man should be happy with suffrage and perhaps one day would qualify for offices requiring "lower capacity."

> The leading men of the colored race themselves make no such unreasonable claim. They understand their situation,

> and have no purpose to be made the catspaws of politicians. As one of their number, Major Delany, who, in his experience as a volunteer, learned something of self-discipline and of men, very sensibly says in a letter upon the subject: "Let colored men be satisfied to take things like other men in their natural course and time, preparing themselves in every particular for local municipal positions, and they may expect to attain to some others in time."

The *Times* added its own conclusions from that. "Neither would the election of a negro as Vice-President make him or prove him to be the social equal of the white man. Social equality is an unnatural and impossible state."

Delany had not meant that in his letter to Henry Highland Garnet, which the newspaper quoted. However, the debate went on. Phillips had put boundless hope and ambition in the hearts of black men which, Delany believed, the realities did not justify. In the South Carolina Republican party convention that July, his own friend Jonathan J. Wright, had offered a resolution demanding a black nomination for vice-president. One of the better young editors of the black press, Rev. R. L. Perry of the Columbus (Ohio), *People's Journal*, even nominated another friend of Delany's for the vice-presidency, John Mercer Langston of Ohio, a most capable young man. Perry also repeated some of the attacks on Delany's position, and his reply was printed in the *Christian Recorder*. It is a curiously self-revealing letter. Delany viewed himself as an elder statesman among the black leadership of the country and blamed all the furor on a generation gap.

> A great issue is before us; the fate of a destiny of a race the consumation (*sic*) of nearly forty years of incessant agitation, struggle, and political contest, commenced and continued by our fathers, carried on and aided by their successors and our friends. And I hesitate not to tell our young men plainly; and should indeed feel that we had "no men qualified" for so high a position as leaders, if we did not do so; that it requires all the wisdom that we posses (*sic*) as a race in this country, to safely direct our counsels at this time, amidst the wisest statesmen home and foreign, and

most important political issue—next to the Magna Carta —that the world ever witnessed.

And our young men are but waiting to enjoy the fruits of the harvest, planted and cultivated by such men as Pennington, Garnet, Purvis, Vashon, and others, whose counsel they presume to sneer, either of whom and many others that might be named, is amply qualified to fill any political position in the gifts of the people. Prof. Vashon, the junior of these names, is forty-five years of age, the youngest of the others being several years past meridian.

Our young men are sadly mistaken if they presume to lead and direct the counsels of their oppressed race; they can and must be aids (*sic*) and assistants, but not *the* leaders. I respect, admire, and love young men of worth and qualifications—and this our young Perry knows—but Mr. Langston the "Standard Bearer" is but thirty-four years of age, Mr. Wright is twenty-seven, and I doubt whether Mr. Perry the ardent Journalist of the "party" is older than Mr. Langston. And while I take pride in such young men of talents and qualifications among us, I should feel ashamed for our race, before the statesmen of America and Europe, if I or some of us who have been advocating the equality of our race more years than some of these young men have lived; did not speak out and disclaim such leadership for four and a half millions of recently disenthralled people.

You very well know, that there is not a more determined, unyielding, uncompromising advocate and friend of his race than I am, claiming for it all the rights and privileges belonging to man, desiring to see black men (or colored, if you prefer the term) in every position socially and politically, attainable. And the one hundred and four (104) black Policemen, and Chiefs of Police, and one Magistrate holding office and doing duty in my Sub Bureau District, all have attained their position directly through me; and the Magistrate by my recommendation.

I conclude by repeating, that we (our race) are not yet ready to claim the Second office in the Nation, and Presidency of the U.S. Senate, one of the greatest deliberative bodies that ever represented a Nation, and the peer of the British House of Lords; and hope that in the National Convention to take place for the nomination of Candidates, no

> such offer will be accepted; because it would be certain to result in the overthrow of the Republican party, by driving all the conservative Negro hating elements North and South together, and end in the loss of our Cause.

The summer of 1867 was also notable for Gen. Sickles' swift and uncompromising action in several cases in which blacks were abused without interference by the civil authorities. In one case, the flogging of a Negro girl, the eight white defendants sent to jail by Sickles included a justice of the peace. In another case, involving Delany's biographer, Frances Rollin, Gen. Sickles found Capt. W. M. McNelty, skipper of the interisland steamer *Pilot Boy*, guilty of discrimination against Miss Rollin "because of her color" when he refused her first-class passage between Charleston and Beaufort. He was fined $250. General Sickles' decision was also a statement of civil rights.

> So long as the laws imposed civil and political disabilities, because of servitude or color, common carriers were permitted to enforce the same discrimination among passengers.
>
> Such disabilities and usages have ceased with Slavery to have any legal sanction whatever.
>
> Whatever belongs of common right to citizens they must be protected in, and as necessarily follows the recognition of blacks as citizens, they must be protected in whatever of common right belongs to them.

This case was a precedent for the country, coming before the 14th Amendment had been ratified and eight years before Congress itself, in the Civil Rights Act of 1875, applied the same principles to interstate carriers. How much Delany had to do with the case, we do not know, but throughout the summer and fall of 1867 he was working with Miss Rollin on his biography, *The Life and Public Services of Martin R. Delany*, which was published in Boston late in 1868. They conferred often, at Hilton Head, Beaufort, and Charleston. However, from a diary she wrote for the year 1868, Miss Rollin appears to have been a most formidable female and may have instituted this early civil rights test herself. She was to return to South Carolina from Boston the following year, marry William J. Whipper, and become the scourge of Democrats and all who opposed her husband, as editor of the *Barnwell County Times*.

Delany himself did not leave Hilton Head until February 1869 although his final accounts to the War Department and the Freedmen's Bureau were completed by September 3 of the preceding year. He submitted a claim for additional pay, allowances, quarters, and fuel amounting to $191.18 plus postage costs totaling $57. He was paid the postage but the bill for 24 days of service since his muster-out date of August 10 was disputed by the paymasters in South Carolina and Washington. The final disposition of the claim seems to have come from Gen. Howard's office in January 1869 with the decision: "The fact that he voluntarily neglected to obey the order to transfer his funds and accounts to Col. Gils at Beaufort until Sept. 3rd, 1868 gives him no claim for pay to that time."

Failure to receive that pay may have been the reason Miss Rollin frequently complained, in her diary, that Delany had failed to send her money. He was broke—again—but still had his plans to continue his place in the top rank of black leadership. He had those plans even before Gen. Grant was inaugurated as President of the United States and took action two months before. Early in February 1869 he met with Gov. Scott in Charleston to begin his campaign. Delany wanted to be appointed the first black Minister to the Republic of Liberia. He had reason to hope for such an appointment. The precedent was set when Grant appointed the first black to any diplomatic post. Ebenezer E. Bassett, the Connecticut-born black educator was sent to Haiti as Minister Resident and Consul General.

Before leaving South Carolina Delany wrote Scott: "I have fully matured all the contingencies and issues which may arise nationally and internationally and consequently will be prepared to meet any question at the Department of State." He then started toward home and family via a lecture tour through the South, and did not reach Wilberforce until June. All along his route petitions to President Grant and to the new Secretary of State Hamilton Fish for his appointment to Liberia were initiated and signed by a most impressive collection of both blacks and whites. The signatories included legislators, judges, publishers, members of the Electoral College who had voted for Grant, and businessmen from Alabama, Louisiana, and Texas. When he reached home there was a special Bishop's

Council meeting called by the AME Church on July 5, and six bishops signed the following to President Grant:

> We the undersigned Bishops of the African Methodist Episcopal Church in the United States, representing the largest number of colored Christians in the United States and also the largest numbers of Colored voters
>
> Would recommend to your Excellency's favorable consideration, Major Martin R. Delany late of the United Army and now residing in Xenia, Ohio, for the position as minister to the Republic of Liberia, Africa.
>
> In our opinion, Major Delany possesses the educational ability to fill the place that we now ask for him.
>
> He was commissioned by President Lincoln as a Major in the regular Army which position he filled with great acceptability as his record will show.

But Delany heard nothing, from either the President or the Secretary of State. In October of that year he was to adopt the same tactics he had used so successfully with Lincoln, the direct approach. He went to Washington from Wilberforce to see the President. On October 18 he wrote him, making formal application and citing his 1859-1860 explorations and "commercial importance" of Africa. Delany wrote:

> For his knowledge and experience in commercial developments he would most respectfully refer to Major Gen'l Rufus Saxton, under whom he served ten months in South Carolina; also Major General Robert K. Scott, now Governor of South Carolina, under whom he served three years, assisting in the restoration of the Industrial and Agricultural productions of the state; also to Major General Daniel E. Sickles, now Minister to Spain, under whom he received the appointment by special order (No. 148, series of 1865) of Inspector, with direct reference to the Commercial and Domestic relations of the Sea Islands in the southern part of the State, and around about Charleston.

There was no response and Delany did not have an interview with either Grant or Fish. Perhaps he was politically naive. His timing was wrong. There was no diplomatic necessity for appointing a black Minister to Liberia in 1869. There was a political necessity in 1871, however, when Grant appointed a black man, James Milton Turner of Missouri, to that post. The election campaign was approaching and Grant needed the black vote for re-election.

But Delany was dreaming of a new career when he left South Carolina on his lecture tour. By then his biography was published and Delany had copies of *Life and Public Services* to sell to his audiences, and they bought the book as much in reaction to the remarkable notices given it in the press as his powers of oratory. It was reviewed by "Rufus" in the *Christian Recorder*, and undoubtedly the writer knew Delany for he was aware of "Minor errors, historical and statistical" which are in the biography. However, his admiration for Delany overflowed:

> Maj. Delany's life is a vivid illustration of what may be accomplished by a man of indomitable will and perseverance, when actuated by a grand emotion of patriotism and a pure and self-sacrificing love of equal and exact justice.
>
> From verifying facts which have come to our knowledge we are compelled to accord to Maj. Delany a place in the front ranks of American Statesmen and philanthropists. Commencing in his early manhood, he has for a quarter of a century, battled against the terrible cast (*sic*)—prejudice—which has kept his people under the iron heel of oppression for two hundred years; and, though battling under the trying disadvantages of extreme poverty, sometimes even wanting the necessaries of life. Yet has he succeeded in accomplishing more practical good for his people than any man of his race now living in this country. The highest meed of praise that can be accorded to him is, that Martin R. Delany is now a *poor* man. . . . We venture to predict that the end of Martin R. Delany's usefulness is not yet, and that, in these happy and peaceful times, he will receive a proper recognition of his merits from a grateful and happy people. It is a proud moment to him to find the labor of his life crowned with success, and it is not asking too much of the American people to request that he be permitted to pass the last days of his useful life in some high position of honor and trust in the Republic.

Whoever "Rufus" might have been, he was no prophet. President Grant had ignored Delany's bid for the "high position" to Liberia. By the time he had reached Wilberforce too, the black leaders of the North were again in massed attack against Delany's thinking, as expressed in his widely published lectures, particularly the one in Congo Square, New Orleans, in April.

The nub of Delany's argument that was to induce protest from so many of his old friends and enemies among the blacks, including Frederick Douglass, was a demand that the Republican party—or any political party appealing to blacks—share the patronage of public office on a "pro-rata" basis. In the North, he pointed out, there were no black Federal appointments because only one out of every thirty of the population was black. Don't let that happen in the South, he warned his audiences, because the blacks comprise from a third to one half the population of the South. Nationally, the ratio was "8 whites to 1 black."

> Shall a small faction control a party discarding the rights of the rest because the great majority of that party are composed of people different in race from themselves? Shall the principles as applied to civil rights, so long controlling political actions in the North under the old state of things, now be permitted to be brought to the South, by any faction of intolerant political schemes?

Once more Delany was rocking the boat of political hopes as envisioned by the new and old leaders of the blacks. Why any such thing as a "pro-rata" recognition? Why not standards of ability and education without limit as to proportionate color?

And Delany's continued reply during the next two years of such debate was that neither the blacks nor the whites were ready or willing to live up to the ideals of democracy. And, as ever, that reply was usually expressed in typically Delany fashion, minus tact.

CHAPTER TWENTY-ONE

The Maverick Republican

A sensible black man, not seeking to share the spoils of corruption, would never have returned to South Carolina. Delany knew better than most the problems and perils ahead and, in fact, had often predicted them in his speeches. But Delany was not a sensible man. He was a committed man. South Carolina had a black majority and therefore had the greatest potential for the black man. In Ohio, the few thousands of blacks could not even vote. The 15th Amendment had not yet been ratified. In South Carolina he had been voting since 1867.

When he left Wilberforce in October 1869, Delany had spent only a few months at home, absent only for occasional lectures. He had busied himself with Wilberforce University affairs and was elected a trustee at the annual meeting held that summer, and had seen to it that Gov. Scott would be a Wilberforce trustee too. And when he left, he had just one plan in mind. He would go to Washington, get the appointment to Liberia, and then send for his family, except for Faustin Soulouque and Alexander Dumas who were preparing to enter the University. Nowhere was an intent to return to South Carolina mentioned.

Delany waited in Washington for two months, expecting word either from President Grant or Secretary Fish. While waiting for a response that never came, Delany was not idle. Many of his friends were in the city, almost all former black abolitionists, and they were planning a new newspaper, a national weekly, "in the interest of the colored people of America: and its purpose was not only to educate but to direct the new black political power." Rev. J. Sella Martin of Massachusetts was named the editor of *The New Era* and Frederick Douglass its corresponding editor. In charge of printing production was Lewis Douglass who had worked in his father's print shop in Rochester before joining the 54th Massachusetts. Lewis had undergone the revelation that his gallant military service, emancipation of his people, and the various civil rights acts by Congress did not mean a thing to the District of Columbia Typographical Union. His application for membership had been rejected on account of his color.

Delany was the author of a series of four articles that appeared in the first issues of *The New Era*, beginning on January 13, 1870. These were elementary lessons and primary definitions on "Citizenship," "Civil Rights," the "Constitution," and "Secession." They were written simply, without Delany's usual adornment of language and for the freedmen, because he believed "It is now important that men of the black race make themselves masters of political science." This series was later printed in pamphlet form as the first of a projected group of University pamphlets entitled "A Series of Four Tracts on National Policy: to the Students of Wilberforce University; Being Adapted to the Capacity of the Newly-Enfranchised Citizens, THE FREEDMEN."

During his fruitless wait in Washington, there occurred an historic event in which Delany played a prominent role, the founding of the Negro National Labor Union. At its first mass meeting on the evening of December 6 at the Union League Hall, he was the principal speaker and delivered a highly informative address on the importance of black labor to the American economy. It was exactly the kind of meaningful self-importance needed by the delegates who just a few months before had been so totally rejected by the white National Labor Union meeting in Philadelphia. Apparently, the "blue collar" worker of early American trade unionism differed little from his counterpart of today in regard to race prejudice, a fact which no doubt has Samuel W. Gompers, founder of the A F of L spinning in his grave.

Isaac Myers of Baltimore, representing the Colored Caulkers Trades Union Society, appealed to the whites:

> I speak today for the colored man of the whole country, from the lakes to the Gulf—from the Atlantic to the Pacific—from every hill-top, valley and plain throughout our vast domain, when I tell you that all they ask for themselves is a fair chance; that you shall be no worse off by giving

> them that chance; that you and they will dwell in peace and harmony together; that you and they may make one steady and strong pull until the laboring men of this country shall receive such pay for time made as will secure them a comfortable living for their families, educate their children and leave a dollar for a rainy day and old age. Slavery, or slave labor, the main cause of the degradation of white labor, is no more. And it is the proud boast of my life that the slave himself had a large share in the work of striking off the fetters that bound him by the ankle, while the other end bound you by the neck.

The white labor leaders disregarded this eloquent appeal for unity of color against the common enemy, the employers, and in so doing they cast the laboring blacks into the roles of strikebreakers and "scabs," much to the delight of the industrialists. The Negro National Labor Union was a form of separatism not desired by the blacks which has continued to this day, particularly in the American Federation of Labor old-line unions.

Delany's speech was calculated to give the delegates a sense of the importance of black labor, according to the report in *The New Era*. The freedman, Delany said, "without education, has been taught in the last few years that labor was the source of wealth." The country's greatest money crops—tobacco, cotton, rice, and sugar—were raised by black labor.

> It was the negro, he said, that controlled the wealth of the South and ruled Wall street today, and the gold market of the country. All the coffee in the universe, except Mocca (*sic*) and Java, is raised by negroes, and the speaker inquired whether this fact was not an acknowledgement of the important position for the negro to occupy. In conclusion he advised his hearers to be united, and be true to themselves and their race, and be respectful to good men.

The more than 200 delegates to the convention decided on a separate organization, adopted a constitution, and explained that among other reasons for such separation a major one was "the exclusion of colored men and apprentices from the right to labor in . . . industry or workshops . . . by what is known as Trades' Unions," a most contemporary condition in the building trades. They also expressed a practical idealism not shared by today's "blue collar" workers.

> In our organization we make no discrimination as to nationality, sex or color. Any labor movement based upon such discrimination and embracing a small part of the great working masses of the country, while repelling others because of its partial or sectional character, will prove to be of very little value. Indeed, such a movement, narrow and divisional, will be suicidal, for it arrays against the classes represented by it all other laboring classes which ought to be rather allied in the closest union, and avoid these dissensions and divisions which in the past have given wealth the advantage over labor.

The advantage held by white wealth over black labor was the problem of his people in South Carolina and, on his return to Charleston, he concerned himself with that.

Delany was dismayed by what he found in South Carolina among his people. They were not making the progress he had hoped for. They were following blindly the political leaders who were labeled "Republican" with no regard for their abilities or honesty. The "Browns" were again setting up a caste system among mulattoes, and the blacks were not exerting enough pressure on the state authorities in behalf of education. He found many things to criticize, having apparently anticipated a metamorphosis among the blacks during his absence. His views were expressed bluntly in the *New National Era*, the Washington newspaper now taken over and edited by Frederick Douglass. Douglass himself replied to Delany in the paper, but this time in a gently chiding fashion, "even where I dissent from your views, I am compelled to respect your boldness, candor, and manly independence in the utterance of your convictions. Especially and sincerely do I thank you for your masterly exposure of the malign influences which surrounded the whole business of reconstruction in South Carolina and the other seceding States."

On one point—one that was to govern Delany's political thinking for some years—Douglass differed sharply. Delany had criticized the blacks for not seeking a greater number of public offices in accord with their population, his old "quota" theory.

> As a matter of arithmetic, your figures are faultless. The mulattoes, on a solid census basis ought to have so many offices, the blacks so many, and the whites so many, the Germans so many, the Irish so many, and other classes and nationalities should have offices according to their respective numbers. The idea is equal and admirable in theory; but does it not already seem to you a little absurd as a matter of practice? The fact is, friend Delany, these things are not fixed by figures, and while men are what they are cannot be so fixed.

If Delany had had any illusions about staying out of politics on his return to South Carolina early in 1870, they were soon blasted, for 1870 was an election year in the state and the whites were making noises about ending their voting boycott and actually launching a campaign. They were needled into it by a meeting of a group of the state's editors, those who were not sharing in the graft, in Charleston on March 16. Almost without exception the South Carolinian press was Democratic.

A few weeks after that editorial entry into politics, Gov. Scott reacted with several key patronage appointments. That is why, without his solicitation, Delany was appointed one of seven lieutenant colonels and aide to the commander in chief of the South Carolina Militia, Gov. Scott. It was a purely honorary appointment and made solely in recognition of Delany's popularity among the freedmen of the lower part of the state. Except in crises, it called for no duties beyond an all-expense-paid trip to Columbia for a banquet or a formal occasion. Franklin J. Moses, Jr., was in actual executive command of the militia as adjutant, inspector, and adjutant general all in one.

The one and only time Delany did ask Gov. Scott for a patronage appointment was like his application to President Grant for the Liberia post. His timing was off. The election was over. Delany applied to Scott for appointment as jury commissioner of Charleston County in March 1871, an extremely low-scale post in the patronage pay and ladder. There was a vacancy for the job, and Delany wrote:

> I am in hopes that your Excellency will give me this little appointment, as I have never received any remunerative position at the hands of your Excellency, and this will pay something, and thus help to bear expenses till I can begin to make money by my Business, which it will not at all interfere with.

The result was that Scott himself nominated and the Senate approved appointment of Nathaniel T. Spencer, a white man, to the vacancy.

Delany's political influence among the freedmen did receive some slight recognition in December 1870 when the General Assembly met in joint session to elect the first U.S. Senator since readmission of South Carolina into the Union. Neither House had awarded any nominee a majority, and it required a joint session to elect Thomas Jefferson Robertson, wealthiest white "scalawag" in the state, to the six-year term beginning March 4, 1871. However, there were only three blacks nominated in the balloting and Col. M. R. Delany was one of them.

The second U.S. Senator to be elected was also a white, Frederick A. Sawyer, a native of Massachusetts, but a highly respected teacher who had come to Charleston in 1856 and therefore was not considered a carpetbagger. Sawyer is credited with the remark, "The Negroes in office in South Carolina were honest men until the white men seduced them."

Before the Republican state convention on July 26 to nominate candidates for the state election, Delany spoke up publicly and vehemently in a demand that his "quota" system for black representation be observed. He demanded, and was publicly supported in it, "a colored Lieutenant Governor, and two colored men in the House of Representatives (Congress) and one in the Senate, and our quota of State and county offices." Strangely enough, his demand was met in all respects except the election of Robertson and Sawyer. Alonzo J. Ransier was elected lieutenant governor with Scott in a contest with the white candidates of the new Union Reform party. Three of the four Congressmen were blacks, including Delany's particular friend, Rev. Richard H. Cain, a Wilberforce graduate from Ohio who was later to become a Congressman and a bishop in the AME Church. It was Cain who, in 1872, persuaded Delany to become an active politician, something he had avoided for two years. Until the Moses campaign of 1872 Delany made his ever popular speeches on the potential of his race in South Carolina and in Africa, and he endorsed several applications to Gov. Scott for political appointments, but his time and effort were devoted to earning a living. Delany was now a businessman in Charleston.

He had set up offices in the Fire Proof Building at Meeting and Chalmers streets as a real estate agent, "note broker," and Notary Public. One of his advertisements described his services as follows: "Lands, plantations and city property bought and sold. Money negotiated on Notes with good security by endorsement, or Mortgage on Real Estate and other vouchers. All transactions at this office strictly reliable and honorable, as no other will be entertained. Northern Capitalists desiring to secure Real Estate in South Carolina, by purchase or mortgage on such property will do well by first consulting this office."

The wisdom of also adding his references to the advertisement is highly questionable. Their composition reflects the black and white leadership of the state, all Republicans, but it was chiefly the white Democrats who needed brokers for such transactions. They owned the land.

> He is permitted to refer to Gov. R. K. Scott; Hon. S. D. Bryan, U.S. District Judge; Hon. F. J. Moses, Chief Justice Supreme Court; Hon. J. J. Wright, Associate Justice Supreme Court; Hon. F. L. Cardozo, Sec'y of State; Hon. D. H. Chamberlain, Attny. Genl.; Hon. G. Pillsbury, Mayor (Charleston); S. G. Trott, Postmaster; Wm. Whaley, Esq. Messrs. Whaley, Mitchel & Clancy (attorneys).

After all of Delany's experience with the Freedmen's Bureau and the Bureau of Agricultural Statistics, no doubt it was a logical kind of business for him. He was to return to the practice of medicine some years later, but the opportunities for a physician were nil in 1870. The freedmen could not pay a black doctor for his services.

Delany was far from successful in this business venture. The times were totally out of kilter for anyone dealing in money or deriving an income from cash or credit transactions. The financial shenanigans by northern capital, which were to culminate in the failure of the impregnable Jay Cooke & Co. in 1873 and bring on that particular depression, were already under way.

In South Carolina particularly a goodly proportion of land and other transactions were being held in abeyance until its Supreme Court ruled on the key case of *Calhoun* v *Calhoun* relating to indebtedness from the sale or purchase of slaves prior to the Emancipation Proclamation. This case, dating from an 1854 transaction, was a test of the Constitution of 1868 by which all such debts were declared null and void in South Carolina. The decisive opinion was rendered by Chief Justice Franklin J. Moses, Sr., of the South Carolina Supreme Court on April 5, 1871, and there was weeping and wailing throughout the state. Moses had agreed with the lower courts that Section 34, Article 4, of the new South Carolina Constitution, since it did not contravene the Constitution of the United States, was a valid and legal action by the duly elected authority of the state. Indebtedness due to slave transactions was not collectible. Thus, finally and for all time, not only was the black extinct for the status of chattel property, but the entire structure of mortgaging and credit agreements based on the blacks as a monetary asset was destroyed. Many planters and merchants held worthless paper and required a new credit structure.

There just was no cash, except from the North, and very few of the blacks had any of it. The freedmen who did and could heed the calls to thrift through the Freedmen's Savings & Trust Company endorsed by Gen. Howard and every black spokesman North and South, were few and far between. Their deposits of pennies, for all 400,000 of them in the state was, at its highest, $320,937 in the Beaufort and Charleston branches. They lost even that when the bank became insolvent in 1872, due to its white financial advisers in New York. Most of these savings had been sweated out of the soil in order to purchase land. Delany could no longer expect them to patronize him.

Thus South Carolina was in the situation where lands for sale—good, productive lands—were available at low cash prices. There were uncounted thousands of freedmen whose only objective in life was to own that land. The wall between the two complementary needs was cash. As he had five years before, Delany tried to break down that wall. He proposed that northern individuals or philanthropic societies finance, *on a loan basis*, the purchase of ten acres of land for each qualifying freedman. His ambitious quota was 80,000 self-sufficient, proud, and happy black families. The figure was arrived at by averaging five to a family of the 400,000 blacks in South Carolina. His entire plan was well expressed in a letter to Sen. Henry Wilson of Massachusetts who had been most active in Congress in behalf of the Civil Rights Acts.

> I would call the attention of the philanthropic capitalists to this suggestion, which would benefit both black and white, and amply secure themselves in the capital invested. . . . There is at present an abundance of surplus lands in this State, which could be purchased at such a figure as to enable the purchaser to dispose of them to the freedmen at an average advance of fifty percent on the original purchase money, and then be fully within their reach to meet with all their contingencies, such as improving and stocking their little farms. . . . What the freedman wants is land of his own, with time to pay for it. What the land owner wants is cash for his surplus lands . . . I am continually being called upon by gentlemen who are willing to sell lands at the lowest figure, to secure such homes to the freedmen, because they know that it would be mutually beneficial to themselves, the freedmen and the commonwealth at large.

This was the proposal of the Constitutional Convention of 1868, to ask that the freedmen be helped to buy lands by Congressional appropriation. Delany's revision was that it be made a private enterprise with every chance of multiple benefit among the entrepreneurs, the landowners, and the freedmen. His letter was printed in the *Charleston News* and had such impact that he continued the series under the title "Homes for Freedmen," which was published in pamphlet form in 1871.

In the second of the series, Delany raised a pertinent question for those days and years of corruption. Why should those who are destitute, such as the freedmen, care much what their elected officials did with tax revenues if they themselves paid none?

> Land in South Carolina is greatly depreciated, while taxes have become proportionably (*sic*) higher. These taxes are mainly paid by a very few of the citizens, as the great majority own little or no real estate, paying little else than the simple capitation tax. . . . By securing homes to the homeless, it

> must be effected by the much desirable division of lands, and by this division of lands, a division of the taxes, the source of the public revenue. . . .
>
> Let the people then—those now homeless—generally become freeholders, possessors of the land, with improved real estate, and they at once become proportionably interested in all the affairs of the State, and they, who are the principal voters, will see to it that reckless and incompetent men will not be sent a second time to misrepresent them and the interests of the State.

Delany made just as good sense in the last letter of the series in which he dealt with the permanent social as well as monetary values of providing "the possession of fixed homes, owned in fee simple by the laboring classes, once slaves."

He used the new German immigrant as an example of "the best agriculturalist to be found." The reason was because he was intelligent, he was educated, his children were provided schools, "and learn to read, write and cipher."

> The freedmen too, must be educated, but it will be impossible to establish facilities for education till they become settled and fixed in neighborhoods. It would be a waste of time and money to build school houses and make other outlays for such purposes where there is no certainty of the people remaining beyond one planting season. And to expect the same development from the freed people as other citizens, without the same kind of facilities for moral, intellectual and religious culture, is to expect an impossibility.

Without such facilities for the freedmen, as a "social and political element to the society," Delany argued, they would become "a curse instead of a blessing. But before either the church or schoolhouse can be erected, the people themselves must be settled in *homes of their own.*"

There were many reactions but no concrete results from Delany's well-conceived plan for social and fiscal health in South Carolina. For one thing, there were no "capitalists" in the North philanthropic enough to be satisfied with a mere 7 percent interest on their money invested in homestead mortgages in South Carolina, not when they could make an overnight killing on state or state-guaranteed "paper" through Howard Kimpton right in New York. Not that the money men hesitated to invest in South Carolina. They poured the financing into the newly discovered phosphate deposits along the rivers of the low country and employed black labor. But homes for blacks in order to stabilize the state? Delany was confusing the social with the profit motive, the long-term investment with speculation. As the bankruptcies of 1873 were to show, American capital at that time had no social purpose whatsoever. The Gerrit Smiths and Tappan brothers of anti-slavery years were no more, and none took their places.

However, by 1871, when Delany proposed "Homes for Freedmen," the twin revolt of white against black and of both races against the highly organized corruption under Gov. Scott had just begun. Delany was involved in both.

Among the whites, there were three approaches to the problem of returning the Negroes to their subordinate position. There was violence against them and the Klan rode openly and brazenly. They not only killed, beat, and burned out blacks but intimidated white officials who were impartial in their treatment of blacks and whites. As an example, in April 1871, the following was sent to Gov. Scott:

> General Order No. 97
> KKK, Fairfield County
> Attention: John Martin
>
> Patience has ceased to be a virtue. Beware. Beware. Once said, done. You are ordered to resign your office at once or in ten days you will be visited.
>
> By order of the Grand Chief A.D. Secretary, KKK
>
> *Take heed while you have the chance and shun the penalty.*

Gov. Scott received this from Fairfield County Commissioner John N. Martin. It accompanied his resignation.

The Klan was operating openly until the fall of 1871 when Gov. Scott persuaded President Grant to suspend *habeas corpus* rights in nine counties, and hundreds of whites were arrested. But very few were ever punished after extended trials.

But the Klan was unnecessary in the strategy of the white Democrats in driving black voters out of the polls or the state.

All localities had their armed whites to terrorize the blacks. John B. Hubbard, the Chief Constable of the state, on September 21, 1870, reported to Gov. Scott about the preparations for the coming elections.

> I am satisfied that a complete organization exists from the Savannah river to Chester, a distance of nearly two hundred miles in length, and embracing and including all the counties above Edgefield, and that its object is to intimidate Republican voters on Election Day, and if necessary murder leading Republicans. I learn also that large numbers of the citizens of Georgia and North Carolina are employed for the purpose of coming into this State just before the Election, with the object of voting and aiding this organization. I have learned also that five thousand Winchester rifles have been shipped to the upper country within the last month from one firm in this city (Columbia).

Either the blacks did not scare easily on that Election Day 1870, or the mobilization of the black militia throughout the state negated the imported and native white armies, because Scott was re-elected by a comfortable margin of some 34,000 votes, and his black running mate, Lt. Gov. Alonzo J. Ransier, beat his opponent, former Confederate General Matthew C. Butler, by approximately the same margin. This result caused the white Democrats to begin their campaign of disarming the blacks.

A second white strategy against the black majority was largely Democratic in participation, but under another name. In fact, Daniel H. Chamberlain, Scott's attorney general, and later Republican governor, was a member of the Taxpayers' Convention held in Columbia in May 1871.

This was a curious gathering of a handful of blacks, some carpetbaggers and scalawags, but chiefly what one speaker described as "the representative men of the once glorious old State of South Carolina." By that he meant the "old family" as well as propertied wealth of the state. Butler and another former Confederate General, Martin S. Gary, were prime movers in the convention and were also the state's lobbyists in the pay of a syndicate of speculators in New York engaged in manipulating South Carolina bonds.

This convention was an effort to recruit all elements against the black majority behind legislation that would give the state a proportional, representative form of balloting thus guaranteeing the whites a minimum of one third of the state legislature, if not more. Often expressed was the belief that taxation should dictate representation, or a reverse of the slogan, No representation without taxation. The hand of paternal friendship was held out to the blacks who, after all, did the best they could, the taxpayers said.

> The newly enfranchised were not only jealous of their acquired liberty, but suspicious of the feeling and intentions of their late owners. They were ignorant of political affairs, totally uninstructed in the science of government, and naturally turned to the men who had flocked here as birds of prey. It was equally natural for the native, respectable and intelligent white people who had heretofore controlled affairs, to feel a supreme disgust, and to hold themselves aloof from this mass of ignorance and vice.

However, this hand of friendship extended to the blacks, was never clasped. The memory of slavery was too recent and the annual haggle over work contracts too bitter to trust the whites. The Taxpayers' Convention had no influence whatsoever in reducing the black vote for any and all Republican candidates.

A third appeal by the whites lay in accentuating the extent of the governmental fraud in hopes that the blacks could be brought into a "reform" movement. In this effort, the whites were aided by the state government itself, from Gov. Scott on. Kimpton's correspondence with Gov. Scott (and all the later governors) shows that the "take" was pretty extensive. As early as January 13, 1869, one letter begins with an offer of "time drafts for yourself" of between $15,000 and $20,000. The same letter concludes, "Your note due 20th will be paid."

In organizing the internal state graft Scott had imported some hometown friends from Napoleon, Ohio, and they saw to it that the money was properly channeled. But the attitude of the blacks toward the widely known frauds which were emphasized daily in the press was that anything was preferable to a return to the Black Code, which was a certainty if the black majority was not sustained.

An example of local self-government that eventually caused

Delany the worst difficulty he encountered in his life—a question of his integrity—came to Gov. Scott from Charleston County in 1872. It was an unsigned petition.

> We pen this note knowing you to be a friend of the coloured people. You always did attend to our rights when you was a general and we chose you to be our Governor on that account. We have been working for the County for the past nine months and during all that time we never received any money except from the store we took provisions from. Mr. Sherman told us that he has to charge us 20 cents on every dollar as he has to pay the county commissioners 10 cents on each dollar and he had to make 10 cents for the loan of this money. We don't find fault with the store man needing something but we do find fault with the county commissioners who has been elected by our votes, charging 10 cents on the dollar out of our labor. The store man say he would not charge us any percentage on our groceries. Now then, if we had the money, if he had to pay the county commissioners 10 cents on the dollar on our groceries, I don't see why we can't get our money and buy our own things. This is just what the Democrats promised the Republicans would do to us. We don't believe all this as we know how these people treated us in former times. We believe there has been some bad men put in office but we know you to be a friend of ours, and we thought we would write you how we have been treated to see if you could do something for us. We would sign our names to this but we are afraid we would be removed and get no work.

Needless to say, the Charleston County commissioners did not change their ways and, in fact, stole so much that eventually the county's warrants were repudiated, just as the state's bonds were, and Delany personally experienced the financial loss.

By that year 1872 Delany himself had had enough. He allowed his friend Rev. Cain to persuade him that a reform movement was imperative if the blacks were to retain equality in the state. He also persuaded Delany to accept membership on the Republican State Committee of which Cong. Robert B. Elliot was chairman. Delany made his decision early, for on January 24,

1872, he sent in his resignation as lieutenant colonel to Gov. Scott.

As ever, once he had adopted a course he did not hesitate. He sailed into action against the Scott clique which was backing a man for governor respected and admired by Delany for his work as State Superintendent of Education, Reuben Tomlinson. He had been one of the few state officials never tied in with any "pay-off." On the other hand, Delany had to go along with the reform movement, and his candidate for governor was none other than Franklin J. Moses, Jr., the "reformed" reformer. Moses was to prove to be a less skillful but far more hungry crook than Scott and Chamberlain combined.

But there was one compensation for Delany. In the campaign of 1872 he had as his candidate for lieutenant governor none other than Richard H. Gleaves, his fellow Freemason who had helped found St. Cyprian's Lodge in Pittsburgh so many years before. Gleaves had come to South Carolina after the war and entered into business with Robert Smalls at Beaufort.

The issues of the campaign were clearly stated by Rev. Cain in his Charleston newspaper, the *Missionary Record.*

> This government of South Carolina is in the hands of white men, placed there by colored men's votes, and they control everything in the State. If there is stealing being done, they do it; if there is robbery of the State of its millions, it is not the Negro who does these things. If there have been over-issues of bonds for any purpose, we tell the country that no Negro has had any hand in this matter; the Legislature passed laws authorizing the issuing of certain amounts of bonds to meet the liabilities of the State. If there are over-issues the State officers who control the matter have done the wrong to the country and the people of this State.
>
> The colored population are as poor today as ever they were, so far as the State bonds has anything to do with their augmented wealth. These facts suggest to the people a new Capital and new Departure here. With the credit of the State gone and the Treasury empty, with the report of frauds in the issue of bonds, with the reputation of the class of men who now guide affairs, is it not the duty of the people to rise up in their might and cast off the present incubus and select

another class of men to guide the State? There must be a change, there must be a uniting of all honest men of every class and race in the State for the maintenance of honest government. These public servants proving to be false in trust must be put out of power and honest men put in their places. There are honest men in both parties who can agree to put down the wholesale robbery of the people, and it is plainly their duty to unite for this great object.

This was the classic campaign of 1872 made famous five years later by the Congressional Fraud Commission whose hearings elicited a shocker with every witness. Delany was one of those witnesses. He had been in Columbia to confer with Cong. Elliot on election strategy and thereby became involved in the incident. John J. Patterson, known as "Honest John," was the most blatantly dishonest of all the white carpetbaggers. He became U.S. Senator from South Carolina, not solely by vote of the state legislature, but by its purchase. He openly revealed that, aside from wine, women, and song in a huge mansion near the State Capitol in Columbia, he offered and paid $40,000 for his seat in the Senate. His opposition was Gov. Scott and Elliot, the latter by far the most dangerous because of his excellent Congressional record and the fact that he was black. "Honest John" had plenty of cash because he was one of the key men in both the Blue Ridge and the Columbia and Greenville Railroad raids. And so he tried to buy Elliot out of the contest. Delany testified before the Fraud Commission:

Major M. R. Delany being duly sworn, deposes on oath as follows:

"My name is Martin R. Delany. I reside in Charleston. My occupation is Trial Justice. I was in Columbia in 1872 at the time of the election of Col. John J. Patterson to the United States Senate. I was then a member of the Republic(an) State Executive Committee of which Gen. R. B. Elliot was chairman. I remember on one occasion at the building where the Executive Committee rooms were at the time, that Gen. John B. Dennis remarked to Elliot that he could get a large sum of money and named some ten thousand or fifteen thousand dollars, perhaps twenty thousand dollars, I do not now recall the amount, if Elliot

> would withdraw from the contest in Patterson's favor for the United States Senate. Elliot became very angry and swore about it, and I had to interpose to quiet him. I think there would have been a serious difficulty and perhaps bloodshed about it."

The voting at the 1872 election was low but Moses won handily. Gleaves proved an even more popular vote-getter than Moses, for he received nearly 500 more votes than the gubernatorial total.

It had been a particularly dirty campaign, even for South Carolina. With the exception of Tomlinson himself, neither side had any genuine intent to reform or even reduce the corruption. At their respective conventions the regular Republican and the so-called true Republican political machines took over. The latter party was the one through which the Democrats and the taxpayers' associations operated. Both were anti-Scott as well as opposed to each other. And each intended to take command of the loot.

Curiously, before the conventions, there was a genuine reform movement begun in Charleston and much of it was based on Delany's "Homes for Freedmen" political plan. A group of blacks formed a Young Men's Progressive Association and won support among the freedmen by basing their program on Delany's plan. In an appeal "To the Colored Men of South Carolina," written under the pen name of "Kush," they repeated Delany's demand for 80,000 homesteads, within the next two years.

> By putting good men in office, black and white, such as we want and must have to carry out this measure, the land for these rural homesteads can be purchased at such a low rate, as to enable the freedmen to live, and pay off the entire cost of each farm in four years from the date of purchase.
>
> The State must purchase the land, and give the people time to pay for it. The time desired is only four years, and this can easily be accomplished by the plans and measures which we have already devised, the leading features of which may be seen in Delany's letters on "Homes for the Freedmen. . . ."

In a militant statement of condemnation of the whites in state government, "Kush" declared, "The first duty of any race of people is to see to their own interests specially, and after that the interest of others. This is what white people do." Before they were elected to office, he continued, the whites made "loud and big promises to the freedmen . . . then did not one single thing for the blacks, but managed so as to have everything done for themselves." The whites had made the same promises in 1870.

> We were willing to give them a fair trial, and as you know at the last voting for State officers, re-elected them. And what do we see?
>
> Why, they have done not a thing for the blacks, and worse for the State than they did before; and now swear that they do not care for us; and have the brazen impudence to say, that they will be elected again, in spite of any opposition that can be brought against them by intelligent, honest men of our own race. That they "can buy the majority of ignorant niggers with fair promises, and their plantation leaders with a little money."

These were the sentiments expressed so often by Delany, the most recent having been the letter in the *New National Era* which drew lengthy response from Frederick Douglass. But we do not know how much Delany had to do with the entire pamphlet by "Kush." Its full title was "The Political Battle Axe for the Use of the Colored Men of the State of South Carolina in the Year 1872."

Another result of the early reform movement in Charleston was the proposal that the two blacks of most unblemished character in the state be nominated for office. They chose Francis L. Cardozo as their candidate for governor and Martin R. Delany for secretary of state. But the Republican machine decided otherwise, nominating Cardozo for treasurer and eliminating Delany. At the state convention in Columbia on August 21 Delany was the only black among the five candidates for governor to be nominated. But, of course, he was quickly dropped. The regular Republicans knew that their party would be over with an honest black governor.

Delany collected a great deal of abuse during the Moses campaign and, strangely, much of it came from the *Beaufort Republican*, a newspaper influenced by William J. Whipper, representative in the House of Representatives of the state and husband of Delany's biographer. The two had known each other long before either thought of South Carolina. They had met in January 1863 at the Michigan State Convention of Colored Men in Ypsilanti where Delany made a speech and Whipper was an active member of the business committee. In South Carolina, though, the two never saw eye to eye.

Early in the campaign, the *Beaufort Republican* began a continuing attack on Delany, right after the August convention nominating Moses. On September 5, 1872, the newspaper endorsed Tomlinson and added:

> The "loudest" Moses man in the State is Major M. R. Delany. He has been in Beaufort trying to collect money to carry on the campaign. He told a friend of ours that $10,000. had to be paid to the *Columbia Union* for its support of Moses. Our Moses men will find use for all the money they have during the campaign in this County, and feel little disposed to start Delany in business. He didn't pay expenses.

The Moses political strategy was to depend on the black majority and therefore Delany was extremely important to him. And the reverse was true. Moses' strategy, or at least one element of it, was extremely important to Delany. It was idle and fruitless to talk about his homestead plan so long as the state's depleted financial condition existed. If its currently due bond issues were being defaulted and commanded losses as high as 75 percent on redemption, how in the world could the state hope to finance so large a capital investment as 80,000 homesteads?

Besides, the stench from the Land Commission operations, begun by the first legislature, fouled the financial picture, too. A total of $746,724.07 had been spent on the purchase of 104,078 acres, about twice as much as had been authorized. That would have been all right however, if the land was useful for anything. It consisted of "sandhill, swamp and otherwise" at an average of $7 an acre unloaded by planters who paid off the Land Commissioner, Robert C. DeLarge, a black. That was the sum total of the effort made by 1872 in the direction of homesteading.

Moses' plan and promise to the blacks was *more taxes*. This would seem suicidal for a politician, but not for South Carolina. He proposed an additional 3 mills levied on property and, since almost all land was owned by the whites, such a tax would be no burden to the landless blacks. In other words, politically Moses would lose no votes since the landed whites were Democrats anyway. Such an additional tax, assigned to payment of interest on South Carolina bonds, would go far toward gaining acceptance of a new bond issue to finance a homestead plan.

That is why Delany worked so hard for Moses, to the neglect and practical dissolution of his business. That is why he was sent to New York by the Republicans in October, to determine whether or not the financiers would cooperate with such a plan. There he learned from Kimpton the depth of the morass into which Scott had plunged the state's credit. It was a disheartening experience for him, but Delany also knew that the prevailing winds of the Sea Islands, erratic as they may be, were still more constant than the bond market. Today's catastrophe could be tomorrow's bonanza. If that additional tax were inviolably tagged for homesteads, they could be financed.

The *Beaufort Republican* again analyzed Delany's activities as sinister. It wrote: "A vote for Moses means a special tax to pay interest on the fraudulent bonds which he voted to validate. His emissary Delany is in New York collecting money from the holders of these fraudulent bonds to help elect Moses."

When the *Charleston News,* definitely pro-Moses, approved the plan, the Beaufort newspaper again aimed at Delany.

> The *Charleston News* (Moses) strives to convince taxpayers that its candidate is in favor of repudiating six or seven millions of the State bonds issued by Scott and Parker, and made valid by the votes of Moses and the men who nominated him.
>
> M. R. Delany (also for Moses) is in New York trying to convince the holders of these very bonds that his chief is in favor of paying the interest on the bonds at the earliest date; that he will, if elected, order a special tax laid for that purpose in accordance with the provisions of the Validating Bill, and that he is in favor of paying the principal at maturity.
>
> Which of these two advocates are we to believe? Neither of them are worthy of much notice as they are both paid

> to say what they do say, and both would say just the contrary for the same inducement.
>
> Delany is trying to raise a fund out of the timid bond holders to help elect his chief, while *The News* hopes to get a slice of the public printing next winter. The people of Charleston have just as much respect for one as the other.

The fact was that Moses knew Delany too well to assign campaign fund-raising to him. Nor was Delany necessary for that purpose. It was his reputation for honesty that Moses needed in New York, as well as in South Carolina. It was his appearance as the symbol of the black majority that would guarantee his victory for which Moses needed Delany. As it turned out, Moses had many and varied methods of raising campaign money, all of them nefarious.

After the Moses victory, Delany learned about politics in still another way. He learned that the only man he could trust was himself. There was no additional millage to help the homestead plan. There was no change in Howard Kimpton's operations in New York except that the pay-off was to Moses instead of Scott. There was no change at all in the corruption except that Moses stole more openly than Scott had or Chamberlain was to.

The future was apparent within a few days after Moses was inaugurated. He attempted to steal $25,000 from the state deposits, but now Cardozo was treasurer and caught him. Cardozo was so infuriated that he immediately sought court action against Moses, knowing that impeachment would be impossible with so many members of the legislature in one form of graft or another. Moses, by exercise of his executive powers, was fully able to halt any court proceedings against him. It did not matter because Moses had many other sources of illicit revenue. He extended the pardon racket, initiated by Trescot five years before, into the penal system and practically emptied the state penitentiary—at a price for each pardon. During his two years, and aside from directing judges in criminal cases, Moses issued 457 pardons to those convicted and serving sentences. As a going-away present to himself during the last month of his term, Moses sold 46 pardons.

As for himself, Delany was broke. His business was gone. He had to earn a living and he went in person to the Collector of

Customs in Charleston to beg a job, any job. He was given a low-paying clerical job under Federal, not state, patronage. He was a bitter man in 1872 and thereafter, not only because he had sacrificed in a false cause but because his hopes for his people were deteriorating from that time on. Delany did not complain, however, although his friends did. The following letter by his friend Rev. Richard H. Cain is a more graphic complaint than any other.

Columbia, S.C. May 8th, 1873

To his Excellency
Gov. F. J. Moses, Jr.
Dear Sir:

Your precious time and arduous duties are so pressing that I cannot intrude upon you in person to express my impressions and desires. I therefore drop you these few lines hoping that the same respectful consideration which you have always accorded me in person, may be awarded to my written communication. Dear Sir, we have ever been the best of friends since we first met in your office in Sumpter (*sic*) in 1866. I have reposed confidence in you—and whatever promises made to me. You will remember the mutual pledges made between us prior to your nomination for Governor relative to Charleston appointments. I do not ask you to do anything that would embarres (*sic*) your administration, or make the appointment of a man, who would do harm by his appointment. I have felt much concern about my friend Delany and my pledges to him made, before he consented to abandon his opposition to your nomination for Governor. It was principly (*sic*) on my personal representations to him and my declarations, that you had been grossly malined (*sic*) and misrepresented by those men who sought your defeat that I brought him over from the opposition—believing what I stated relative to your honorably maintaining our rights, and keeping your pledges made to the Colored men who would stand by you. He became your advocate, and our mutual friend. I had assured him on the honor of a gentleman that you would not brake (*sic*) faith, he has consistently held on while all others have declared to him, that you would not give him an appointment nor keep faith with me in his behalf. I do hope, Sir, that you may disappoint those who thus traduce you. Permit me to say, that it is certainly impolitic to break faith with friends, it is dangerous however insignificant they may be, it would be better to have one unwise officer than to have a thousand of his friends against you in the future. Gov. Scott broke faith with those who served him most faithfully, and when the time came none would trust him. I hope Sir you will not make his mistake. Keep this promise and if he proves inefficient, remove him and you throw on him the blame, and disprove those who are now, or may be in the future, too ready to find a flaw against your Re-Election of further advancement Gov. Col. Delany's condition is a needy one and he has staked all on *your word;* for heavens sake do not cast him away. He has many strong friends, who sympathize with him, and desire to see him placed where he may render the state some services while he makes a living for his wife and children you know doubtless what it is to be without money, without friends, without a position, with pressing necessities. I appeal to your generous nature, to your Honorable pledges made to him to me and to others. Do not permit other considerations less potent prevent you doing a simple act of justice, to those who have done much to serve you in the past and are ready to do so in the future. Dear Sir, you will pardon this seeming importunity on my part. Nothing but the unbounded regard and confidence in your noble and generous consideration would have prompted me to venture this freedom, with the highest consideration for your Excellency, and the complete and triumphat (*sic*) success of your Administration, I remain your Obt. Servt

R. H. Cain

Perhaps the most amazing result of Delany's first venture into politics was his rebound. As soon as he realized that not he nor any other black man would benefit from another of the regular Republican party operations, he began his four-year labor of fighting that political machine, both internally and externally, state-wide and nationally.

A lesser man might have given up. But not Delany. He began his preparations for 1874 immediately after his victimization of 1872.

CHAPTER TWENTY-TWO

The "Black Prophet"

The lessons learned by Delany from the state and national elections of 1872 were to dictate his course in 1874 and alienate him from most of the black leadership in South Carolina.

Essentially, it was a bitter lesson learned by each political generation, that while the brand names may remain the same in political parties, the product changes. The magic of "Republicanism" remained, but the content did not and, by 1872, its differences with the label "Democratic" had become largely a matter of personnel rather than platform. It was the Grant versus Greeley campaign for the presidency that taught Delany and a handful of others that the black majority in South Carolina must break out of the web of the past. The Republicanism of the past was born of dissent, had accomplished its limited objectives, and now trapped both the blacks and the whites. None expressed the change better than the Congressman who had brought the impeachment charges against President Johnson, James M. Ashley of Ohio. In a campaign speech for Greeley in Toledo in 1872 he declared:

> Fellow-citizens, this presidential canvass is unlike any in our history. Greeley, who was nominated at Cincinnati by the old Abolitionists, and in fact by a new party, which in their national convention, they called the "Liberal Republican Party" has been nominated as you know, by the regular national Democratic convention at Baltimore, and thus Greeley, who never was a Democrat, is made the Democratic candidate, and General Grant, who was all his life a regular Bourbon Democrat, and never a Republican, until after he was nominated by that party for President, is a candidate of the machine Republicans. From a philosophical standpoint,

> and as I look at the situation, this unprecedented condition of national affairs, is not bad for the nation, nor for the people, however undesirable it may be for the machine politician, or the office-holder and office-seeker.

In 1874, as a dissenter from machine Republicanism, Delany too had the "machine politician" and the officeholder against him. But the reasons for the birth of the liberal Republican party nationally in 1872 and in South Carolina in 1874 were identical. Ashley said:

> I do not believe that General Grant is a corrupt or bad meaning man, as many of our blind partisans charge, but I do believe that the corrupt rings, which now dominate and control his administration, must be driven from power. . . . In an unfortunate hour, to prevent our opponents from taking this man, who never belonged to our party, we took Grant and elected him; and one of his first acts was the selection of a Cabinet that was a surprise and an offense to the American people. With an exception or two he has continued in the same course until he has surrounded himself with men who have been a trouble and a disgrace to the nation. Not one of the Cabinet ministers—save the Secretary of the Interior, and his affairs have not been examined into—but has been convicted of a violation of the law.

That did not differ an iota from South Carolina's executive structure in 1874 and the man nominated by the machine politicians, to be elected by the black majority, was Daniel H. Chamberlain whose function under Gov. Scott had been that of attorney general, theoretically the legal watch-dog of the state! And Delany could have duplicated Ashley's final plea to the black:

> I appeal to every black man, not only here but everywhere in America. . . . Of the grand army of men who compose this Liberal Republican movement, you find four-fifths of all the men who, in the early struggle in forming the Republican party, constituted its advance guard, while the camp-followers and thieves, who came in afterward and took possession of it, were fighting us till victory was achieved.

The answer, nationally and in South Carolina, was to throw out the thieves. But then what? A new set of thieves, such as Moses introduced? Moses was a "reform" candidate and now Chamberlain was another. To Delany there was small choice and, in 1874, he believed that the problems of black Republicanism were far more fundamental than mere corruption.

In his thinking and writing, Delany maintained and argued consistently with Wright, Cain, Smalls, Elliot, Whipper—all of the black leadership—that, in politics, property rules. He revived Elizur Wright's famous and impatient comment in the *Boston Commonwealth* of 1867 demanding confiscation of land for the freedmen.

> O ye mighty "practical" men! don't you know—are you not sensible—does it not enter your noodles to suspect—that if you have thirty thousand disloyal nabobs to own more than half the land of the South, they, and nobody else, will *be* the South? That they laugh, now in their sleeves, and bye-and-bye will laugh out of their sleeves, at your school-ma'ams and ballot-boxes? *They who own the real estate of a country control its vote.*

The black leadership did not agree with him. The black people would never desert the Republican party and their only danger lay, not in the maladministration they had elected for the third time but in the growth of the white population and reduction in black voting. Immigration was implementing the first and intimidation the latter. Delany persisted in arguing that the black majority vote was transitory so long as it disregarded program, that even collaboration with the most die-hard Democrat was preferable if a fundamental need, such as a valid homestead plan, could be realized by working with the whites.

Not even Joseph H. Rainey, who served four terms in Congress, agreed with that and answered an attack by a white New York Democrat in the 42d Congress with the statement, "We are republicans by instinct, and we will be republicans so long as God will allow our proper senses to hold sway over us."

In the same speech Rainey pointed out that, in Congress at least, the Democrats showed their political attitudes.

> Now you come to us and say that you are our best friends . . . But your votes, your actions, and the constant culti-

> vation of your cherished prejudices prove to the Negroes of the entire country that the Democrats are in opposition to them, and if they (the Democrats) could have sway our race would have no foothold here.

Delany had greater foresight than Rainey, perhaps because the U.S. Congress is no place to plan ahead longer than two years. Delany saw that the North, whether Democrat or Republican, was no longer interested in the blacks. They were a nuisance. They were free, weren't they? There had never been any intention of making them equal, too. Let the blacks in the South get back to shipping cotton north and quit interfering with white men's affairs. By then Stevens was dead, Sumner was ill, and there was nobody in Congress to stir the country's conscience. Rainey was a black man, and when he talked about the black majority in South Carolina, he showed his political naivete. A white majority would never act that way.

> Sir, I ask this House, I ask the country, I ask white men, I ask Democrats, I ask Republicans whether the Negroes have presumed to take improper advantage of the majority they hold in that State by disregarding the interest of the minority? They have not . . . You cannot point me to a single act passed by our Legislature, at any time, which had a tendency to reflect upon or oppress any white citizen of South Carolina. You cannot show me one enactment by which the majority in our State have undertaken to crush the white man because the latter are in a minority.

That was entirely true and among "practical" politicians, it proved nothing more than that the blacks were new at the game. They were not satisfied with orating about democracy, they practiced it. That black majority might continue in the vital statistics but not in votes, because of the unity of northern money and southern property.

There was another aspect of agreement between northern and southern whites. Both feared a black exodus from the South to the North. That was one reason Congress threw out the various Black Codes enacted in the rebel states with Johnson's encouragement. The whites of the North feared an influx of blacks from the peonage of the South. Emancipation had given the blacks freedom of movement now, and they did not even need an Underground Railroad. Conversely, the whites of the South feared such an exodus because they needed black labor. Some of them even protested Ku Klux Klan and other terrorist activities, except at election times, for fear of driving away their subservient labor.

In the early 1870s it was not a question whether the black majority would prop up Republicanism. It was only a question when they would realize that if they wished any part in government at all, they would switch from one group of whites to another, under any political label. That is why Hampton and Conner remained in the background, busily organizing white rifle clubs and awaiting *Der Tag*. That is why they ordered the Democrats to support Delany to the hilt in 1874.

Delany opened his campaign for fundamental political change among the blacks of South Carolina early in February 1874. He seized an opportunity to reply to a speech made in Columbia by his good friend Judge Jonathan J. Wright and what he wrote amounted to political heresy. However, being Martin R. Delany and known to owe no politico any favors, and having received none, he was given a wide hearing. Among the blacks he was considered a prophet of doom. To the whites he was the most thoughtful spokesman for his race. In fact, Johnson's provisional governor, Benjamin F. Perry remarked publicly in 1874: "I must say he has exhibited, in his speeches and addresses, more wisdom and prudence, more honor and patriotism, than any other Republican in South Carolina, white or black. I say this deliberately and after mature reflection."

In commenting on the fear that white immigration would once again put the black back under the white heel, a point discussed at Wright's meeting, Delany recalled that since 1866 he had been sounding that warning. He predicted that within five years the whites would be sufficiently numerous to become political challenges.

> I simply desire to say that this tide of emigration having now set in will go on to completion—that is, it will not cease till the white population in the State sufficiently outnumbers

> the blacks to secure to the whites the basis of a ruling element. . . . The object of the "Granges" or immigration movement in this State, as you very well know, is to neutralize the black ruling element, by reducing or exceeding its majority. And my candid opinion is that the whites in the South generally, and South Carolina in particular, prefer as agricultural, mechanical and laboring elements the blacks to the whites; and that this immigration scheme would never have been organized had they, from the past and present aspect of things, not been led to believe that we, the blacks, were influenced, controlled and led in our political notions without principle or a will of our own, and that so long as we outnumbered them, they would never get a chance to participate in the political affairs of the State.

Two years later, the election of 1876 was to present proof of Delany's warnings, for it was found that the black political majority could be whittled down by the white rifle clubs, making immigration unnecessary. But Delany raised the question in order to propose something which, had it been adopted, might have granted the blacks of South Carolina a share in their government to this day. He suggested:

> That, having prospectively lost the popular preponderance and consequent certainty of representation in all the departments of government, local, State and national, our only hope and chance of its future security is in the principle of cumulative voting, which secures minority representation as well as majority. Let our Legislature be wise enough now, while it is in the power of our race to do so, to take such measures as to secure, by constitutional amendment, the right of minority representation, which, while it immediately secures to the whites of the State, irrespective of party, a pro rata representation, or representation in proportion to numbers, it secures to the black race the same ratio of representation in counties where the whites have the majority, and when they shall preponderate in population in the State, which they most assuredly will, at no distant day.

This was Delany's first, and far from his last, call to his people to "Save what you can while you have the chance." The whites never intended, he continued, to allow the blacks to rule in giving them "liberty and equality of rights."

> And the blacks may as well know this at once; that there is no scheme that can be laid, no measure that may be entered into, nor expense so great, which they will not incur to change such a relation between the blacks and whites in this country. Rest assured of this, that there are no white people North or South who will submit to see the blacks rule over the whites in America. We may as well be plain and candid on this point, look each other in the face, and let the truth be known. Radicalism, as taught by political leaders for selfish motives and personal gain, has led the masses of our untutored race to believe otherwise, and act accordingly.

Delany's letter was widely reprinted, north and south, and editorial opinion on it depended on the political complexion of the periodical. The Democratic press generally recognized it as an indication "that the sympathies of the country were with the white minority of South Carolina." But Francis Warrington Dawson, the English-educated and politically ambivalent editor of the *Charleston News and Courier*, devoted a full column to commentary, and reprinted the entire letter. His editorial, under the heading "A Black Prophet," was also an attack on Judge Wright as an example of a black man who held public office solely because of his color, not his fitness.

> The letter of Maj. Delany is, however, a solemn warning to the people of his race—a warning which they may, to their sorrow, despise and disregard, as they have the arguments and entreaties of the White citizens of the State. They cannot hereafter complain that there was not one of their race who possessed the boldness and ability to expose their faults, and point out to them the edge of the precipice on which, in blind security, they stand.

Dawson agreed with Delany's point that in order to protect their own futures the blacks must grant the white minority some representation. He pointed out that a switch of ten or twelve thousand votes in a general election could take the government away from the blacks. And Dawson quite frankly expanded on Delany's emphasis on the abyss that separated the races.

> One statement is made by Maj. Delany, which will prove exceedingly unpalatable to the State officials and other centres of the Rings. There are, says he, "no white people, North nor South, who will submit to see the blacks rule over the whites in America." This is a profound truth. The instinct of race will assert itself, and, besides, the freedmen have proved, to the satisfaction of their best friends, that they cannot be trusted with absolute power in any Commonwealth. South Carolina stands to-day before the people of the Union a burning example of the extravagance and corruption which must prevail where the voting majority are so constituted that they fall an easy prey to Black rogues and white adventurers. The colored people must be protected in the enjoyment of their every privilege, but they will not be permitted to hold three hundred thousand white Americans in bondage, to make them their playthings which they may shatter at pleasure, to make them their prey whom they may rob and fleece as they will. There is no political question in this, as Maj. Delany knows. The issue is between intelligence and ignorance, honesty and rascality, and in this contest the sympathies of the country are with the minority in South Carolina, and not with the majority, whose crafty and unscrupulous leaders have swamped the State, brought disgrace on the National Republican party, and made the Columbia Rings a stench in the nostrils of all honest men.
>
> Maj. Delany will, doubtless, be soundly abused for talking plainly to his people, but he has done his duty, and can trust to time for the vindication that will surely come.

Change was in the South Carolina air. For the second time, the Union of Taxpayers' Leagues met and sent a delegation to see President Grant, to ask his intercession in ending the waste and corruption. But their visit was fruitless for the regular Republicans hurriedly met and sent another delegation to Grant to counter the complaints by the white men.

Through Cong. Robert B. Elliot the national Republican

party told the black majority of South Carolina in early February that their record was besmirching that of the entire party. Elliot made a speech in Columbia that the *New York Times* characterized as "Plain and Sensible Talk from a Colored Congressman" in its headline. He carried a warning from the national Republican leaders:

> They beseech us to rally, one and all, to the great work of restoring good government to South Carolina. They tell us in plain terms that our own safety depends on reform in our State affairs, in cutting off those who have proved unworthy of the trusts confided to their care, in recalling and reinstating honor and ability in our high places of public trust. They do not ask us to forsake the Republican Party, but rather to be true to that Party, to vindicate its fair name, to make it, as it is, the party of progress, of intelligence, of public economy, and good faith. They warn us that, unless the Republicans of South Carolina take heed to their way, purify their administration of public affairs, select upright officers, expend the public revenues for the public good, the national Republicans will no longer recognize them as members of that party, or permit them to affiliate with the national organization.

There were other threats and warnings, including one that was most prophetic, from the white carpetbagger E. W. M. Mackay of Charleston in July of that year. "Without a great change, in less than two years from now the Republican Party of this State will be dead. If we want to save it we must at once commence a fight against the band of thieves in our midst."

The Republican State Executive Committee met in July and agreed that "reform" would be the slogan for 1874. They admitted that was a demand of the national party. Immediately Daniel H. Chamberlain began to stump the state in search of delegates for his nomination. To most of the county Republicans, both those who were part of the corruption and those who remained honest, Chamberlain seemed a logical reform candidate. He had been out of office practicing law in Columbia for the past two years, usually another name for lobbying, but was in no way involved in the Moses scandals. He might even have been honest, after a fashion, although he did confess his involvement in the

Blue Ridge Railroad bond clean-up and was closest of all South Carolinians to Kimpton.

Another and much smaller group of blacks did not trust Chamberlain's sincerity at all. There were Cain and Rainey, Wright and Cardozo—but most of all—Delany. This handful of influential blacks that summer founded a number of Honest Government Leagues in most of the counties. These were Republican clubs directly in opposition to the regular Republican Union Leagues. Stressing the need for the blacks to clean house before the whites did it for them, the leagues had a certain influence, particularly in the cities. But even the machine Republicans knew it was time for a change. The Speaker of the House during the Moses administration, Samuel J. Lee from Aiken, himself not altogether pure, announced:

> We, as a people, are blameless of misgovernment. It is owing to bad men, adventurers, persons who, after having reaped millions almost from our party, turn traitors and stab us in the dark. Ingratitude is the worst of crimes, and yet the men we have fostered, the men we have elevated and made rich, now speak of our corruption and venality, and charge us with every conceivable crime.

There were two attitudes definite when the Republicans held their state convention in Columbia beginning on September 8. Moses would not be considered for re-election, and the platform would stress reform. Otherwise, through five stormy days of discussion, loyalty to the party as it was then constituted in the counties was a must, and therefore any fundamental change was not even considered.

In the balloting for nominations the battle for governor boiled down to Chamberlain and the highly esteemed native white, Judge John T. Green of Sumter, which the former won by a vote of 72 to 40, quite a decisive margin. Two blacks vied for the lieutenant governor nomination, two friends, the incumbent Richard H. Gleaves and Martin R. Delany. Gleaves won by a landslide of 97 to 11. But the vote came after a revolt from the opening day of the convention.

The rebellion began two nights later and it was then that Delany set the pattern of the coming campaign. An angry Cong. Rainey called a caucus of dissidents at the State House on September 10 and its circumstances thrust Delany to the front. A full report of the affair was made by the *Charleston News and Courier*, whose editor and co-owner, Francis Warrington Dawson, was a Hampton man (although secretly, since he was taking some of the Republican graft).

> The Republican caucus at the State House tonight was an escape valve for the surplus gas which the Committee on Credentials has so far succeeded in bottling during the sessions of the Convention. There was a large crowd in attendance, composed of delegates, State and Federal office holders, and a good sprinkling of colored residents of the city.

It must have been a riotous meeting. There was a call for Cong. Elliot, who was president of the State Executive Committee, but it was shouted down by a demand for Gov. Moses to answer some questions. Either Moses was not there or he sneaked out, for a committee was appointed to find him and bring him before the caucus. They soon returned with the report that Gov. Moses had disappeared. It was then that Rainey called on "Col. Martin R. Delany, the black Major."

According to Dawson's account, Delany began by warning his audience that they might not like what he had to say and "then supplemented this remark by a broad hint that he didn't care a cent whether it was acceptable or not."

> He intended to talk to his own race, to look men in the face and to call things by the right name. The black man had been purposely misled by the white politicians for selfish and interested motives. He warned the black men if they didn't stop in the course they had been led to pursue, they would be deprived of all political privileges which they now enjoyed. The colored people in South Carolina had a great and important duty to perform and the most important duty that they owed was to the white people of the State who are not in the Republican Party. The whites had the education, owned the land, and had the capital. The black man owned the labor, and it was easy to see that it was the interest of both races to go hand in hand together. This might not be called orthodox Republicanism, but it was sound political economy (cheers). He urged the black

men to take this matter into serious consideration. The Democrats, he said, were accustomed to regard the term Republican as a bugaboo, and Republicans on the other hand, had been taught to be frightened by mention of the word Democrat. It was all a mistake, Democracy and Republicanism were synonymous terms, both meant the right of the people to rule, the slaves were set at liberty by democratic teachings. He warned the Negroes of the mistake that they had made and impressed upon them the fact that they had nothing to hope from Grant unless they mended their ways and quit the evil practices that they had been led into by designing politicians. They need not be misled into the belief that Grant, who was a white man, loved the black man better than he did his own race. A war of races could only result in the extermination of the black race. He called their attention to the recent enactments of Congress, fixing an educational qualification for jurors in the United States Court, and to the failure of the Civil Rights Bill. These were significant facts, he said, and all pointed to the fact that unless the black race changed their course, all their political rights would eventually be curtailed. It was not a sufficient excuse that they were misled by men of another race who knew no better.

All in all, it was an eminently wise speech, and was very well received by his hearers, whose attention he managed to keep by an occasional reference to the Ku Klux.

Delany's frankness seemed to open the avenues of communication between the blacks who opposed the Republican machine and the whites who were not, as yet, Hampton men. They named themselves conservatives rather than Democrats, and the state was startled by an event without precedent in its history. On the night of September 21 there gathered in Military Hall in Charleston between 700 and 800 whites and blacks about evenly divided, with the sole purpose of acting in political concert. It was a meeting called by the Honest Government League of Charleston and it was here proposed that there be nominated a ticket for the coming elections composed half of white and half of black men. Their political affiliations were to be discarded and the only criterion for selection was unquestioned honesty. In recognition of the black majority and its attachment to the Republican label, the ticket should bear that in its name. Let the conservatives and Republicans differ as much as they pleased on platform, so long as they agreed on one plank—the election of honest men to office.

Delany was called upon to make the keynote speech which, Dawson reported, was "one of those sensible speeches so characteristic of the man."

He explained his attitude toward Chamberlain as one of "high esteem" but that, if elected, he would not be permitted to pursue an honest course.

"He was surrounded by the most infamous set of scoundrels that ever lived." But now that the Honest Government League existed, there was an entirely new day possible. It could not have been done years ago because blacks and whites did not trust each other. Now both were coming to the realization that there was an interdependence between black labor and white capital and that "it was manifestly to the interests of both races to fulfill the eternal fitness of things and go hand in hand together, to live on the very best terms with each other, without seeking to invalidate each others' rights." Delany continued that he had no thought of advising his people to fight white men.

> His advice was for the two races to stand side by side together, each conceding to the other what belongs to it, and working together for the good of the State. He did not ask the Democrats to become Republicans, nor to give up their political principles. He only asked them to throw aside their politics for the time and unite with honest Republicans in securing an honest State government.

If they did this, he predicted that at the next convention, "there would be no little ring in Columbia with a money-changing shop on the corner" to name the next governor.

About a week later, on October 1, there was still another occasion on which the blacks and the whites of Charleston could unite and discard their party affiliations. They demanded a fair election, no matter who won, and that signified the removal of the present election commissioners of Charleston County, all appointed by Moses to manipulate the up-coming count. The *News and Courier* reported that about 4,000 people crowded in front of City Hall that night. "The crowd was composed of white and colored citizens, and it was the most quiet, and at the same time, the most thoughtful and deliberate mass meeting that has been held in Charleston since the close of the war."

Once more Delany was chosen to speak for the blacks and once more he brought cheers with his proposal of mutual effort for mutual gain of both blacks and whites, not only in obtaining an honest election. Again he stressed the interdependence of the races.

This meeting resulted in a petition and a series of resolutions addressed to Gov. Moses and demanding a reply from him. The accompanying letter declared its purpose was to obtain a fair election, freedom of the voter to pick his choice of ticket, timely announcement of polling places so that the voter can cast a ballot, "impartial conduct" by election officials, and an honest count. With their current election commissioners they did not expect this at all.

> WHEREAS, the Citizens of Charleston County have seen with anxiety and alarm that C. C. Bowen, B. H. Hoyt and P. H. Gregorie have been appointed commissioners of election for Charleston County and; WHEREAS, there is no assurance whatsoever that under the management of these commissioners, there will be a free vote and a fair count at the approaching elections; and WHEREAS, the violent and avowed partisanship of these commissioners gives good ground for the belief that they were appointed for the purpose of defeating the popular will by an unscrupulous exercise of the large power which the election laws of the State confer upon them. . . .

it was resolved, in the names of combined "Republican and Conservative citizens" that Moses fire these men.

Moses did not fire them, but did fire others on October 22 throughout the state in order to appoint in their stead men pledged to the regular Republican machine. It was one of the last pay-offs of his administration.

On the day following the mass meeting, the convention of the independent Republicans opened at noon in Hibernian Hall. There were eighteen counties represented on the opening day and more delegates expected. Most encouraging too was the fact that both the low- and the up-country counties were represented, indicating a widespread interest in breaking up the Republican machine. Again, Delany was the first speaker called upon.

In this speech, he bid welcome to the whites among the delegates, telling them that it was because the native whites had not offered their political support in establishing an equitable government that the blacks had turned to northerners without ethics. These "Sixth Ward New York politicians" taught the colored people that anything goes in politics, even the belief that "it was right to vote minors, women and girls, even to go to the graveyard and rake up the names of the dead and vote them."

The only worthwhile effort made by these "teachers" for the benefit of the blacks, Delany said, was establishment of the Land Commission, and that was destroyed by theft. He also made the accurate prediction that if the independent Republicans nominated an honest ticket, they would receive the support not only of the Honest Government League and the Taxpayers' Convention but also of the conservatives, who were to hold their nominating convention the following week. And he repeated his economic theme that the blacks and whites together could "enable the laborer to demand his highest price for his labor and the capitalist to pay it."

But from the account of the speech in the *News and Courier*, Delany got his greatest reaction when he dealt with a topic avoided by speakers before mixed audiences, what he called "the great bugbear, SOCIAL EQUALITY."

> He said he had a family of which he was just as proud as anybody. But social equality must regulate itself. He would not allow anybody to dictate to him who should sit at his table. (Applause) The blacks were imitative creatures, and until it became fashionable for white men to sit down at the table with black men there was no danger of black men insisting on sitting down to the table with white people. (Applause and laughter.)

During the following sessions both the platform and rules of the regular Republican party convention were adopted, so as to prove to the state that it was not the principles of the party to which the independent Republicans objected but rather those who had failed to live and govern by them.

At no time during the campaign that was to follow did Delany make a more characteristic assertion of his beliefs and his pride than his speech of acceptance of the nomination as lieutenant governor. He was nominated by J. P. M. Epping of Beaufort, the interesting carpetbagger who had become wealthy through the introduction of bottled soda water in the state. Delany was introduced as "the honest exemplar of the honest colored men of South Carolina." His speech was reported verbatim in the *News and Courier:*

> This is one of the most extraordinary occasions of my life. I have not words to express my gratitude to you for this manifestation of your regard and confidence in nominating me for the second office in the gift of the people of South Carolina. I have but little to say to you now, for you have already heard me frequently upon the various phases of our relations to each other. But this much I will say to you, that I have entered into this great movement with no other design than, if elected to second to the utmost extent the integrity of the chief magistrate of the State. I will go further than this, I will pledge all of the intelligence, all of the powers of intellect that I possess, all of the integrity of character, to bring about between the two peoples in this State, black and white, those relations that shall tend to the promotion of each others' mutual welfare. (Cheers) I shall not act in the sense it is understood as a party man. I shall know no other party than that which shall have for its object the interest of the whole people, black and white, of the State of South Carolina. (Cheers) I shall try to correct, so far as my own race is concerned, one or two errors in the Republican party as it formerly existed. We are now standing upon a new platform, so far as party acts are concerned. In our party there were three points of consideration: 1st: We were formed as a Republican Party in contradistinction to the Democratic party; next, we were taught first and foremost an antagonism to the Democratic party which, as a whole party, was all right; Next, we had factions in our own party, which was all wrong; and next, one part of our party was taught as a fundamental principle that they must stand in direct hostility to one portion of the people which formed the community in which they

lived. I shall endeavor to correct this. It is my province to say that because, when I look upon my race, I see that it has all and everything to lose in a contest such as might be brought about by antagonism of races. This being true, I have but one more remark to make. I do not intend to lower my standard of manhood in regard to the claims of my race one single step. I do not intend to recede from the rights that have been given us by the beneficence of a just Congress of the nation one single hairsbreadth; but I do intend, in demanding all this, to demand the same equal rights and justice to every citizen, black and white, of the State of South Carolina. And upon this line I will fight it out if it takes all winter. (Cheers)

Judge Green was an ideal running-mate for Delany. Not even the machine Republicans, black or white, could find a point of departure for criticism beyond his intention to clean up the party. Son of a Sumter Methodist preacher, lawyer, and successful planter, he had been elected and served in the pre-war state legislature for six successive years. In 1866 he had been appointed president of the Sumter County Provost Court by the military. As soon as civil government was established, Judge Green was unanimously elected to the Third Judicial Circuit by the General Assembly and kept there by re-election.

One aspect of Judge Green's life probably was an asset among the blacks, though perhaps undeservedly. He was considered a Unionist by the whites because he had not participated in South Carolina's affairs throughout the Civil War. This may or may not have been so. The fact was that he rejected certain re-election to the state legislature or any other public office in 1858 due to a recurrent illness, and that could have been the reason for his inactivity during the war. In his speech of acceptance of the nomination by the independent Republicans he said: "It is true, gentlemen, that I am weak in body . . . ," and he was to outlast the campaign by only a few months. He died in January 1875.

Most of the rigors of campaigning were taken by Delany, due to Judge Green's poor health, and he even ventured up country where blacks were in the minority. One of the old-line South Carolina aristocrats, Joseph B. Kershaw, a Confederate general, threw his hat in the ring for Congressman under the independent Republican ticket and he reported from Camden that "Col. Delany's speaking has had great effect on the old hard-shelled Democrats who had vowed they would have nothing to do with a ticket that had a Negro on it."

Editorially, Dawson wrote in the *Charleston News and Courier* about Delany's

> gallant work in the Up Country. It is a surprise and gratification to the whites to hear wise, generous and statesmanlike words from the lips of a black man, and the colored people are proud to see that a man of their own race can worthily stand side by side with Kershaw and McGowan in the advocacy of fair dealing and peace. Major Delany has, by his good work, strengthened the cause of honesty and reform.

Naturally, the contest was of national import, and the press followed its course closely. The general newspapers reported it objectively but, strangely, Frederick Douglass editorialized his correspondence in the *New National Era.* In fact, one story was printed in the October 22 issue, in time to reach its South Carolina black subscribers before Election Day.

> If Green should be elected, it would be by Democratic votes, for the Republicans who support him are not sufficient to elect him. Having been elected by Democratic vote, he would be virtually a Democratic governor, and the best offices in the different counties he would fill by the appointment of Democrats, thus giving that party supreme control of the government. . . . I am indeed surprised that such men as Lee (Samuel J. of Aiken), McKinlay (William J. of Charleston) and others, active workers for Green, are so blinded as not to see the inevitable destruction of Republicanism which would follow the success of the movement they so persistently champion.

Douglass also predicted: "The Green-Delany movement will be one of the grandest fizzles of the age, and deservedly so for it is a deliberate attempt to break up the Republican party and turn the State over to the Democrats." Douglass, of course, was still in the thrall of the Washington political world and could not, until too late, realize what Delany already knew, that some attempt to salvage his people's gains must be made.

The result of the election was not quite the "grandest fizzle" that Douglass predicted, though the Green-Delany ticket lost. It was likely that the usual dishonest counts and "lost" ballot boxes were arranged for as in every election. Still, over 149,000 citizens, black and white, cast their ballots. Green lost to Chamberlain by 11,585 votes, and Delany lost to Gleaves by 15,985 ballots. It was by far the largest vote and the closest result in any South Carolina election. The distribution of the sectional votes shows that Green and Delany lost in the low-country counties with the heaviest black population. The machine Republicans had been effective in all but one respect.

For the first time since its creation in 1867 the state legislature now had a white majority—by three members—but it was a turning point in the race war. It was exactly what Delany had feared and why he had been a candidate. In 14 of the state's 32 counties the conservatives, meaning the Democrats, who had joined the independent Republican ticket swept the local offices, and white men dominated the black majorities.

One thing was certain, and was demonstrated as soon as Chamberlain was inaugurated. The state was mired in a financial morass so deep that all of the evils of public bankruptcy faced the new governor. Even with the most honorable intentions and without any obligation to his thieving associates, Chamberlain was laden with repudiation of the swollen state debt, with unpaid public employees, unperformed public services, and an actual, if not organized, tax strike—and this situation was duplicated in all of the counties and cities.

A note of horror was added to the situation when it was learned that Chamberlain's old Yale Law School classmate, Howard H. Kimpton, had been given a financial settlement by Moses. The total in *commissions alone* paid the New York financial agent was $735,969.13, and no one could even begin to estimate his totals on over-sale of bond issues, receipt of interest of monies guaranteed by him, or his profits from participation in the two railroad frauds that made dozens rich. It must be allowed though, that without doubt Kimpton had to "kick back" some of his share. And it was quite fitting that the man who originally gave Kimpton to South Carolina, Chamberlain, should have the impossible task of cleaning up his financial mess.

The real winners in the election of 1874 had been the Democrats. While Hampton and Conner had named no state ticket, the Democrats were far from inactive. On February 24, 1874, Adjutant and Inspector General H. W. Purvis begged Gov. Moses not to issue any more requisitions for arms and equipment to rifle clubs because "the present number of guns on hand are inadequate to supply the regularly organized Militia of the State. . . ." That did not prevent Moses from authorizing issues of guns to the Irish Rifle Club and the Mackey Zouaves when there were just 500 left in the state armory.

Chamberlain was to testify before a Congressional committee that when he was inaugurated in 1875 there were 290 white rifle clubs in the state. They were under command of Gen. Conner and were highly organized. That was attested to by the historian of the Carolina Rifle Club of Charleston who extolled its membership as "a brave, spirited and enthusiastic body of men and they were easily held back by their officers, because our party leaders and particularly the leaders of the Rifle Club organization, were men who had gone through the War and their courage was unquestioned and recognized. If Gen. James Conner said 'be quiet,' we knew and felt that it was not because he was afraid, but because he knew that thus he could best subserve the high interests he and we were contesting for. During these troublous days, there never was even a chance of a fight, but down would come a telegram from Hampton 'Preserve the peace at all hazards.' "

While the Republicans were splitting apart in 1874, the Democrats were drilling for the military campaign of 1876.

CHAPTER TWENTY-THREE

The Justice on Trial

Delany certainly did not plan it, but his unremitting efforts to find a formula whereby black and white could live in amity were responsible for the questionable inauguration of Rutherford B. Hayes as 19th President of the United States.

The polite terminology given in the historical texts is that the national election of 1876 was "resolved by a compromise," an agreement between the conservative Republicans of the North and the white Democrats of the South that they would bury the Civil War hatchet. The fact that the blacks were buried with it is not mentioned. The texts have been fumigated and the stench of the "sell-out" of 1876 no longer disturbs the placid American hypocrisy. Instead of sowing the seeds of today's menacing *apartheid,* this election opened a golden era of peace and westward economic expansion, according to the standard versions.

In South Carolina, at least, the "sell-out" of the state's electoral votes amounted to Hampton proposing to Hayes, in devious Washington ways, of course, "You make me Governor of the State of South Carolina and I'll make you President of the United States." Hampton might never have been in a position to make such a deal if it had not been for Martin R. Delany. It was a bizarre situation Delany put himself into. He had repeatedly warned audiences and readers that southern whites would utilize any conceivable means, fair or foul, to restore their absolute political power. He was right in 1876, for they used Delany too.

It would be expected that Delany, as a defeated candidate in 1874, might be relegated to the obscurity of the "outs" in politics in the succeeding years. Quite the reverse took place. In public service, without public office, in the local problems and commemorative events of his race, in both the black and white need for an honest arbiter, throughout the turbulence of the changes he had predicted, Delany became again what he had so often been before—a personality of wide influence.

As he had for years, Delany continued to be the principal speaker at the annual St. John's Day celebrations of the Colored Freemasons of Charleston, and at them again sat beside Richard Gleaves, the man who had beaten him. He was still called upon for the Emancipation Day speeches and the 4th of July celebrations. Independence Day of 1876 was also Delany's day. His Delany's Rifles led the parade, and he was the speaker of the day at the Battery where, according to the *News and Courier*, approximately 10,000 blacks gathered. The reporter unconsciously put his finger on Delany's inveterate habit of telling it as he saw it. He wrote: "Col. M. R. Delany was next introduced and made one of those sound, sensible speeches which have always made him so unpopular with his own race."

Delany had told audiences the same thing before and they took it from him. He told them they were *not* the equals of the whites and "never could become their equals until they did as the white man did, educate their children and honor and respect their females."

> Their females, said he, were the types of every race. Men never attained the higher grade of civilization than the women of their race. The way therefore for them to make themselves equal to the whites was to educate their children, and watch with jealous care their women. No father should allow his daughter to leave her home after dark.

It was a strange kind of speech for a flag-waving day, but Delany had been all through with such speeches years before when he learned that the Declaration of Independence did not apply to blacks. Not even in the centennial year of Independence Day would he deviate from that stand.

For part of 1875 he spoke out weekly, being once more editor of a newspaper for blacks, the *Charleston Independent*. At the same time, having resigned his customs house job in order to be a candidate for state office, Delany began the restoration of his medical practice, but it was the same story as in Pittsburgh, Chatham, and Wilberforce. He simply could not afford to make a living. Each time he had been faced with the decision whether to support his family or his people, the latter won, and Catherine patiently kept on sewing far away in Wilberforce.

An example came soon after he had set up offices and a practice following the election. He received an invitation from New York to make a speech. It came from the venerable abolitionist, poet, and editor of the Republican *New York Evening Post,* William Cullen Bryant, and was signed by a number of the city's intellectual and civic leaders. Naturally, Delany accepted, and made the speech on March 5, 1875, in Irving Hall, with "a number of ladies, and many colored people" in the audience, according to the news story. Delany was introduced by Bryant himself, somewhat inaccurately but sufficiently flowery unto the day. Delany, he said,

> had fought in the war of opinion and in the war of physical force for his colored brethren. In the war of opinion he wielded his pen with Frederick Douglass. In the war of physical force, he drew his sword under Grant, leading his Company for four years during the war. He was here to speak of the relations that now exist between the two races at the South in which there had been so many opinions that some have gone wild over them.

Delany gave his audience the blunt truth. He told them they were uninformed as to the South because they received their information from "interested politicians." Should his listeners suspect that he spoke for a political party in opposition to the Republicans and "that he was not a true friend to the cause of the blacks," Delany told them about his work with John Brown in Chatham and about starting the *North Star* with Douglass.

At the close of the war, he stated, the blacks could have become "a political force that the country would have taken pride in." But they knew nothing of politics or the responsibilities of freedom and were faced with a totally new relationship between what had been master and slave, "a relation so new that neither party knew its own position."

> But the men who at last undertook at this time to lead the blacks in the South in their political life were men who had no interest in the colored people of the South, and no interest in the white people of the South. These men passed

> themselves off upon the innocent colored people as representatives of the government, and they taught the blacks that it was their right and duty to distrust and keep down as much as possible the whites. These men stood between the whites and the blacks, keeping them apart, but with their arms to the elbows in the black man's pocket, and to the armpit in the pocket of the white man—stealing from each.

After further castigation of the carpetbaggers, he declared that the only benefits thus far received by the blacks was misguidance. "These meddling politicians taught the blacks that democracy meant slavery and republicanism meant freedom." His own definition, he declared, was that "Democracy . . . was an institution of the Americans in opposition to aristocracy and monarchy, and republicanism was nothing but democracy carried out."

> Mr. Delany said that there is no feeling of antagonism between the whites of the South and the blacks of the South, but on the contrary, the two races would confide in each other were it not for the class of miserable political adventurers who go down among them. The two races must continue to dwell together, for the blacks represent the labor and the whites of the South the capital. The two must exist together. The idea of the war between the races, the speaker pronounced absurd, as there are seven whites to every black, and such a war would lead to the extermination of the blacks.
>
> "There can be no war of races. There shan't be a war of races," he exclaimed, and continued with an appeal to the people of the North to acquaint themselves thoroughly with the real facts of the situation, and to discourage the scheming politicians and acknowledge the position of political importance of the colored people.

There was not a great deal said in New York by Delany that he had not already said in South Carolina, but apparently it was new in the North, where corruption had already been classified as "all black," and the whites, as Democrats and planters, had no real repentance for the Civil War, even seven years after Johnson Reconstruction. This, too, was before his next disillusionment, and Delany actually believed that the freedmen and the old aristocracy were so interdependent that they could make a just peace. He was to repeat the argument of New York in other speeches in South Carolina and in the *Independent.* In fact, it was to be several years before Delany again completed his lifelong cycle from hope for an equitable relationship between whites and blacks to total rejection of whites. For five years he believed that democracy was possible in South Carolina.

The *Independent* was an obvious attempt to consolidate the blacks behind an "honest government" program and to assert the black viewpoint, which, of course, was Delany's. Its first issue, published on August 21, 1875, left not a single doubt as to his intent with the newspaper which would be "a true representative organ of our race, to go side by side with the organs of the white race" in obtaining recognition for the blacks. The *Independent* also would be the eternal enemy of "all persons and classes who promote discord or distrust, who seek to destroy confidence between the races under any pretext whatever."

Delany, in the same announcement, declared war on any and all who had brought South Carolina "to discredit and disgrace, and well nigh to the brink of ruin."

> Our position is: "Measures, not men" and we care not who the persons are, or what their pretended party may be, they who pervert the true principles upon which the rights of the entire people as citizens, irrespective of race or color were based, we shall endeavor to overthrow, and dash from power and place in the State.
>
> Indeed, it has become unendurable and no people above the level of well fed serfs would longer submit to the intolerable misrule and imposition of the class of persons who have led in the politics of South Carolina during the first six years of pretended Republicanism, or "Radical" rule, as it was called.
>
> Every species of infamy, however atrocious, private and public, bare faced and in open daylight, was defiantly perpetrated under the direction and guidance of the despicable political leaders in the sacred name of "Republicanism" and "Reconstruction."
>
> To such an extent this has been carried, not only in our own State, but we dare venture to assert in every Recon-

> structed State where Republicanism prevails, till the idea of the colored race as a political element in American politics has become—especially in the North—a sneer, a hiss and a by-word. As a part of the race, it becomes our bounden duty to aid in obliterating this disgrace by the clearing of our State Government of the pests who have heretofore held the rule in their power. This we are determined to do, by unfurling aloft the banner we this day fling to the breeze "In the name of our God" the God of all the people and God of Justice.
>
> One thing we are determined upon—which is the great object of our paper—and that is to prevent the colored race from the further imposition of these men who have heretofore misled them in politics and their domestic affairs. They are not the friends, but the worst enemies of our race, and it is high time that a stop was put to it by leading men among ourselves.

Whether the *Independent* lived up to these lofty aspirations is not known since, like *The Mystery*, so little of the newspaper's contents have been found. At least one gem has not escaped extinction, since it related a classic election story for the city of Charleston in the municipal elections of October 1875. It was a political joke relished all over the state, probably because the joke was on "Honest John" Patterson, who had paid $40,000 for his Senate seat. His political pal in Charleston was former Congressman Christopher Columbus Bowen, an ex-captain in the Confederacy, whose political reputation was most unsavory. However, he bought consistent election support from the blacks.

The *Independent* did not disclose whose idea it was, but the week-end before the Charleston municipal election, plans were made to import enough votes to carry the balloting for Bowen's candidates. This was standard practice. As a result, some smart young colored men, chiefly from Greenville in the up country, decided on an excursion to Charleston. "Honest John" wired Bowen from Columbia that he had chartered thirteen cars and that the young men should be met, given their voting tickets, wined, dined, and lodged and, after voting, be sent back home. The *Independent*'s version of what happened is so delightful that it should be accepted:

> They were met at the depot in Charleston by special committees, and members of them were carried to lodging houses which had been provided and where they were taken in and fed, but on Monday night, the 1,100 hypothetical voters, according to the program, embarked on the train and returned to their homes, greatly to the disgust of the committees who had fed and feasted them during their stay. (The election was on Tuesday.)

Apparently the *Independent* was intended to be in politics with all fonts. It was to fill the need so long proclaimed by Delany, political education for the blacks. The editor himself was seemingly a daily political activist. There were numerous reports of his organization, a citizens conservative organization, in three of Charleston's heavily black wards. In Ward Four that August before the municipal elections, there was not only a split from the Republicans but among the Conservatives, too, and Delany wound up on one of the three executive committees. While this internecine battle was going on the *Independent* continued to startle its readers into political thought. One editorial entitled "Who is He?" annoyingly does not give the answer it asks. But Delany's opinion of the gentleman is clear.

> We understand that a deep-laid scheme is completed, by bargain and sale, whereby to make one of the most despicable, unprincipled demagogues the next Governor of South Carolina. This was intended, and doubtless supposed to be, a deep-laid scheme, but it is too shallow for concealment. Heaven and earth may pass away, but that man can never be the Governor of this State. Nay, he shall not be. As one of the people, we speak for the people.
>
> We shall stifle this monster in embryo, not permitting it to develop its horrible deformity; and all colored men concerned in bringing it to maturity, if they persist in standing by it, will be strangled to death along with it. The free, independent people of the State will not longer submit to the base political outrages heretofore committed upon them.

The readers of the newspapers may have known who the despicable creature was but the reader of history can find a dozen candidates for such identification in the state legislature of the day.

Delany's last issue of the *Charleston Independent* was published on Christmas Day 1875. It had lasted barely four months and there was a publication lapse until April 8, 1876, when two new editors took over and Delany wrote a "Valedictory" for it, announcing that thereafter he would not be editor, merely an occasional contributor. "My withdrawal as the editor was simply in consequence of the pressure of my official engagements, which taxed all of my time, and not because of any want of interest or patronage on the part of the public and friends of the enterprise."

Those "official engagements" constitute some of the amazing anomalies of those years and illustrate the mercurial character of political purpose in South Carolina, right until the final deal was made in Washington in early 1877. The following appeared in the October 18 issue of the *Independent* as a display advertisement:

M. R. DELANY

TRIAL JUSTICE

Ward Number 3

ANSON STREET

One door from Market

CIVIL CASES PARTICULARY (*sic*)

ATTENDED TO

The Rights and Feelings of all persons however humble, coming into this office, shall be sacredly respected.

The candidate he had opposed so vehemently a year before, Governor Daniel H. Chamberlain, on October 8, 1875, had officially removed the trial justice in Ward 3, Charleston, a Moses appointee, and appointed Martin R. Delany in his stead.

It was one of those illogical turnabouts of politics in which two opponents court each other. Chamberlain knew that he would need a man as influential as Delany on his side in the coming campaign for re-election. He could sew him up with such an appointment.

On the other hand, Delany knew that he needed the $1,200 annual salary and the prestige of the office if he himself were ever to run for office again.

The function of trial justice in South Carolina was, theoretically, similar to that of police courts today. Its duties were to enforce the common laws of property, public order, and private peace. Like the police courts, too, a "fix" was frowned upon from the moment it became public. But a trial justice in South Carolina was more than a judge, he was *the* local political authority as well, ever since Gov. Scott changed the name of the function from "magistrate" and made the dispensation of justice a political process. Perhaps the baldest kind of political use was given the office by Moses, who often sold the appointments. Once he made out a pardon for four men found guilty in Richland County of kidnaping some cattle and demanding $5 for their ransom. A Justice Goodson made the mistake of finding them guilty and giving each a $10 fine and ten days imprisonment. They complained to the then Speaker of the House, Robert B. Elliot, and being loyal, active Republicans, they were promptly pardoned and their sentences remitted. On the back of Justice Goodson's indictment is the notation, in Moses' handwriting: "Make out pardon for these men on the ground that they had been illegally convicted and *do not let it get into the papers*" (emphasis Moses'). Later that same day Speaker Elliot handed Moses a petition from both Houses, and Justice Goodson was ordered removed from office.

Delany's appointment was first proposed in July 1875 by the Negro Senator S. E. Gaillard of Charleston, but apparently Chamberlain was reluctant to honor the petition. He did have a problem with the current trial justice in Ward 3, one W. A. Grant, who appeared to make each decision on the basis of the highest bid. He did have a substitute, but when the residents of Charleston heard about it, they sent Chamberlain a searing document about the candidate, David Riker, who was from an old Charleston family. Among the kinder things mentioned was

Riker's thievery. "Knowing how he has wronged and cheated us out of our small earnings we could not keep silent and have him set over us. And in conclusion we do earnestly beg and supplicate that your honor will not do us the injustice to appoint Mr. Riker Trial Justice, but select some respectable man of honest worth."

Whether or not Delany was that man in Chamberlain's estimation, is not known. In August the Charleston municipal campaign for mayor was boiling over and a candidate named Cunningham won the support of the conservatives, as well as both Alonzo Ransier and Martin Delany. The "prime movers" in Charleston, the old families, merchants, and professional men wanted Cunningham badly, chiefly to see if they could pull the county out of its financial mess. With a population of 89,883 blacks and 33,606 whites in 1875, it was apparent that the black majority was an absolute necessity for Cunningham. Otherwise, they would be forced to accept another of Christopher Columbus Bowen's profligates. They needed Delany badly, on the stump as well as on committees.

The aristocrats of Charleston deluged Chamberlain with petitions in behalf of appointing Delany. Doctors, lawyers, former mayors, senators, and representatives signed. Each petition was mixed with black and white signatures, and the total comprised most of the city's leadership.

Delany delayed the inevitable and the reason may have been that he made no promises. Only once did he communicate with the Chamberlain and that was when the petition campaign first began. On July 13 he wrote the governor:

> Sir: I have the honor to communicate, that having been requested by a number of respectable citizens of Charleston, induced by Senator S. A. Gaillard, to become a Trial Justice, and learning that such Application was forwarded yesterday, I write in deference to your Excellency to say that such an appointment would be acceptable to me.
>
> I have the honor to be, Governor,
>
> M. R. Delany

That is all Delany ever promised Chamberlain, that he would accept the job. The point becomes important in the light of events of 1876. In addition, when the appointment finally was made, Chamberlain never sent it to the Senate for confirmation as required by the judicial code. It was obvious that both Chamberlain and Delany were keeping a gap between them.

But once he did get the appointment, Delany went at his duties with his characteristic thoroughness and dedication. He gave the office a flair and prestige it had never had before. Usually, the court was held in the back of a store or in the trial justice's livingroom. But Delany decided that the site of justice required more dignity. The *News and Courier* reported,

> Col. M. R. Delany, recently appointed trial justice for the Third Ward has inaugurated a happy change in the hitherto unsightly locations of these special Courts in our City. He has fitted up for his use as a Trial Justice of Charleston an office in Anson St., above the Market, which far surpasses those of his brother justices. There are six trim settees in the room, 2 chairs especially intended and labeled as "Constables Seats", a long office table furnished with writing materials for the use of reporters and lawyers, besides the private table of the Justice. There is an inner room, suitably furnished, for private conferences. The walls are neatly papered and the whole office is creditable to its use.

From the records, Delany judged a huge number of assault cases and seemed to prefer any alternative to imprisonment for those he found guilty. He fined them and placed them on peace bonds, often had the disputing parties shake hands and leave as friends, all charges dropped, but he sent few to the county jail. His office was extremely busy as he became as much an arbitrator in disputes as a formal judge hearing charges and evidence.

Without question, it was work that Delany relished, but he soon learned that the office, like most positions under state and county authority, was never certain as to its funds. All of the trial justices in Charleston held a meeting on December 2 to plan a petition to the state legislature for that body to appropriate money for their pay. As yet, Delany had received none. The General Assembly consequently met and allocated 1/4 mill of the Tax Act for the year 1866 for payment of these salaries. On January 28 the trial justices again met to take further action in getting their pay. If the full millage allocated them was collected, and that was doubtful, they would still be $9,000 short in meeting the salaries, to say nothing of the back pay owed for the prior year. Again a petition was sent to Columbia.

Meanwhile, Delany's poverty was responsible for circumstances that were to embitter him for the rest of his life. On February 8, 1876, in the First Circuit Court of Sessions, sitting in Charleston, Judge J. P. Reed and a jury found Delany guilty of "Breach of Trust with Fraudulent Intent" and a separate charge of "Grand Larceny." He was sentenced to twelve months in the state penitentiary and was released on $1,000 bond pending an application for a new trial. Delany returned to his office and duties. Legally, he knew that the guilty verdict of larceny was correct, for he did owe $212. But he also knew that the finding of guilt in breach of trust and fraudulent intent was entirely false. It was an attack on his most prized possession, that integrity for which he had sacrificed so much.

The court records make the whole sordid story clear and explain why Delany, in the fall of 1876, decided to help drive the moneychangers out of the South Carolina government.

It began in 1871 when Delany had his short-lived brokerage business in Charleston. On John's Island, where Delany had been well known as a Freedmen's Bureau officer and as the Black Major who helped the blacks with many contracts, the John Wesley Methodist Church congregation decided to build a new church and collected money for that purpose. The amount—$212—was placed in the hands of the treasurer of the church trustees, Telemachus Baynard, when, suddenly, Baynard died. His widow, fearful of keeping such a large amount of money in her house, selected the only honest black she knew, Delany, to keep the money until the new board of trustees decided what to do.

Delany too had a problem in keeping that amount of cash around. The logical step would have been to deposit it in the Freedmen's Savings Bank but Delany had been up North and knew that the white speculators from New York had their hands in the till. (Jay Cooke borrowed $500,000 from the Freedmen's Bank at 5 percent interest, just before he went bankrupt.)

And so Delany decided to put the money into the safest kind of investment known, government obligations, where it would earn interest. He bought Charleston County Tax Anticipation Warrants with the money. Gilbert Pillsbury, mayor of Charleston, had finally straightened out its tangled finances and balanced the budget. Merchants and bankers were putting their money into these warrants because the county's future was bright. John's Island was a part of Charleston County. What could be more logical than to invest in one's own home county?

However, the following year Moses and "Honest John" were elected, and C. C. Bowen ran the precincts in Charleston County. Not only were the city and county budgets unbalanced, but tax revenues disappeared into various pockets. Charleston County tax warrants became even more worthless than state bonds. There was absolutely no negotiable value to them. So, when the new chairman of the Board of Trustees of the John Wesley Church, a Dr. A. Webster, requested the church's money, Delany could only offer them the tax warrants which were refused. There the matter rested for three years, awaiting payment of the warrants by the county. At no time did Delany have any amount even approaching $212.

Then Delany entered the political campaign of 1874 and was fair game for Bowen's regular Republican organization. Honesty? Hadn't he stolen $212 from a church, a black church at that? It wasn't so much the stealing, but a church! It was the depths of dishonesty to steal from even a white church.

On June 29, 1875, one Cyrus B. Rivers ("a colored man") appeared before Bowen's Ward 6 Trial Justice W. E. Hutchinson and made the charges in behalf of the church. Hutchinson bound Delany in $1,000 bond for trial at the next term of the Court of Sessions, where he was found guilty. In announcing the charge the *News and Courier* in June reported: "This case is based on the story that was so popular at all the Radical pow-wows in the late State campaign, and Delany says he is very glad that it has come to a head at last, when he will have an opportunity of nailing the lie."

At the trial before Judge Reed, "The wife of the deceased (Telemachus Baynard) trustee testified that Delany was her business agent, that her daughter had given him the money for safekeeping because the trustees had quarrelled over it when they applied to her to turn it over to them." Delany's lawyer was E. B. Seabrook, of the old Sea Islands family with whose father Delany had negotiated many labor contracts. His defense charged that the entire case was brought for political reasons, that his client had never disclaimed responsibility for the money even though he had acted only in a trustee capacity. As proof of Delany's assumption of responsibility, he had given Dr. Webster his own note for the amount. But he just plain did not have the cash and the tax warrants were still worthless. Who was the culprit, Delany or the county?

Legally, it was Delany, and the verdict of guilty was assured by the fact that the state Solicitor was the radical Republican C. W. Buttz, and there was a gubernatorial campaign coming up.

But a storm of protest spread across the state and into Chamberlain's office. It was true that Delany owed the money. He was the first to admit that guilt. But "Breach of Trust" and "Fraudulent Intent"? Judge Reed was severely criticized for not instructing the jury against those charges. Even Buttz and Bowen joined hundreds of others in asking Gov. Chamberlain to pardon Delany immediately. In fact, on April 3 Bowen was able to notify Chamberlain that Delany had given him the money which "upon his request for executive clemency being granted, will be immediately turned over to the Trustees of said Society." He therefore recommended the pardon. Turning the money over to one of Chamberlain's own political henchmen was a sagacious move. Chamberlain needed Bowen as much as he needed Delany in the coming campaign.

Once more the outstanding citizens, black and white, of Charleston put together a petition. There were 93 signatures on this one and again they included a cross-section of government, commerce, and old families. In the city government, the mayor, chief of police, chief of detectives, a 2d lieutenant of police, and the police department's clerk all signed. The substance of their petition was the same as in all the others. They were certain that "after strict inquiry into the matter your Excellency will arrive at the conclusion that the conviction was unjust. The intent to defraud was not proven, and further we assert that there is now in the hands of the Court subject to Delany's orders more than sufficient money to cover the amount alleged to have been fraudulently appropriated by him, and we who are many of Delany's race pledge ourselves, if necessary, to pay the amount claimed to have been fraudulently appropriated. We do so because we sympathize greatly in the trouble of one who has from his acknowledged ability reflected so much credit on his race.

We feel convinced that your Excellency will exert in his favor that mercy which the people of this state have placed in your hands."

That petition was sent to Chamberlain and, on the same day, the Chamberlain's private secretary, Walter Jones, wrote to Delany as follows:

> I am directed by His Excellency the Governor to inform you that recent events occurring in the Court of General Sessions in Charleston seem to compel him to ask your resignation of the office of Trial Justice for the City of Charleston.
>
> The Governor directs me to say that in taking this step he acts wholly from a sense of official propriety—and duty, and not from personal motives.
>
> He does not assume that you are necessarily guilty of the offence of which you have been convicted, but when a case has progressed to a verdict of sentence, he feels that it is his duty to ask you to vacate your office pending the further and final disposition of the case.
>
> He earnestly hopes for a solution of the case favorable to you and if such shall be the result he will rejoice in it for many reasons, and he will feel it to be his duty to restore you to your office whenever the charges against you shall be disposed of or shall no longer be confirmed by the subsisting verdict of a jury and the sentence of the Court.
>
> The Governor requests me to express his best wishes for your speedy vindication and your personal welfare in all respects, and that he awaits your early reply.

Delany's reply to Jones was that he would be in Columbia to see the governor in three days. It must have been a hot session. Delany told the governor that he would not resign as trial justice until and if the state Supreme Court confirmed his conviction. His appeal was already entered in that court by Seabrook and the witnesses to be summoned would include quite a few political figures, beginning at the precinct level. This could be embarrassing. Another thing Delany told Chamberlain was that the loss of the money had been accepted by him but not the conditions which caused the county to repudiate its tax warrants, a situation the governor knew well. He was sitting on complaints from the teachers and health officers of Charleston County that they had not been paid in a year. Finally, Delany told him, probably at length, that he didn't give a damn about a pardon since his conscience was clear and the Supreme Court would absolve him anyway.

What Delany did *not* tell Chamberlain was that he would support him for re-election that fall. This left the situation in a stalemate that seemed to bother everybody but Delany. Chamberlain's files have numerous letters from individuals, demanding a pardon for Delany, even one from Daniel Riker. Chamberlain took no action and Delany kept court every day on schedule. On April 27 Judge Reed himself, growing unhappy over the coming term of the Supreme Court made a journal entry himself:

> In view of the former good character of Defendant and a doubt that may be reasonably entertained as to whether he acted with a fraudulent intent in the breach of Trust of which he was convicted, I recommend that the Imprisonment in the Penitentiary to which he was sentenced, be remitted and pardoned, upon condition that he first pay to the Trustees of the John Wesley Church the Sum of money which he converted—Two Hundred and Ten dollars—with Interest from the date of the conversion, and also the costs of the prosecution, that the church and the country may be saved harmless.
>
> J. P. Reed
> Judge 1st Circuit
> April 27th 1876

A week later Seabrook replied curtly to an inquiry from Chamberlain regarding a complaint made from James Island by a Rev. H. H. Hunter concerning some money owed, this time, to a Presbyterian church. Delany's name appeared because he, as a broker, had signed the lease on some land involved. He had been a witness in litigation connected with it and Seabrook replied to Chamberlain that Delany's friends "earnestly hope that you will not allow Delany to be put at the mercy of everyone who may think to blackmail him." Delany himself no longer wrote directly to Chamberlain, only to his secretary, and finally the governor acted.

On June 23 Delany received notification from the Secretary

of State that since the Senate had not confirmed his appointment as trial justice, he was to cease the function immediately. Actually, the Senate had never been asked to vote on the appointment in all the eight months Delany had been holding Court. Delany replied that it would take him five days to wind up the affairs of his court. He did not communicate with Chamberlain at all.

However, Delany made several speeches during this time, before the Shaw Veteran Volunteer Association, an organization of 54th Massachusetts veterans, and he was the principal speaker at that year's July 4th celebration by the colored population of Charleston. His loss of the trial justice spot, his situation in regard to the conviction, his all-around political independence did not seem to affect his popularity.

As a result, on July 7 he received a letter from another of Chamberlain's private secretaries, W. R. Ives, asking where the receipt was showing that he had paid the money as ordered by the Court. Otherwise, how could the governor pardon him? Bowen had done nothing about it! Delany replied that same day that friends, known very well to the governor, had been handling that for him.

> I saw after the reception of your note today, one who has communicated between me and the others in this matter, showed him the note, and stated my ultimatum, which is that I shall proceed immediately among my friends of another party—as I have not got means within myself—to raise the money necessary to meet these requirements, and communicate directly through you with his Excellency on the subject. It shall be attended to at once by myself in person as I shall wait no longer on friends.
>
> I should say to his Excellency, in justice to myself, that I once raised the money since this litigation ended to meet these demands, when it was placed in the hands of a party who volunteered to attend to it as a friend—two weeks previous to the offering of these gentlemen now acting for me—but instead of paying in my behalf, they expended it, in paying on a mortgage against real estate of theirs!
>
> This was severe on me but of course I had to bear it, and would not disclose it on any account, so as to expose them.

> I shall hope to communicate to you in a few days my progress in this, to me, very important and very delicate matter.

And then nothing happened. It did not bother Delany, apparently, for his appeal was on the calendar for the fall term of the Supreme Court, but his friends were annoyed. On August 19—with Wade Hampton already making noises in Chamberlain's ear about the coming campaign—a delegation of the signatories of one of the original petitions for a pardon sat down and wrote at length to the governor. Since they represented a large part of both the black and white vote in populous Charleston, there is no doubt that Chamberlain read it and between the lines too.

> We the undersigned Colored Citizens of Charleston County, most humbly petition and ask your Excellency's attention and consideration to the unfortunate situation of our friend, "Brother" and "Companion" *Col. M. R. Delany*. We some months ago sent to your Excellency a petition based on certain conditions for his pardon (namely the paying of certain Moneys $282.00) Two hundred and eighty-two Dollars. At that time, if your Excellency will please to look among the papers then sent to you you will find a letter from the Hon. C. C. Bowen, telling your Excellency that the Money for the Wesley Chapel was paid, and was in his hands, waiting for the Trustees to forward receipt for and receive the same. The Trustees did go and have receipted for the Money and their receipts if not in your possession are in the hands of C. C. Bowen, and have kept back for reason best known to himself (C C B) M. R. Delany is dear to us, what ever may be his faults, and if we had the money we would willingly pay, *yes* a hundred times over, rather than seeing him going to the Penitentiary. Some of us are public Officers. Doubtless you are aware, of the County affairs, for paying her creditors, but a large number of your petitioners have no Money and find it hard work at this time to make daily bread for ourselves and family's, we can safely say that two thirds 2/3 of the people of Charleston today and living on one meal per day, but we hope, the above clause will not be wanted to impress you

> with our unfortunate condition for that is not the subject which compels us to ask of you, and from the interposition of your Executive Clemency in his behalf, we want and only want *Delany* pardoned, the records of the Court will show that the Money original sued for, and claimed by the Wesley Church of Johns Island, is today in their hands of the Court. M. R. Delany, Governor, happened to be one of the few of our Race of whom, we are proud to claim, we have waited long to hear from you on the letter of C. C. Bowen, we trust that you will soon relieve us of our painful anxiety by an early reply, being satisfied that its issue is sufficient to justify you in granting the pardon prayed for by your petitioners, and believing and hoping it will come.

Chamberlain signed the pardon ten days later, on August 29, almost seven months after the conviction. He used one of the left-over pardons printed and sold by Moses, scratching out the printed name of his predecessor. There was no notification to Delany, no communication at all with him, no restoration to his post as trial justice. But Delany wrote directly to Chamberlain as soon as he learned of the action. His letter is dated September 1 from Charleston and, after thanking Chamberlain "for great and beneficient (*sic*) favors," he then committed himself. "The first thing now to be done should be the *securing* of your *nomination* by the Convention."

Delany himself offered to assure that nomination through the chairman of the Republican State Executive Committee.

> General Elliot and I are personal friends, though we differ in political matters, and I think I can do more with him than most any other colored man in the state, when I have occasion to approach him on any matter of public policy or interest.
>
> He knows that I am sincere in all of my measures, do not dissemble, have no duplicity, and therefore, he always listens with respectful attention to my propositions. I must have an interview with him immediately, to show him the importance of putting you in nomination, which I think he will adhere to.

He also proposed that he begin canvassing the state in Chamberlain's behalf and therefore requested a 1,000-mile railroad ticket so that he could travel. Having just resumed the practice of medicine, he explained, he would necessarily have to travel by railroad.

The letter was an unequivocal offer to repay Chamberlain for the pardon by supporting him for re-election in a most active fashion. Yet, two weeks later, on September 14, in Hibernian Hall before 400 mixed white and colored members of the 4th Ward Democratic Club, Delany startled the state by declaring that there was no reason why any colored man could not be a Democrat and vote for Hampton.

Two weeks after that, on September 26 through the *News and Courier*, Delany announced that he was going to campaign for Hampton and he began the course that was to cost Chamberlain the governor's chair and Tilden the presidency. His decision was made after the Republican state convention in Columbia had nominated Chamberlain and the Democratic state convention in Orangeburg had made the expected nomination of Hampton. It was a characteristically independent and most unexpected political switch. Chamberlain might have been acceptable to Delany but nominated with him were the same old set of thieves. Therefore, nothing would be changed by a Republican victory in the election of 1876.

CHAPTER TWENTY-FOUR

"The Spirit of (18)76"

The whole truth about that election will never be known. Who received the highest popular vote, Chamberlain or Hampton? We know that a Congressional committee gave it to Hampton by 1,134 votes while Chamberlain claimed it by 3,194 votes. It was very much a case of thieves quarreling over division of the loot because both Republicans and Democrats were guilty of every conceivable election fraud in every one of the 32 South Carolina counties. Perhaps Chamberlain had a justifiable complaint, in one example, when he expressed disbelief about the vote count in Edgefield and Laurens counties where he *did not get a single vote*. He had made enough political appointments in these counties to win at least one vote of gratitude.

On the other hand, in the low country, such as Colleton and Charleston counties, Hampton no doubt had absolutely valid claim to fraud when, as was reported among other ridiculous details, black women refused to sleep with their husbands if they voted for that Democrat.

But these gems of political history are unimportant. The fact is that to this day nobody knows who won the gubernatorial popular vote in South Carolina, and in Washington, D.C., in the White House, and the halls of Congress, nobody wanted to know. Any recount, any new popular vote with an effort to reduce the fraud, any effort to evaluate that count in any county might rock the Hayes boat. One count they wanted untouched was the electoral college vote of 816 for Hayes over Tilden, giving the Republican the South Carolina electoral delegation in toto. The same problem had existed in Florida and Louisiana, and it had been settled nicely in Hayes' favor simply by selling out the blacks to the Democrats. With South Carolina, Hayes had 185 electoral votes to Tilden's 184, and they don't come much closer in American history.

Perhaps the only tabulation to be accepted as semi-valid was the official count of the total vote—183,388. By some 40,000 votes this would make it the highest turnout of any election in the state. The Democrats claimed that the increase was due to the final acceptance by the whites of their duty to vote. The Republicans claimed that much of the increase consisted of Hampton's "Redshirts" at the polling booths "marching in and out again" and voting each time. They said that gallant white Democrats across the Savannah River in Georgia donned red shirts to vote in Edgefield County to the number of 5,000. No doubt this was an exaggeration and was offset in the low country where the black militia did the same thing for the Republicans.

In fact, the election of 1876 in South Carolina was a burlesque of American Democracy, and would be laughable if it were not for its sinister purpose, the structuring of American *apartheid*. What did happen to that black majority which had made its presence known in five elections? After it was all over, Chamberlain claimed that Hampton had received approximately 3,000 votes, black Republicans turned Democrat. Hampton claimed 17,000 black votes. In either case, since the final accepted majority of 1,134 votes won for Hampton, then the black Democrats were the decisive factor in the election, and Delany's role as the leading black to desert the Republicans was also decisive.

But this would be misleading, too, for there is no tabulation of the number of black Republicans terrorized into staying away from the polling booths on that November 7, 1876. They had been subjected to a military, not a political, campaign. There were four Confederate generals in command—Hampton, Conner, Matthew C. Butler of Edgefield, and Martin W. Gary of Richland County. It was General Gary who wrote the manual for the members of the white rifle clubs whose assignments were spelled out. One example is: "Every Democrat must feel honor bound to control the vote of at least one Negro, by intimidation, purchase, keeping him away or as each individual may determine, how he may best accomplish it." It was Gary, too, in his handy manual, who coined the definition, "A dead Radical is very harmless. . . ." An estimated 14,000 whites were in the rifle clubs and, on one occasion in Columbia, Gary was able to muster over 3,000, most of them mounted and all of them armed, and including a company of artillery. This was accomplished on 24-hour notice via the telegraph.

The black militia were far from as well organized and commanded, but they too served their political purpose in keeping blacks Republican and making reprisals against the white rifle clubs for intimidation. But one thing both the armed whites and armed blacks agreed upon was to laugh at Chamberlain and President Grant when they were ordered to disband and the U.S. Army was reinforced in South Carolina. Neither side took the duly constituted authorities very seriously.

Chamberlain first appealed to President Grant on July 22, when the riots at Hamburg threatened to set off a series of armed clashes between the black militia and white rifle clubs all over the state. Chamberlain wanted U.S. troops, and he received what amounted to pious sympathy from Grant.

EXECUTIVE MANSION

Washington, D.C. July 26, 1876

Dear Sir:

I am in receipt of your letter of the 22nd of July and all the enclosures enumerated therein, giving an account of the late barbarous massacre of innocent men at the town of Hamburg, South Carolina. The views which you express as to the duty you owe your oath of office—and to the citizen—to secure to all their civil rights, including the right to vote according to the dictates of their own consciences, and the further duty of the Executive of the Nation to give all needful aid, when properly called on to do so, to enable you to insure this inalienable right, I fully concur in. The scene at Hamburg, as cruel, bloodthirsty, wanton, unprovoked and as uncalled for as it was, is only a repetition of the course that has been pursued in other Southern States within the last few years—notably in Mississippi and Louisiana—Mississippi is governed today by officials chosen through fraud and violence such as would scarcely be accredited to savages, much less to a civilized and Christian people. How long these things are to continue, or what is to be the final remedy, the Great Ruler of the Universe only knows. But I have an abiding faith that the remedy will come, and come speedily, and earnestly hope that it will come peacefully. There has never been a desire on the part of the North to humiliate the South—nothing is claimed for one State that is not freely accorded to all the others, unless it may be the right to kill negroes and republicans without fear of punishment, and without loss of caste or reputation. This has seemed to be a privilege claimed by a few States.

I repeat again that I fully agree with you as to the measure of your duties in the present emergency, and as to my duties—Go on, and let every Governor where the same danger threatens the peace of his State, go on in the conscientious performance of his duties to the humblest as well as proudest citizen, and I will give every aid for which I can find law, or constitutional power. Government that cannot give protection to the life, property and all guaranteed civil rights (in this country the greatest is an untrammeled ballot) to the citizen, is in so far a failure, and every energy of the oppressed should be exerted (Always within the law and by constitutional means) to regain lost privileges or protection. Too long denial of guaranteed rights is sure to lead to revolution, bloody revolution, where suffering must fall upon the guilty as well as the innocent.

Expressing the hope that the better judgment and cooperation of the citizens of the State over which you have presided so ably, may enable you to secure a fair trial and punishment of all offenders, without distinctions of "race, color, or previous condition of servitude" and without aid from the Federal Government—but with the promise of such aid on the conditions named in the foregoing. I subscribe myself

Very respectfully,
Your obedient servant
U. S. Grant

Hon. D. H. Chamberlain
Governor of South Carolina

The rifle clubs grew bolder every day of the campaign but Chamberlain took no further legal action against them. He was dickering with the Democrats to become their candidate as well as the Republicans'. If they nominated no Democrat for governor, he, in turn, would give the bounce to Robert B. Elliot, Christopher Columbus Bowen, and the radical Republican leadership for the rest of the ticket. For a time, even Wade Hampton considered this agreement—named "Fusionist"—a logical stepping-stone to ultimate white Democratic control. But there were too many other generals involved in the Democratic strategy, and they demanded a totally Democratic ticket—win or lose—"straightout."

After the Fusion plan failed and Chamberlain was snowed under with complaints that Republicans could not hold meetings without disturbances by the rifle clubs, and blacks complained about the beatings and black bodies resulting from the military campaign, he gave up and formally appealed to the President.

State of South Carolina
EXECUTIVE CHAMBER

Columbia, Oct. 8, 1876

To His Excellency
Ulysses S. Grant
President of the United States:
Sir:

I have to inform you, that insurrection and domestic violence exist in various portions of this State, especially in the Counties of Aiken, Barnwell and Edgefield against the peace and government of this State, to such an extent that I am unable with any means at my command to suppress the same;—that the Legislature of the State is not in Session and cannot be convened. Wherefore, by virtue of the power in me vested by the Constitution and laws of the State, and in accordance with Article *IV*, Section *IV* of the Constitution of the United States and of Section 5297 of the Revised Statutes of the United States, I do call upon you to aid me in suppressing said insurrection and domestic violence (and to suppress said insurrection and domestic violence) by the powers conferred upon you by the Constitution and laws of the United States.

In witness whereof I have hereunto set
my hand and caused the Great Seal of

the State to be affixed at Columbia
this Eighth day of October, A.D. 1876
and in the 101st Year of American
Independence.
By the Governor
D. H. Chamberlain

President Grant declared martial law on October 17 and ordered troops. There was a tongue in every Democratic cheek on October 18 when the state Executive Committee "disbanded" the rifle clubs even though President Grant had acted on the "misrepresentations of the Governor." They even "disbanded" their names and disavowed any political control over them. But nothing really changed except the names of public derision adopted by the clubs. The well-drilled troops now wore red shirts to "religious meetings" instead of Hampton meetings. They continued to break up Republican meetings and prevented Chamberlain from speaking in the up country.

The riots at Hamburg, Ellenton, Edgefield, Beaufort, Cainhoy, Charleston, and other places took their toll, usually black, but there are no mortality statistics for the month-long night-riding, just as in the KKK years of 1870 and 1871. But the swamps and by-roads yielded their black bodies once more. Actually, by Election Day, most of South Carolina was "captured" by whites whose historians named them "Redeemers," having redeemed the proud white state from black rule.

On the whole, these were curious allies for a man with Delany's fierce racial loyalty. However, he believed in Hampton's promises and not in Chamberlain's. On September 12, when Chamberlain accepted Robert B. Elliot and others like him on the same ticket, at the Republican state convention, Delany knew that nothing had changed and his people faced even greater disaster. That is why, two nights later, Delany really launched the campaign with his speech at the 4th Ward Democratic Club. He had accepted the invitation to speak there because he wished to assure the colored members that they had every right to be Democrats. In effect, he expanded on his New York speech of the year before. The *News and Courier* report of his arguments went all over the state.

His advice to his race would be to accept any good officer who was tendered them without regard to his politics, and he would say this in a Republican or Democratic meeting. There could be no equality of race if the colored man was not allowed to join the Democratic party (applause). White men had the right to become Republicans, why should not the colored man have the same right to change his politics. The fact that colored men have all been Republicans has done more than anything else to injure them. Again, they had been taught to believe that everything done by the Republicans was right, from the stealing of a watermelon to assassination. He was here to utter his unqualified condemnation of such teachings and no number of lying suits could deter him from uttering that condemnation (applause). He wanted to see one great party formed by the native whites and blacks of South Carolina for the common good of South Carolina, and for the common prosperity of her people (applause). He could not rest until this was done, and he didn't care a fig for the name it went by. It was the height of presumption for adventurers from abroad to come here and tell the laborer of the country that they must not strike hands with the capital of the country. What was wanted was union, friendship, confidence and reliance, and that was what they intended to have. (applause) These fellows who tell his race that the worst Republican was preferable to the best Democrat were fools and rascals. Was it not better for the colored people to accept the friendship of the Democrats if they could get it on the same terms. It was better to live on terms of friendship with one's neighbors than for both to be afraid to go out without being shot. Instead of this, some were trying to get up a war of races which they could never get up. (applause) He had never been a Radical Republican, nor never would be, because to be one he must be in favor of every rascality that took place. He was an Independent Republican. He saw Gen. Hampton's addresses and his kindly expressions to the colored race had entirely satisfied him. He knew he was earnest, but while he would state that his first preference would be for Governor Chamberlain, he saw nothing that would prevent him from voting for Gen. Hampton.

Naturally, there was anger and dismay among the Republicans. But there was also serious consideration given Delany's logic. Some 64,000 of them had thought enough of Delany to vote for him two years before, when he had warned his people to "Save what you can." But his most telling argument was that they were bound to no single party, as they had been to a single master while slaves. He was besieged with more invitations to speak.

But, as yet, Delany had not unmistakably "plumped" for Hampton. He had only told his people that they had the right to be Democrats if they chose. It was not until a few days after the state Democratic convention had met and decided that they would present the state with a complete ticket—the "Straight-out" Democratic ticket—that Delany took his stand and found himself Hampton's outstanding black spokesman. The *Charleston News and Courier* not only printed every word of his statement but editorialized with abandon. Its editor, Francis W. Dawson, had also switched sides, although it is likely he did so for pecuniary reasons rather than principles. The state treasury had been empty for two years of Chamberlain tenure, and Dawson's private correspondence reveals his unhappiness over this situation. Quite suddenly, the *News and Courier* had become a Hampton newspaper and thus joined most of the South Carolina press. Prominently displayed on September 26 was Delany's letter.

DELANY FOR HAMPTON

A Black Man's View of the Interest and Duty of His Race

A cool and intelligent statement of the aspects of politics and the relations of the races in South Carolina—the logic of events compels a conscientious National Republican to declare for Hampton and Good Government.

Charleston, S.C. September 25, 1876

To the Editor of The News and Courier: The present condition of things in the State, by the relation of the two races in hostile array against each other, is most anomalous, and, to the thoughtful observer, capable of comprehending the true state of the situation, and interested in the welfare of the people and State, is alarming to the extreme. I cannot, nor will not, believe otherwise than that political motives, by unscrupulous leaders, have induced it; as the general feelings between the races, till after the last canvass in 1874 for Governor, were kindly and cordial. The canvass of that year was the first great mutual effort made to unite the two races in one political movement, which came near being successful. Why then, now, this great divergence and extraordinary estrangement: From whichever side it comes, or whether from those on both sides, it evidently is intended to prevent a union of the two races in one common home or State interest.

In such an issue as that now pending, if not permanently checked, my race can have but one terminal destiny, political nonentity and race extermination. And what care the promoters of the fearful strife when that is the end they desire to obtain? This thing can and must be stopped. There are virtue and intelligence enough among the people to do it; but each race must perform its part and do its duty. Shall it be said that at such a crisis the blacks had no statesmen, no men of diplomatic wisdom among them equal to the emergency, the demands of the hour? For statesmanship is not necessary simply to diplomatic shrewdness, since even among savages (as the Indians of America) shrewd diplomatists are met with. Shall we, the blacks, be less than they?

When my race were in bondage I did not hesitate in using my judgment in aiding to free them. Now that they are free I shall not hesitate in using that judgment in aiding to preserve that freedom and promote their happiness. What I did and desired for my own race, I desire and would do if duty required for any other race. The exercise of all their rights, unimpaired and unobstructed, is that desire.

I have then but one line of duty left me, and that is to aid that effort which in my judgment best tends to bring about *a union of the two races, white and black,* (By black I mean all colored people) *in one common interest in the State,* with all the rights and privileges of each inviolate and sacredly respected.

The present Democratic movement promises this, and asks us, the blacks, simply to aid them and try them once; if they do not fulfill their promises, to trust them no more. This is simply fair. This was asked by the Republicans (colored people) in 1868 of the Democrats at the beginning of reconstruction, which they then refused, but have long since seen and felt the results of their error. I am not willing, now that an occasion requires our cooperation, that with their example before our eyes we should commit the same error.

As Gen. Wade Hampton is the candidate for Governor, no one will question him as speaking the sentiments of his party in the present issue and campaign. I quote:

In his speech at Abbeville, as in every county where he has spoken, he has pledged his word that, if elected Governor of South Carolina, he "*Render to the whole people of the State equal and impartial justice*." And that his meaning should be unmistakable he said: "If there is a white man in this assembly who, because he is a Democrat or because he is a white man, believes that when I am elected Governor, if I should be, I will stand between him and the law, or grant to him any privileges or immunities that shall not be granted to the colored man, he is mistaken; and I will tell him now, if that is his reason for voting for me, not to vote at all."

Again, as late as Saturday, the 23rd, at Darlington, he said: "We wish to show the colored people that their rights are fixed and immovable, and furthermore, we would not abridge them if we could. I do here, what I did in the Convention, *I pledge myself solemnly, in the presence of the people of South Carolina, and in the presence of my God that, if the Democratic ticket is elected, I shall know no party, nor race, in the administration of the law. So sure as the law pronounces a man guilty, so sure shall that man be punished. I shall know nothing but the law and the Constitution of South Carolina and of the United States.* (Immense applause) We recognize the thirteenth, fourteenth and fifteenth amendments of the Constitution of the United States, and so kept them in good faith. The colored people know that it is under these amendments they enjoy the rights they now have. We stand upon that platform and *not one single right enjoyed by the colored people today shall be taken from them. They shall be the equals, under the law, of any man in South Carolina.* And we further pledge that we will give better facilities for education than they have ever had before. (Loud cheering) Let me say one word more to the colored people. I was the first man in the State of South Carolina after the war, who advised the white people of South Carolina to give the right of voting to the colored people. I made the proposition at several public meetings in Columbia, and I took the ground that they had been made citizens and that they should not be excluded from the right to vote."

These are, indeed, most definite, strong, impressive and extraordinary words, and must have been candidly meant, or they never would have been spoken; and I shall hold Gen. Hampton on behalf of my race, before the civilized world, responsible for them; and if they are not verified in every particular the moral sentiment of all Christendom will be a swift and condemning witness against him. And not only him, but Mr. W. D. Simpson, candidate for Lieutenant Governor, and all others of his colleagues who have pledged their party for equal rights and justice before the law to all the people of both races, shall be held equally responsible for their utterances. I desire in this that my race shall see that the veracity, honor and integrity of the party have been pledged to them.

And since the Carolinians of the white race do not hesitate to take me at my word, and honor me with their support in the general State canvass of 1874 for Lieutenant Governor on the Independent Republican ticket, in an effort to redeem the State of incompetence and corruption, I shall now not hesitate to take them at their word, and aid them in a similar effort in 1876, by supporting the State movement and voting the State Democratic ticket as put forth and avowed in the present issue, for the good of all the people of both races. In doing this, I change no principles, but adhere as an American to the Democratic-Republican principles of the *right of the common people to rule.*

This is a step taken after the matured deliberation, as the claims of race are far above those of faction and party; and duty to the claims of community, far above the dictation and requirements of factional and party leaders.

My design was fixed after the adjournment of the Republican Convention recently held at Columbia, and my conclusion only reached after the Straight-Out nominations at the County Convention at Orangeburg, Thursday last, by which was proven to my satisfaction that the policy of the party recognizes both races, as three colored men were put in nomination on the ticket.

In this step, impelled by my own promptings for the benefit of my race with that of the white, as when, buckling on my sword, I entered the United States Army, as a field officer, for the same object and purposes, I have the honor to be, sir, your most obedient servant,

M. R. DELANY

From publication of this letter until the day of election Delany stumped for Hampton. He spoke only to and for his race. He reminded them again and again that not a single promise had been kept by the white Republicans and their black dependents in office. How many had "forty acres and a mule"? Where had their savings in the Freedmen's Bank gone? Was it not slavery to be bound to vote for the same people who built private fortunes from public money when so many schools were needed for black children? Here are another group of whites who promise things. They are mostly natives of South Carolina and the blacks must work for and with them. Therefore, they could be concerned with the welfare of the blacks and act honorably toward them. And, finally, what more do the blacks have to lose by switching to Hampton beyond what they already have lost by sticking with the Republicans?

Many times, particularly when he invaded the low country, Delany was not allowed to speak by the black militia. He was even shouted down at the very spot on Edisto Island where he had negotiated good contracts while on the special mission for Gen. Sickles in 1868. The very same people for whom he had negotiated interrupted his speech. He had gone to Edisto with a party of mixed white and black Democrats on the promise made by the Republican boss C. C. Bowen that they would be given a hearing, just as Republican speakers were given "equal time" at the Democratic meetings. The *News and Courier* reporter with the party called the audience of some 500 or 600 "African citizens" by far "the most uncouth, savage and uncivilized that I have ever seen."

> There was but one power that charmed them and held their inborn viciousness in check, and that was the magic name of "Bowen". . . . When it was understood that Col. M. R.

> Delany who is probably the most intelligent man of his race in the State was to be one of the speakers on the Democratic side, your correspondent asked Mr. Bowen if they would hear him speak. "Yes," replied Bowen, "I reckon I can keep them still but it will be just about as hard as to hold a wild elephant or a lion without tying him."

But if the reporter's account is credible, Delany was as tough as any of them. He wrote:

> After speaking twenty minutes, Mr. Smythe gave way to Col. M. R. Delany who was introduced by the chairman as the next Democratic speaker. As soon as Col. Delany mounted the wagon, the Negroes started to beat their drums and left in a body. They would not listen to "De damned Nigger Democrat". In vain, the chairman called them to come back and shouted to them to stop their drum beating. They paid no attention to his orders. They marched off and the women crowded around the wagon with their bludgeons, with threats, curses and imprecations. Even Bowen was unable to restore quiet until he leaped from the wagon and brought them back by main force. A semblance of order after a half hour's work was restored, and Col. Delany was invited to go on with his speech. This, however, he declined to do. He simply said that he had been in Europe and Africa in the presence of the nobility of many countries, and black as he was, he had never been insulted as he had been today by the people of his own race. Amid frequent interruptions, he reminded them of the fact that he had come to South Carolina with his sword drawn, to fight for the freedom of the black man; that being a black man himself, he had been a leading abolitionist; that he had warned them against trusting their money to the Freedmen's Bank; and that they had, to their sorrow, paid no heed to his warnings. His only object was to give them warning now that the northern white people were altogether in sympathy with the southern whites. They could see that by reading the northern newspapers. He was a friend of his own race and had always held the position that it was the duty of those who had education to teach them that their best interests were identical with the white natives of the State.

Delany was the target for the Cainhoy black militia on October 16, during which six whites and one Negro were killed and many were wounded. The village, ten miles upriver from Charleston, was under siege for several days. Delany was with other Democrats both black and white, when the militia opened fire on the gentle, inoffensive W. J. McKinlay, the Charleston teacher, whom they mistook for Delany.

However, it was generally agreed among the Democrats that Delany's voice and influence and his reputation for integrity had won whatever black vote Hampton received and that black vote was sufficient to allow him to strike the bargain electing Hayes and himself.

The results of the election were in doubt for some time and there was worriment in both camps. Gen. Conner, who was holding down command in Charleston, had sent his wife to Richmond, Va., for safety, and he wrote her two days before the election: "What the result will be is hard to say. It will be a very close election, whoever wins. The chances are that the State will go for Hayes, but will elect our State ticket. It all depends on the darkey, and no human being can tell you how he will vote."

Three days after the election, on November 10, Gen. Conner again wrote his wife:

> The election passed off quietly enough, but the negroes went back on us fearfully. They fooled us to death. Thousands who had promised Hayes and Hampton voted the solid Republican ticket. The pressure of race and religion was brought to bear upon them. All their preachers had harped on the election in their Sunday discourses, and the ignorant ones had told their hearers in so many words that to vote the Democratic ticket was to go to hell sure. We lost at least twenty-eight hundred votes that were pledged to us in the City alone, and we could not buy votes on election day. They wanted it as badly as ever, but they dared not touch it.

The story of the four months of "dual government" in Columbia is a familiar one. It amounted to a military occupation of the counties and assumption of local authority by Democrats designated by Hampton's generals. Chamberlain and his Republicans held the State House while Hampton and his Redshirts held the state. Only the U.S. soldiers kept the remnants of the black militia and the Redshirts apart.

Finally, at the end of March, both Chamberlain and Hampton went to Washington for interviews with the newly inaugurated Hayes. There had been no re-count of the vote in South Carolina. That 816 margin of the presidential electors committed to Hayes was too small to be risked. But the question still remained, Who was Governor of South Carolina?

Hampton had kept his side of the bargain. He was in a position to command any kind of re-count he named, made by Democrats, of course. Chamberlain could not even command a mobilization of the blacks. The result of the interviews was a certainty, and Hampton sat in his room in the Willard Hotel in Washington and sent his bill for services rendered to the President of the United States. It repeats the conditions of the deal and, as blackmail with finesse, has no parallel in American history.

WILLARD'S HOTEL

Mar. 31, 1877
Washington, D.C.

To The President
Sir

The result of the conference to which you did me the honor to invite me, has been to leave on my mind the conviction that you sincerely desire to see a peaceful and just settlement of the questions which are distracting our people and injuring so seriously the material interests of our State and I trust that you are equally convinced of my earnest wish to aid in accomplishing this happy end. As I may not have the pleasure of seeing you again on this subject, it may be proper to put before you in the fullest and most definite form, the assurance given to you verbally. I repeat therefore, that if the Federal Troops are withdrawn from the State House, there shall be on my part, or that of my friends no resort to violence, to assert our claims, but that we shall look for their maintenance solely to such peaceful remedies as the Constitution and laws of the State provide. I shall use all my authority to repress the use or the exhibition of force, in the settlement of all disputed questions, and this authority shall be exercised in such a manner that the peace shall be preserved. We only desire the establishment in our State of a Government, which will secure to every citizen, the lowest as well as the highest, black as well as white, full and equal protection in the enjoyment of all his rights under the Constitution of the United States. No one can be more deeply impressed than myself with the imperative necessity of establishing cordial relations between all classes and both races in So. Ca. for it is only by these means, that the true and enduring welfare of the State can be secured. With the recognition of the perfect equality of every citizen before the law, with a just and impartial administration of the laws; with a practical secure exercise of the right of suffrage; with a system of public education which will open the services of knowledge to all classes we may hope to see our State soon take the position to which she is entitled. It was the patriotic hope to aid in the accomplishment of these high aims, that called me from my retirement to become a candidate for the office of Governor of So. Ca. It was through the confidence of the people of that State that I would honestly and faithfully carry out all these purposes, that I was elected their Chief Magistrate: and I feel profoundly that peace can be surely preserved there, and prosperity restored, by assuring our people, that the right of "local self-government" so prominently brought forward in your Inaugural and so favorably received by the whole country, is to be promptly carried out as the rule of your Administration. I anticipate the ready fulfilment of the just and reasonable hopes inspired by the announcement of the policy you have unfolded,—a policy which found a responsive echo in every patriotic heart as indicating a purpose to administer the government in the true spirit of the Constitution. In conclusion, permit me to assure you that I feel the strongest confidence that the wise and patriotic policy announced in your Inaugural, will, as soon as it takes shape in action produce such fruits, that the whole country will enjoy the blessings of peace, prosperity and harmony. Thanking you, Sir, for the courtesy you have extended to me and with my good wishes, I am

Very Respy Yr. obt Sevt
Wade Hampton
Governor of So Ca

On April 10 all Federal troops were withdrawn from Columbia, and so was Chamberlain. He left quite hurriedly, and it appeared that the long war was over. It also appeared that a new era had dawned for the blacks, for in his inaugural address Hampton had repeated the pledges of civil rights made to Delany and to the blacks throughout the campaign that

> they declared solemnly that all citizens of South Carolina, of both races and both parties, should be regarded as equals in the eyes of the law; all to be protected in the enjoyment of every political right now possessed by them.
>
> To the faithful observance of these pledges we stand committed, and I, as the representative of the conservative party, hold myself bound by every dictate of honor and good faith, to use every effort to have these pledges redeemed fully and honestly. It is due not only to ourselves but to the colored people of the State that wise, just and liberal measures should prevail in our legislation. We owe much of our late success to these colored voters who were brave enough to rise above the prejudice of race and honest enough to throw off the shackles of their party in their determination to save the State. To those who, misled by their fears, their ignorance, or by evil counseling, turned a deaf ear to our appeals, we should not be vindictive but magnanimous. Let us show to all of them that the true interests of both races can best be secured by cultivating peace and promoting prosperity among all classes of our fellow citizens.

These were fine, reassuring words, and Hampton may even have meant them. They expressed all that Delany had in his heart. Now the black people of South Carolina and the country could begin again. Delany was so happy that he paid no attention to Chamberlain's answer to the question, on July 4, 1877, "What is the President's Southern policy?" in a speech in Connecticut.

> In point of actual present results, it consists in the abandonment of Southern Republicans, and especially the colored race, to the control and rule not only of the Democratic party, but of that class at the South which regarded slavery as a Divine Institution, which waged four years of destructive

> war for its perpetuation, which steadily opposed citizenship and suffrage for the negro—in a word, a class whose traditions, principles, and history are opposed to every step and feature of what Republicans call our national progress since 1860.
>
> In point of general political and moral significance it consists in the proclamation to the country and the world that the will of the majority of the voters of a State, lawfully and regularly expressed, is no longer the ruling power in our States, and that the constitutional guaranty to every State in this Union of a republican form of government and of protection against domestic violence, is henceforth ineffectual and worthless.

It was two years before Delany would agree that Chamberlain was right. Meanwhile, for the first months of 1877 he himself was caught between the two "governors" keeping their governments in Columbia. One of Hampton's first acts after having himself inaugurated was to appoint four trial justices in Charleston, and Delany was one of them. But the largely Republican city of Charleston refused to recognize any of the Hampton appointments. That was true throughout the state where there was a Republican majority, and in the Democratic counties, the Chamberlain officials were boycotted.

In Charleston the difficulty was not resolved until C. C. Bowen was deposed as sheriff of the county. Bowen simply refused to arrest anybody or accept anybody in his jail if they were to come before a Hampton-appointed trial justice. The *News and Courier* went editorially wild about this situation, demanding action from the Hampton appointees.

> We answer for it, that the business of the bogus justices will come to an end very quickly, if any of the Hampton Justices will give notice upon proper information he will arrest and hold for trial any person calling himself Constable or Trial Justice other than the Hampton Justices and their Constables, who shall arrest or in any way molest any citizen. The Trial Justice giving this notice can make the necessary arrests. *There is power enough in Charleston for that* (italics mine), but he must be prepared to arrest any person who refuses to obey his process and he must be prepared to clap

> the prisoners in jail, and to arrest and imprison any person who refuse to receive them at the jail. This is no time for milk and water talk or rose water remedies. We want men, not grannies.

The writer of this editorial was Francis W. Dawson and he, with fourteen others knew very well that "There is power enough in Charleston. . . ." They comprised a secret, all-white Charleston County Democratic executive committee which had been meeting in the Bank of Charleston since January 3, 1876. One word to Gen. Conner who was a member and half a dozen rifle clubs would have any Chamberlain trial justice and Bowen lodged in the jail, if they survived.

This group operated in secret throughout 1876 and thereafter controlled the Democratic organization in the county in continued sworn secrecy. At their second meeting, on January 8, a surviving Minute Book reveals that the chairman, G. Lamb Buist, delineated their structure.

> This Committee should consider the entire responsibility in them and be the dictators for the time being without imparting their knowledge to the Party. . . . We have accepted the trust to organize the County. It must be successfully done regardless of mountains of offense. The offended will be louder in their praises where the good work is done. With the white people there is no choice, hence our power. . . ."

The entire county was to be organized and controlled, ward by ward, parish by parish, island by island. No member of the committee was to assume a purely party office but rather was to select the Democratic leader and retain control over him. Only announcements and propaganda approved by the committee were to appear in the *News and Courier*.

Organizationally, the presidents of each ward were to operate in two directions (1) the white vote—to list registered Democrats and those who refused to so register to be publicly named radicals, and (2) the colored vote . . .

> 1. Make a complete census of the qualified colored voters in your respective precincts, in which shall appear: 1) the name

and aliases of the voter; 2) with whom he works, and in what capacity, and who advances him money; 3) when enrolled, the Negro should know we have his name.

Those blacks who were Democrats were to be organized into clubs. With such instructions, it would be difficult for any black in Charleston County to eat without going Democratic. Within two *local* elections, all blacks in Charleston understood the message. With another *state* election, all blacks in South Carolina got the message, and the black majority was no more.

Delany watched this happen but neither he nor most blacks could complain of Hampton. He kept every one of his promises to the blacks and more, thereby becoming the first white politician to do so. Hampton even vetoed a legal peonage bill in the 1877 legislative session which the blacks felt was aimed at them. It was to allow the use of penal labor on public works, such as roads, and during the Black Code years of the Provisional Government, had been applied by county authorities against blacks under the broad "vagrancy" clauses. It was not until 1936 in Arkansas that legal peonage was attacked successfully in the South after it had become common practice. Hampton was perhaps the first and last of the southern governors to recognize the injustice in this phase of American *apartheid.*

Delany had a personal reason to admire Hampton. He stood by him in the spring of 1878 when the official Charleston Democratic delegation—not the secret committee—decided that they did not want a black man as trial justice. On March 18, 1878, over 26 signatures, a petition went to Gov. Hampton asking for Delany's removal. The reason given was "Because the office is conducted by the said M. R. Delany in a manner discreditable to the present Administration of the State of South Carolina and repugnant to the feelings of both races in this community."

There followed a petition campaign for and against Delany, begun by the concurrence of the titular Democratic committee—not the secret committee—with the original removal request but without stating any reasons.

When this action was taken, Delany wrote his one and only letter to Hampton in regard to it: "I have the honor to state to you that the Charleston Delegation has selected my name for removal from office; I know of no cause to merit this. And I hope, Sir, that this shall not be done without giving me an opportunity of vindicating myself."

There was no need to "vindicate" himself. An amazing campaign began, without question begun by decision of the secret committee. The president of the Charleston Chamber of Commerce, George Y. Tupper, wrote to Hampton concerning some legislation and ended: "Permit me to say a word in favor of Maj. Delany, a colored man, whose removal as a trial justice has been recommended by our delegation. A good deal of sympathy is felt for him by many of your friends. He was warmly and actively with us during the late gubernatorial contest and I cannot learn of any well founded objection to him."

Gen. Conner, too, could not understand why the Charleston delegation wanted to get rid of Delany but promised Hampton he would try to find out. "The colored people are moving in behalf of Delany. The latter was very much ostracized when he became a Hampton Democrat but the 'panning out' has led the brethren to think that Delany's head was black on top, and they have come back to him and gave him a very prominent place on the flag reception of the *Azor*, so that unless there is good reasons (*sic*) for removal, it would not be politic."

But on April 5 the *News and Courier* carried the following note:

> A petition has been put in circulation for the retention of Trial Justice Delany in office. A number of persons have already signed it, and it will be presented to the citizens again today. A copy of the petition will be at this office for the convenience of any who desire to sign.

And, of course, among the old families, former mayors, business, and civic leaders who signed the petition was Francis W. Dawson, editor of the newspaper. It is quite likely that he wrote the message over those signatures.

> We the undersigned citizens of Charleston City and County, do most earnestly recommend to your Excellency the retention of Maj. M. R. Delany in office as a Trial Justice in and for said City and County.
>
> We know that Maj. M. R. Delany is a man of coolness, deliberateness and broad experience, which enabled him to

differ widely with many persons of his own race and party and especially with the extravagant and ultra men.

His record speaks louder than this paper.

It was a repetition of his experience with Chamberlain, except that Hampton stood by him and Delany was trial justice as long as Hampton was governor, until Hampton was elected to the U.S. Senate in 1879.

But Wade Hampton was not typical of the South or the southerners whose "word" was piously vaunted. In all of the rebel states there began the evasion of the 13th, 14th, and 15th Amendments on which their readmission into the Union as equals was based. Putting the "nigger" back in his place was a procedure quite easy to rationalize. Those rights for the blacks were forced on the South at the point of a bayonet, were they not? Therefore, there was no moral obligation to observe them. Nor was there any longer a political obligation. By 1877 the Yankees too were honoring in the breach the very guarantees to the blacks that they had forced down the throats of the vanquished South. The nation was once again indivisible in one intent—return the blacks to the inferiority from which fratricidal war had so briefly lifted them.

This was quite easy to accomplish, for semi-starvation and total dependency for bread alone will render slaves of all humans, yet it keeps the 13th Amendment pristine. Share-cropping, labor paid in script or credit, vagrancy laws, intimidation and outright robbery of land, livestock, and crops from blacks who had achieved a measure of economic independence—all restored slavery. There were only two differences. No white was obligated to feed any black, as under the slave codes, nor could a white prevent the physical departure of black labor except by legal imprisonment—which deprived him of that labor—or keeping families as hostages. All of these practices were adopted in all of the South by 1877.

The denial of guarantees of the 14th and 15th Amendments followed in due course with "grandfather" clauses, poll taxes, and the familiar methods of eliminating black voting power utilized today. State by state, constitutions were amended into the formal structure of American *apartheid*.

With the loss of suffrage came, of course, the loss of protest and civil rights, the loss of schools, health care, and civic assets —loss of an equal share in the benefits of the tax dollar. In substance, the blacks returned to inferiority status in all respects, and the only representatives of the race allowed any hearing at all were the "Uncle Tom's" like Booker T. Washington. It was a gradual process and varied from state to state from 1877 on. In fact, it was not until 1902 that white perfection returned to the land. For the first time since the Civil War not a single black was in any state legislature or in Congress.

The old process of change from hope to despair was again repeated in Delany. Once more he was completing the cycle and, by 1878 it was emigrate, for the fight was over. Gen. Conner's reference to the *Azor* was Delany's last desperate effort to help others realize his African dream of twenty years before.

In the spring of that year he was in communication with the American Colonization Society from Hilton Head when that organization had chartered the *Golconda* to carry disillusioned blacks to Liberia. On January 16 of that year Delany wrote William Coppinger, Secretary, asking free passage for a young freedwoman from Savannah, who had found refuge in Hilton Head. "She deserves a better fate, and desires to take the highest step in life attainable. . . . I believe that her going will be but the precursor of many more leaving the South for Africa, my beloved fatherland, who ought to leave for their own good and that of posterity."

However, at that time the Colonization Society was broke. It had lost its chief source of revenue—the slaveholder—and Congress was no more interested in appropriating money to get rid of the blacks than it was to change their economic position. Lincoln was dead and the South needed cheap black labor.

It was not strange nor out of character that Delany should engage in the struggle by the blacks for position in the new America and still remain an emigrationist. He was criticized for mixing his objectives—fight or emigrate—but he quite candidly answered his critics in the *Christian Recorder* of April 18, 1868, from Hilton Head.

> All men of maturely intelligent experience in social affairs know that discontentment is, next to famine and a prevailing mortality, the most disastrous in its consequences, of any thing that can be brought upon any people. It enervates

them, makes them nonentities; they simply do nothing from discouragement, and are, therefore, in life useless.

There are now, in different parts of the South, several thousand freed people, who are determined not to remain, desirous of going to Africa, and really impatiently anxious to get off. It is not to be a question why this is so; in fact, it gives its own question and answer: simply because they are the people, therefore, just like all other peoples under similar circumstances—Germans and Irish for example, leaving their nativity in Europe—when dissatisfied.

I am here—so far as I am desirous—for the benefit of my race, and whatever I conceive to be conducive to their interests, I am ready and willing to advise, which has been the course of my actions, ever since my station in the South.

To the end of aiding, and thereby saving from moral destruction, all who desire to emigrate to our father and mother land, I hope that the next expedition or voyage of the "Golconda" out, may consist of a "squadron" of at least four large vessels, instead of one, that there may be no discouraging disappointments to the three thousand people who would most certainly go, if only assured that there will be an opportunity.

The desires of this people should be complied with, because being people, they are in their affections and passions, just like others, and wont (*sic*) be satisfied where they are.

Nor will this prejudicially affect that part of our brethren who never will leave America, but rather favorably; because experience and observation teach us, that wherever there are the *fewest* colored people in the United States, there is the *least* objection to them.

Ten years later, when a group of despairing blacks from all parts of South Carolina formed an organization to escape to Liberia, naturally they turned to Delany for guidance. They were not alone in what came to be known as the "Exodus" movement of 1878–1879 when blacks from every black belt state once more faced the question—where to go? Thousands from Louisiana and Mississippi found their way up the Mississippi River to join "Pap" Singleton's colonies in Kansas, which were begun by Tennessee fugitives. Once again, a few found their way northward to

Indiana, then to Canada, and some trekked through Texas to the Mexican border. But they were few in number compared with the millions in servitude.

One, a 28-year-old black teacher named H. N. Bouey who was to escape from Edgefield Court House to Charleston and then work with Delany on the *Azor* project, early in 1877 wrote of his people's fate in Edgefield County in a letter asking Bishop Henry M. Turner of the AME Church for direction.

> Dear Sir: I write to inform you, that as soon as I can arrange my business in America, I am going to Liberia to teach school. Not to come back either. I am a colored man or yellow man as you may have it. I have become satisfied that the colored man has no home in America. I have manhood in me that I would sooner die than compromise. You may not know me but I have seen you, and know you too well to undertake to tell you, anything of our humiliations socially, our degradation politically, and our afflictions financially, in the south. We have no chance to rise from begars (*sic*). Men own the capital that we work, who believe that they still have a right to either use us or our value from the general Government. Hence they believe that my race have no more right to any of the profits of their labor than one of their mules. The majority of colored men who work with the heartless Democrats, get just about what the mule gets of the profits of labor. In five years from now the public schools will be closed on the negro. In a few of the southern states they have fine schools; but only in the cities, towns and villages where they can be seen by visitors. But my *God*, the masses of our people just behind the vail (*sic*) are piteous. You know educations make unprofitable labor in the south,—hence my people must, and will, be kept ignorant. Some of their leaders such as have property own farms, and some ministers, who have fine congregations supporting them, are standing against immigration to Liberia. But you know, our people must be kept poor and ignorant, so that they may be profitable laborers. I live in this miserable County Edgefield and every pulsation of my heart prays God to speed next fall, when I shall leave for Liberia.

But Bouey did not go to Liberia in the fall of 1878. He joined with a New Guinea native named George Curtis in

Charleston, and they interested Rev. B. F. Porter, an AME pastor who was occupied in black education; and by the end of 1877 Delany had joined them as a member of the Board of Directors of the Liberian Exodus Joint Steam Ship Company. This was a nonprofit stock company in which the purchase of a single share at $10 entitled the stockholder to passage to Liberia. These subscriptions were utilized for a down payment on the *Azor*, a 190-foot clipper-built bark of 412 tons. It was to make a regular run to Monrovia from Charleston, carrying emigrants there and pay-cargo back. The goal of the emigrants was a settlement seventy miles up the St. Paul's River established by an emigrant from Charleston who had gone out on the *Golconda* in 1866.

While Delany was involved in the entire project, his chief contribution was to handle the negotiations with the Liberian government whereby each emigrant received a land-grant of 25 acres without cost and additional land as desired at a cost of fifty cents an acre.

The group announced the project in the fall of 1877 and almost immediately were swamped with eager fugitives. Even before the stock was issued the rumor ran all through South Caro lina, Georgia, and as far as New Orleans that a ship was to sail o of Charleston Harbor for free Liberia on November 15. Hund of families left their homes for Charleston.

Within three months after organization of the stock pany there were sufficient subscriptions to purchase th and it was brought into Charleston Harbor to be ref passenger use. Soon the first voyage was booked to r capacity, and the waiting list, even before the *Azor* sa April 1878, was sufficient to account for six more cro

There was a strange reaction from the whites began to feel almost a religious frenzy in their call The exodus movement became a unifying force a of such proportions that it affected their lab planters began to complain. The exodus was posal of the peonage law in the state legislatu ton. It was one thing to return black labor for exploitation but a calamity to lose it er that by the summer of 1877 approximatel the process of joining the movement.

Delany was spokesman for the m and, in his speeches, stressed that pa

whites was al

Exodus Association declaring it a result of "a desire to prepare for the rising generation of colored men and women who have had the advantages of education, a sphere in life in which they can maintain a position equivalent to their attainments and talents, and not to be confined, as they would be in this country, to a subordinate and menial position in society." He was called upon to speak at the Liberian Independence Day celebration of July 26 when 7,000 blacks massed to hear about their fatherland from a man who had been there. The July 4th American Independence Day celebration of 1878 was converted into an Exodus Day, as was the Emancipation Day celebration of that year.

When Dawson of the *News and Courier* sought an explanation for the exodus movement, he questioned Delany just before the *Azor* sailed about whether the political change in South Carolina and the election of Hampton were responsible for the "cry . . . raised throughout the entire South by the black race that their liberty had been wrested from them and that Africa, their fatherland, was their only place of refuge."

> Major M. R. Delany, a prominent officer in the Exodus Association and a man who has in person explored the wilds of Africa, says that this political aspect was given to the movement not so much by the fear of ill treatment from the whites as by apprehension on the part of the blacks that they could not live in a subordinate position where, for ten years, they had held the reins of government and had been led to believe that they would always retain the supremacy. The blacks, he says, had enjoyed such license and such unbridled liberty from the time of their emancipation, that when the check came the shock was too great. They could not see how they could live without their accustomed license. The let-down had come so suddenly and so unexpectedly that the result was general discontent and unwillingness to remain in any community where they could not be the predominant element.

Delany also predicted to Dawson (quite accurately) that [illegible] would replace black labor in the near future, and this [illegible]eady taking place in the skilled trades. Black artisans were

being supplanted by emigrants or workers from the North. "The colored people are fast coming to the conclusion that the tide of white labor is setting southward. It will not be many years before white men will be performing much of the labor which they are now dependent upon for their support."

But like so many "back-to-Africa" movements since, the *Azor* venture was destined to fail, not for want of emigrants (some 300 were waiting) but because of financial difficulties beginning with the very first voyage. The crisis was placed on Delany's shoulders. He was named chairman of the Committee on Finance and also of a special committee to negotiate a new financial structure. He needed $1,680 within ten days of July 8 when he wrote to the president of the American Colonization Society in Baltimore, asking for a loan in that amount for four months. By October, when crops would begin coming in, the emigrants would be able to buy sufficient stock to rescue the company.

> We solicit no money or donations as our movement is intended to be self-sustaining in order to make our people self reliant. Among the whites here we have no friends to the movement who would aid us by loan; but would rather contribute to prevent success. We would not have these drafts (for $1,680.) dishonored under any consideration. Our prospect is very encouraging and we desire that nothing should impede our progress.

The obligation had been incurred on the first voyage when Capt. W. E. Holmes, white, apparently began a series of maneuvers to take over the *Azor*. He had been trying to buy it and was outbid by the Exodus Association. When he reached Sierra Leone on May 28, 1878, Capt. Holmes incurred towing charges, then an additional amount for supplies. This might have been overcome, but he returned from Africa in ballast, not even having sought a cargo. Even this might have been overcome too with a well-paying cargo to London, but Capt. Holmes used all of the freight charges for expenses, then sued the Association for back pay.

On January 1, 1879, the Exodus Association owed $4,600, all lost in operation of the *Azor*, and the ship was held in Charleston Harbor for debt by the U.S. Admiralty Court. A mass meeting to raise $5,000 was unsuccessful, and a wealthy Boston merchant named F. S. Rodgers bid for the vessel at the ridiculously low price of $2,675, of which $450 was forwarded by the Exodus Association. The understanding was that the cost to Rodgers would be met by November 11, 1880. The money was offered on time, and only then did Delany learn that Rodgers had sold the *Azor* at a fat profit five months before. On December 18, 1880, he wrote to Coppinger of the American Colonization Society:

> The transaction has surprised everybody, as this merchant is very wealthy, was commended as being very reliable, and generally reputed to be a gentleman of unswerving integrity. A suit has been entered for $10,000, but I have no hopes of success except through his clemency, as he has plenty of means and we have none.

The litigation dragged on until 1884 and then disappeared with the Exodus Association. All its resources were gone in the legal snarl. Once again white speculators in the North had punctured a black dream.

CHAPTER TWENTY-FIVE

"Shall Have Lived in Vain"

There was little satisfaction for Delany in seeing his predictions coming true daily. All through the Hampton years—in fact for the rest of his life—he watched American *apartheid* take its present shape. He did not try to make his compromises with the structure after Hampton had gone to the Senate, and the new governor did not see fit to reappoint Delany as trial justice. Economically, he again returned to the practice of medicine; emotionally, he again turned to Africa. Intellectually, he continued to fight the whites. He could not, like Frederick Douglass and Booker T. Washington, accept as final for his lifetime the dictate that he and his people were inferior to any and all whites. He refused to agree that there are natural or social limitations inherent in blackness. He continued to dispute, as he had since the 1830s, any compromise with equality of opportunity in a democracy such as this country claimed to be.

When a man does not know when he is licked, he fumbles. This is what Delany did for the last six years of his life. He sang his "Swan Song" in 1879 with publication of *Principia of Ethnology*, etc., which was written during his preoccupation with the duties of trial justice and the problems of the exodus. But during those busy years he also had had some joy in his sons. How often he visited his family in Wilberforce, we do not know.

We do not know if Delany returned to Wilberforce for the commencement exercises of the Class of '73 when Alexander Dumas graduated or to the commencement of the Class of '78 for Faustin Soulouque's graduation. But he lived to see Alexander Dumas become principal of the colored schools in Urbana, Ohio, and Faustin become a professor at Lincoln University in Jefferson City, Mo.

For a time he lived with St. Cyprian and Charles Lenox

Remond in Charleston. St. Cyprian came to him first and served as a secretary in the Liberian Exodus offices until he was given an appointment as a postal clerk and carrier and spent the rest of his life working in the Charleston post office. Charles Lenox Remond was not with his father long. He was working somewhere near Savannah and was drowned in the Savannah River in mid-December 1879 at the age of 29. All that is known of the circumstances is the terse news item announcing the accidental drowning of Maj. Delany's son. If not for the relationship, even that would not have been reported. Black deaths were not news.

Toussaint, by then, was a wanderer, frequently ill with an eye affliction. He taught in colored schools in Louisiana and Mississippi, worked as a barber in Nashville, and in a saloon in St. Louis. After many years of effort he was awarded a pension of $6 a month as a veteran of the 54th Massachusetts.

At home with Catherine and still at school were Placido and Hallie. Why didn't Delany return home by 1880, when he was so clearly defeated? From his own correspondence the pitiable truth was that he did not know that his kind of rebellion had ended. He did not know that a black man could no longer afford to dream, and he still had the African dream. As late as December 1880, when he had reached 68 years of age, Delany still believed that he and his family would one day emigrate to Africa. He wrote then: "By God's help I shall hope before long to help forward the glorious work. I have the hope and expectation of having to aid me (in Africa) at least two of my sons who shall be Civil Engineers and Mineralogists."

In August of that same year he corresponded with William Coppinger of the American Colonization Society and explained his plans quite at length. He lacked the money to pursue them, he told Coppinger. But

> my course has been laid out, and my work in Africa all fixed and clear before me. My expenses in supporting my family and educating my children very great, and as I could not be a corrupt politician, you see that I found no favor with those in influence and authority. . . . I am at my old profession of Medicine, as the best I can do for the present. And I have been thus particular, and in letting you know something about myself and *my* interests in this greatest, and to me,

> all absorbing to the black man, movements of Africa's future. If I could get some one of the many government favors worth from $2,000. to $3,000. a year for about two (2) years, this would give me the command of available means sufficient, so as to enable me to leave my family, and children in school, and go at once to Africa, the field of my destined labor.

Delany wrote as though unaware of his age. Within two years he would be seventy, surely an advanced age at which to launch a new life in Africa. He suggested to Coppinger that some such position as Superintendent of the Freedmen's Hospital in Washington would be the ideal type of appointment. Only at the conclusion of this long and autobiographical letter was there a hint of complaint.

> I have thus brought these matters in connection with myself before you—as an old friend, that you may see how studiously and completely I have been ignored by my "friends" after all my services faithfully performed under the government, in the Army, during four years and ten months.

By the end of the year he had another proposal for Coppinger, inspired by Hayes' appointment of his old friend and rival, Frederick Douglass, as Marshal of the District of Columbia. Delany wanted Coppinger's help in obtaining an appointment of some kind but particularly as "Doorkeeper of the U.S. Senate." He told the Colonization Society official that he would be in Washington in February 1881 in search of some appointment. He was still in Washington, jobless, although he did some lecturing, in June when he applied to the Secretary of the Treasury, William Windom, and once more expressed some hopes of a diplomatic post.

> Pending my appointment to a position secured as Consul to a foreign Post, I have the honor to make Application for a position as Special Agent, or Inspector, in your Department, for a limited time previous to my assignment to duty as Consul. I can bring with me the experience of several

years practice in such duties as would be required in such agencies.

With this he enclosed a letter of recommendation from Samuel J. Lee, former Speaker of the South Carolina House and of dubious reputation. Lee was now a candidate for Congress from the Charleston District (and was defeated).

Delany was never to receive a political appointment. For a time he stumped Virginia for Republican Congressional candidates. He joined a host of famous blacks in the Washington Emancipation Day celebration of 1883 on New Year's Day, and despite the presence of both old and new leadership this 20th anniversary of the Emancipation Proclamation had all the characteristics of a wake, even though the *Washington Bee* characterized it as the "grandest event on record in the history of the colored race." Senator Blanche K. Bruce from Mississippi was the main speaker and there was a banquet for Frederick Douglass. Delany was one of the speakers too and his subject was still Africa, "The Republic of Liberia." Socially, it no doubt was a great occasion but in 1883 everyone knew that emancipation had proved to be a mockery of freedom. Only the younger men there, the new black leadership, like T. Thomas Fortune, the black historian George Williams, young Lewis Douglass, John Cromwell, the black scholar—they were yet to experience the frustrations of a structured *apartheid*.

Before going home to Catherine, a sick and dying man, Delany tried other things, such as an appointment to manage a fruit plantation in Central America which fell through. And he lectured, so long as he was physically able, and sold his *Principia of Ethnology* to the audiences.

Actually, this book was Delany's last gesture of defiance to the white world. It was published in 1879 by the firm of Harper & Brother in Philadelphia, and undoubtedly, in the light of today's knowledge, added little to the ethnological mysticism considered a science at that time. It is a pseudo-scientific tract in behalf of the Negro in general and Africa in particular, and it could be dismissed as a flight of Delany's racial fancy, read today. But if the reader were also to read Thomas Carlyle's "Occasional Discourse on the Nigger Question," pertaining to the West Indian Negroes, or anything by Dr. Samuel G. Morton of Philadelphia, founder of the "cranial difference" school of Negro inferiority, or perhaps Dr. Josiah Clark Nott of Mobile, Ala., whose theories in "Types of Mankind" were gospel in America until an atheist named Charles Darwin came along—in fact, if one were to read any of the anthropological and ethnological treatises of the day, Delany's work is refreshing. Whether his premise is right or wrong, at least his argument has a semblance of logic. This is surprising, since it was written out of the deep roots of Delany's pride in his race, from an emotional necessity to tell the white man that the black *is* now co-equal and once *was* superior. As he wrote, in a letter to his old mentor, Dr. William Elder: "I desire to dare do, what white men have ever dared and done." He was the first black American to attempt it.

The title of the book is descriptive: *Principia of Ethnology: The Origin of Races with an Archeological Compendium of Ethiopian and Egyptian Civilization.* After his name, as author, he added: "Formerly Physician, Surgeon and Practitioner in the Diseases of Women and Children; Member of the International Statistical Congress, London, His Royal Highness Albert Prince Consort of England, President; Member of the National Association for the Promotion of Social Science, and Member of the Social Science Congress, Glasgow, Scotland, 1860, Rt. Honorable Lord Henry Brougham and Vaux, President; late Major in the United States Army, now one of the Justices of Charleston, by Commission of the Governor." It was dedicated to the Earl of Shaftesbury, patron of many intellectual endeavors and particularly helpful to Delany in 1860, so much so that Delany wrote in the dedication, "the writer may dare venture to claim the moral aid of His Lordship, in this his second adventure, in the regeneration of his Race and Fatherland, and that Race the attainment of a promised inheritance."

Today's anthropologists might quarrel with the basis Delany assumed in order to attach the blacks to the unquestioned wonders of the Ethiopian and Egyptian civilizations. He took the Hamitic thesis that the sons of Noah were Shem, Ham, and Japheth.

> That Shem was of the same complexion as Noah his father, and mother—the Adamic complexion—there is no doubt in our mind. And that Ham the second son was swarthy in complexion, we have as little doubt. Indeed, we believe it is generally conceded by scholars, though dis-

> puted by some, that the word Ham means "dark", "swarthy", "sable". And it has always been conceded, and never as we know of seriously disputed, that Japheth was white.

And Shem settled in Asia to establish the yellow race; Japheth settled in the northwest to begin the Caucasian, or white race; and Ham went into Africa where he and his sons achieved the highest degree of civilization known in the years before Christ. Delany's authority is, of course, the New Testament.

Then Delany resurrected his Harvard Medical School lectures on blood chemistry to prove that all three colors were identical, being *rouge*, but in differing concentrations. Thus was the wisdom of the all-wise Creator effectuated.

A goodly portion of the book is given over to repetitious proof of the ascendancy—intellectually, economically, politically, and socially—of the early Ethiopian and Egyptian empires under the sons of Ham and their descendants. The Pyramids could only be built as a result of Ethiopian mathematical genius, and the Sphinx is negroid in feature. As he had believed in his years of youthful study in Pittsburgh, Delany was convinced that these lost civilizations were man's highest achievements, not even yet duplicated by any modern society. They preceded the commonly accepted Chaldean and Assyrian civilizations; thus "The African branch of this family is that which was the earliest developed, taking the first strides in the progress of the highest civilization known to the world, and for this cause, if for no other, it may be regarded as the oldest race of man, having doubtless centuries prior to the others, reared imperishable monuments of their superior attainments." And never forget—these were *black* men.

The alphabet was an Ethiopian device for communication never before known to man, and "the literature of the Israelites, both in the science of letters and government, also religion, was derived from the Africans. . . ." The authority for this is in the Scriptures themselves, for they tell us that Moses "was learned in all the wisdom of the Egyptians." The historian Lucian is the authority that the Ethiopians "invented Astronomy and Astrology." The Garden of Hesperides was no myth either. It was deep in the heart of Ethiopia and its greatest treasure.

To what does all this lead? To the clear path of the black

man today. "All that is good and desirable in African polity and economy—and there is much for which they get no credit—we shall retain and endeavor to improve; and all that is good and desirable in the civilization of other races and peoples, we shall emulate and endeavor to profit by, and all that is demoralizing and objectionable in all races and peoples, of whatever degree of civilization, we shall reject in this our progress of civilization, as tending to degeneration, and thereby fatally pernicious to the desirable social polity."

How far toward this ideal has the African come? Delany answered by excluding all Africans on the coasts and held up the Yorubas as "equal in susceptibility and moral integrity to the ancient Africans." Their moral and social standards were beyond reproach, Delany asserted, and using once again the position of the female as the standard of a society, he translated Bishop Samuel Crowther's words:

When the day dawns,
The trader takes his money,
The spinner takes *her* spindle,
The warrior takes his shield,
The weaver takes his batten,
The farmer wakes himself and his hoe,
The hunter wakes with his fiddle and his bow.

This allocation of vocations among the Yoruba, according to Delany, keeps the woman in the home, and that is her sole task. Thus the Yoruba have achieved, in his day, the desirable epitome of a social structure.

Nor did Delany fear the dread miscegnation about which white supremacists shuddered. Blacks would be equally fearful if the loss of their race was threatened, he wrote. Besides, after thousands of years of copulation between and among all races, there still remained the three dominant colors—black, yellow, and white. Isn't that proof enough that destruction of any one of them is impossible? It is not possible genetically, nor is it God's will. "Nay, verily, as long as earth endure so long shall the original races in their purity, as designed by God, the Creator of all things, continue the three sterling races—yellow, black and white,—naming them in the order given in Genesis of Shem, Ham and Japheth."

Delany concluded his study with a summation of his lifetime preachings, much milder in tone and expression. Throughout the book, he tempered his language and purified it of the polemic, for he had assumed a "scientific objectivity." But his final writing is more of wish expression than assertion.

> Finally, the African race in Africa should not be adjudged by those portions of that race found out of Africa. The difference is too great for comparison. Untrammeled in its native purity, the race is a noble one, and worthy to emulate the noble Caucasian and Anglo-Saxon, now at the top round of the ladder of moral and intellectual grandeur in the progress of civilization.
>
> The regeneration of the African race can only be effected by its own efforts, the efforts of its own self, whatever aid may come from other sources; and it must in this venture succeed, as God leads the movement and his hand guides the way. And now the advanced civilization of the Christianity of the world is called upon to recognize an overture to their consideration.
>
> "Princes shall come out of Egypt; Ethiopia shall soon stretch forth her hands unto God." Ps. lxviii. 31.
>
> With faith in this blessed promise, thank God, in this our grand advent into Africa, we want
>
> No kettle-drums nor flageolets,
> Bag-pipes, trombones nor bayonets,
>
> but with an abiding trust in God our Heavenly King, we shall boldly advance, singing the sweet songs of redemption, in the regeneration of our race and restoration of our fatherland from the gloom and darkness of superstition and ignorance, to the glorious light of a more than pristine brightness—the light of the highest godly civilization.

This was Delany's last meaningful expression, his last real effort to fight the white intellectually. The book is a remarkable display of erudition, the work of a man whose knowledge of the ancients is beyond question. But in the 1880s it was so much spindrift. A few blacks found in it the profound truth of their capacity to excel. The whites? Had they known that the classical Latin dramatist Terence was a black man, his work would have been spurned by the academies. They took no black scholar seriously, including Delany.

Late in 1884 Delany went home. At his death, on January 24, 1885, at the age of 73, he could claim at least half a century of dedication to his people in more roles than most men—black or white—are cast in a lifetime. In that time black voices had first been heard, black soldiers had a vital part in saving the Union, and black freedmen had attempted to govern. But never had blacks become a part of the United States, not in all those fifty years. Before his death Delany may have read an announcement: "The Colored Men's Central Committee of Illinois have issued a call for a convention, to be held in Pittsburgh in April to effectually determine whether in times of peace questions of public concern are to be settled by the ballot or the bullet."

This was 1884, and by then Judge Lynch was busily enforcing the unwritten laws of American *apartheid*. Since then the Americans have dealt with the blacks in two of the three ways Delany wrote about. "Civilization is promoted by three agencies, Revolution, Conquest, and Emigration. . . ." Blacks have been part of every American war of conquest, and there is no foreign battlefield without its black American bodies. Blacks have been driven to emigrate, not just back to Africa but to every country where the degree of freedom or oppression is shared equally. As yet, there has been no revolution, and therefore American *apartheid* remains unchanged, despite the febrile apologists who claim such change in "tokenism."

Martin R. Delany has been forgotten by American history. Not even the black militants of today know his name or know that they are expressing, in today's language, his pride in race, pride in self, and hatred of whites as he began speaking and writing in the 1830s. Their thoughts and opinions are identical. It is doubtful whether any but the most ardent scholars of black history, such as Carter G. Woodson, have singled out Delany as a vital example of black manhood and intellect. American historians disregard him, and so do the black people themselves.

Only once since his death in 1885 has any black community recognized Delany as an example for their children. In Pittsburgh, just after the Spanish-American War, a Negro lawyer named Frank Stewart organized the "Delany Rifles" as a black drill team. The team later developed into a locally famous athletic organization, with football and basketball teams playing under the same name. Stewart once explained to one of the three surviving members of these teams: "I organized the Delany Rifles to keep our boys out of trouble." For the same reasons and in the same locale, Delany had once organized his study and intellectual groups. But beyond this one example none, black or white, have even noticed his contributions to his times and his people. Only recently have some of his writings been considered sufficiently important to make available to the general public, and only now is his newspaper correspondence being examined.

For nearly a century, Delany has been forgotten and perhaps might never have been recalled if not for the second Negro awakening of the 1960s. In his own eyes he had lived and striven in vain.

But had he?

We must consider his total message to his people and to the whites as well. One message so often expressed was heard in many countries. It was something new for his day and its power is underrated to this day.

There were many tribunes for the black people, and each presented a valid argument for their freedom—political, moral, or religious. Some even pleaded for a measure of equality as well.

Delany was the first to *demand*—not *appeal*—for black freedom and equality for the very simplest of reasons—because "*I am a Man.*" To hell with justice, which man has never granted, or godliness, which man has never achieved, or political equality, which always has been a chimera whether in the guise of democracy or autocracy. Delany demanded recognition as a member of the human race, in good standing.

Today, such status is called "black pride." It is a total denial of centuries of weeping over the burden of a black skin. Delany expressed it from his earliest efforts in Pittsburgh. He fought with other black leaders to adopt it as an essential element in any black nationalist movement. He could not forgive any of his fellows—including Frederick Douglass—for their "Uncle Tomism" in licking the white hand for favors long overdue.

That is why there was no compromise with whites in Delany's make-up as a man. He had infinite love and compassion, openly demonstrated paternalism for any and all members of his own race—except those who had adopted the white man's vices.

There was a duality in him which could either result from egomania or from the purest integrity. The whites considered it the former and, as one prominent South Carolina white said: "Sir, I do not believe Delany considers any white man as good as himself."

On the other hand, Delany's pride of race was such as to distinguish him among his fellows and command their slavish following.

Delany's philosophical descendants of today—the black militants—have recently discovered black pride, but he knew it, felt it, demanded it, and defined it to his very first and youthful audiences in Pittsburgh during the 1830s. Throughout the fifty years of service to his people Delany did not deviate from his definition though he did vary in his technique of its presentation.

"*I am a Man*" meant solely and exclusively that he *must* enjoy all of the favors or suffer all of the pains of being a man, no matter what his color or physical characteristics. To Delany that was the First Commandment.

It was this unequivocal stand that made enemies and friends, fierce opponents and stalwart followers. It is true that his arrogantly asserted beliefs won over few whites, but it did win the respect of all. And Delany perhaps had a good reason for his militant expression. He had read the ancients and very few of his day, of any color, had done the same. There *had* been great black civilizations.

But such proof and the mere statement "*I am a Man*" was not enough for the color phobia, then or now. Black pride is an empty phrase and becomes a form of separatism without the ingredient of hope. What if there had been mighty and learned black civilizations in Africa? What were the glories of Greece? The entire world needed an inferior race to exploit through colonialism, and the United States needed slavery. That need dictated the inferiority of the blacks, and so a Christian civilization, a modern economy, and a political system called democracy all were perverted in proof that the "nigger" was not a man.

And so Delany called upon the future as well as the past to prove his thesis. He gave his people hope that "*I am a Man*" had concrete meaning by raising the ghost haunting all whites today. During his early writings and speeches Delany seldom failed to tell his black audiences that there was a reality in black pride that the almost immediate future would prove. He said it in many ways but perhaps most succinctly at his Emigration Convention in Cleveland in 1854:

> The white race are but one-third of the population of the globe—or one of them to two of us—and it cannot much longer continue that two-thirds will passively submit to the universal domination of this one-third. . . .

Here was the fact to buttress the wish expression of black pride. It was a future in keeping with the past shown by Delany to his people. It was hope for the blacks.

For the whites it was a slashing reality threatening their racial house of cards and remains today the foundation for existence of all of the WASP organizations. A century ago the whites could laugh at it, but today they are frightened. Why, Delany signified "black supremacy," and that is simply inconceivable! Yet throughout the world the blacks are awakening too, and in the United States their minority more and more militantly demands a share in democracy. In the North and South even the opponents of American *apartheid* are reacting in horror to the inevitable results of such demands.

Perhaps Delany should be remembered for this alone: he gave black pride existence with a past and a future. That is why American *apartheid* will not be eliminated without bloodshed, because black pride is, year by year, implementing its demand for black equality. American whites will not willingly grant black equality because they believe it would be a step toward black supremacy. It is not only economic and political exploitation that buttresses American *apartheid;* it is white fear.

There is no American political leader, preacher, educator, or industrialist to assume the task of changing white attitudes. There is nobody to convince the American whites that it is possible for the races to live together in amity, as Delany attempted to do during the last ten years of his life. There has been no white leadership in American history, from Presidents to preachers, who have attempted to duplicate his effort to avoid race war.

Therefore such a war is inevitable and only a moral conversion of the American white can avert it by an attack on *apartheid*. White Americans appear more inclined to attack "black pride" as their enemy instead of understanding it as an asset to the country, an inevitable result of the revitalizing of a large minority.

Such a race war would prove that Delany was our country's leading realist. The chief casualty of such a war would be even the faulty democracy we now possess.

Sources of Materials

It is certain that for years after publication of this book investigators will be finding new and original material on Martin R. Delany. He was so articulate, both with his pen and on the platform, that his work is hidden in as yet undiscovered letters, news reports, and pamphlets. Very few historians have dealt with Delany from the primary sources, and none has detailed any particular phase of his life. Therefore, this writer sought and found original sources of information and opinion, chiefly written by Delany himself. These sources are to be found in many cities and villages, pamphlets and newspapers.

Such a search would take one man a lifetime, but it was accomplished with the skilled assistance of two individuals. One was Dorothy Sterling, whose books on black history—written for young readers—have opened young eyes to totally neglected aspects of American history. Her assistance and research skills have been invaluable. And Floyd J. Miller, while working on his doctorate on Martin Delany at the University of Minnesota, transmitted many valuable pieces of information. Dr. Miller, now in the Oberlin College history department, discovered the balance of Delany's novel *Blake*, so long reported by all historians as lost.

Delany's books, pamphlets, and newspaper correspondence, as well as the letters in his handwriting found everywhere are, of course, the most useful. Delany's books are:

1. *The Condition, Elevation, Emigration and Destiny of the Colored People of the United States Politically Considered* (Philadelphia, published by the author, 1852). Reprinted by Arno Press, 1968.

2. *Blake, or The Huts of America; A Tale of the Mississippi Valley, the Southern United States and Cuba* (serialized 1859 in

The Anglo-African Magazine; 1861 and 1862 in the *Weekly Anglo-African Magazine*). Beacon Press, 1970.

3. *Official Report of The Niger Valley Exploring Party*, by M. R. Delany, Chief Commissioner to Africa (New York and London, Eng., 1861). Reprinted in *Search for a Place*, edited by Howard Bell (University of Michigan Press, 1969).

4. *Principia of Ethnology: The Origin of Races and Color with an Archeological Compendium and Egyptian Civilization, From Years of Careful Examination and Enquiry* (Philadelphia, 1879).

Delany's many pamphlets were found in totally unrelated places. As an example, the fundamental and lengthy booklet, *Freemasonry*, was not in any Freemason's library, not even in the collection of Alvin McCurdy, Amherstburg, Ontario. It is in the Western Reserve Historical Society collection in Cleveland, Ohio. I did not find No. 4 of the tracts on *National Policy* address to the students at Wilberforce University anywhere in that institution. It is in the Dawson Pamphlet Collection at the University of North Carolina. A copy of *Homes for the Freedmen* printed in Charleston, S.C., in 1871 is in none of the customary libraries, although the Boston Public Library has one. A few libraries have the proceedings of the 1854 Emigration Convention with Delany's report in it, but the most certain source of *Political Destiny of the Colored Race on the American Continent* is in the Index of the Report of the Select Committee on House Resolution No. 576, printed in July 1862 by the House of Representatives.

Delany's two weekly newspapers have been accepted as extinct by historians. But the writer found two copies uncatalogued and among a pile of miscellaneous old Pittsburgh newspapers, at the Carnegie Library, Pittsburgh. The two copies are revealing but more so are the stories reprinted in the white Pittsburgh press, in *The Liberator*, the *Pennsylvania Freeman*, and all of the transitory Negro press in the country. They used *The Mystery* of Pittsburgh from 1843 through 1847 as a source of black reporting, thinking, and a refreshing new voice.

Delany had a newspaper, the *Charleston* (S.C.) *Independent*, during most of 1875 but the writer could discover only one copy, the last one Delany wrote and edited. This is in the American Antiquarian Society library in Worcester, Mass.

However, the researcher must scan miles of microfilm and columns in all the newspapers of his times, for Delany was a person to report and to quote. Of course, for the nearly two years he was co-editor of the *North Star* with Frederick Douglass (microfilm in the Schomburg Collection, New York Public Library), he wrote weekly from all over the country. And for the Canadian blacks, he wrote regularly in the *Provincial Freeman* (Chatham, Ont., Public Library). But since he made speeches at one time or another in almost every city, North and South, no newspaper really should be neglected, from the *New South* in the Sea Islands of South Carolina to the *New York Times* and *Tribune*.

In Canada his leadership was recognized by the Ontario press, and some of the few newspapers there are in the Treasure Room of the University of Western Ontario Library, as well as the rich papers of the late Dr. Fred Landon, Canada's leading historian of the Negro. Other valuable sources are in the Baldwin Room of the Toronto Metropolitan Library, and the Kent Co. Historical Society in Chatham. As for private individuals of importance in Canada as guides in Negro history, there are Drs. Farrell (University of Windsor) and Simpson (University of Western Ontario), both of whom are from London and took doctorals in black history. One of the two leading collectors of John Brown material is Stanley Smith, whose spare rooms and cellar in Ingersoll, Ontario, are filled with valuable material.

The other is the late Boyd B. Stutler of Charleston, W. Va., whose enormous collection on John Brown is neatly filed and was gathered during the past 25 years while he was writing his histories of West Virginia.

In New England where the white abolitionists held forth there are a few helpful documents on Delany, such as the Harvard Medical School Archives, the Widener Library, the Boston Public Library, the Boston Athenaeum, and some historical societies.

As ever, the most willing and valuable help in Washington, D.C., may be obtained from Mrs. Dorothy Porter of the Howard University Moorland-Spingarn collections. A good deal of key documentary material may be found there, as well as the National Archives, the State Department Archives, and the Library of Congress.

Resources in the Midwest are fragmentary and far-flung. The Burton Collection of the Detroit Public Library is exceptional for background information. In Pittsburgh the Carnegie Library historical collection and the Allegheny Historical Society are replete with Delany's 25 years of activities there. In Salem, Ohio, are located the records of the Western Anti-Slavery Society, and at Wilberforce University are the Bishop's papers and the old African Methodist Episcopal Church files. But copies of the AME newspaper, *Christian Recorder*, containing so much of Delany's correspondence are available only at the Microfilm Library on the Berkeley campus of the University of California. This is true, even though the national headquarters of the AME Church are in Nashville, Tenn., and original files of the *Christian Recorder* are closely held in the Bethel Mother Church in Philadelphia.

Records of Delany's youth in Charles Town, W. Va., and Chambersburg, Pa., are scanty, but for both it is rewarding to search the historical society's small collections and the public libraries. The record of Delany's father's manumission may be found only in the Winchester County (Va.), Courthouse, and the family's residence in Chambersburg is verified by payment of an "Occupation Tax" recorded in the Town Hall.

It might be asked why the writer did not depend more on the biography of Delany, *The Life and Services of Martin R. Delany* by Frank A. Rollin, published in Boston by Lee and Shepard in 1868, and widely available. The major reasons are errors of omission and its lack of the all-important South Carolina decade. The book was written, with Delany's close collaboration, by Frances Rollin who returned from a year in Boston to meet and marry William Whipper, the Beaufort politician.

While in search of Delany material only in South Carolina, my findings indicated that any historian in search of new Reconstruction evidence will find it and rewrite the entire period.

For instance, the State Archives documents in Columbia have been in the process of being organized and catalogued for some years. Here were found Delany's letters to each Reconstruction governor and in some cases copies of the governors' letters to him. Here also were found the circumstances and pardon issued Delany for his guilty verdict of grand larceny and embezzlement. In their own handwriting were the reports of the lobbying with President Andrew Johnson and the bond manipulations in New York which were to bankrupt the state.

From governor to governor in these letters and documents is the first-hand story of the road of corruption and the failure of democracy. Just a few steps away is more evidence at the South Caroliniana Library on the University of South Carolina campus. Not far south in Beaufort the story of the Sea Islands and the death of the "forty acres and a mule" fiction are shown in its public library. In Charleston, S.C., the Library Society has a remarkably complete file of the newspapers of the day which named Delany the spokesman of his people.

There are other sources of primary material concerning all the fifty years of Delany's dedication to his people. They have yet to be sought and found. And it is this writer's opinion that they should be. The chronicle of American history will never be complete without the full and documented chronicle of black history in the United States.

Index